Capitalism Reconnected

"We are in a race against time to transition to a net-zero and sustainable economy. This is a must read for anyone seeking to learn more on how Europe can help set the world on a new development pathway to make us more resilient to future shocks."
—Ban Ki-moon, 8th Secretary-General of the United Nations

"Only if we address the basic human values on which humanity is based will we address the most burning issues. Learn why Europe is well placed for a leading role in creating a new inclusive and sustainable world order. *Capitalism Reconnected* convincingly explains how we should focus on the things that matter and apply cooperative leadership to attack today's biggest challenges."
—Paul Polman, Former CEO Unilever
Author of *Net Positive. How Courageous Companies Thrive by Giving More Than They Take*

"The road to sustainability is a shared assignment, for citizens, civil society, businesses, national and European authorities. Cooperation is a value in itself. A renewed economy requires a renewed society. A book full of ideas, values, and especially hope, which we badly need."
—Herman van Rompuy
President Emeritus European Council,
Minister of State Belgium

"As we move into a multipolar world in the 21st century, Europe's role will be critical. Sadly, in many ways, Europe has lost its way. This volume by Balkenende and Buijs is timely as it provides a deep analysis of Europe's challenges and prescribes many thoughtful solutions. It's a must read for all friends of Europe around the world."
—Kishore Mahbubani
Former UN Permanent Representative of Singapore
Distinguished Fellow at the Asia Research Institute of NUS,
Author of *Has China Won?*

Capitalism Reconnected

Toward a Sustainable, Inclusive and Innovative Market Economy in Europe

Jan Peter Balkenende and Govert Buijs

Amsterdam University Press

The publication of this book is made possible by grants from the Templeton World Charity Foundation, Inc. and the Goldschmeding Foundation.

Cover design: Lyanne Tonk
Back cover photograph of Jan Peter Balkenende: © Michel Porro
Back cover photograph of Govert Buijs: © David Meulenbeld
Lay-out: Crius Group, Hulshout

ISBN	9789048562633
e-ISBN	9789048562640 (pdf)
DOI	10.5117/9789048562633
NUR	801

Printed and bound by CPI Group (UK) Ltd, Croydon, CR0 4YY

By way of introduction

An idea

The origins of this book lie in a conversation that took place sometime in 2019 between ourselves (the authors) after one of us, Jan Peter Balkenende, gave a lecture at a conference of Finance and Control students in Amsterdam. The short talk covered topics like 'integrated reporting,' 'purpose,' and 'values.' The students hadn't paid too much attention to what was said from the podium during the day, but this changed quickly when Jan Peter started to talk: after one or two sentences, they started to pay attention; the chatter waned, and they apparently noticed that themes were now being addressed that really mattered to them – both personally and professionally. "Are you going to write about this?" Govert asked Jan Peter when we met a few weeks later. He didn't have any plans to do so at that time, and – as a former prime minister, Jan Peter was hesitant to speak out publicly too much on issues connected with current politics and policies. But, Govert asked, wouldn't it be important, given the perspective he had gained and the views that he had developed over the years, to see if something could be produced to reach a larger audience than just those who attended lectures, and in a more lasting form? Isn't there some responsibility as well, particularly for the next generation, the students you meet so often? Govert was working on a project at that time on 'Markets and Morality' and was developing the closing phase of this project with an academic conference. And then a certain 'flow' started to form: Couldn't we combine this into a larger 'consultation' on the future and morality of market economies, an exploration of the 'future of capitalism'? Such a consultation could bring together new insights that were emerging now – at first as a late response to the credit crisis and then as an answer to ecological and social challenges – in what seemed almost to become an avalanche of intellectual and political innovation.

Jan Peter had already worked on the idea of a responsible economy in many publications during his time as a researcher at the Research Institute for the Dutch Christian Democratic Party (CDA) and as a professor of Christian Social Thought at the Vrije Universiteit Amsterdam during the 1990s. As Prime Minister, he began a European-wide dialogue on European values when the Netherlands held the presidency of the EU Council in 2004.[1] He has given many lectures in recent years on these topics all over the world, in addition to his work as Professor of Governance, Institutions and Internationalization at Erasmus University Rotterdam. As holder of the Goldschmeding Research Chair for Economic and Social Innovation at the Vrije Universiteit, Govert has been working on markets and morality, European culture, and the future of our economy.

A Consultation

A consultation was therefore organized on 'The Future of Capitalism' with several elements. At first a starter paper was presented: 'Toward a New Market Economy in Europe for Future Generations.' The original plan was to start the actual consultation with an expert seminar with visionary economists who were forging new paths in answering the challenges of the future. Because of Covid, this plan was eventually transformed, in the fall of 2020, into a series of online dialogues in cooperation with the Amsterdam debating house Pakhuis de Zwijger, which developed into a rather monumental series.[2]

In addition, an ad hoc think tank of young economists was organized who would write their own report as one of the sources of input for this book. Apart from delivering columns during the dialogues just mentioned, they published two reports: *Towards the Wellbeing Economy: Implications for Public, Environmental and Financial Policy* (February 2021) and *Renewing the Welfare State: The Right Mix Ensuring Jobs, Income and Services* (April 2021) which were presented during online seminars and have drawn quite a bit of attention in the Dutch press.[3]

For the purposes of involving other young scholars, an essay contest was organized for students at the MA level and one at the young scholars/young professionals level. Fourth, consultation sessions were held with representatives from the business sector and NGOs, as well as research institutes of Dutch political parties across the political spectrum. The idea behind this was to gain a proper understanding, often an insider's view, of how they saw the future of the market economy. The fifth element was an open call to deliver 'viewpoints' for the consultation, a call that was open to anybody who wanted to do so.

Another book will be published after this one, probably called 'Reconnectors.' This is the sixth element of the project. It will contain interviews with people who in one way or the other can be seen as frontrunners of a new economy, from the business sector, from politics, from civil society and from the domain that in this book we call 'imaginative reflection.'

Europe

From the start, an important focus of the project was on Europe. In the late 19th century, provoked by the rise of socialism and very much inspired by Christian social thinking – both Catholic and Protestant – Europe had started to search for a way to reconcile capitalism and basic human and social rights. It was a search for possible 'third ways' between unfettered capitalism and full-blown socialism, often called the 'Rhine model' of capitalism over against the 'Anglo-Saxon model' or 'stakeholder' vs 'shareholder capitalism' (see below for more details). Eventually, this resulted in (various types of) welfare states. When these welfare states ran into all kinds of (financial, administrative, and social) difficulties in the 1970s, this particular type of European economic thinking fell into near oblivion and was not kept up to date – at least not at a publicly relevant level. The next decades saw the unchallenged rise of what later came to be called – correctly or incorrectly – 'neoliberalism.' In light of today's challenges, however, the search for a 'third way' is as relevant as ever. So, one of the ideas behind our consultation was to contribute to a renewal of European economic thinking and European economic practices in which a workable and wholesome mix of market, state, and civil society has a positive influence on the wellbeing of all, this time including nature. This renewal is all the more necessary in light of the new challenges that Europe finds itself confronted with: climate change, rising inequality, political turmoil within many democratic nations, the geoeconomic need to secure energy and raw materials, and the geopolitical realities of a multipolar world, and the continuing, and even increasing, need for global cooperation.

When this consultation started, Donald Trump had been in power for almost four years and his reelection was certainly a possibility. His administration had had incisive implications for the relations between Europe and the USA and laid bare deep differences regarding the future of the market economy (for example, Trump took America out of the Paris Agreement). So it was clear from the beginning that geopolitical and geoeconomic considerations had to be a substantial part of the consultation's outcomes. This was strongly reinforced twice. The Covid pandemic struck in January 2020. And in February 2022, when we had just finished the first draft of this book, another geopolitical earthquake took place: Russia invaded Ukraine, forcing us to rethink and reformulate key elements of the book (though not its central message). Many of the elements that were already discussed in the manuscript took on much greater urgency, for example the geopolitical and geoeconomic position of Europe. Moreover, the general mood in which the book was going to be published had changed drastically. With the book as we present it now, we hope to have found a tone that fits the present, unprecedented context.

It is not possible to mention by name all those who were involved in these consultations. But there are people whom we would like to thank explicitly for their contribution.

First of course are the participants in the online dialogues that gave so many new insights, often authors of inspiring books.[4]

Here we mention with deep gratitude – following the order of appearance in the dialogues – Joseph Stiglitz (USA), Herman van Rompuy (Belgium), Rebecca Henderson (USA), Colin Mayer (UK), Raghuram Rajan (USA), Paul Collier (UK), Isabelle Ferreras (Belgium), Josh Ryan-Collins (UK), Elizabeth Anderson (USA), François Bourguignon (France), Mohammad Yunus (Bangladesh), Jeffrey Sachs (USA), Julia Steinberger (Switzerland), Ann Pettifor (UK), Rana Foroohar (USA), Jonathan Taplin (USA), Christian Felber (Austria), Luigi Zingales (Italy/USA), Tito Boeri (Italy), Luis Garicano (Spain), Dalia Marin (Austria/Germany), and Geert Noels (Belgium). Among these participants, we cannot help but note with pride, gratitude and humility, three Nobel prizewinners: Stiglitz for economics, Yunus for peace (especially in relation to global poverty), and Van Rompuy (who received the prize on behalf of the European Union for international peace and cooperation). The dialogues were moderated by David van Overbeek and Natasja van den Berg, and Julia Muller was involved as coordinator.

We would also like to thank the members of the Think Tank of Young Economists: Sam de Muijnck, Elisa Terragno Bogliaccini, Jim Richard Surie, Kees Buitendijk, David van Overbeek, Eefje de Gelder, and Rens van Tilburg. Some of them were involved with different organizations that also facilitated their participation: Rethinking Economics, Our New Economy, Socires, and the Sustainable Finance Lab. Of course, we also thank all those who contributed to the essay contests, and we would like to mention the winners: Camila Posada from Bogota, Colombia, winner of the MA level contest, and Fausto Corvino from Turin, Italy in the young scholars/young professionals category.

Consultations were held with representatives of the research institutes of Dutch political parties. The participants were Klara Boonstra (Wiardi Beckman Foundation, PvdA, the labor party), Coen Brummer (Mr. Hans van Mierlo Stichting, D66, the social liberal party), Arjen Siegmann (Wetenschappelijk Instituut CDA, the Christian Democratic Party), Hans Rodenburg (Wetenschappelijk Instituut GroenLinks – the Green Party), Laurens Wijmenga (Groenstichting, Christian Union), Roelof Salomons and Maartje

Schulz (Teldersstichting, VVD, liberal party, which hosted the events and made the facilities of the Telderstichting available for the meetings that had to take place under Covid restrictions).

Several drafts of this book were discussed in an advisory board consisting mainly of (Dutch) economists: Arnoud Boot, Wimar Bolhuis, Dirk Bezemer, Lans Bovenberg, Barbara Baarsma, Bas van Bavel (given the first letter of their family names, together with Balkenende and Buijs, this was almost a 'B corporation' in itself), Rutger Claassen, Peter d'Angremond, Steven van Eijck, Johan Graafland, Irene van Staveren, Rens van Tilburg, and Jaap Winter.

Sessions with representatives from both various markets sectors and from civil society organizations were organized by Achmea-De Kamers, thanks to Timo van Voorden, and by the Dutch chapter of the Caux Round Table for Moral Capitalism, organized by Herman Mulder and Karel Noordzij. Global Compact Netherlands and the think tank Socires organized a special input session for young professionals in the business, NGO and government sectors, in which Kees Buitendijk and Linda van Beek took the lead.

Parts of the manuscript, or sometimes even the entire manuscript in one of its phases, were read as well by Cor van Beuningen, Kees Buitendijk (both staff members of Socires), Paul Schenderling, Jan van Wijngaarden, Boudewijn Hogeboom, Andrew Basden, Shirley Roels, Pieter Jan Dijkman, Kees Cools, Marcel Canoy, Charan van Krevel, those working on the new BA program 'Humane Economy/Social Economy' at the Vrije Universiteit, Henry de Groot, Arjo Klamer, Koen Bruning, and Paul Koster, and members of the Ethos Center of the Vrije Universiteit: Muhammed Akbas, Jelle van Baardewijk, Gabriël van den Brink, Paul Bosman, Thijs Janssen, Joris Peereboom, Ad Verbrugge, and Bram Verhulst.

During 2023, the Ethos Center of the Vrije Universiteit also organized an ad hoc think tank on the geopolitical situation and its geoeconomic implications, resulting in a separate essay volume, edited by Govert Buijs and Paul Bosman, *Ontwaken uit de geopolitieke sluimer* (Waking up from geopolitical slumber: Repositioning europe in a world adrift). In addition to the editors,

René Cuperus, Monika Sie Dhian Ho, Eelke de Jong, Luuk van Middelaar, Trineke Palm, Frans-Paul van der Putten, Paul Scheffer, Haroon Sheikh, and Paul Timmers contributed to this volume.

Many of the ideas in this book originated in the context of the research project 'What Good Markets Are Good For,' led by Govert Buijs and Johan Graafland (Tilburg University), cooperating in a team consisting of researchers from Erasmus University Rotterdam, Radboud University Nijmegen, Tilburg University, and Vrije Universiteit Amsterdam: Jelle van Baardewijk, Jordan Ballor, Iwan Bos, Iwan Boldyrev, Lans Bovenberg, Martijn Burger, Marcel Canoy, Harry Commandeur, Paul van Geest, Eefje de Gelder, Martijn Hendriks, Eelke de Jong, Kees van der Kooi, Ilse Oosterlaken, Antoinette Rijsenbilt, Daan van Schalkwijk, Annemiek Schilpzand, Ad Verbrugge, and Rudi Verburg.

Eefje de Gelder and Ilse Oosterlaken also worked hard on the organizational and digital infrastructure that made both the Good Markets project and the specific consultation of which this book is the result possible (see https://www.moralmarkets.org/researchproject/ and https://www.moralmarkets.org/futuremarketsconsultation/).

Funding for this project was provided by the Templeton World Charity Foundation, Inc. (which funded the larger project on markets and morality just mentioned above) as well as by the Goldschmeding Foundation. (Neither organization had any say over the content of the publications.)

Draft texts of the book were written by Govert Buijs, while Jan Peter Balkenende provided both input (articles, lectures, lecture notes) as well as extensive comments on the drafts, which then led to revisions of the texts. Short drafts of some sections of this book were written by Marcus van Toor (on ecology), Paul Bosman (on research innovation) and Kees Buitendijk (on the financial sector). Marcus van Toor is also co-editing the interview book that will appear later. The Canadian Henry Jansen did a great job in correcting the language and removing as many 'Dutchisms' as possible. We would like to express our thanks as well to Inge van der Bijl, Inge Klompmakers, Vicky Blud and Randy Lemaire from Amsterdam University Press for their great efforts to see this book through the press. Thanks as well to Beatrijs Kostelijk en Daniël Rijfers for compiling the indices.

To be sure, none of the people mentioned above is responsible for the text as presented here, and especially for any mistakes it may contain. At the same time, it may be clear that without their willingness to generously share their knowledge and experience, we couldn't have accomplished what we did, so we extend a heartfelt thanks to all of them.

While the focus is on Europe, we do not intend this book to advocate a Europe for Europe's sake. But we have to acknowledge that today's world is radically different from that of yesterday. From European world domination in the 19th century, two world wars, a Cold War and American hegemony in the 20th century, we are moving today toward a multipolar world, in which Europe has to define its own place anew. And that entails reformulating its key values, asking what type of economy it wants to develop, and how it can position itself in this multipolar world. We believe that Europe, both the European nations individually and their common Union, has a crucial role to play in today's world. It needs to once more take on the task of mitigating capitalism, both for the sake of social fairness and inclusivity and for the sake of the long-term ecological integrity of our planet, less for the generation that has built the present world than for the generations to come – and not just in Europe but the whole world. That is why we used the term 'Reconnected' as key word in our title, thereby indicating a new, values-driven connectedness between generations, between different layers and 'bubbles' within nations, between the European nations themselves (and their Union), between Europe and the other 'poles' of the world, between our economies and the natural environment. We present this work so that Europe and the world are better able to face the challenges of the present and of the future.

September 2023, Jan Peter Balkenende and Govert Buijs

Table of contents

Analytical Table of Contents

Part I
Europe's Present Condition: A Diagnosis

Part II
Europe's Mission:
Developing Responsible Capitalism

Part III
Europe's New Position:
A Global Player for the Common Good

Part I

Europe's Present Condition:
A Diagnosis

In Part I, 'Europe's Present Condition: A Diagnosis,' we start from the most recent developments in Europe and look back upon the great European (and more broadly, Western) project of the last 250 years – the escape from poverty, in which a market economy/ capitalism was an important driver. This system turned out, however, to have destructive tendencies as well, and therefore was and still is in need of correction and political and social embedding. This insight has tended to become lost in recent decades. The balances between markets, states, and civil society/communities were once again abandoned in favor of 'markets alone.' This eventually led to a number of distortions that require a new response, a new phase of correction and embedding of the market economy. European nations and their cooperative association, the European Union, have to reorient their market economies to make them ecologically and socially robust, while at the same time (re)connecting with their own populations and reckoning with a new geopolitical constellation in which the US, China, and Russia have each recently adopted new positions. To navigate these challenges, a new sense of shared values within Europe is essential.

.

Chapter 1

Introduction: From the Challenge of 2015 to the Shock of 2022

2022, and the Seven Years that Preceded It...

It is always risky to mark a certain year as 'historical,' but it may well be that 2022 will qualify as one of the important turning points in modern history, along with years like 1948 (the Declaration of Human Rights after the end of World War II), 1989 (the fall of the Berlin Wall, marking the end of the Cold War that had divided the world in the decades prior to that) and 2001 (the attack on the New York World Trade Center, a sign perhaps that the post–Cold War order would not be as peaceful and harmonious as was assumed after 1989).

In February 2022, Russia invaded Ukraine. In itself, the Ukraine war could have been interpreted as a 'regional conflict,' of which there have been – and still are – many in the world. That, however, is probably a severe underestimation of its significance. It seems to be the better part of wisdom to see this war as a turning point for Europe, for the Western world in general, and even for the world. But its significance for Europe – and the serious challenges it creates – can only be gauged against the background of the seven years that preceded it.

The seven years, the 'septennium,' from 2015 to 2022 may later well come to be considered crucial for defining the long-term future of Europe – the European nations individually, the European Union, and the European continent – in the world. Let us briefly recapitulate, starting with that most remarkable year of 2015. (In the various sections along the way we will formulate some key observations that will inform the remainder of this book in italics.)

The 2015 Agenda: A Clarion Call

In 2015, the United Nations formulated the Sustainable Development Goals, with 2030 as its time horizon – an ambitious global agenda. The earlier Millennium Development Goals, formulated in 2000, which called for – among other things – a 50% reduction of poverty by 2015, were largely met and in some respects even exceeded. This induced confidence in the realizability of the new set of goals that focused less exclusively on the 'underdeveloped' Global South but also targeted the 'overdeveloped' North, calling for a global effort:

1. No poverty
2. Zero hunger
3. Good health and wellbeing
4. Quality education
5. Gender equality
6. Clean water and sanitation
7. Affordable and clean energy
8. Decent work and economic growth
9. Industry, innovation, and infrastructure
10. Reduced inequalities
11. Sustainable cities and communities
12. Responsible consumption and production
13. Climate action
14. Life below water
15. Life on land
16. Peace, justice and strong institutions
17. Partnerships for the goals

Moreover, in May 2015, Pope Francis issued his most important encyclical by thus far, *Laudato Si'*, in which he called for new, swift global action to save the world's precious ecological system that he described as "our common home." As an integral part of his message, he also called attention to the fate of the world's poorest people: they are estimated to suffer the most from ecological problems and have no resources to shield themselves from them. The Pope thus intricately connected ecological and social issues with each other. This remarkable year concluded in December 2015 with the landmark Paris Agreement, or Paris Climate Accords, that was adopted by no less than 195 countries, including all European countries, and the European Union itself. The agreement could be seen as well as a response to the Fifth Synthesis Assessment Report of the International Panel on Climate Change (IPCC) with its alarming message on global warming, published in November 2014. The message of 2015, the '2015 agenda,' was clear, and hence our first key observation:

The world, and hence Europe as one of the largest, if not the largest, economies (and therefore also one of the biggest polluters in the world), has to reorient its market economy to long-term social and ecological sustainability for itself but also for the world as a whole and future generations. This requires global cooperation.

In the meantime, Europe had already started to respond to this agenda. To mention just two examples: in December 2019 an ambitious 'European Green Deal' was proposed to make Europe carbon neutral in 2050, and in February 2022 the EU Corporate Sustainability Due Diligence Directive was issued, stimulating large companies to pay attention to the human rights and sustainability issues in their entire production chain.[1]

...And Beyond (2016): Brexit and a Fragmented Populace

In June 2016, however, Great Britain decided to leave the European Union. The decision sent shock waves through Europe. Of course, every country has the right to leave the EU, but the reason for Britain's exit was worrying for the entire project of European cooperation: apparently, there were large groups in Britain that felt disconnected from the European project. 'Taking back control' was the motto that inspired the Brexiteers. Perhaps, it was feared, similar groups of similar size with the same attitude would emerge in other countries that could be easily mobilized by those known as 'populist' politicians, resisting international cooperation in a world and time that urgently needs it. The UK was indeed no exception. In November that same year, Donald Trump was elected President of the United States. This sent further shock waves through Europe. It felt like a repetition of Brexit. Evidently, there are large groups in society that look to the nation state for the shelter and protection they do not find in the rapidly globalizing economy. A similar message was sounded in 2018 in France in the 'Yellow Vests' protests, which in some way confirmed the message of Brexit: this time not targeted against Europe but against the national leadership itself. It made clear that even a 'green' policy, that is, making an economy sustainable in the long run, can only be achieved if the economy is (re)connected to the population. Comparable anti-establishment and/or nationalist movements can be seen in other countries such as the Netherlands, Austria, Poland, and Italy. Democracies – in Europe and worldwide – seem to be coming under increasing pressure. Autocratic tendencies are on the rise. Although the causes for these developments are not only economic, it is clear that a sense of economic insecurity and marginalization plays an important role. The message, again, is clear, and, hence, our second observation:

Europe has to organize its market economy in such a way that people feel protected and connected, or else people may turn against the 'elites' and may even turn against long-term goals like sustainability, even if – 'objectively' seen – a long-term sustainable economy is urgently needed and can be brought about only through national and international cooperation.

...And Beyond (2017): Trump and 'America First'

The election of Donald Trump had another impact on Europe. In his inaugural speech on January 20, 2017, Trump made it immediately clear that his motto from now on would be 'America First,' effectively abandoning America's postwar role of 'leader of the free world' and even as 'leader of the world – period.' In his encounters with European leaders, both in the context of EU–US economic relations and in the context of NATO, he made it clear that he would no longer be willing to have America act as the great fixer of Europe's problems and the guarantor of Europe's security, nor would America act as the world's policeman. No longer would Europe be the natural and preferred partner of the US. To be sure, Joe Biden replaced Donald Trump in 2020 and immediately started to reconnect with Europe and to take an active global role (for example in the Ukraine crisis), but this does not alter the possibility of a Trump-like figure (or even Trump himself) becoming president again. And even Biden himself has somehow continued parts of Trump's 'America First' policies, as is evident from the 2022 Inflation Reduction Act that clearly favors American companies and helps companies reduce emissions on the condition that their production takes place in the USA itself – 'America First.' A rock-solid geopolitical partnership that has lasted for decades suddenly seems to be faltering. Therefore:

Geopolitically, and geoeconomically, Europe has to learn to stand on its own feet.

…And Beyond (2020): Covid, Vulnerability and Europe's New Strength

In 2020, the Covid crisis broke out, a health crisis of a magnitude the world had not seen for decades. At first, the responses in Europe were very nation-based. Later on, governments increasingly came to realize that a more internationally coordinated approach regarding medical supplies and vaccines, for example, would be much better for all individual nations. Only together would they be able to stand up against the new 'big powers' of today's world – in this case, 'Big Pharma.' The crisis also became a geopolitical chess game, with China and Russia trying to provide medical supplies and vaccines both in Europe and worldwide and thus investing in new relationships. In general, European nations started to realize that only a coordinated, solidary effort would suffice to deal with the economic consequences of the Covid pandemic. A large 'rescue package' was negotiated in a relatively short time. And the already emerging discussion on 'strategic autonomy' entered a new phase. The lesson:

In today's world, European nations need each other, or else they will be set against each other by outside players, both countries/ empires (China, Russia) and 'Big Business' (e.g., 'Big Tech,' 'Big Pharma,' 'Big Finance') which would, on balance, weaken all of them substantially.

...And Beyond (2022): The Ukraine War and a New Geopolitical Constellation

And then came 2022. Russia decided to invade Ukraine, starting the first interstate war on the European continent since the end of World War II. As noted above, the Ukraine war in itself could have been interpreted as a 'regional conflict' (and many countries in the world prefer to see it that way, to the surprise of Western countries). The long-term geopolitical implications are becoming all too visible, however. Russia had secured the support – a 'friendship with no limits,' of the rising superpower, China (for whom, perhaps, this war was an interesting test case for how the world would respond to a possible invasion of Taiwan). Other important countries in the world stayed 'neutral,' such as India, South Africa, Indonesia, and Brazil, unwilling to condemn what was a clear break of the post–World War II international order. Under President Biden, the US took a leading role in orchestrating the Western response to Russia, and Europe was more united than ever before in recent years. NATO was revitalized. But it also became clear that the war prefigured a new constellation in which the non-Western world, often under the leadership of autocratic rulers, is going to claim a larger role in the world and will no longer simply comply with the international order that was created after World War II. The sovereignty of nations and human rights as basic principles seem to give way to the clashes and claims of empires. The Western world responded with unprecedented sanctions against Russia. But at the same time, it became evident as never before that, in an interconnected world, the boycott of a large nation is backfiring: it not only hurts the target nation but one's own nation as well and creates immense economic risks. It is a new world in which Europe has suddenly realized how vulnerable it is, given its dependence on foreign oil, gas and many other raw materials from all over the world, as well as on a constant flow of consumer goods produced in China. The question arises whether market globalization is always the best solution. Should European nations not be able to produce some essential supplies themselves (an issue that arose as well during the Covid crisis)?

What the Ukraine crisis also revealed is that Europe and the US – say, the Western countries or the global North – cannot count on any automatic loyalty and support worldwide. On the contrary, they are increasingly seen as former colonial powers that still profit from their earlier position and should somehow play a different role in the world than the leading one they had in the postwar international order and previously in colonial times. Whatever the exact outcome of the Ukraine war will be (if there will ever be a more or less clear outcome), many countries seem to think that perhaps China should take that leading role, and China itself seems to think this too.

Comparable patterns emerged during the COP27 conference in Sharm el Sheikh in November 2022. Global South countries displayed a new self-consciousness, demanding compensatory payments for the climate damage caused by CO_2 emissions in or on behalf of the Global North (70% of global emissions are related to Northern production and consumption, including emissions that are taking place in the Global South but are part of production chains of Northern consumer goods). Instead of reduction of emissions tabled by the North, this request for compensation initiated by the Global South became the key point on the agenda. Pakistan claimed $30 billion US to repair the damage caused by recent floods, the severity of which was ascribed to climate change. Therefore our fifth observation is:

The European economies have to reposition itself economically in a new geopolitical constellation in which the non-Western world is assuming, and will continue to assume, a new, self-conscious role.

Beyond 2022: A New World Order, New Questions and the Need for New Responses

A new world order is emerging. Crucial questions are now forcing themselves on all global players about the economic order they would like to establish for themselves and what type of world they would like to see. Some of them seem to have already formulated clear answers that differ substantially from each other: from a US-led market-oriented capitalist order to a state-oriented capitalism dominated by China.

The European nations and the European Union also urgently need to answer these questions: What role does Europe want to play in the 21st century? What type of economy does it want to pursue internally? What type of economy does it want to see in the world at large? What kind of geopolitical order does it want to see (and thus help bring about)? Who are its most important allies going to be? Will it let itself be marginalized in a clash between 'the West and the rest' – ultimately, between the US and China? Will it become nothing more than an extension of the American economy and American capitalism? Will it want to become part of the New Chinese Century that is developing as a counterpart to what was once called the New American Century? Will it let itself be torn between the US and China, with some European countries leaning toward the US and some leaning toward China? Or does Europe want to pursue its own course, in relative independence?

If so, for what reason? What does it want to bring to the world, not just in terms of power but also in terms of ideals, of values? What is Europe's mission going to be? Will it indeed choose to become an incubator for furthering the '2015 agenda' of the SDGs and the Paris Agreement? And if the answer is yes, what does this imply? Or will Europe, under the pressure of the shockwaves of the Ukraine war, quietly sideline the '2015 agenda' and adopt a 'survival mode,' making sure that its way of life can be continued as before, and nothing else? Will 2022 trump 2015?

This was certainly not the first response; on the contrary, the Ukraine crisis seems to be accelerating Europe's green ambitions. At the same time, however, the use of coal has also increased, and Germany expanded a lignite mine in Lützerath, despite heavy protests by environmental activists. And what will happen when, via various chains of effects, Europe will witness continuing economic hardships with further inflation, new financial crises, rising debts, increasing poverty, an energy crisis, perhaps even a new immigration crisis due to food shortages in Africa and an avalanche of political crises in a substantial number of European countries? How strong, how 'connected' will Europe show itself to be? We have to reckon with the possibility that the Ukraine war won't be over soon and that Russia will give itself all the time it needs to test Europe's resolve, its unity, and its financial and economic resilience again and again. It may well be enough to stoke relatively minor unrest every now and then, play at *divide et impera*, and in that way try to break the unity of European nations. If Russia breaks the will of Europe after a couple of years, it will not only have eliminated one contender in the superpower arena, but it will also have taken a major step toward isolating another one, the US. And – an added bonus – Russia may have effectively sidelined the 2015 agenda with its goal of complete independence from fossil fuels, a goal that is close to an existential threat for Russia.[2] The stakes are high for Russia, way beyond Ukraine, and Europe should be aware of this.

In our view, as we will argue later in this book, Europe has no choice but to show strong resolve not to give in but to stand firm together, not just for the continuation of its own position and interests but just as much for the future it wants to see in the world, its values and ideals – and even be prepared to suffer for it.

One of the central messages of 2022 is that a new, grimmer, era has begun, and it will require a new response from Europe, a response in which Europe has to find its own place in the new world order and still promote global cooperation as much as possible in order to save and further the 2015 agenda. The year 2022 is also the year in which the sixth period of the IPCC, the Intergovernmental Panel on Climate Change, came to a close with a series of highly alarming reports, culminating in the 6th Synthesis Assessment Report (published in the spring of 2023). This report once again makes clear beyond any reasonable doubt that the earth is in very dire ecological straits.

The Challenges Ahead: Reorientation, Reconnection, Repositioning, Revaluation

Against the background of these defining seven years, this book argues that Europe, both the European nations individually as well as their cooperative structures such as the European Union, have to deal with unprecedented challenges that are arising from this 'septennium' and have to restructure their economies in such a way that they simultaneously:

1. **reorient** their economies toward a circular, or even regenerative, economy in Europe itself that is in long-term harmony with the ecological resources of the planet but at the same time play a leading role in furthering this goal worldwide as the ecological challenges are truly global challenges;
2. **reconnect** and reintegrate the economy with different layers of the European population, and with key institutions such as governments and civil society, establishing a new 'social contract'

or 'covenant' between people and elites, and building an economy 'of the people, for the people, by the people (to use Lincoln's description of democratic government to the economy) and also 'with the people,' within ecological boundaries;

3. reposition Europe in the geoeconomic and geopolitical world of the 21st century, recognizing the drastically changing power relations in the global economy and squaring its own interests with a long-term global orientation.

In a number of publications since 2000, the economist Dani Rodrik formulated the 'globalization paradox' or the 'globalization trilemma.'[3] It is hard, if not impossible, Rodrik claims, to combine full economic globalization – he uses the term 'hyperglobalization' – with national sovereignty and democracy. One can only have two of these completely – the third will always lose out. Rodrik's warnings should be taken seriously. In recent years, an autocratic regime in China has presented the semblance of economic effectiveness by rigorously directing its production toward the globalizing economy at the expense of democracy. The USA has recently started to reconsider globalization and to reclaim its sovereignty ('America First'), and even risked its democracy at one point. And Europe may also have been playing the card of hyperglobalization too much, at the risk of losing legitimacy with important parts of its own populations. All those who claim that 'the markets require...' or 'the markets force us to ... so and so' cannot at the same time promise that 'the people may decide on ... so and so.'

However, Rodrik's formulation of the trilemma may be a bit too harsh and may not be entirely able to meet the present challenges of Europe. It seems wiser to speak of a balance that every political actor has to find between globalization, sovereignty, and democracy time and again. The European nations and the European Union have to constantly find and keep this balance as well. And the European Union can be a crucial player in this respect as a community of sovereign nations, each of which individually runs the risk in today's world of being marginalized but together are able to shelter their citizens from the winds of globalization and, even more, to influence the nature and direction of the world economy itself.

Moreover, Rodrik's scheme is in a sense rather abstract. It does not distinguish between what types of globalization can be pursued, nor does it say much about the way 'democracy' should really function to maintain its legitimacy. And what can full sovereignty actually mean in today's highly interdependent world? So, the actual dilemmas for European nations run more along the lines of: Is it realistic to assume that relatively small nation states in today's world can keep their commitments to their own people without associating with likeminded nations? Can Europe expect globalization to go in the desired direction sketched by the SDGs and the Paris Agreement without the European Union taking on a role comparable to the world's so-called superpowers (and hence developing its own global agenda)? Is it acceptable to incur a certain amount of loss of GDP by restricting globalization for the sake of protecting once's own citizens (against economic theory in which David Ricardo's so-called 'law of comparative advantage' suggests that unlimited globalization is a recipe for wealth)? What type and which degree of sovereignty is possible and needed for nation states in an interconnected world for states to be able to act in the interests of their own citizens? And: How can the cooperation between nation states, large or small – but particularly smaller ones – be organized in such way that it becomes a resource for all, precisely because all have their own strength?[4]

What is also missing from Rodrik's trilemma is the responsibility and role of the private sector itself – in particular business and finance – in supporting the legitimacy of a country and its economic order. He gives the impression that government bears sole responsibility for the social and moral infrastructure of a country and of the world as a whole. Research has indicated that political turmoil is often the result of a financial crisis, and the most recent financial crisis was not induced by governments but originated in the banking sector itself.[5] It is unfair to make governments alone responsible for the globalization dilemmas

– the private sector has to face these dilemmas as well. Business companies are citizens, too (as we will argue).

One of the basic convictions of this book is that the time when we could separate the economic from the political, the social, or the ecological is past. As Feike Sijbesma, a former CEO of the Dutch chemical corporation DSM, once said, "Nobody can be successful in a world that fails."[6] This adage has some quite far-reaching implications: 'No government can be successful in a world where business fails'; 'No business can be successful in a world where governments fail'; 'No business nor government can be successful in a world that fails ecologically.' And if one brings civil society, families, educational institutions and media into the equation – which we should – the number of formulations grow exponentially. So the task of 'reorientation, reconnection, and repositioning' is a *multiactor endeavor*, as will be argued in this book. As the late British rabbi Jonathan Sacks said, "Society is a home we build together."[7]

Moreover, the current challenge for Europe is no longer how to attain as much globalization as possible but to (1) reorient our economies toward sustainability and inclusivity, to develop a new form of capitalism, and to approach the question of globalization from that angle. But in this process, it is (2) crucial to organize this as a common project for all strata of the population, protecting them from economic and geopolitical turmoil within their different nation states while (3) pursuing a geopolitical and geoeconomic strategy that furthers the global renewal of the economy and at the same time keeps Europe in a strong economic position, defending its own interests. Instead of Rodrik's trilemma, we would therefore propose a triangle of three goals that have to be met at the same time and within which policies constantly have to move, sometimes leaning toward one point and at other times toward another. But the third corner can never be abandoned. We call this a 'thorny transition triangle' or 'triangular challenge.'

For this huge and ever-recurring task, a fourth challenge may turn out to be key (one that is not mentioned by Rodrik but may well

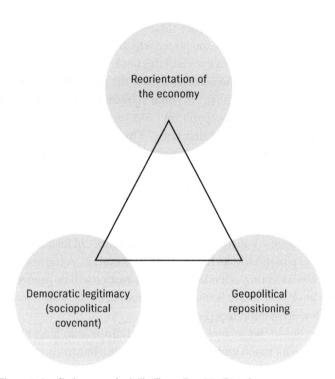

Figure 1a (preliminary version): *The Thorny Transition Triangle*

prove to be essential for dealing with this trilemma): to formulate one's own values and goals, tell a story about what it means to be 'European' and what European nations, apart and together, want to be, a 'European dream' of sorts (which should also acknowledge Europe's dark sides!). Only if one has a clear sense of what one considers to be truly valuable can one find the overall direction in which to navigate within the 'thorny triangle' just sketched. So, the fourth challenge for the European nations and their economies is to

4. revaluate Europe's own leading principles, values and sources of inspiration and to reorient its economy accordingly. Human dignity, inclusivity and ecological sustainability, together with an emphasis on co-creativity and innovation, can be seen as key values for Europe (as we will expound later on).

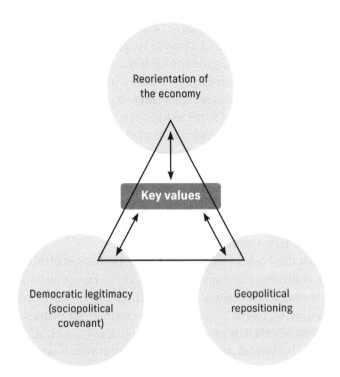

Reorientation of
the economy

Key values

Democratic legitimacy
(sociopolitical
covenant)

Geopolitical
repositioning

Figure 1b: *Value-orientation within the Thorny Triangle of the Transition Towards a Sustainable, Inclusive and Innovative Economy*

New Intellectual Resources: Rethinking Capitalism

With this fourfold challenge we are engaging in what can be called 'reflexive modernization': not simply taking the economy as it has emerged in modern times at face value but, given the problems it has created, engaging in 'rethinking our economy,' what needs to be kept, what needs to be changed, what new direction can we find?[8] The challenge may easily cause a sense of powerlessness. In this endeavor, however, we have at our disposal a true avalanche of recent literature, mostly by economists, that breaks through the sometimes rather dogmatic sterility of economic thinking in earlier decades and breaks new ground. After the credit crisis, new reflection on the nature of capitalism started, consisting at first of more direct analyses of 'when did what happen and how did it go wrong.' Later on, this was expanded and deepened by fresh analyses of the ecological problems caused by our current economy. It then developed into more in-depth analyses of capitalism and proposals about how the idea and reality of a free market can be reoriented toward furthering the common good, instead of undermining it.

This new literature has promulgated new terms like 're-sponsible capitalism,' 'moral capitalism,' 'conscious capitalism,' 'progressive capitalism,' an 'economy for the common good,' 'regenerative capitalism,' 'doughnut economics,' 'economy of arrival,' 're-imagined capitalism,' 'democratic capitalism,' or whatever term one wants to use.[9]

What this book intends to do is to reap the harvest of this new body of literature and apply it specifically to European nations and their central cooperative organization, the European Union. Moreover, we intend to sketch ways to actually get there, steps that can be taken by all of us, a multiplicity of actors, such as citizens, businesses, and governments. In this vein, it sketches a possible 'European Economic Approach' as distinguished from both unfettered capitalism and autocratic capitalism – continuing and renewing the typical European search for a 'third way' (see below). We prefer to call this 'responsible capitalism' but sometimes will use other phrases such as 'an economy for the common good.'

Much of the literature on 'rethinking capitalism' focuses on either the ecological agenda or the social agenda (inequality) but has difficulty integrating these two, let alone taking the geopolitical context into account. However, the latter is the context in which a new economic order actually has to be developed. As both the SDGs and Francis's encyclical *Laudato Si'* – both mentioned earlier as landmarks of 2015 – strongly emphasize, it is impossible to separate the ecological from the social and vice versa. And realism demands that we look as well at the geopolitical arena in which a renewed capitalism has to take shape. This book therefore intends to take steps toward integrating these various elements because they are all crucial elements of the transitions ahead. It becomes increasingly clear that, in some sense, each element functions as precondition for the others.

Another theme that is often missing from the literature on 'rethinking capitalism' is reflection on what 'European values' are and why Europe should be a leading agent in this process (at least as long as others are not taking that role). One of the outcomes of our public discussions with leading economists included in the input for this book was that almost all, including those with an American background such as Stiglitz, Sachs, and Rajan, pointed to Europe as the continent that needs to take a leading role in the global reorientation toward a more sustainable and inclusive type of market economy.[10] In this book, we aim to substantiate this claim by outlining moral, and sometimes also spiritual, resources that have developed in Europe and may provide the needed orientation for a new future (while not closing our eyes at all to the darker sides of Europe and its history).

Thus, this book is an attempt to integrate various discourses that urgently need each other to make the move from dreams to reality: ecological, sociopolitical, geopolitical, and moral/cultural discourses. Why this attempt at integrating these discourses? Taken individually and on their own, each of these discourses risks creating its own 'bubble' and 'tunnel' and therefore runs the risk of staying on the margins of real developments. In retrospect, we can say that the ecological discourse as well as the protests against the growing inequality within countries has been relegated to the margins far too long. The wrong type of 'realism' prevailed: 'This is not how the real world works.' In our present predicament, however, the entire opposition between 'realism' and 'idealism,' between 'morality' and 'markets,' between 'a better world' and 'realist politics' is evaporating. In the present context, these former oppositions come together. If we don't work toward a more sustainable and fairer world, the world as we know it may collapse. As Paul Polman, former CEO of Unilever, has been saying at multiple occasions in recent years: "The price of doing nothing is now greater than the costs of acting." This concerns the direct costs of climate adaptation but also the consequences of ecological degradation such as political instability both at a global level, resulting in, among other things, massive migration and, at a national level, in growing distrust and resentment that may threaten the democratic order. So 'mainstreaming the margin' is the call of the day. Idealism has become realism.

Some Working Definitions: Market Economy, Capitalism, Market Society, Market Ideology

Terms like 'market economy' and 'capitalism' can be defined in many ways.[11] We will not go into a lengthy discussion but will give some working definitions that can help us throughout this book.

Market Economy. We would describe a 'market economy' (anticipating some arguments presented later in this book) as an economic system in which:
- the means of production – labor, capital, natural resources, knowledge – are privately owned and brought together in 'cooperative hubs' of people with a diversity of talents, led by entrepreneurs/enterprises
- which together produce goods and services that are freely exchanged with buyers in free competition with other suppliers at a mutually agreed price (market)
- which enables the entrepreneur to make a profit, pay his employees, and cover other production costs, including the cost of capital, and
- last but not least, governments do not directly interfere in the market process but do ensure a legal framework within which the enterprises can operate, and in which the 'external effects' of the production processes are fairly addressed. Moreover, governments also play a role in defining and partly organizing or providing public goods that are not delivered, cannot be delivered, or may even be undermined by the market.

Capitalism. But why then speak of 'capitalism'? 'Capitalism' is often used simply as a synonym for market economies, and we will sometimes use it in this loose way as well. But if one wants to be more precise, it may prove useful to reserve the term 'capitalism' for a specific phase in market economies in which the role of shareholders and other providers of capital becomes more and more important.[12] Financiers may become less and less interested in *what* is produced and for whatever reason and become focused more and more exclusively on whether something is able to produce a profit. A substantial assessment of whether a new investment is adding real value for people, for society, has become increasingly superseded by an assessment of what gives the highest return on investment, preferably in the short term, for the capital providers. The classic short formulation of this tendency was already given by Marx in *Das Kapital* where he describes the role of money (M) in 'ordinary' market economies as a means to facilitate the exchange of goods (G), hence $G \rightarrow M \rightarrow G$.[13] In capitalist economies, however, the role of money and goods have swapped places. The exchange of goods facilitates the growth of money, hence $M \rightarrow G \rightarrow M^+$. If we look at capitalism in this 'pure' form, it then refers to an impersonal system in which the incentives for the financiers are clear: search the entire globe for investment opportunities that give the 'biggest bang for your buck.' In this vein, almost everything can become 'tradable' or 'commodified.'[14]

Moreover, what we have seen in recent decades is that financial markets can become almost fully independent markets where derivative financial products are traded, with almost no reference any longer to underlying real value – 'footloose,' as it were. Money and financial assets become a tradable commodity themselves. The Marxian formula would then read: $M \rightarrow M^+ \rightarrow M^{++}$. Any connection with the 'real economy' of goods and services is lost. This results in the total amount of money in the world vastly outnumbering the value of the real economy. We will come back to this later when we discuss 'financialization' (chapter 3).

To conclude, we will sometimes use 'capitalism' and 'market economies' loosely as synonyms (especially when capitalism is used with an adjective: 'moral,' 'regenerative,' 'progressive,' 'responsible,' etc.), but we will sometimes use it as a critical description of a market economy that has become entirely 'financialized.' In those cases, we will often employ adjectives like 'unfettered,' 'unrestricted,' or 'disembedded' capitalism (or 'unfettered markets').

Market Society. This brings us close to the concept of a 'market society.'[15] A 'market society' is one in which the market-type of transactions – and more precisely, a specific truncated subset of market relations, namely buying, selling, accounting, and private profitmaking – is increasingly institutionalized and viewed as the sole mode of interaction between people. Everything is for sale – even a Nobel Prize, if that were possible! A distinction is often made between the various ways in which societies or, better, people within societies coordinate their mutual activities: by living in communities where love, loyalty and cooperation are the primary means of relating to each other (without profit, so the mutual 'gift' is crucial), by organizing political bodies that can establish and enforce rules for everybody, and by market relations, in which people freely buy and sell, pick and choose, cash and carry.[16] The theory on this often says that, in a well-developed, balanced society, all three presuppose and need each other, like three pillars for one roof.[17] In a market society however, this balance is disrupted. The argument is often made that, in the long run, a market society is self-destructive: growing inequality, together with dysfunctional public institutions ('private wealth, public poverty') and marketized private lives instead of communities and cooperation, causing the social context for healthy businesses to be destroyed in the long run, resulting in a low trust society where transaction costs go sky high. From win-win-win, the dynamics swing to lose-lose-lose. This self-defeating dynamics of market societies will be our concern throughout this book.[18]

Market Ideology. The development toward a 'market society' is propelled by what can be called a 'market ideology': stories and intellectual reflections (we wouldn't necessarily call them scientific, although universities have played an active role in promulgating them) that state that markets always provide the best solutions to societal problems.[19] All these narratives and reflections repudiate the importance of the role of states, communities, morality, spirituality, and other domains for a well-functioning economy.

Outline of the Book

This book is divided into three parts:
- Part I: Europe's Present Condition: A Diagnosis
- Part II: Europe's Mission: Developing Responsible Capitalism
- Part III: Europe's New Position: A Global Player for the Common Good

In Part I, **Europe's Present Condition**, we start from the most recent developments in Europe and look back upon the great European – and more broadly, Western – project of the last 250 years, the escape from poverty, for which a market economy/capitalism was an important driver. This system, however, proved to have destructive tendencies as well and therefore was – still is – in need of correction and political embedding. In recent decades, this insight has tended to become lost to view. The balances between markets, states, and civil society/communities were abandoned in favor of 'markets alone.' This leads to a number of distortions that require a new response, a new phase of correction and embedding of the market economy. European nations and their cooperative association, the European Union, have to reorient their market economies to make them ecologically and socially robust, while at the same time (re) connect them with their own populations and reckon with a new geopolitical constellation, in which the US, China, and Russia have each recently adopted new positions. To navigate these challenges, a new sense of shared values within Europe is essential.

In Part II, **Europe's Mission**, we sketch what such a new embedding of the market economy could entail. We lay out a fivefold agenda of renewal, an agenda that revolves around five I's: renewing *Ideals* (1), renewing *Inspiration* (2), renewing economic *Ideas* (3), renewing economic *Indicators* (4) and renewing *Institutions* (5). We make this case against the background of an interpretation of European culture and European history, with all its ambivalences, its hope-giving upsides and terrible downsides. A well-functioning economy, from a European perspective, requires a broad range of actors who all play their own roles in cooperation and, if necessary, in conflict. Old oppositions like 'either market or state' are simply no longer up to the task. The 'multiactor approach' that we propose – as a further development of a stakeholder approach – runs the risk that each actor waits until the other takes the initiative, the risk that ethicists have dubbed the 'problem of many hands.' Therefore, we strongly emphasize the 'power of initiative': each actor – businesses, governments (local, national, international), consumers, civil society, intellectual and religious leaders, and so on – can, or even has to, take initiatives to address problems that they observe from their own perspective and build coalitions with other actors to deal with these problems.

In Part III, **Europe's New Position**, we discuss the attitude and strategy that Europe can follow in the geoeconomic and geopolitical context of the 21st century, as a self-conscious geopolitical and geoeconomic actor that is aware at the same time of the implications of the condition of a multipolar world order. In today's world, Europe is not an island. Formulating new ideals and nurturing new practices can hardly succeed if it is a 'stand-alone' exercise. We have entered into an age of globalization and there is no way back. Efforts for a reorientation of the market economy have to reckon with this new reality of living together in a multipolar world.

Our Intended Readership

The people we have in mind in particular as readers of this book are policy advisors, politicians, business leaders, thought leaders, all those who are in a position to actually shape our future, old and young. But we could also ask: Who is not in such a position? Each of us individually, and each company or NGO (small or large) has, as we argue later in this book, 'the power of initiative.' Many of us who may feel unease or even outrage about our present economic system may also have a feeling that 'There Is No Alternative'(the infamous phrase uttered by Margaret Thatcher about capitalism). Many people, in all these positions, when they long for change, feel the urgency and are willing to take steps toward a different future, but may still lack a perspective on what this might look like and how another type of market economy can ever become reality. The current domestic political situation in quite a few countries as well as the geopolitical situation is a matter of great concern and may cause paralysis and pessimism among the younger generations or cynicism among the elderly. The almost natural response in such situations is to cling to the supposed certainties of a bygone era. This book aims to sketch new ways for an undoubtedly different, but certainly not worse and perhaps even better, future – for all humans, and for the earth itself, 'our common home.' There Are Alternatives.

The Title of this Book

We have called this book 'Capitalism Reconnected.' This refers first of all to the connection with the next generations. The generation that is in power right now has not given enough consideration to future generations and has broken what the conservative philosopher Edmund Burke once called the "partnership not only between those who are living, but between those who are living, those who are dead, and those who are to be born."[20] There is a lot of anger and anxiety among the younger generations, anger about the past, anxiety about the future. Greta Thunberg's activities and those of Extinction Rebellion can be seen as indicative here.[21] This book intends to restore some parts of this contract, this covenant among the generations, perhaps turning anger into action and anxiety into hope.

But 'reconnected' also refers as well to the European nations internally. Almost all European nations face internal rifts and clashes. The economy has in recent decades propelled various types of inequality and by consequence divisions between 'winners' and 'losers,' a division that is sealed by a strong 'meritocratic' discourse: 'You only have yourself to blame.' More and more people are no longer buying into this and are starting to resist in various ways and starting – to borrow the language of the sociologist Manuel Castells – "to exclude the excluders," which even threatens our democratic order.[22] Reconnection is needed between economy and society, between political and business leaders on the one hand and voters and customers on the other.

Furthermore, 'reconnected' is a key term in the relationship between human beings and nature. In modern times this relation was characterized by separation, by an instrumental view of nature, as some 'thing' out there that we can manipulate at will, not as a larger whole that we ourselves are part of and that we therefore have to respect and preserve. 'Reconnected' therefore also aims at a new relationship with nature.

'Reconnected' also refers to the European nations together that, inside or outside the European Union, share a continent together and have to live with each other and are in the same boat geopolitically, whether they like it or not. There is the risk that, in the present fearful geopolitical situation, after the Russian invasion of Ukraine and all that this entails and will still prove to entail and after an initial phase of unity, European nations will let themselves be played out against each other, some drawing closer to the US, others to China, others perhaps even to Russia. Given Europe's mission, as we outline it in this book, there is a need as well for a new long-term connection between the European nations, for what they have in common with respect to values, history, inspiration, and aspiration is much more and much stronger than whatever separates them (as anyone can tell who travels outside Europe and then looks at Europe from that outside perspective).

Last but not least, 'reconnected' also refers to the relation of Europe with the non-European world, especially the global South.

Up until the present, the world economy has been and is centered to a high degree around the global North. Although this book has a strong focus on Europe, that is not meant to stimulate European isolationism, on the contrary: Europe should design its economy in such a way that the global South is no longer exploited, but can really find its own just and dignified role in the global economy.

The Book in Three Figures

The content of the book can be briefly rendered in three figures, one of which has already been presented above.

First Figure:

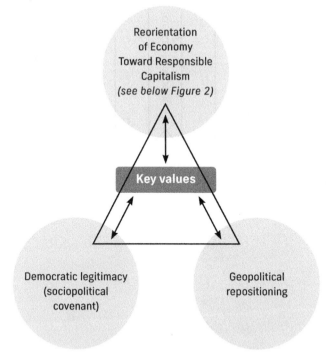

Figure 1: *Value-orientation within the Thorny Triangle of the Transition Towards a Sustainable, Inclusive and Innovative Economy*

Second Figure:

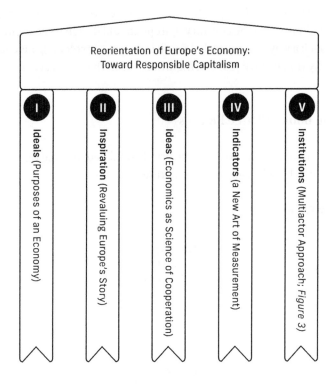

Figure 2: *The Reorientation of the Economy: Five Pillars of Renewal (5 I's)*

Third figure:

Figure 3: *The Institutional Platform of Responsible Capitalism*

How (not) to Use this Book

This book can be used in many different ways. One can of course read it from beginning to end and follow the argument from step to step.

But it is not a novel. One can also follow different paths through the book. The heart of our argument is found in chapter 3 (on the problems of today's capitalism), the final section of chapter 6 on the new set of common values that Europeans should adopt, and in chapter 9 where we outline the multiactor approach – and, of course, the 'Challenges and Recommendations' at the end.

People who are especially interested in the way businesses can operate in the context of 'responsible capitalism' can refer to chapters 8 and 10. Those who want to read more about the role of economic education and research can read chapters 7 and 12.

The geopolitical aspects are elaborated in chapters 13 and 14. People who are interested in Europe's history of dealing with economics can refer to chapters 2 and 6.

All this comes down to: Use the book as you see fit.

Chapter 2
Europe's 250-Year Project...

The Age of the 'Great Enrichment' or the 'Escape from Poverty'

The seven years that we described above may well turn out to be the end of several eras at once. First of all, they mark the end of an era that started about 250 years ago in which Western societies embarked on a project of overcoming poverty by creating new sources of wealth. It was what has often been called the 'Industrial Age,' which at the same time became a 'Free Market Age.' It entailed the transition from what had been (by and large) a 'zero-sum economy' for millennia, to an economy of new wealth creation, which Deirdre McCloskey has called 'the Great Enrichment'[1] and can also be called the 'Escape from Poverty Project.'[2] Through a mixture of technology, the division of labor/ specialization, entrepreneurship, trade, and the growing availability of cheap labor (the 'working class' within Europe, slavery outside Europe), energy and raw materials, it turned out to be possible to escape widespread poverty and to create the "wealth of nations," as the herald of this new age, Adam Smith, called it in his 1776 landmark book. What he actually meant was wealth for "the different ranks of the people." Now it became possible, Smith claimed, for the standard of living of "an industrious and frugal peasant [to exceed] that of many an African king."[3]

It was – and still is – a new era in the history of humankind. Indeed, an entire class of people of non-aristocratic descent was able to liberate itself from feudal and aristocratic bondage. The 'bourgeois' class, as they came to be called, developed many new initiatives: new businesses were founded that made new technologies fruitful for what came to be called 'progress.' What Acemoglu and Robinson have called "extractive institutions" were curbed and replaced by institutions that were much more responsive to the needs of people. As a whole, it has been a truly amazing age in the history of humankind, indeed an age of progress. We live longer than any generation before us, are much better educated, have more political rights, more individual freedom, are much better equipped to deal with illnesses and diseases, live more comfortably, and so on.[4]

But this new age developed its own downsides and ambivalences as well: the great heights were often accompanied by severe depths. Within this new era, this 'escape from poverty,' we can distinguish four stages, each with its own mix of achievements and downsides.

Heights and Depths: Four Phases, from Unfettered Markets to 'Unfettered Markets 2.0'

Market Potential Unleashed. The first launch phase in the 19th century included the creation of economic and technological growth. The Industrial Revolution went hand in hand with a revolution in entrepreneurship. New factories were established, new industries started, first in Britain and then other countries followed suit. The innovative potential of markets showed itself, almost for the first time in history. Older ways of producing materials were abandoned in favor of new techniques in a process that the Austrian economist Schumpeter would later call "creative destruction." This also created a sense of progress and hope.[5] People started to move from the countryside to new cities where the industrial action was, hoping to make a better living.

But the downsides became manifest as well. A growing number of them, including women and children, had to work in harsh circumstances in coal mines and in dirty factories. They had to live in crowded slums. People suffered from new dependencies and even exploitation. Karl Marx, the philosopher-economist who made incisive analyses of these developments, would come to identify them as proletarians. It was a situation that still occurs, at the present time, in quite a few countries in the global South. In reference to this, it must be stated that labor, technology and trade were certainly not the only drivers of the 'Great Enrichment': this age was increasingly also driven by drawing 'resources,' both material as well as human (slave labor), from the global South that had been colonized.

So, this first phase of the market revolution, the first phase of capitalism (coinciding with the Industrial Revolution), called for substantial corrections. The lesson of the 19th century was clear: markets create economic growth, but they do not automatically create a just society, neither nationally nor internationally. Economic growth can go together with social deprivation, extraction, and exploitation. It is very well possible for market economies and the governments that harbor them to create oppressive, extractive structures not all that different from earlier feudal exploitation – making a bad situation worse.

Protective Legislation. Important corrections were indeed made in a *second* phase, in which critical analyses were made of the derailment of the market economy, first by various types of socialists (among them of course Karl Marx, already mentioned above) and later as well by various types of Christian social thinkers, both Roman Catholic and Protestant. This led, toward the end of the 19th century, to protective legislation for children and women, and later for all workers, in most European countries. Yes, this took a long time: it is not only old habits that die hard – new habits, such as market ideologies, do as well. Civil society initiatives were taken to improve the living conditions of the underprivileged classes regarding housing, health, and education. Some of these initiatives were supported or even adopted by states. In this way, gradual steps toward a threshold level of decent living conditions were made, albeit only in the West itself. The non-Western world did not partake in this first correction of capitalism, although the abolition of slavery was a part of this phase. This second phase can be characterized as a socio-moral counteroffensive against a derailed market economy:

this is proof that such a counter-offensive is possible and can be effective – which is something worth remembering.

Welfare States. A *third* phase in Europe began as a response to the economic crisis of the 1930s that was followed by World War II, a period in which the need for and reality of broadly shared common interests among the entire population – so many people of all ranks cooperating to win the war – had made itself felt. This phase was marked by the development of various types of welfare states. Both in the US, with Franklin Roosevelt's New Deal, and in Europe, where, in the UK, Lord Beveridge wrote a very influential report on the need for a welfare state, the idea was implemented that the state had to ensure basic living standards for every citizen, regardless of their economic position: general education, health care, housing. The exact organizational arrangements could vary from country to country, with a much greater role in some cases for civil society (family, labor unions, housing corporations, mutual health insurances, etc.), and in other cases a larger role for the state or for market players, thus creating different types or 'worlds' of welfare capitalism, as Esping-Anderson would call them.[6] This period, roughly between 1930 and 1975, has been called the 'Long Exception,' for only in this phase did inequality really decrease, whereas it increased in all three other phases.[7] Only in this period do we see a gradual development toward a more balanced relation between labor and capital, as the French economist Piketty has shown.[8]

This was often combined with the idea that states should play an active role in the economy by public investments in times in which the market economy suffered setbacks or outright recessions, a policy advocated by John Maynard Keynes. Globally, both geopolitically and geoeconomically, this third phase was marked as well by the emergence of communist countries, first of all the USSR and China, along with quite a number of smaller states (often newly formed in the wake of decolonization). The complex relationship between the superpowers was characterized as a 'Cold War.' Decolonialization was part of this phase as well, although most of the time this was not the result of new human-itarian insights but of the loss of power of the European nations in the wake of two world wars. Steps were taken to improve growth opportunities for non-Western countries (the World Bank, development cooperation, etc.) but this didn't amount to much in this phase. Economic relations throughout the world remained very unequal.

Triumphant Capitalism. A *fourth* phase in the age of the 'Great Enrichment' started with the economic stagnation in the early 1970s, partly induced by one of the first manifestations of the rising power of the non-Western world and hence of the growing dependency of the North: the Arab Oil Crisis. Inflation and stag-nation went hand in hand, causing a theoretically unexpected 'stagflation.' Toward the end of the third phase, quite a few states were less successful in maintaining a balance between state, market, and civil society. States had grown to such a level that they ran into serious financial difficulties. They were no longer able to play their Keynesian balancing role in the economy but had started to 'crowd out' the market economy and civil society as well. The welfare state ran into severe problems concerning its bureaucratic (in)effectiveness, its costs, and its moral legiti-macy (creating dependent people). This stagnation triggered the election of Margaret Thatcher in the UK and later Ronald Reagan in the US, in 1979 and 1980 respectively.

The new economic wind that they unleashed had been prepared by the growing influence of economists like Friedrich Hayek and Milton Friedman, both strong advocates of limited states, unfettered markets, and strict monetary policies, severe critics of welfare states, and vehemently anti-Keynesian.[9] Both were awarded the so-called 'Nobel Prize for Economics' – actually the Sveriges Riksbank Prize in Economic Sciences in Memory of Alfred Nobel, given that Nobel himself didn't institute a Nobel Prize for economics – in 1974 and 1976 respectively. The period between 1980 and 2007 is often called the phase of 'neoliber-alism' and is characterized by both budget cuts and tax cuts, privatization or 'marketization' of services that were, entirely or partly, organized by states or civil society in earlier phases (e.g., public transport, social housing, electricity, parts of health care provisions), and great confidence in the self-regulating forces of the free market – hence deregulation. The private business sector was considered to be much more efficient and innovative than the public sector. The cultural 'icon' of a successful person came increasingly to be the entrepreneur (whereas earlier he often was seen as a somewhat dubious figure). What remained of services arranged by the government or civil society – which are still very considerable at present, despite the lengthy history of anti-government rhetoric – were reorganized preferably in a business-like manner, hierarchically, with a focus on quantitative results, often referred to as 'New Public Management.' In this way, despite the emphasis on freedom in free market discourse, governments and civil society organizations turned this fourth stage into quite a technocratic endeavor. Apparently, market freedom and technocratic control can go well together.

A defining turning point of this age was the fall of the Berlin Wall, marking the collapse of the Soviet Union, and the gradual opening up of China and its subsequent participation in the world economy. Capitalism had won the world-historical contest over how to successfully organize an economy, completing the 'Great Enrichment' – or so it seemed. A period of unprecedented economic globalization followed, with the establishment of the World Trade Organization (WTO) in 1994, replacing the much more piecemeal trade arrangements known as GATT (General Agreement on Tariffs and Trade, established in 1947) as a both symbolic and real culmination point. In 2001, China joined the WTO as well.

This fourth phase of the 'Great Enrichment' was also marked by the digital revolution and the emergence of an entirely new kind of company. These companies have relatively few employees compared to their financial worth and market power: the high-tech companies, the largest of whom are now called MAGMA or GAMMA (Google, Apple, Microsoft, Meta, and Amazon). This is, again, a curious development: free markets and extensive technocratic control of data and humans can go together indeed – also in the relation between (big) companies and their customers. An extensive apparatus of algorithmic surveillance has been designed to 'mine' the private data of customers and turn these data into profitable material, with a much higher return on investment than raw materials in the 'old economy.' In this 'free market,' all people are free, but some, apparently, are much freer than others. And all are equal, but this equality pertains in particular to the profitability of one's personal data. The term 'surveillance capitalism' has been introduced to capture this new and very curious stage in what was earlier hailed as the 'epitome of freedom.'[10]

The most consequential development, perhaps, in this phase is the financialization of the economy (also see below, chapter 3). The financial economy grew disproportionately, compared to the real economy of goods and services. Financial investments were more profitable than investment in the real economy and the results of labor, so the labor share of income has been decreasing (a phenomenon that is also occurring in the high-tech sector). More and more economies in this fourth phase of the 'escape from poverty' are therefore starting to look like rentiers economies that by nature tend to produce inequality, as labor income tends to be (much) less profitable than income based on financial assets.

Learning Processes: Embedding Markets

What was learned throughout the first three phases, in a difficult and tortuous learning process, was to embed the free market in an extensive sociopolitical framework. Markets cannot be left to their own devices. Their great innovative potential can easily become destructive because many of the so-called 'external effects' of innovation are not accounted for. Therefore, embedding markets in a sociopolitical framework is essential to truly turning market innovations into general contributions to human wellbeing. And this framework needs to be inspired by basic values, focused on human dignity, justice, and solidarity, and by basic virtues practiced by the market participants, such as honesty, temperance, prudence (here: long-term orientation), courage, and even benevolence/love (as some studies suggest). Neither markets – nor states for that matter – can do without a guiding moral orientation, although it may be very difficult to align moral values and virtues with economic and political behavior and policies.[11]

The various nations that had embarked on the project to overcome poverty by economic development therefore had to learn to take on a critical-reflective stance toward the market economy, seeing both its innovative, poverty-overcoming, wealth-creating potential as well as its destructive potential. This critical-reflective stance and the articulation of these leading values very often occurs in civil society at first, outside the market and the state: in religious organizations, in social movements, in labor movements, and so on.

This core idea of 'socially embedded markets' later went under several names such as the 'Third Way,' or 'civil economy,' 'Rhine model,' 'mixed economies,' or 'social market economy' (German *soziale Marktwirtschaft*), or, in the English context, the attempts to formulate a 'Red Tory' or 'Blue Labour' vision.[12] The common core is the ongoing quest for a good society (not just a maximizing economy), with an economy that works for all, respects individual freedom, safeguards each person's dignity, stimulates innovation, and prevents oppressive conglomerate power and corporate monopolies (and today we would add ecological sustainability).

In retrospect, the broad popular support for these kinds of arrangements in most Western countries is remarkable. Although the specific histories are quite different from country to country, the general idea of some kind of market economy combined with broadly available social, medical, and educational services went together with an almost unquestioned legitimacy of a democratic order, in which sometimes more right-wing, sometimes more left-wing parties were in power. Stagflation and unemployment in the 1970s triggered political unrest, but the idea of democracy itself survived relatively uncontested.

Compared to the third phase, by contrast, one can say that the critical reflective way of dealing with the market was given up in favor of an uncritical endorsement of markets in the fourth phase. Compared to phases two and three, the fourth has been one of 'unlearning,' of decline in wisdom and moral sensibility. The similarities to the first phase are striking: unfettered markets have returned, and so have their results. This has serious consequences. Remarkably, in various countries in the world, we see that democracy itself is coming under fire at the end of the fourth stage: the democracy-supporting 'social capital' that was built up in phases two and three is being wasted.[13] A widespread sense that the 'traditional' political parties no longer channel the will of substantial parts of the population allows the emergence of what have been called 'populist' movements that sometimes quite bluntly question the legitimacy of the constitutional democratic order.[14] One wonders why. In the next chapter we will attempt to give a deeper analysis of the inherent problems of this fourth phase. And calling this fourth phase a 'phase' may imply that that it will not be the 'end of history' but may require a new, fifth, phase...

Chapter 3

Triumphant Capitalism: The Bold Assumptions of an Overconfident Age

Seven Assumptions

Within the 250-year project of the Escape from Poverty/Great Enrichment, it is this fourth phase that is now apparently drawing to an end, culminating in the septennium that we described earlier. But what is the connection between the fourth phase and the problems we identified in the first chapter? To clarify this, it is helpful to have a closer look at the dynamics and key assumptions of this fourth phase.

This phase can be called 'triumphant capitalism.' The collapse of its global rivals and the improving economic performance of the US and the UK in the later 1980s (GDP growth, reduced inflation, dropping unemployment figures, lower taxes) gave wings to their economic policies of deregulation, privatization, cutting government spending and cutting taxes. Francis Fukuyama caught the mood of the age very well with his phrase "the end of history."[1] The triumphant mood was boosted as well by the fact that in the 1990s the digital revolution started to reach the masses seemingly as a pure result of free entrepreneurship (although the basis for this was actually laid by public investments, particularly in the defense industry).[2] In retrospect, '1989' wasn't interpreted as the collapse or the conscious abandonment of one system – communism – but as the victory, the triumph of the other system: unfettered capitalism. And according to a well-known American custom, 'winner takes all.'

Triumph – especially when accompanied by this 'winner takes all' mentality – is closely related to overconfidence and overstretch. The Belgian political scientist Jonathan Holslag even spoke of a period of consumerist decadence in which the Western world – in particular Europe – failed to adequately prepare for the long-term future, geopolitically and geoeconomically, making its future adversaries stronger and stronger.[3] And, we may add, it didn't adequately prepare for the internal challenges within their own societies either. The 'overconfidence' manifested itself in at least seven ways, seven assumptions that guided mentalities and policies in Western countries and beyond (for example, via the so-called 'Washington consensus').

'The Market Will Solve it' Assumption. "This is what we believe," Margaret Thatcher is supposed to have said in 1975 during a meeting, throwing a copy of Friedrich Hayek's *The Constitution of Liberty* (1960) on the table. The book is a passionate defense of the self-organizing power, the 'spontaneous forces' and 'spontaneous order' of free markets and a strong indictment of the welfare state and of government intervention in the economy. It can therefore be read indeed as manifesto for the fourth phase of the 'Escape from Poverty' project. The trust in the salutary effects of free markets now grew to the stage that more and more of those safety valves for markets, the checks and balances established in the earlier phases, were removed. The basic idea was that money always looks for the most efficient ways to produce more money and will thus always come up with the most desired products and best solutions. Possible negative 'external effects' will be solved by the very same dynamic: when external effects become a real burden for people, sales will drop and businesses will be replaced by better operating businesses with less negative external effects. The mantra thus now becomes 'deregulation,' based on the presumption, as FED president Alan Greenspan would state later, "that the self-interest of organizations, specifically banks and others, is such that they are best capable of protecting shareholders and their equity in firms."[4]

The role of governments came to be seen, ideally, as that of creators and facilitators of markets, small but strong. They were to be small: governments were no longer seen as active economic agents themselves, making investments, as Keynes would have it. And they were to be strong: the regulating function of governments is supposed to be strong in order to prevent monopolies and cartels. Governments were also to be strong in that they should try to create new markets in areas where cooperative or public arrangements previously provided certain services (e.g., housing, education, health care). So both government and civil society had to be pushed back forcefully, in favor of the private, for-profit sector. Markets should be everywhere.

This overconfidence in the regulatory and self-regulatory power of markets obtained especially for the financial sector, particularly in the UK and the US. The Glass–Steagall Act, a precautionary law enacted following the earlier economic crisis in the early 1930s, was repealed in 1999, removing the wall between commercial banking and investment banking. Deregulation in the UK also stimulated the emergence of the City of London as a financial hub in the world. All kinds of highly complex financial products were created that turned out to be extremely risky and evaded any supervision by financial authorities. Crediting consumer spending and business investments started to turn into over-crediting. After this, a whole new layer of financial products, derivatives, was designed to offset the risks that were involved in the primary credit process, so-called Credit Default Swaps, adding layer to layer of risk insurance, with financial firms even insuring themselves against their own products. The 'financial industry' and the global money supply grew astronomically, perhaps one of the most defining characteristics of this fourth phase. How risky this was became apparent during the credit crisis of 2007 and the following years. The financial sector had created what Warren Buffet would call "financial weapons of mass destruction." Instead of solving problems, deregulated financial markets created new ones.[5]

In Greenspan's 2010 statement given above, another key characteristic of this phase was inadvertently highlighted: the first and foremost obligation of firms to protect and enhance their shareholder value. This loyalty to – often anonymous

– shareholders trumped the connection with other parties involved with the company, either in the production, chain in the customer chain, or in the physical, geographical, or social environment of the company who are affected by the company's action, the so-called 'stakeholders.' Theoretically and practically, a company came to be seen not as a group of people cooperating to create long-term added value, real worth, for stakeholders, but as a money-making machine for shareholders. They became unfettered, not really connected with or embedded in a social and ecological environment, and with a short-term horizon. Here, the distinction between 'market economy' as we defined it in the introductory chapter, and 'capitalism' is highly pertinent! Capitalism became a threat to the market economy.[6]

The 'Quantitative Bigger is Better' Assumption/Gigantism. The financial sector was not the only sector that expanded exponentially, compared to the real economy. New companies in the tech and digital communication sector also grew to gigantic proportions, not only with respect to their stock value but also with respect to their global digital power. They created something that has been called 'surveillance capitalism' in which citizen's data were transformed into massive profit resources.[7] In addition to Big Finance and Big Tech, something like Big Pharma emerged that, contrary to the fundamental preconditions for free markets, acquired *de facto* global monopolies or proxy monopolies on various types of medical drugs, often making use of scientific discoveries in the public domain that led to large profits. The model that the Giga sectors actually used came to be known as 'collectivizing debts and losses, privatizing profits.' Once big, it is easy to grow even bigger because 'Big Finance' loves to fund the other 'Bigs': they can borrow money at very low interest rates to finance takeovers of other companies, especially startups, in their sector.

One of the consequences of this 'gigantism' (a term coined by the Belgian economist Geert Noels[8]) in the market sector is that the amount of income that results from actual labor diminishes compared to the income that emerges from capital investment. The 'Bigs' are all highly oriented to shareholder value and have huge political power that they can use to prevent fair taxation and regulation, what is often called 'regulatory capture.'[9] In this they are often supported by 'Big Con,' highly influential, globally operating consultancy firms.[10]

Their sheer power puts them at odds with what – especially in the fourth phase of the market economy – was one of the key legitimations for capitalism: it frees people and protects them from domination by external powers.[11] How they operate has led several observers to talk about a 'new feudalism' in which ordinary people become 'serfs' under powerful 'lords.'[12] The ubiquitous power of the Giga companies contributes greatly to the feeling among large groups of the population that a powerful 'elite' is reaping the profits of the economic developments, while common people are suffering and paying the full price. Inequality is on the rise everywhere, resulting in what can be called a kind of oligarchic capitalism. More and more people are feeling uncertainty about their future, as large companies give the impression that they can come and go at will and hire and fire at will.

So, the final stage of the fourth phase, the phase dominated by free markets, gives rise to widespread dissatisfaction and distrust among citizens, even to the point that conspiracy theories are gaining increasing clout. Curiously enough, however, this distrust is often projected onto the political domain instead of onto the companies concerned. Companies spend an enormous amount on creating a good image of themselves and their products – the PR budget is growing to gigantic proportions as well, and this continuous PR warfare is paying off. It is the political domain that is considered to be failing at protecting people and has let itself be captured by 'Big Business.' So, the paradoxical outcome of the fourth phase is that the very government that has been withdrawing itself and was supposed to become less of a nuisance ended up being nevertheless distrusted and at the center of social turmoil as a useful scapegoat. "Government isn't the solution, government is the problem," is one of Ronald Reagan's most famous quotes, which seems to have been adopted by large groups of voters, neglecting the threats of the 'Bigs.'

The quantitative Bigger is Better assumption also becomes manifest in how the achievements of key economic actors, including the government itself, are measured. Instead of critically assessing how the economy or a company is doing in various domains, a 'mono-indicator policy' was followed, giving the semblance of certainty and of 'being in control.' For decades, the GDP was taken as *pars pro toto* for all the values that we identified as part of the common good. We thus installed and submitted to what can be called a 'mono-indicator tyranny,' relegating the responsibility of evaluation to one formal, abstract indicator. Something similar happened at the corporate level. We assumed that companies were doing fine if they made financial profits and hence increased shareholder value – despite, for example, health problems (e.g., the tobacco industry) or the environmental problems they sometimes created: 'the bigger, the better,' rather than 'the better, the better.'

The 'Money is Everything and Everything is Money' Assumption: Financialization. We have already mentioned how the development of free markets in Europe soon tended toward (unfettered) capitalism due to the ever-increasing role of money, not simply as a facilitator but as a commodity itself. What we witness today is that this process is still ongoing. The role of money in all kinds of decisions, political and corporate as well as those involving non-profit organizations, households, and personal choices, seems to be ever increasing. It is exactly for this reason that books have to remind us of what money can't buy.[13]

In the meantime, money can buy a lot. We see financialization in the increasing focus by companies on 'shareholder value,' including the increase in share buybacks.[14] We see it in the increasing decoupling of the financial world from the real economy as, as indicated earlier, money is increasingly becoming a tradable commodity itself, leading to an astronomical increase in the total amount of money in the world, exceeding the size of the real economy multiple times, and precisely therefore able to have influence on the real economy, often leading to 'short-termism.'

We also see it in the amount of outstanding debt in the world, which gives great power to the lenders (banks, equity funds, insurance companies) that do not have an intrinsic bond with the 'object' they are investing in, nor with the people involved. Increasingly, it is only the quantitative level of expected profits that guides the decision to participate. Often, it is not even that: many investment decisions regarding shares are made on the basis of the expectation of the share itself rising, quite independent of the underlying value (and, as the early 2021 case of GameStop showed, this is open to manipulation). Debts itself are now tradable assets. A layer of a whole range of derivatives has grown on top of financial markets.

Is all this a problem? Not necessarily, but it does distort our sense of how an economy is doing. It even distorts the very limited measure we have: GDP. The growth of the financial industry may give the impression that an economy is growing, while almost nothing can be seen of this growth in the real economy, for it is mainly financial. The result is that an economy may appear to be growing for decades, even though almost nobody experiences growth in real income. Moreover, the public sector continues to be underfunded because financial transactions often do not contribute much to a country's tax base. Therefore, we may experience 'phantom growth'[15] and even growing poverty at the very same time that governments are claiming 'growth' – a sure recipe for institutional distrust on the part of the citizens.[16]

The Citizen as Selfish Consumer Assumption. The fourth phase was also the age in which what Walt Rostow would call the "final stage of growth" was achieved, that of mass consumption.[17] This led in this phase to a new assumption as a basic principle for designing and 'selling' policies: citizens have no other desires and needs than the maximalization of consumption. They do not, it was assumed, see themselves as belonging to a nation or to other group identities. They do not even see themselves as workers who are proud of making certain products. They are no longer concerned with solidarity with the less advantaged, for each human being is responsible for their own success and hence for their own failures. You can easily take away jobs as long as you can compensate for that by increasing consumption. And the only question that counts with elections is – as both Ronald Reagan and Bill Clinton asked – "Are you better off today than you were four years ago?" Politics is therefore becoming more and more 'economized': it is not about how we create a good society together for everybody but how one's individual paychecks increase (that is ideally how the overall GDP growth is made tangible for voters). The *homo economicus* replaces the *homo politicus* and the *homo cooperans*.[18] This fostered an almost exclusive focus on economic growth as well, to make sure that each year we – or better, I – can consume more than the year before. And it was assumed that this longing concerns all people equally, worldwide: we are a humanity of consumers. This brings us to the fifth assumption.

The 'There is No Such Thing as Society' Assumption. It may be giving her a bit too much honor in this chapter, but there is another assumption that is often attributed directly to Margaret Thatcher. In an interview in September 1987 she said, referring to the many people who were living on state provisions, and hence on 'society':

Who is society? There is no such thing! There are individual men and women and there are families and no government can do anything except through people and people look to themselves first. It is our duty to look after ourselves and then also to help look after our neighbour and life is a reciprocal business .... There is no such thing as society. There is living tapestry of men and women and people and the beauty of that tapestry and the quality of our lives will depend upon how much each of us is prepared to take responsibility for ourselves and each of us prepared to turn round and help by our own efforts those who are unfortunate.[19]

It is good to provide the quote with some more context than is often done, for Thatcher certainly was not an Ayn Rand type defender of egoism and selfishness. She had a clear sense of the mutual responsibility of people for each other (hear, hear, let all 'neoliberalists' hear!).

And yet, her overall view of society is fraught with difficulties. For it is indeed the case that a view of society has become dominant in which society is seen as nothing but an empty platform for acting out individual life projects and individual interests. And it is certainly the case that, for Thatcher, there should be no institutional arrangements that somehow connect people, from all income levels of society, with each other. For her, and for many political and business leaders in her wake, the outcomes of the economic process are always right, whatever the distribution of income may turn out to be. "I've earned it" is the mistaken meritocratic adage that denies what we receive before any earning takes place: from parents, from 'society' (a well-organized country, education, health care, a judicial system, safety, etc.), from life itself (as no one is able to give oneself life).[20]

In recent years, the consequences of huge inequalities have become known in astonishing, often shocking, detail and are well documented in research literature. Joseph Stiglitz speaks of "the price of inequality."[21] This may be too much of a financial metaphor, but in reality the total 'costs' of inequality are indeed shocking, not just in moral terms of 'fairness' but also in terms of psychological health, lost creativity, educational underperformance, physical health, even plain death and suicide.[22] Moreover, inequality affects people's sense of belonging to society and may make them susceptible to radicalism, exclusionary collective identity movements, conspiracy theories, and so on. So, there are many reasons to develop a sense of 'togetherness' that takes material form in a fair distribution of primary goods (as John Rawls already advocated in the early 1970s), ensuring a balance between competition and solidarity. Or, in short: a sense that there is indeed something like 'society.'

The 'One World Assumption': Hyperglobalization. A sixth domain of overconfidence regarded globalization. In this phase of the era of the 'Great Enrichment,' an almost fully globalized economy was created with a global 'division of labor.' More and more, the global production of consumer goods was left to the South, especially first Taiwan and Japan and then China. Economies in the North developed more and more into knowledge-intensive service economies. The majority of the goods produced in the world, however, as well as the majority of the world fuel production were consumed in the North. By implication, this resulted in a North highly dependent on the South for its way of life. Moreover, a very dense global network of logistical supply chains was woven to make sure that all the goods arrived with 'just in time' delivery, as it came to be called. One ship running aground in the Suez Canal – the 'Ever Given' in March 2021 – symbolically revealed the vulnerability of the network. And during the Covid pandemic, the North realized that almost all basic medical supplies were being produced elsewhere. The same was true for energy. The countries in the North became highly dependent first upon oil from the Arab countries and Europe in particular later as well on the Russian supply of natural gas. Thanks to shale drilling, the US was able to become more or less energy independent after 2000. But its dependence on consumer goods produced elsewhere in the world remained. What, according to economic theory, was always profitable – international specialization and global trade, the 'law of comparative advantages' formulated by David Ricardo – turned out in reality to entail severe geopolitical risks.

In addition to the consumption of goods and energy, the dependence of the North concerns other raw materials, metals and minerals, especially those that are vital for a 'green transition' (see below). Electrification requires immense quantities of relatively precious raw materials like lithium, cobalt, and even copper will become more precious as demands increase substantially.[23] In recent decades, China has been much more proactive in securing these materials than Europe and the US have been.

Beyond the logistical vulnerability of the North, globalization has had a huge impact as well on the labor market in the North. Blue-collar jobs came under pressure, causing feelings of abandonment and uncertainty in large parts of the population for which blue-collar work was the key area of professional specialization. The stress on so-called 'higher education' undermined the professional pride formerly associated with craftsmanship and practical knowledge. Social analysts started to talk about the 'winners' and 'losers' of globalization, and the growing divide between the cosmopolitically oriented 'anywheres' and the locally oriented 'somewheres' that felt unprotected.[24]

The legitimation of what Dani Rodrik already earlier called "hyperglobalization"[25] was sought partly in the *doux commerce* thesis, formulated for the first time in the 18th century, that stated that trade makes people peaceful toward each other (in German: *Wandel durch Handel*, 'change through trade'). This was enhanced by a kind of world-historical expectation that the world would now finally move toward more peace, equality and democracy (we referred already to Francis Fukuyama's famous phrase "the end of history" at the beginning of this chapter). This 'One World Assumption' not only became an eschatological hope but was increasingly viewed as reality itself, making the global North blind to the still existing and newly emerging power differences in the world as well as to long-lasting cultural differences, even in the modern, globalized world. Moreover, part of this assumption was that the global division of labor that had newly emerged was going to last forever: knowledge and high tech in the West (not in China), consumer goods in China (not in the West), raw materials in Africa and Russia – as if this is both just and sustainable, let alone a reflection of reality rather than a passing neocolonial framework. This all contributed to what – with hindsight – can be characterized as geopolitical and geo-economic naiveté – a naiveté that was exposed during the Ukraine crisis in particular.

The Inexhaustible Resources Assumption. A seventh domain of overconfidence, last but certainly not least, concerned the ecological preconditions for a long-term healthy economy. The economic development of the entire age of the 'Great Enrichment,' and especially of the fourth phase of mass production and consumption, was based on a crucial but unarticulated assumption: that of unlimited natural resources and an inexhaustible and always automatically regenerative earth, regardless of what humans do, regardless of what they produce. The reality of 'planetary boundaries' was entirely unthinkable for centuries. Early warnings by the Club of Rome were largely neglected. Only gradually did the awareness of potential problems in this respect grow. The Brundtland Report of 1987 launched the felicitous term 'sustainability,' and this was a landmark, for now there was global recognition that our relations as humans with our natural environment is a vital matter of concern.

Here the big project of the 'Great Enrichment,' the 'Escape from Poverty,' is biting its own tail. As it turns out, the more successful the project is, the more vulnerable it becomes. The growing standards of living, and hence the rising consumer levels, combined with a rapidly growing world population, have resulted in a quantum leap in material production and energy consumption, and hence pollution (waste, plastics, PFAS and other non-degradable substances, etc.) and emissions (CO_2, nitrogen, ultrafine particles, etc.). In itself, it is not population growth that is the problem. The problem is what has come to be known as the 'ecological footprint.' The ecological footprint per person in those areas in the world where the population is not growing or even shrinking, in particular the North and China, is many times that of people in Africa, where the population is growing strongly. As Gandhi once observed, the earth provides enough to satisfy everyone's needs, but not everyone's greed. Earth Overshoot Day, the day of the year in which humanity – that is, that part of humanity that lives in the rich and developed countries – has used more resources in that year than the earth can regenerate, occurs earlier and earlier with each passing year. In 2022, it was on July 28. Planetary boundaries are becoming more visible by the day. In 2009, Johan Rockström and his team identified nine such boundaries: climate change, ocean acidification, stratospheric ozone depletion, interference with the global phosphorus and nitrogen cycles, rate of biodiversity loss, global freshwater use, land-system change and aerosol loading. Only regarding the ozone layer is the trend positive.[26] Moreover, the reservoir of natural resources isn't inexhaustible either. As Harald Sverdrup and Kristin Ragnarsdottir have shown, there are clear limits to the (exploitable) amount of not only oil and natural gas but also of iron, nickel, cobalt, copper, gold, and phosphorus (to mention a few) that the earth harbors, some of which are crucial for any energy transition that we may envisage.[27]

During the entire age of 'Great Enrichment,' production chains were organized along the lines of 'take, make, waste' linear production. It almost never occurred to people that both the production process and the end of a product's lifecycle may require as much creativity and innovative efforts as its beginning. For centuries, product design ended at the very moment a product reached the consumer, while the production process was evaluated only in terms of financial efficiency and the amount of (costly) labor needed. Everything beyond that – production waste, energy, pollution – was considered an 'externality' in economic theory. The implications are becoming clearer by the day: climate change, decreasing biodiversity, deforestation, pollution such as plastic soup in our oceans, abused animals, endangered species – none of which is accounted for in economic models, let alone in prices.

A key problem is that all resources are commodified in one way or another and hence are profitable for extraction and use. According to this logic, a tree in the rainforest is worthless alive but becomes valuable only when it is cut down and dead, sold as tropical hardwood and – doubly profitable – makes room for a palm plantation. In the final stage of the 'Escape from Poverty' commodification – together with the easy way in which negative 'side effects' can be externalized – trumps the need to preserve nature and the earth for the next generations as a habitable place. Capitalism, if it is defined as nothing more than the constant search by capital for the expansion of capital, can hardly be squared with the need to preserve – and hence not to exploit – nature and its delicate ecosystems.

The Results: A Tendency toward a Rentier Economy

Together, the seven assumptions yield the uneasy impression that in the global North a development has begun (adopted in many other parts of the world) toward something that can be called an extractive rentier economy, that is, an economy that draws on human, political, and ecological resources that are unrenewable and hence is unsustainable.[28] Economic growth is increasingly being achieved at the cost of future generations, both financially (growing debt, both public and private) and substantially, using resources that are not renewable. None of the assumptions can stand the 'able to last forever' test, a test that should be a key test from now on for all human activities: Can we perpetuate this activity and this pattern of activities in the long-term future? (More on this below). See here a brief review of the assumptions.

1. Markets cannot solve all social problems, but only some, and they create others. Markets are great at stimulating new solutions and propagating them. But they have also come to be organized as shareholder-oriented, financialized platforms where externalization of negative effects has become very attractive. Parasitizing non-renewable resources – via commodification and externalization – has become easy, and even if a company would like to behave differently, market forces will hardly allow this (race to the bottom, waterbed effects, etc.). Therefore, critical reflection and more effective regulation is urgently needed. If the market truly belongs to all of us and should work for all of us, for this and succeeding generations, we all should be able to participate in this critical reflection and design effective

regulations. A free market is a great value in itself and is an important vehicle for innovation, but it requires embedding, socially, politically, morally (the lessons of the second and third phase of the 'escape from poverty' project identified above) and ecologically (a later lesson).

2. The emphasis on quantitative growth both in macro terms (GDP) and at the corporate level ('shareholder value,' financial profits) blurs negative effects that are somehow not represented in prices and puts a premium on actively hiding these effects ('externalization'). The sheer size of many corporations, and the combined size of sectors, gives them the power to either block regulation or escape it via international routes.

3. Financialization has made us blind to the ups and downs of the 'real economy.' It marks the transition from a well-functioning 'market economy' to 'unfettered capitalism' (we refer here to the section on key terms in chapter 1), the release of money that is only searching for more money, 'accumulation,' without asking what real value is.

4. As it turns out, there is a growing political and social unrest in the final stage of the 'Great Enrichment.' People are not only consumers: they belong to communities – local, national, international – in which they demand to be recognized as citizens and as human beings and not be excluded from participation and from a dignified life. A certain amount of inequality doesn't necessarily constitute a problem, but when growing inequality induces widespread feeling that one cannot make a decent living by decent work, it becomes a source of despair and anger and gives a feeling of being excluded.

5. This implies that people do live in societies that have to be organized in such a way that all "different ranks of the people" (to use Adam Smith's phrase again) have a sense of belonging, of being recognized. And this belonging will have to be made tangible, not in a vague sense of cultural 'identity' but in something that can be called an "economics of belonging."[29] We should think of society as based on a 'social covenant' of people who belong together and in which a healthy balance between competition and solidarity is ensured.[30]

6. Geopolitically, older structural imbalances between East and West as well as between North and South have remained (in spite of the formal end of colonialism), and new imbalances have emerged. It turns out to be highly risky to assume that this world will be an eternally peaceful one. Indeed, trade is an important driver of peace, but the main political actors should always maintain something like 'strategic autonomy' regarding raw materials, basic resources, energy, military equipment, and so on, so that, in times in which the global peace is under pressure, one isn't suddenly robbed of the potential to act independently. In the meantime, it is an urgent task to work toward a more just and sustainable world, both for intrinsic moral reasons and to remedy geopolitical risks.

7. Nature is the domain where the implications of the rentier economy become most pungently visible: the 'take-make-waste' economy is in full swing, and – given how markets are currently organized – it is virtually impossible to abstain from certain activities when a profit can be made. Nature doesn't sit at the table where the decisions are made. Nor does nature, as long as it remains nature, have a price attached to it. The drive to commodify and exploit nature is almost irresistible, given the way the market economy is organized at this moment.

Conclusion

Can we perpetuate this pattern of activities in the long-term future? The answer may be clear from the analysis just given: we are living in an unsustainable economy. A thorough reorientation, a true transition, is needed, comparable in magnitude perhaps to the transition that we identified as the 'escape from poverty,' with which it all started. It is now time to escape from the negative consequences of this earlier project, while retaining the key gains that it has given us in terms of wellbeing.

Chapter 4
Europe's Confusion and Reorientation

Europe's Confusion

During the second and especially the third phase of the age of the 'Great Enrichment,' Europe in general had started to develop a balanced approach to markets. It recognizes their innovative strength while at the same time taking measures to embed the market in a sociopolitical framework of guaranteed rights and bringing the market into balance with non-profit civil society initiatives.

As a general outcome, one can say that Europe has been able, on the basis of the values it has discovered over time, to find a way beyond authoritarianism and free market individualism in the form of a social market economy. Europe – this gigantic world-historical social, political and economic laboratory – has experienced the terrible risks and costs of totalitarian state rule. But it has discovered as well that a market that is just left to its own devices as a self-regulating mechanism also runs the risk of new power concentrations, new feudalism, new oppression. Therefore, a dynamic balance between market, state and civil society/community is an essential precondition for inclusive well-being – such was Europe's discovery.

This all changed during the fourth phase. In the light of the impressive semblance of successes of the fourth phase of capitalism, Europe started to have doubts and second thoughts about what it had learned from the earlier derailments of free market capitalism. The reflective-responsible attitude toward the capitalist market seemed to evaporate as an unnecessary pastime. During this fourth phase, the tradition of 'balancing,' of 'third ways,' of social market economies fell into disrepute and even oblivion, especially in academic economics. The result is that younger economists and managers have no systematic awareness of alternatives to what was established as 'mainstream' economic thinking after Hayek and Friedman (also due in part to a very clever educational strategy of 'neoliberal' economists and think tanks).

There were some exceptions. Michel Albert, a French economist and banker, published a small book in 1991 called *Capitalism Against Capitalism* in which he clearly distinguished between the 'American model capitalism' and the 'Rhine model capitalism,' not hiding his preference for the Rhine model. And in the 1990s the British Prime Minister Tony Blair, the American President Bill Clinton, and the Dutch Prime Minister Wim Kok together advocated the idea of a 'third way,' joined later by the German Chancellor Gerhard Schröder. It remains questionable, however, how much critical substance this had: both Blair and Clinton, for example, substantially deregulated their financial sectors. And Albert's work did not lead to a solid tradition of European economic thinking and research as an alternative to what often came to be called the 'neoliberal' paradigm. The 'third way' discourse almost seemed to justify leaving the Rhine model and moving toward the American model. The 'third way' was less a bridge to invite others to come closer to Europe than a freeway for Europeans to move elsewhere, to the US model. When Margaret Thatcher was asked in 2002 what she considered to be her greatest achievement, she said, "Tony Blair and New Labour. We forced our opponents to change their minds."

The original idea that there are different possible ways to organize the economy seems to have given way to the impression that history has culminated in, as Branco Milanovic calls it, "capitalism alone." Both communism and the 'third way' have disappeared, it seems. Milanovic now distinguishes between "liberal meritocratic capitalism," still exemplified by the Anglo-Saxon world, particularly the US, on the one hand and "political capitalism," exemplified by China on the other. But, as Milanovic fears, there is even the possibility that the actual differences between the two remaining options may disappear, for in both variants one can see a "tying up the knot on wealth and power," resulting in plutocracies.[1]

In practice – and we are inclined to say, happily – many elements of a distinct 'European capitalism' remained intact, despite the different rhetoric. In quite a few European nations as well as at the level of the EU, we still find policies and institutions that attempt to curb unfettered capitalism, to an extent that would be considered unacceptable either in the US or in China (obviously for very different reasons). But it seems that a somewhat elaborate, and self-conscious, exposition and justification of what in reality is still a 'European Economic Model' is missing.

This demise of European self-confidence is remarkable since, in terms of human flourishing, most European countries are on the top of the world – probably due precisely to the still-extant elements of a European Economic Model. While they are not necessarily the countries with the highest GDP per capita, their ratings in terms of happiness, health, moderate inequality, education, and income are the highest in the world (e.g., World Happiness Index, Human Development Index/Inequality-adjusted Human Development Index, OECD Better Life Index, etc.). Apparently, a social market economy is in many respects superior to its rivals, unfettered capitalism or state capitalism/communism. But what might it look like in the 21st century?

The Task of this Book: A Reorientation of Capitalism

That is where this book comes in. What is distinctive for Europe perhaps is the very practice of evaluating, of taking one step back and asking whether either a government or the economy is doing what it should do in terms of key values such as human dignity. And if not, we should take action, not simply comply with an ideological recipe – either fully pro- or fully anti-market. We believe that this realistic, undogmatic, and morally inspired attitude that led to a first reorientation of capitalism in the late

19th and the 20th centuries is also crucial for the future attitude of Europe toward the market economy. It is, after all, clear that a 'reorientation' of capitalism is once again urgently on the agenda.

During the last 250 years, it appears that the development of free market capitalism was like that of a young adolescent who leaves home with a large allowance, excited about new things, with almost free space to explore the world, to develop himself, without any obligation to take long-term responsibility. Given the problems and crises it has caused over the years, it is time for capitalism to grow up and become responsible for the society in which it functions, responsible for the future generations, responsible for what economists tend to call 'externalities,' the external effects of the system and of the actors who play by its rules. The ecological consequences in particular, as well as the social consequences in terms of inequality and (job) insecurity, the disproportionate role of financial incentives throughout the system ('financialization') and the power concentrations of new companies that base their profits on the algorithmic intrusion in the private spheres of humans are all urgent matters that require a new, mature phase in capitalism. We call this 'responsible capitalism' or a 'common good economy.'[2]

The general direction – and in a sense the political legitima-tion as well – for this new type of market economy is provided by the '2015 agenda': the Sustainable Development Goals, as formulated by the United Nations, the call of *Laudato Si'* and the Paris Agreement. Increasingly, the 17 SDGs have become the concrete manifestation of a new global awareness of the importance of what can be called human flourishing or wellbeing as the central goals of our economies beyond GDP growth. Despite rising tensions between the geopolitical superpowers, the SDGs have still been able to mobilize strong support.

But it is crucial that geopolitical players should really commit themselves to this agenda to prevent this from becoming an empty vessel, a mere token. The new economy is searching for 'carriers,' for 'levers,' that are able to really have an impact. The first reorientation of capitalism could to a large extent take place at the level of nation states. We can no longer look exclusively at this level. In terms of financial size, some single corporations are already larger than the entire GDP of quite a few nation states. So we need to talk about nations working together in larger regions and ultimately globally.

But it is impossible to just 'jump' to the global level. Before this movement toward a renewed economy can take on real global dimensions, it might be more conceivable, and even mandatory, to look for at least one global player that has the size and leverage to really make a difference, and that has intrinsic reasons to embark on this transition. This is why we look to Europe, to the European economies separately and jointly, as the European Union or, more broadly, the European economic zone (which may well include the UK, which is after all not only the birthplace of Margaret Thatcher but also the inventor of the welfare state and the NHS, and therefore part of the search for 'third ways'). Based on the analysis given earlier, we believe that Europe has a strong motivation and solid reasons for becoming a champion of the SDGs and, beyond that, of a reoriented 'responsible capitalism.' Hopefully not the only champion, but at least Europe will take up the challenge. So the central question that we ask ourselves is:

How can we reorient our economies in such a way that the upsides of free markets, with respect to freedom and innovative problem-solving potential, can be maintained and stimulated, while the downsides, that is, the ecological, social, and psychological costs, can be remedied?

Or, to put it in a much more straightforward and somewhat simple way:

How can markets be equipped to achieve the SDGs?

And one can also read other sets of indicators for 'SDGs,' as we will discuss in part II of this book, that are connected to concepts like 'wellbeing' and 'a better life' (OECD). We believe that Europe is still, and is once again, in a good position to pioneer a new phase of the market economy. Therefore, the second central question that we ask is:

What should Europe's role (both the European nations and the EU) be in this reorientation of the economy?

In the introductory chapter, we stated that this reorientation can be meaningful only if it leads at the same time to a reconnection between the different layers and groups of the European population, between 'the elite' and 'the people.' And of course, all this has to take place in a very complicated geopolitical context that has to be reckoned with.

A task of this magnitude cannot be a pragmatic affair, with some pluses here and some minuses there. It also requires a new orientation to the question 'why,' the purpose of an economy. This can only be answered by (re)discovering driving ideals and inspiration. What is Europe about?

Fortunately, as indicated in the introductory chapter, we do not have to do this in a vacuum. In recent years an unprecedented creativity has been invested in reformulating the goal and direction of our economies. From GDP growth alone, by whatever means, we have now moved to a much more realistic way of assessing how we are doing by formulating indicators that take into account ecological exhaustion as well the quality of human life in many respects, not only financially but also with respect to health, education, inequality, the quality of institutions, and so on. New sets of indicators have been developed, at first by the UNDP (Human Development Index), which later gave way to, for example, the OECD Better Life Index and an avalanche of similar attempts, and in recent years as well, as mentioned above, the Sustainable Development Goals. There is also a wealth of literature on 'Rethinking Capitalism,' on the reform of 'derailed capitalism,' sometimes leading to very similar book titles as happened with *Reimagining Capitalism*.[3]

What this new phase will entail has therefore become increasingly clear in recent years, at least on a general, abstract level. Many insights that were formulated earlier in the dissident margins of economic thinking are becoming more and more mainstream. New ideas are being developed all over the place. What we are witnessing is perhaps something of the magnitude of a paradigm change in economic thinking, blurring the distinction between mainstream and margin, between 'orthodox' and 'heterodox.' On this basis, we will formulate in the next part of this book Europe's mission as working toward a renewal of capitalism in the direction of responsible capitalism. This reorientation consists of a fivefold renewal, which we identify as five 'pillars,' each marked by an 'I.' These five I's, the five pillars of economic renewal, are listed below and rendered graphically in Figure 2:

I.   Renewing Ideals (chapter 5)
II.   Renewing Inspiration (chapter 6)
III. Renewing Ideas (about economics, chapter 7)
IV.   Renewing Indicators (how to measure what really counts, chapter 8)
V.   Renewing Institutions (who needs to do what, chapters 9 through 12).

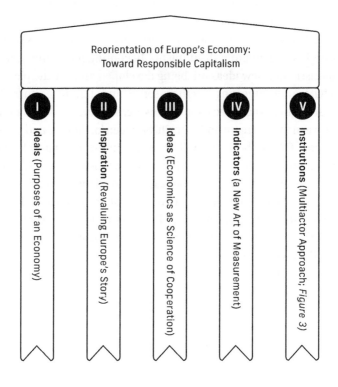

Figure 2: *The Reorientation of the Economy: Five Pillars of Renewal (5 I's)*

Part II

Europe's Mission:
Developing Responsible Capitalism

In Part II we lay out what a new embedding of the market economy could entail. We lay out a fivefold agenda of renewal, structured around five I's, hence five pillars of renewal: Ideals, Inspiration, Ideas, Indicators, and Institutions. We argue this against the background of an interpretation of European culture and European history with all its ambivalences, upsides, and terrible downsides. From the European perspective, a well-functioning economy requires a broad range of actors, each of whom play their own role in cooperation and, if necessary, in conflict. Old oppositions like 'either market or state' no longer suffice. Instead, we advocate a 'multiactor approach' as a further development of the stakeholder approach that, from our perspective, is too reactive and not proactive. A risk the multiactor approach entails is that each actor waits until another takes the initiative – the famous 'problem of many hands.' Therefore, we strongly emphasize the 'power of initiative': each actor – businesses, governments (local, national, international), consumers, civil society, intellectual and religious opinion leaders, etc. – can (even more strongly: must) take initiatives to address problems that each observes from their own perspective and build coalitions with other actors to deal with these problems.

Part II

Kumar Bhattacharyya

Developing Resonsible Capitalism

Chapter 5
The First Pillar of Renewal: Ideals about a Good Economy

What kind of society do we want, and does our economy contribute to that? And if it doesn't, what can we do about it? Quite a few formal constitutions of countries indicate that the outcomes of economic processes should not just be accepted in the same way we accept changes in the weather but evaluated in light of larger goals, of some notion of the common good. For example, the German Constitution reads (Art. 14), "Property entails obligations. Its use shall also serve the public good." The Bavarian Constitution even includes the far-reaching clause "The entirety of economic activity shall serve the public good, in particular the guarantee of a decent existence for every person and the gradual increase of the standard of living of all social classes" (Art. 151).[1] And the Dutch Constitution states: "It shall be the concern of the authorities to promote the provision of sufficient employment" (Art. 19.1) and "It shall be the concern of the authorities to secure the means of subsistence of the population and to achieve the distribution of wealth" (Art. 20.1). Moreover, this Constitution also declares: "It shall be the concern of the authorities to keep the country habitable and to protect and improve the environment" (Art. 21). Similar articles refer to the health of the population, sufficient living accommodations and education as well as social and cultural development and leisure activities (Art. 22, 23). The Preamble to the French Constitution (1946) reads: "The Nation shall provide the individual and the family with the conditions necessary to their development" (Art. 10) and to the "protection of their health, material security, rest and leisure" (Art. 11) as well as "equal access to instruction, vocational training and culture" (Art. 13). And the Italian Constitution declares, regarding the economy: "There is freedom of private economic initiative. It cannot be conducted in conflict with social utility or in a manner that could damage safety, liberty, and human dignity. The Law determines appropriate planning and controls so that public and private economic activity is given direction and coordinated to social objectives" (Art. 41). Bhutan has even famously included the promotion of "Gross National Happiness" as part of its Constitution (Art. 9.2). These examples will suffice.

This is of course in line with longstanding spiritual and philosophical traditions in which, for example, the 'Golden Rule' ('do to others as you have them do to you,' and all variations of it) has been articulated.[2] For example, churches have formulated ideas about the good society and a good economy throughout their long history up until the present, as attested by the stream of social encyclicals issued by the Catholic Church since 1891 (*Rerum Novarum* by Leo XIII) and very recently (*Caritas in Veritate* by Benedict XVI, *Laudato Si'* and *Fratelli Tutti* by Francis). Quite a number of Protestant theologians and economists have developed similar views, as have communitarian philosophers.[3] The core is always: we humans are not individuals but responsible participants in communities, and therefore we need to care for each other and for our life together in a society. Recently, our responsibility for our 'common home,' that is, the earth, has been added to this. China, to mention an interesting example, has recently added the aim of becoming an 'ecological civilization' to its constitution.

'Mono-Indicator Tyranny' and a New Understanding of Value(s)

In this respect, one can distinguish between two types of argumentation. According to one type, the economy is a self-sustaining mechanism, and we have to accept the outcomes as the 'optimum,' just because they have been produced by this mechanism. As human beings (i.e., nation states, regions, larger economic zones), we are not in a position to judge its outcomes, let alone correct them. That is basically Friedrich Hayek's view: the economy is, indeed, like the weather. It is a "spontaneous order" the outcomes of which we shouldn't question at all.[4] This view has substantively informed the practical policies of Western nations in recent decades.

Almost all economists – certainly Adam Smith himself (about whom more below) and almost all influential economists in the 19th and 20th centuries followed him – had a different view.[5] We have to formulate goals, a mission (e.g., reducing poverty), and then look how our economies can best achieve these goals. Economies shouldn't have us, but we, the public, have economies, in order to realize the values, the ideals, that we deem important. Viewed from this angle, which we adopt in this book, economic policy and, by implication, the science of economics, is values-driven through and through. There is no mathematical or metaphysical 'objectivity' to it, but the way we organize our economies helps us to realize certain values. And nothing is more logical than 'to evaluate' (from the French 18th-century *évaluer*, derived from the Latin *valeo*: to make the value of something explicit, to show the value of) from time to time in order to see whether the expected outcomes have been realized. The acknowledgement that economic policy and the science of economics are not just 'value-based' but even more 'values-based' forces us to constantly think and rethink what values we want to organize our economic policy around.[6]

But a strange thing happened in our economic thinking and in our economic policies: we relegated this crucial task of critically evaluating our economic performance in line with the public ideals or values to one, actually very narrow, measure: GDP growth. For decades, GDP was taken as the *pars pro toto* for all the values that we identified as part of the common good: we installed and submitted ourselves to what can be called a 'mono-indicator tyranny,' relegating the responsibility for evaluation to one formal, abstract indicator.

Something similar happened at the corporate level. Businesses achieve a great number of different values at the same time:

providing jobs, educating people, teaching them to collaborate, playing a part in developing communities, providing goods and services for customers, making profits (some of which may go to investors), and so on. Here again, however, we find another example of the 'mono-indicator tyranny': for decades we assumed that companies were doing fine as long as they made a financial profit – despite, for example, health problems (e.g., the tobacco industry) or the environmental problems they created. On the other hand, we did not really appreciate their positive impact in society. There was no way to really account for both the negative and the positive external effects of companies. The balance sheets were strictly financial.

In recent decades, however, and especially in recent years, we have been seeing a highly interesting change, almost revolutionary in nature. We are seeing a return of the value dimension in a broad sense: What are our ideals, our standards for a truly good economy, beyond GDP growth? What does 'value' really mean, apart from the numerical financial indicator that we so easily use as a proxy?[7] What is it that we really want our economies to deliver, both as a process and as outcome? Is the economy a platform for the exercise of personal and corporate greed? Or do ideals, moral inspiration, and virtues play a – perhaps crucial – role? How can we achieve a less prejudiced view of what people do and of what motivates them beyond personal greed? What is the role of values and 'pro-social preferences' in behavior of humans and even that of companies? This conscious reentry of ideals, values and virtues can be observed at three distinct levels: the macro, meso and micro levels.

Macro-Values and Macro-Virtues: Beyond GDP Towards 'Flourishing'

At the macro level, in the various constitutions that we mentioned, we already saw a very early reflection of this development after World War II, but this was largely hidden from view by the focus on GDP. In recent years, however, this reentry of ideals and values has been fleshed out by introducing concepts like 'happiness,' 'wellbeing, 'human flourishing,' and 'sustainability.'[8] Gradually, more and more indicators are being developed to keep track of the respective achievements in these domains (see below). The key development where this all comes together is the formulation of the Sustainable Development Goals at the UN level that were the result of a highly significant global consultation process. And the movement is gathering pace: more and more countries are starting to formulate what they want to achieve in substantive terms. Bhutan started with the Gross National Happiness and developed an elaborate method to track how it is doing in this respect. One of the most recent examples is New Zealand, which has adopted a 'human wellbeing' framework as a basis for its policies, entailing attention to mental health, minority groups, child wellbeing, and a sustainable economy, in addition to the more 'classical' focus on productivity.[9] In the meantime a 'Wellbeing Economy Governments' coalition (WEGo) is formed with next to New Zealand also Finland, Iceland, Canada, Scotland, and Wales as members.[10]

But values have not only reentered the discussion in relation to the desired outcome of economic processes, there is renewed attention for values and virtues as well in regard to how economies operate, the processes themselves through which the results are realized. Already in the 1990s, a great deal of research showed that there is a huge difference between 'high trust societies' and 'low trust societies' in terms of the happiness and wellbeing of citizens as well their economic efficacy. High trust societies perform better on almost all indicators. The same holds for related concepts like 'social capital,' which refers to the quantity and quality of social relations and 'moral capital,' a term coined by, among others, the Polish sociologist Piotr Sztompka. For him, the term refers to the presence of values or virtues like trust, loyalty, reciprocity, solidarity, respect, and justice in any given society.[11] These 'soft' elements are increasingly proving to be very 'hard' economic factors. And in recent years, the analysis by Acemoglu and Robinson has also shown that trustworthy, inclusive – or, one might say, 'virtuous' – governments are crucial to economic success.[12]

Meso-Values and Meso-Virtues: Purpose beyond Financial Indicators

A similar process of the (re)discovery of the significance of ideals, values, and virtues is happening at the corporate level. The idea that the only "social responsibility of business is to increase its profits," (in)famously posited by Milton Friedman in his 1970 essay, seems very much 'old school' these days.[13] Corporations today are working on 'added value' for society and are formulating their 'purpose' or 'mission,' in contradistinction to the maximalization of profits. As Harvard's Rebecca Henderson claims: "People will work hard for money, status, and power – 'extrinsic' motivators. But for many people, once their core needs are met, the sheer interest and joy of the work itself – 'intrinsic' motivation – is much more powerful. Shared purpose creates a sense that one's work has *meaning*."[14] In her view, a truly good company is able to formulate its purpose and direct its activities accordingly. Similar views, in a clear break – at least on paper -with earlier statements by the same networks, have been expressed by the American Business Round Table in their "Statement on the Purpose of a Corporation" and the 2020 Davos Manifesto of the World Economic Forum: both documents announced a transition from a strict shareholder to a stakeholder orientation, from short-term maximum profits to long-term value creation.

The 'purpose' or 'mission' of a company has both internal and external aspects. Inside the company, it can give all employees a sense of dignity and responsibility. For the outside world, as long as words and deeds are consistent, the purpose-driven company is trustworthy, and therefore such a company may play a role in overcoming the current institutional mistrust that is a driving force in today's populist uprisings.[15] Graafland has shown that, in countries in which the business sector shows a high degree of corporate social responsibility, human flourishing is significantly higher than elsewhere.[16]

The terms 'mission-driven' and 'purpose-driven' are, in themselves, still quite empty concepts. They need to be given content and substance, and we have recently been seeing numerous attempts to do exactly that when companies formulate their long-term ambitions in terms of 'people, planet, profit' or, more recently, in terms of ESG (Environmental, Social and Governance standards), or even in terms of contributing to the realization of the SDGs. There also is an emerging literature on 'love' as a key organizational virtue, looking both internally at businesses' attitude toward employees as well as externally at outside stakeholders.[17]

The dilemma that companies face, or perhaps only falsely fear to face, is that integrating a substantial idea of the good into the mission or purpose of the company implies that the company cannot survive in the brutal world of competitive markets. But it is increasingly proving to be the case that this dilemma is indeed a false one. Profit and purpose can quite often not only go together but can reinforce each other, especially in the long run. So 'doing good' and 'doing well' are apparently becoming more and more aligned: companies can become 'net positive.'[18] There even are strong indications of a positive relationship between the emphasis on 'purpose' and the long-term profitability of companies.[19]

Moreover, serious attempts are made to demonstrate this in very elaborate balance sheets, that give insight, beyond financial achievements, into the positive and negative external effects of businesses, allowing us to judge whether a certain business is 'net positive' or 'net negative.'[20] We will deal with this at greater length in the chapter on the renewal of Indicators (chapter 8).

Micro-Values and Micro-Virtues: Moral Leadership, Conscious Employees, Critical Consumers

Finally, at the micro level of individual workers and leaders, the very same word 'purpose' has almost become a buzzword. There is even talk of a "purpose economy."[21] And buzzwords are seldom without significance.

We see the idea of values and virtues operating at the level of leadership in companies.[22] The idea that leaders have to be focused on just one thing, that is, the maximalization of profits for the shareholders, is increasingly being unmasked as a psycho-pathological deformation of character.[23] Leadership is much more multidimensional and therefore requires skills of listening to a diversity of perspectives and the ability to convey an intrinsic sense of what the work to be done together is all about. There is a long history here to back this up. Numerous biographies of socially engaged entrepreneurs – James O'Toole calls them "enlightened capitalists" – show how they succeeded in bringing their moral engagement to successful businesses, trying to see and treat their employees not just as 'production factors' but as fellow human beings with their own needs and skills.[24]

A similar development can be observed regarding the recruitment of young talented people. It is becoming increasingly clear that it is no longer sufficient to just offer the highest wage: the company also has to deliver on immaterial values such as sustainability, societal impact, and work-life balance. There has to be a credible answer to the question that especially young people, often the most talented, pose: What is the real added value of this company?

Employees are often also participants in pension funds. Here again, we see a movement toward responsible and sustainable investments at the initiative of participants in the funds who are increasingly showing resistance to having their (future) pensions based on morally unacceptable earning models.

A final manifestation of values and virtues, also at the personal level, the micro level, is found in the behavior of consumers. We see growing movements of critical consumers who don't want to buy goods that involve child labor or don't want to buy from companies that have a bad tax record or are known to contribute greatly to the pollution of the environment.

An Enlarged Conception of the Common Good: Discovering and Rediscovering Values

A market economy is an intrinsically moral endeavor organized by humans to make life better for each other. Presenting a market economy as a neutral allocation mechanism robs it of this moral dimension and propels a view of the economy as something that we aren't required – and perhaps aren't even intellectually allowed – to assess morally. We have indicated earlier that asking moral questions lies at the heart of a free market economy: Does it really promote the common good? That is why we as humans have an economy in the first place. Answering that question is critical for any economy.

A new awareness of the importance of inspiring values, both old and new, is therefore crucial, especially for Europe. We may recall here Jacques Delors's call for a "soul for Europe." And we may remember the condescending phrase uttered by Donald Rumsfeld, then the American Secretary of Defense, about 'old Europe' as a continent without spirit, tired, exhausted, not able to create any enthusiasm. But that is completely off the mark. As we will explain in more depth in the next chapter, we believe that a European approach to the market economy can be a highly inspiring project that – in an updated form – really prepares Europe for a new future. There is, we believe, something like a 'New European Dream' centered around old and new values, a new conception of the common good.[25]

But what might this conception of 'the common good' consist of in the first half of the 21st century? What values should we articulate as a standard for assessing how our economy is performing, at least in Europe? How can the common good be interpreted in a way that is suited to Europe?

The Sources of Values: The Role of (Hi)stories

The common good may or may not be the same everywhere. Where do values come from? As humans, we tend to live our lives under the guidance of stories and histories that somehow provide background and context for our basic values. We even tend to talk about our economic life in terms of stories, of orientating narratives. China, for example, has invested heavily in recent years in the development of the story of the 'Century of Humiliation,' the period from the 19th century up until the end of the Japanese invasion. During this period, China, despite its millennia-long history and many periods of greatness, was humiliated by foreign powers, lost wars, and became economically and technologically backward compared to Western countries and Japan.[26] The implication is that the time has now arrived to restore China to its natural, hegemonic role – and hence the economic and technological projects of modern China such as the Belt and Road initiative. It shows that stories can have huge economic consequences.

In the US, the narrative of the 'American Dream' is still very influential: the idea of the US as a 'city on a hill,' shining as a beacon of freedom for the nations and the individual 'pursuit of happiness,' the country where democracy was institutionalized for the first time on a large scale and where every citizen is entitled to pursue their own dreams without government or collective interference. Here we see the background of Reagan's famous dictum: "Government is not the solution to our problem; government is the problem." And this is also the background for decades of budget cuts and austerity. Stories have economic consequences indeed.

For a long time – at least since the Enlightenment until the end of World War I – modern Europe lived with the story of its own superiority, of being 'modern,' 'civilized,' and 'enlightened.' And this story served to justify both its contempt for other cultures and peoples as well as its self-appointed mission to bring its own culture, 'modernization' and 'enlightenment' to other cultures. Likewise, it previously saw itself as the torchbearer of Christianity.[27]

Telling stories always entails risk: the darker sides of one's past or present (and future) often tend to be left out. Stories frequently identify 'good guys' and 'bad guys' in a rather binary way. This turns stories into risky affairs: What is left out? What is allowed in? Who is left out? Who is allowed in? The selection may therefore give rise to a plurality of stories and even to conflict between various stories. Postmodern philosophers, with their keen sense of the arbitrariness and power-oriented nature of stories, can always have a field day exposing the inclusion and exclusion that takes place in stories, and are often right to do so.

And yet, although we might want to do so, it is virtually impossible to live without stories, without a narrative of where we come from and where we want to go, a narrative about 'this is the past we want to leave behind,' or 'this is the past we want to preserve,' 'this is the present we face,' and above all 'this is the future we are striving for.' Stories help us identify key values, what is really important to us, and what should thus guide our actions. They inspire us – for better or for worse – and give orientation for future courses of action.[28]

But stories should aspire to truth and to including as many facts as possible – for the sake of plausibility. The stories should therefore not simply be 'myths,' popularly known as 'made-up fantasies.' Rather, they should give an account of cultural and societal developments that have brought a certain group or society to 'where they are right now' in combination with a sense of 'where they want to go.' Telling a story about who you are and what you aspire to be is not a matter of cultural exclusivism, let alone supremacism: cultures have learned from each other, can learn from each other, should learn from each other, and hence be willing to 'unlearn' as well. An acceptable or plausible story should include, and learn from, dark pages.

A key question is: Does Europe have a – more or less common – story? Or better: What story can be told about Europe? And what shape can that narrative take if we are looking for orientation for the future? Is there a story that can align with, and give a kind of background, to a more multidimensional view on the economy, as an economy of 'wellbeing' or 'human flourishing'? Any simple story of civilizational superiority is no longer acceptable. But what can then be identified as characteristic of Europe? Or is there only a diversity of national or even regional stories? In the next chapter, we will take a deep dive into the history of Europe, with all its ambivalences, to see if we can identify a common core of values and what criticism and updates are needed to prepare Europeans for the challenges of the 21st century: What did Europe learn, what did it forget and should perhaps relearn, and what should it unlearn to make it fit to meet the future? We thus embark on a risky adventure: a story of Europe. By way of anticipation, we will argue that, both in light of its past – the bright and the dark pages – and the future, Europe should (re) adopt the following four values: human dignity, regenerativity, inclusivity, and co-creativity.

Chapter 6

The Second Pillar of Renewal: Inspiration from Revaluing Europe's Story

The Dark Ambivalence of Europe: Conflicting Histories

It is very challenging to explore Europe's story today. European history has become a highly contentious affair – and rightly so. A 'culture war' of sorts is taking place around this issue, particularly between the 'right' (the simplistic view: 'Europe is great') and the 'left' (the simplistic view: 'Europe is terrible'). And if one travels around the world today and asks about the story of Europe, the answers almost certainly refer to colonialism and slavery. In Europe itself as well, much attention has been paid in recent decades to the dark shadow sides of European history: the crusades, the nationalist and religious wars, the violent persecution of those who were considered 'deviant,' imperialism, colonialism, racism, exploitative capitalism, world wars, the Holocaust, gender discrimination. The list could go on. From this perspective, given its past, Europe should be silent about the global future – it has had its chance and wasted it – so it is claimed. And indeed, when Europe started to play its geopolitical role, it continued the long human history of bloody empires, of 'extracting institutions,' that we have seen throughout the later history of *homo sapiens*, especially after the transition from a hunter-gatherer culture to sedentary agriculture and empires.[1] Europe even doubled down on it, assisted by, among other things, its superior military technology.

At closer inspection, however, there is another story to be told as well. Despite the list of dark elements just given above, Europe has also been the birthplace of the very standards on the basis of which we make our negative judgments of the phenomena mentioned above: human rights were formulated for the first time in Europe, the systematic fight against poverty and exploitation began in Europe (and the academic field of economics even partly finds its original inspiration in the struggle against poverty). States that were set up on the basis of the rule of law and eventually became democracies are also very much a European invention (especially if we include the former European colony that is called the US today), although there have been, often short-lived, earlier attempts to have a democracy.[2] Since medieval times, a group or class of citizens, often identified as 'bourgeois,' formulated new standards for the social, political, and economic order. International law itself originated in Europe.

So, Europe's first history, the dark history, is accompanied by a second history, a counter-history, that criticizes and tried and tries to remedy the dreadful manifestations of its first history. We can, perhaps, even speak of a Europe-I – that of power hierarchy, internal and external exploitation and inequality, religious wars, colonialism, racism, and so on – and a second Europe that is also Europe: Europe-II – that of human dignity, equality, human rights, struggle against poverty, end of slavery, international peace, and so on.[3] The heart of this schizoid split seems to be a pervasive gap between 'in-group ethics' and 'out-group ethics' that has haunted Europe throughout its modern history. The new humane insights and practices that were developed in Europe were tainted by at least two forms of this gap: internally, the in-group/out-group split became visible in the rift between higher and lower classes. This was most emphatically exposed by Marx who pointed to the 'proletariat' as the excluded class. Externally, geopolitically, a comparable split has characterized Europe's dealing with other parts of the world, denying others the prosperity it achieved for itself. An ever-increasing body of postcolonial literature is still exposing the dark consequences of this in both the past and the present. Frantz Fanon can perhaps be called the 'Marx' of colonialism.[4]

In recent times we have also become aware of a second serious flaw of the 'European mentality': its highly instrumentalist attitude toward nature. Nature was increasingly seen in Europe only as 'matter' to be used, to be exhausted, to be disposed of as 'waste.' Respect for nature wasn't part of Europe's dominant culture – and we are experiencing the consequences of that today.

Without belittling the seriousness of this first history in any way (and we will come back to it below), we should not be lured into disregarding that other history, the counter-history of 'bourgeois values' and 'bourgeois virtues.'[5] It would be a mistake to discredit (as Marx did) 'bourgeois values' and 'bourgeois virtues' because they were not widespread enough (not even among the bourgeoisie themselves!). Rejecting something good because it is not widespread enough is a great mistake. Instead all effort should be made to push for its broader application. The fact that Europe hasn't lived up to its own internally formulated standards should not lead us to reject these standards themselves or to a massive rejection of European culture. So, what were these historically rather new standards? What is the heart of the 'second history,' the counter-history of Europe-II?

The Other European Story: The Gradual Discovery of Human Dignity and Four Revolutions

One standard mold in which the European story is often cast follows this pattern: 'from feudal-collective oppression toward individual freedom and rationality.' Although there is a lot to this story, it is not really helpful as a whole in understanding how the European market economies came about. We believe that a kind of amoral individual freedom is not the heart of the European story but a caricature of Europe. Nor is the European story simply about the breakthrough of reason and the growth of science, technology, and efficiency – although these elements are certainly part of it.

This second European history has, in our view, one propelling fundamental motive, a moral one branching out into four rather revolutionary implications. And these four 'revolutions' have given rise to various other institutional 'signposts for a good society.' The one fundamental discovery that – with hindsight – stands out and propels the second history, Europe-II, is *the explicit formulation of human dignity as a fundamental principle and an increasing social and political awareness of the importance of this idea, this ideal.*[6]

Since the High Middle Ages, this second history has become stronger and stronger (and hence the internal conflicts in Europe became more intense). The idea that 'all men are created equal' was perhaps first officially stated in the Bologna *Liber Paradisus* of 1256, when the city released 5,600 slaves at once and granted them their freedom.[7] The argument was that God had not created free people versus slaves in paradise but had originally created all humans in equal freedom (*pristina libertas*: original freedom[8]), an idea that resurfaced centuries later in the work of John Locke and eventually became the resounding opening statement of the Preamble to the American Declaration of Independence and fed into the *Universal Declaration of Human Rights* (1948). In 1949, the precise phrase 'human dignity' reappeared as well in the Constitution of a reborn Germany after the horrors of Nazism, stating: "Die Würde des Menschen ist unantastbar" (Human dignity is inviolable).

In the meantime, the idea of human dignity had also been given intellectual (philosophical and theological) expression. The most famous instance of this was undoubtedly the Oration on the Dignity of Man (*Oratio de hominis dignitate*) by the Italian philosopher Pico della Mirandola in 1486. For him, the dignity of humans is connected to freedom and to the potential to explore and govern nature.

In this entire train of thought, we encounter the first, and foundational, element of the European sociomoral infrastructure (of Europe-II, that is):

a sense that all human beings are created equal and have an inherent equal dignity, regardless of individual or group differences.

The principle of universal human dignity is increasingly and constantly challenging every status quo that is not in line with it. Exploring the implications of this principle is a centuries-long and often painful process that, in many respects, is still ongoing today. Apparently, for many people the 'group identity' is part of their primary experience of life, and this doesn't sit well with the principle of universal human dignity. But once this revolutionary idea has been installed in the minds of people, it starts to invite, and often incite, a social transformation, eroding the legitimacy of hierarchical and/or exploitative relationships and of group identities. This type of relationship can no longer be regarded as 'God-willed' or 'natural.' What should be considered 'God-willed' or 'natural' is human freedom, human dignity.[9] And this inviolability should be given explicit recognition in law, over against the whimsiness of royal (in earlier periods, also papal) powers: human rights – preferably codified in constitutions.[10]

This principle is increasingly becoming the cornerstone of European societies. At no stage was this an easy ride: it often went through periods of deep conflict, especially between the powerful and the less powerful, lower elites, or even the common people. It is this long history that has provided the sociomoral infrastructure for what we would call the first 'moral-institutional signpost for a good society':

(Signpost 1): respect for individual human rights.

The idea or ideal of equal human dignity is one crucial discovery. As indicated already, what is perhaps even more characteristic for European history, however, are the attempts to develop a social order that somehow reflects this idea of human dignity, the *institutionalization of human dignity.* The 19th-century German historian of law Otto von Gierke spoke of a constant conflict between *herrschaftlich* (top-down, hierarchical) and *genossenschaftlich* (bottom-up, community) ideas and practices in Europe.[11] In Europe, the ideal of what a good society should be, the 'social imaginary,' becomes transformed over the course of time into what the philosopher Charles Taylor has called the "Modern Moral Order": society as the coming together of equals to realize mutual benefits and what can be called the common good.[12]

Against the background of this moral horizon, we can identify four different and rather revolutionary institutional developments that reflect the idea of human dignity. Together, these four form a sociomoral infrastructure in Europe that, up until today, has been a somehow deeply felt but often hidden, or unrealized, standard of a good society – and hence the source of constant revolutionary potential. Against the background of these four revolutions, further 'societal and institutional signposts for a good society' have emerged.

A. The Cooperative Revolution: A Community of Equals

The first European revolution can be called the cooperative revolution. Already in medieval times, a new way of organizing human communities was emerging. From about 1050 onwards, starting in northern Italy, we can observe something that can be identified as a real social movement: people started to associate as free and equal persons in newly established communities, the medieval cities. A few decades later, this process began as well in northwestern Europe. In the 13th century, for example, in what is today called Germany, about 200 new towns were founded every decade. Ever since the 19th century, many historians and social theorists have – in retrospect – noted the revolutionary character of this development.[13] The movement had its rural parallels in the formation of 'commons,' arable land that was cultivated and managed collectively by inhabitants of a village or of a city.

Most of the cities were conscious *associations*, and citizens were free members of them. But not only was the city itself an association, the dominant organizational form within the city was again the association. They were often called *universitas,* the bringing into one body of a plurality of members. These included, for example, guilds as well as a myriad of cooperative associations for the establishment of poor houses, hospitals, seniors' homes, and so on.[14] Membership of associations was an important hallmark of being a good citizen.[15]

In most cities, people could become citizens, regardless of their background, after having lived in the city for one year and one day, by swearing an oath of loyalty to the city and its citizens, promising to treat each other as equals and to assist each other when needed (*mutuum adiutorium*: mutual help).[16] In this sense, being a citizen was more a matter of becoming a participant in a 'covenant' – a mutual promise to stick together and care for each other, regardless the unforeseeable circumstances – than being a party in a 'contract,' a deal in which the *quid pro quo* is clearly stipulated (and from which one can walk away if the transaction becomes too costly).[17]

Cities had two economic pillars, labor and trade, and recognized each other all over Europe, together creating something like a European Union *avant la lettre* in the form of the Hanseatic League. At its zenith, this League included around 200 member cities from West to East, covering the entire northern part of Europe in what today are 16 countries, including Russia.

What the cooperative revolution left as a kind of sediment layer in the European sociomoral infrastructure is

a sense that a social order should be seen as an association, a kind of covenant, in which people, as individual persons with their inherent dignity, unite to work together in mutual trust on something like the common good to which everybody contributes and from which everybody profits.

Two moral institutional signposts for a good society have some-how found their way into the European sociomoral infrastructure as a result of this 'cooperative revolution':

(Signpost 2): In a good society there is space for common, 'bottom-up,' initiatives by people, free associations, not based on family relations but on mutual trust and a sense of common purpose. Eventually, this developed into what sociologists today have called 'civil society' or a well-established role for 'NGOs.'

The other institutional signpost that has trickled down in European history out of the 'cooperative revolution' is the value of work and the dignity of workers. But this would be too narrow: traders were valued as long as they did not ask exorbitant prices.[18] So we can safely add trade and tradesmen, and later on the entrepreneur, as well. Thus, the appreciation of work was extended to the entire domain of the 'active life' in distinction from the 'contemplative life.' The 'affirmation of ordinary life,' the entire domain of what we today call 'the economy' became a distinct feature of European culture and a hallmark of its conception of a good society.[19]

(Signpost 3): In a good society, work and the worker, trade, and the tradesperson, as well as the entrepreneur, are held in high esteem and are seen as important contributors to the common good.

B. The Politico-Institutional Revolutions: Establishing Freedom, Responsive Institutions

The second type of revolution that we see in European history, sometimes coinciding with the cooperative revolutions, are political revolutions that try to establish political self-rule/autonomy by a certain community or try to acquire certain rights.[20] Although, as we pointed out earlier, instances of reigning in royal power by assemblies have a long history, perhaps even occurring in some way among hunter gatherers, historians see the first instance in Europe of what we would today call a parliament in the Cortès of Léon in 1188,[21] from where it spread throughout Europe (e.g., the Magna Carta in England in 1215, the Golden Bull in Hungary in 1222), almost always as counterweight to the hierarchical authority of kings (and a 'conciliary movement' even emerged in the church, counterbalancing the authority of popes) – we should recall here the constant clash between 'top-down' and 'bottom-up.'

The most eye-catching instances of this type are of course the real revolutions that took place on a national scale: the

Dutch Revolution of 1568 (with formal independence in 1581), the Glorious Revolution in England in 1688, the American Revolution in 1776 and eventually the French Revolution in 1789 (each with its own context and characteristics of course). These may still be far from any type of formal democracy – one person, one vote – but formal democracy is not the only point here. The key is indeed responsive institutions that do not coerce or manipulate people in ways they have no control over, which is materialized in the 'rule of law.' It calls for all formal institutions – governments, corporations, NGOs – to find ways to meaningfully engage their 'stakeholders' or else run the risk of losing their social 'license to operate.' This second type of revolution added a second layer to the European sociomoral infrastructure:

A longing for and attempts to establish responsive institutions, over against oppressive, 'extractive' or self-centered ones (at first political institutions, but one can easily imagine that this layer would later equally affect religious, economic, and other institutions).

The political revolutions led to further institutional signposts for a good society:

(Signpost 4): In a good society, no one should claim absolute power, but supreme authority should lie in the rule of law.

But once the absolute, often arbitrary power of the most powerful institutions conceivable – states ruled by royal houses, kings and emperors – is limited, the idea of limiting absolute power will not end there. Other institutions are no longer safe from this revolutionary potential.[22]

(Signpost 5): In a good society, institutions (primarily political institutions, as well as guilds, businesses, religious institutions, civil society associations, etc.) should, each in its own way and capacity, be responsive to the public, with an eye to the common good.

C. The Reflective-Cognitive Revolution: Improving Humans' Grasp of the World

A third revolution that can be discerned in Europe is the institutionalization of critical thinking and the pursuit of knowledge as a way to enhance the human being's grasp of the world. This 'reflective-cognitive revolution' is often interpreted in a very narrow way as if it only concerns the rise of natural science and technology or the rise of instrumental rationality (often connected to the 'Enlightenment'). But it also concerns the pursuit of moral and spiritual insights, where traditional knowledge is not necessarily rejected but is no longer taken at face value either. Instead, it is weighed, discussed, and renewed and then used as a critical yardstick to evaluate current and future developments in society. So, scientific curiosity and moral critical reflection go hand in hand.

This pursuit of truth takes place in highly diverse institutional embeddings. At first in the medieval 'cathedral schools,' in monasteries and in universities, a medieval invention (the oldest European university, that of Bologna, was established in 1088 as a guild). But the institutional settings for the pursuit of truth are diverse: religious institutions, educational institutions, research centers, universities, the media. And, as always when there is a diversity of institutions, there may be tension within and between these settings. But a 'sphere' was created throughout all these various institutions, the public sphere that could serve as a platform from which one could 'speak truth to power' and/or give new direction to social and political actors.

The reflective-cognitive revolution not only enhanced our grasp of the natural world but engendered a plethora of ideas for the reform of the social and political world (up to full-blown ideologies, with sometimes fruitful and sometimes disastrous results; more on this below). As a whole, European society has become a highly 'reflective' society in which innovative knowledge and ideas have played an enormous role.[23] There is no way back: we cannot but continue to reflect on what we consider to be a good society, good governance, a good economy, and perhaps above all on what we consider to be the common good that may inform all these spheres in their own way. Here, we encounter a third layer in the sociomoral infrastructure of Europe:

The urge to understand both the natural and the social world and to understand and develop ideas and insights that assist us in getting a better grasp of our lives and our societies.

This third revolution leads again to two institutional signposts for a good society:

(Signpost 6): A good society includes the free pursuit of knowledge, led by truth and truth only, and there is ample room to transpose knowledge into technology in order to deal with all kinds of (practical) problems, hence 'innovation.'

(Signpost 7): A good society includes the free, public exchange of moral and spiritual ideas about what a good life and a good society actually are.

Signpost 6 is the acknowledgement of the great importance of the scientific revolution, education, and research. Signpost 7 refers to what is often called 'the public sphere.' This was earlier partly embodied by the church, but, from the 17th century onwards, it has tended to become a secular sphere in which debates and arguments replace divine authority (although people and institutions who are religiously motivated can certainly participate in the debates).[24]

D. The Economic Revolution: Overcoming Poverty, Creating Wealth for Everybody

The fourth revolution that somehow completed Western development was the economic one. The idea that work and organizing it in a smart way ('division of labor') is the most promising way to escape from poverty can be seen as the foundation of a new type of economic thinking that came to fruition in the work of Adam Smith: wealth is not a zero-sum game but can be created and expanded; economic growth is possible. Many have joined this quest to find ways to improve the lot of all. In an entirely different part of Europe, we encounter the Italian economist Genovesi, a contemporary of Smith, who wrote about a "civil economy" that is part of the same quest (though some of his insights and emphases differ from Smith's).[25] And social protest has also joined this quest. From medieval times onward, via Marxism until the present day, social movements have emerged demanding a full and dignified place at the economic table, particularly as response to economic crises.[26] The economic revolution brings to light a fourth layer of the sociomoral infrastructure: the 'social imaginary' of European societies:

The awareness that human dignity requires that we find ways to improve the concrete life situation of all people, particularly those who are least well off.

The economic revolution leads again to two institutional signposts for a good society:

(Signpost 8): In a good society, people together overcome poverty by organizing an economy in which everyone can participate and in which everyone profits from the wealth that is created.

(Signpost 9): In a good society, the 'public' (the body politic or the state) checks whether the reasonably expected outcomes of the economic process are indeed realized for everyone, and, if not, corrective action is taken by all participants in a process of public goalsetting.

Against this background, it may be clear that a free market should not be seen as a morally neutral mechanism but as a moral phenomenon. In the emergence of free markets, a moral horizon becomes visible in which other forms of production and (re)distribution are found wanting: feudal relations with serfdom or charity and begging as means of (a very limited) redistribution. The market can be seen in principle as a liberating, emancipating platform.[27] And, as a moral phenomenon geared to the equal dignity of humans, its workings and results should be constantly evaluated according to this internal standard.

To be sure, the fact that a culture develops moral standards does not imply that they are realized or that that culture lives up to its own standards. But the public presence of moral standards gives direction to social struggles and social unrest, for example in Europe often between 'left' and 'right.' There is something that people can appeal to. Once the standards have been formulated and have somehow become part of a culture, people will start to protest on that basis against practices that are somehow not up to par (e.g., Martin Luther King's civil rights movement could appeal to the American Constitution). The preservation of human dignity, the space for free cooperation, the rule of law and responsive institutions, respect for science and open debate, an economy that really works for all of us, is never a matter of course, never a secure achievement. It all requires constant vigilance and, if necessary, struggle. If anything, this is clear from Europe's own history.

A Dubious Philosophical Heritage: Ideologies and 'Recipe Thinking'

Europe's history can be seen as a long protracted, largely un-planned search for principles for a good society. This search was more a matter of practical lawmakers than one of philosophers, more Hugo Grotius and less Thomas Hobbes, more a matter of practical experiment and step-by-step discovery than of a Grand Design. Philosophers did increasingly join the search, though not always to its benefit. European philosophers have tended to interpret the search for a good society – and for a good economy – as a search for the One Big Recipe, the ultimate principle, preferably forged on the anvil of the emerging natural sciences, as the one law to explain everything. The search for the One Big Recipe, the panacea that would end this centuries-long search, ushered in what can be called the 'age of ideologies.' The term 'ideology' dates back to the beginning of the 19th century, but the phenomenon itself is older. From the age of Hobbes onward, we see more and more attempts to find this holy grail, this cure-all. We see philosophers and 'would-be' philosophers proposing all kind of alternatives – from royal absolutism to individual liberalism, from free market thinking to collectivism of the left and the right (fascism). Fully totalitarian ideologies such as communism and national socialism emerged later.

Ideologies have a degree of attractiveness in that they bring home one specific point that often does need to be addressed. And yet, in their one-sided and often radicalized oversimplification, they tend to become rather destructive, sometimes even hugely destructive – and Europe has experienced the destructive nature of ideologies firsthand. The great tragedy is that one ideology often provokes its opposite.

This fateful dialectic has manifested itself in a very poignant way in the economic domain. Adam Smith's work can still be described as based on pragmatic principles, combining moral concerns with a keen analysis of actual human behavior and looking for a workable mix of what free markets can do and what public services in the free market should be. But his insights were dogmatically applied soon after him and were treated as 'cure-all recipes,' with disastrous results. We then see 'free market liberalism' as an ideology that refused to address the issue of the deepening poverty of millions of laborers in the 19th century as an issue that concerned the common good. For purely ideological reasons, the state was not allowed to take action. Nor was anybody else for that matter: labor unions were forbidden, thus barring laborers from addressing their problems as shared problems.

In all its radicalness, it was this dogmatic laissez-faire liberalism that provoked the Marxist analysis that eventually developed into a geopolitical and world-historical rival of free market liberalism and vice versa – right up until the present day. Marx acutely analyzed the increasing inequality and exploitation of unfettered free markets. But the Marxian solution was perhaps even more destructive and unrealistic: the dignity of human beings suffers deeply when they are defined as parts of collectivized entities. Moreover, totalistic, radical revolutions have turned out to devour their own children, and Marx-inspired revolutions have never been an exception to that rule. The practical application of various ideologies as well as the fight between them has cost millions and millions of lives.

A Distinct European Model: Combining Principles with Institutional Plurality

The solutions that were eventually found in Europe were not developed by the great philosophers but much more by what can be called 'reflective practitioners' taking concrete steps and designing concrete solutions to problems when they emerged and apparently called for action. The motives for these measures were highly diverse. Real social concern was often mixed with fear that the labor movement would be radicalized and with attempts to prevent an all-out class struggle. Thus, in Germany, we see a typically 'rightwing,' rather authoritarian, regime adopting 'socialist' initiatives (Bismarck's *Sozialgesetzgebung*). We see the influence of Bernstein's 'revisionist socialism' or pressure from Catholic and Protestant social thought and adjacent social movements in other countries. Even in classical free trade, laissez-faire countries like the US and the UK, there have been very significant attempts to break away from ideological orthodoxies and to solve the problems as they manifested themselves in economic crises and in wartime, as is shown both by Roosevelt's New Deal in the US and the huge acclaim for the 1942 Beveridge

Report in the UK. They both tried to find a workable mix of free market institutions and collective protection and correction of market outcomes.

Alongside the combination of principles and the affirmation of the role of both the market and government, there was one other important element that made it possible to keep the free market on track: the age-old tradition of cooperative initiatives, of civil associations (as Alexis de Tocqueville called them) or of civil society (as it is often called today). It was reinvented and reinvigorated in the 19th century and ensured that a whole range of services essential for human wellbeing was organized outside the market sphere: health care, insurance, finance, education, and housing were to a large degree organized in cooperatives and associations. A kind of 'multiactor approach' was thus installed. What Rajan calls the "three pillars of a healthy economy" – markets, government and communities – developed in the 19th century and contributed greatly to a more balanced and humane society beyond autocratic governments and unfettered capitalism.[28]

With Europe's long history of cooperative relations between citizens, its history of reigning in arbitrary power structures, its history of scientific research and moral reflection, and its history of attempts to reduce poverty and improve living conditions for all, the development of practical, often incremental, wisdom combined with institutional plurality, implied that it proved to be possible in Europe as well to develop a distinct type of capitalism that one of its later architects, Wilhelm Röpke, dubbed a "Third Way" or "Economic Humanism."[29] During the 19th and 20th centuries therefore, and thanks to the intellectual activity combined with the social and political action of many different actors – from philosophers and theologians to social activists, from economists to entrepreneurs, from cooperative farmer's banks to labor unions – it turned out to be possible to harvest the advantages of free markets with respect to freedom and innovation. And at the same time, it became possible to remedy the most distressing downsides of free market capitalism and realize some of the underlying ideals: improving the lot of the many, not the few – something like a practical economy for the common good.

This solution has worked as a kind of 'overlapping consensus' (to use a term created by the American philosopher John Rawls): people from very different backgrounds and worldviews, both religious and secular, have found each other in their support for this arrangement, albeit on very different metaphysical and/ or political grounds. For some, human dignity is intimately connected with a view of human beings as created in the image of God, for other humans are worthy of the highest respect by nature. Others may have completely different justifications for this principle. This also applies to the core ideas of an economy for the common good: core ideas of a culture can be supported on very different grounds.

This core idea of an 'economy for the wellbeing of all' has gone by several names in addition to the 'Third Way,' like 'civil economy,' 'Rhine model,' 'mixed economies,' or the 'social market economy.' There are clear differences in how this is organized in detail, which Esping-Anderson has referred to as different 'welfare state regimes' (liberal, social democratic, and conserva-tive-corporatist).[30] Some relied more on a relatively strong role for the state, and others on a relatively strong role for civil society alongside the market. And yet, despite these differences, there is a commonality that becomes evident if one compares Europe as a whole to almost any other part of the world. The common core is the ongoing quest for a good society, as sketched above, with an economy that works for all as a key element.

An Unfinished and Embattled Project

The long history of humankind was very often characterized by the hierarchical, collective oppression of individuals and groups, especially oppressive rulers, kings and emperors, and their 'extractive institutions.'[31] In Europe, this history has continued in many ways, and we called this 'Europe-I' (we will come back to this in the next section).

But there is also this other history – Europe-II – where a different path was carved out for Europeans (and perhaps for humanity) to follow: a history of human rights, of the rule of law, of scientific and technological progress, of responsive/inclusive institutions and an economy for all, a 'narrow corridor' between oppression and anarchy.[32] To be sure, this pathway in Europe was found almost by historical accident, as a result of numerous smaller and bigger fights and numerous concrete practices and solutions that were somehow left over in the sieve of history and time. They were not the result of a masterplan but of numerous factors, actors, and actions. It is remarkable how widespread this has been, from the Cortès in Léon in Spain to England and Hungary, and in innumerable city states in Italy and throughout Europe.

Europe-II has never been fully realized in Europe itself. In a way, it is a 'promissory note' that Europe has been issuing to itself. Moreover, although democratic, 'bottom-up' thinking eventually got the upper hand most of the time, the fascination with hierarchy, dominance, and even violence has never been far away. Europe has a tormented soul. Europe-II still is an unfinished and embattled project, in constant need of critical (self)reflection.[33]

The Terrible Mystery of 'Europe-I'

It is a great and terrible mystery: How is it possible that exactly this part of the world, where the four humanitarian revolutions took place, has – in geopolitical and geoeconomic respects – become the launchpad for the very often violent and oppressive exploitation of other parts of the world and the birthplace of two world wars? How is it possible that 'Europe-I' has played such a major role while 'Europe-II' was developing at the same time?

While Europe has become the birthplace of an impressive set of ideas on how a good society can be organized, it also has practiced everything that is the exact opposite of these ideas and practices. We already presented the list: outside Europe the crusades, slavery and the slave trade, racism, imperialism, and colonialism; inside Europe religious wars, the exploitation of the lower classes, racism, and other discriminatory practices toward women and LHBTQI+, totalitarian regimes with concentration camps, genocide, and the Holocaust; and both inside and outside Europe an exploitative attitude that culminated in depleting nature in all its forms: animals, rain forests, natural resources, biodiversity, landscapes. (Already in 1905, the great sociologist Max Weber warned that there would be no end to industrial development "until the last ton of fossilized coal is burnt").[34]

It would take us too far afield to attempt a full explanation of this paradox – if such an explanation can ever be given. We certainly would have to deal with the issue of evil, both what Hannah Arendt called the "banality of evil" as well as what she, with Immanuel Kant, called "radical evil." So, without claiming to touch on the deepest levels of what has been going on, we can only elucidate some aspects in order to get a better sense of what is necessary for rethinking Europe's current and perhaps future role in the world.

Haunted by Specters

What does Europe need if it is to play a different role in the world than it has in the past? We can identify at least four 'specters' that have apparently haunted Europe and have stimulated 'Europe-I' over against 'Europe-II,' as we have outlined above. The metaphor of 'specter' doesn't imply that Europe, the European elites, and the people who have been involved in the dark sides of Europe are not responsible. They have done what they have done. But at the same time, there seems to have been – in retrospect – several types of blindness, causing entire nations, a whole continent, to not see what we see now. These very same specters have as well fed into the 'age of triumphant capitalism' we identified earlier.

We see two 'specters of the past' and two 'specters of the future' – and all four have huge political and economic implications. The 'specters of the past' concern tendencies that are present in virtually all cultures and civilizations that we know of and that Europe has not been able to break away from, even though it could have done so, given the revolutions we identified. As 'specters of the future,' we can identify derailments that have their background in the revolutions themselves and represent a kind of 'going wild,' a derailment of the humanitarian revolutions.

A. Separationist Ethics in Countries. The discovery of human dignity has been limited from the outset by second thoughts about who then really has 'dignity.' Various distinctions were maintained or even introduced to award dignity to some and withhold it from others. Marx rightly pointed to class distinctions made by the bourgeois class to differentiate itself from the lower classes, the proletarians who were less than human. And we all know how racism, including antisemitism as a special type of this, has been part of Europe's separationist history – in direct contradiction to this principle of human dignity.

In itself, this is a very old phenomenon in human culture throughout known history. Hierarchical thinking and hierarchically organized social relations have been a dominant thought pattern among *homo sapiens* (and it may have many evolutionary ancestors and parallels). But for Europe to continue this practice is a different matter, compared to what other cultures have been doing. After all, in Europe, the counter-position – that of equal human dignity – is formulated very clearly as the ultimate normative position. One could say that Europe could and should have known better.

B. Global Separationist Ethics. The second specter of the past is the use of separationist ethics in the relation between Europe and the rest of the world. As far as we know, almost all cultures have or have had the tendency to distinguish between 'in-group ethics' and 'out-group ethics,' often giving rise to a kind of almost schizoid split. These distinctions can perhaps be seen as residues of a tribal phase in the history of humankind.

And, again, it is Europe's failure that it hasn't been able to overcome these oppositions, although the intellectual, spiritual, legal, and even political resources for overcoming them were present. Europe saw itself as a 'civilized' culture highly elevated above 'uncivilized' cultures and hence felt justified in dominating other parts of the world, turning them into colonies. The history of the slave trade, which, significantly, did not take place in Europe itself but was accomplished by Europeans acting elsewhere, belongs to this second specter. Thus, the momentous discovery of the dignity of all human beings has not led to a global humanitarian ethic or has done so only partially. Supremacist and racist thinking and practices have been part of the European heritage as well.

C. A Materialist-Mechanistic-Mathematical Conception of Life. The third specter is oriented to the future. Part of the reflective-cognitive revolution identified above was the development of the natural sciences in particular. Nature turned out to be susceptible to experimentation, research, and eventually mathematical, law-like description – a truly remarkable discovery! The natural sciences have played a crucial role in enhancing our 'grip' on nature, allowing us to be less susceptible to illnesses and the unknown factors in nature that may make life sometimes so terrible, such as famines, earthquakes, and so on.

The discoveries and their successes, however, have given rise to the idea that nature is 'nothing but' matter, just a collection of manipulable atoms and molecules to be manipulated by us, humans, at will. The millennia-old awareness that nature is not only 'matter' but also Mater, a mother feeding us, nurturing us, a mother to which we are deeply connected and that we have to care for, has been virtually lost along the way.

It didn't have to be this way. Many cultures display a sense of the sacredness of nature and a deep awareness that we humans are part of an encompassing cosmos. And this awareness was also present in Europe itself, as, for example, in the thinking and spirituality of the medieval *homo universalis* Hildegard von Bingen and of course in Francis of Assisi. In their spirituality, we find an entirely different experience of nature. But these views have lost out – unrealized potential – and the mechanistic view has won, including the idea that nature is without limits and simply at the disposal of humankind.

D. Addiction to the 'Not-Yet': Growth. The fourth specter is also the result of the humanization project itself. As soon the possibility of making improvements is seen, the danger arises that we will constantly judge the present by the unknown and unrealized options of the future. So 'growth' becomes the yardstick for all qualitative judgments. Tomorrow is always to be praised above today. This attitude is a key driver of progress.[35]

But this pervasive future orientation also makes it very hard to 'stop and think,' to reflect on what is truly important and meaningful in the present, what needs preservation. The concept of 'path dependency' applies here: in Western societies we are constantly 'extrapolating curves,' that is, assuming that the means and recipes of yesterday and today will bring us to an ever-better future. There is a mental addiction to linear growth and various types of utopian thinking. This ties in very much with the ideological 'One Recipe' thinking. There is always the idea that we can fix the problems of today tomorrow – if only...

The Need to Unlearn, Relearn and Learn: A New European Orientation

Given our analysis thus far, if Europe is to play a new role in the future, oriented toward the common good, and a truly sustainable and inclusive economy, it has to *unlearn, relearn,* and *revive* some basic insights.[36]

Unlearn: Europe has to *unlearn* what the 'specters' just identified tell us and develop an inclusive view of the future economy that does not take the outcomes of a random market process as a substitute for the common good but develops and implements a much more inclusive and broader perspective on human flourishing. And it has to make the utmost effort to make sure that a transition toward a renewed economy does not take place this time at the cost of the global South nor at the cost of the socially and economically less privileged groups within its own territories. The transition should not be another neocolonial project but an inclusive one. And it has to unlearn thinking in terms of perpetual, linear, material growth and learn to start thinking in circular terms, developing a new more balanced relationship between humans and nature.

Relearn: It has to *relearn*, rediscover, some of its own old traditions: cooperation and the potential of cooperative arrangements to protect the provision of basic needs such as housing and health care; cognitive-moral reflection in which the fruits of science and technology are fully affirmed without mathematical models and algorithms taking over our conscious decisions; the determination to improve the conditions of all – the many, not the few. In short, we have to relearn basic notions of the common good, inspired by the awareness of human dignity.

Learn: Europe has to *learn* new insights, especially regarding the interconnectedness of all of life, of human and non-human nature (insights that are not only articulated in various non-Western cultures but are also present in forgotten parts of European culture itself, *pace* Hildegard and Francis). A more integral view on the ecology and the embeddedness of *homo sapiens* within it as its "common home" (in the words of Pope Francis in *Laudato Si'*) has to guide the economy of the future.

Working on a European model of an inclusive and sustainable market is the order of the day. But this focus on Europe is of course in no way meant to be exclusive. A well-functioning 'European model' may be of great significance elsewhere and may well turn out to be a laboratory for market economies of the future.

Four Key Values for a New Future

Based on these considerations, we propose the following mix of 'old' and 'new' values that we believe have been partly adopted by Europe in the past (though Europe itself certainly didn't live up to them very often!) and should partly be adopted now to prepare Europe for the 21st century and beyond.

Human Dignity. The particular conception of the common good that has emerged in Europe was inspired by the key intuition of human dignity and led to a fundamental and broadly recognizable idea of what a good society for Europe is. A good society is one

- in which people participate on a cooperative basis
- in which there are institutions that are responsive to humans and human needs
- in which science, technology and (moral) reflection are taken seriously and stimulated to enhance human's grip on the world, related to the good
- in which poverty is addressed by organizing an economy that works for all.

This idea of the common good did not prevent Europe from terrible mistakes, as we have explained above. So we need to complement this idea of the common good that developed over the centuries with key new ingredients. Therefore, we propose adding three – more or less – new key values to the European 'value portfolio.' The three ideals that we propose for the economy of the future, as further specification and a complement to human dignity (and what this entails) are *regenerativity, inclusivity,* and *co-creativity.*

Regenerativity (or *Circularity*) refers to the ecological limits of our economic activities.[37] In the future, all our economic activities, and hence the aggregate of all our economic activities should be such that they are in balance with nature and therefore should make it possible for nature to continue its natural cycles of recovering and new growth after harvesting or use by humans. Our activities should always allow nature to restore itself, to regenerate. In 2022, Earth Overshoot Day – the day of the year when our consumption of resources exceeded their ability to be renewed – was on July 28, and the date comes earlier with every passing year (with the exception of the first Covid year 2020, when substantial parts of the world economy slowed down). Regenerativity requires a new perspective on nature as 'our common home' and on the balance between that part of nature that we call humanity and all the other living organisms that are part of nature.

No longer can we have a separationist ethics regarding nature, as if nature doesn't count when we make our decisions. In one way or another, we have to take nature into account in all the decisions we make. That means, in the long term, that all our products and processes are to be designed not only from producer to consumer but are also to be always guided intrinsically by the question of what happens when this product's life cycle has finished. Generations from now, people might look back in astonishment and anger at the negligence with which our generation became so accustomed to waste and a throwaway culture. They probably will look with indignation at how we – in a few generations – exhausted the earth's resources and just released our waste into the atmosphere we all have to live in and breathe. Regenerativity has to become one of the cornerstones for judging whether a specific economic activity makes us 'better off' or 'worse off' than before (recalling that awkward question American presidential candidates have thrown at their audiences since Ronald Reagan: "Are you better off today than you were four years ago?"). We are not doing well, if the earth, the environment, is not doing well.

This idea of 'regenerativity' also applies to humans themselves. An economy should be such that all those involved in it have time to recuperate, to rest, to have leisure time. An economy should not allow, let alone make necessary, modern types of slavery – neither in blue-collar jobs (often due to underpayment), nor in white-collar jobs. Forcing people into situations in which they have no choice but to accept terrible working conditions just to stay alive is outright exploitation and a violation of human dignity, whether that happens in a sweatshop in Bangladesh or in a underpaid outsourced delivery job in Europe (as, for example, portrayed in the movie *Sorry We Missed You*). Similarly, often forcing higher educated people into situations of what is known as 'burnout' in Western countries (or *zangyou* and even *karoshi* in Japan) is incompatible with human dignity and regenerativity.

Inclusivity refers to the basic requirement that an economy should work for all of us because we all participate in it, regardless of our starting position and regardless of who we are. We should all get fair chances, and at the same time – as it seems that there are quite a few people in the world who don't end up being Jeff Bezos – it is total nonsense to assume that outcomes are just a matter of individuals taking advantage of their opportunities or failing to do so. So, a true economy that works for all should not leave individuals entirely to themselves but provide both dignified participation for each and every person as well as a safety net in cases where labor participation proves to be really impossible. This is also related to the cooperative nature of economies. Because everyone is supposed to contribute, it is quite unfair when some people really suffer from it while others reap extraordinary profits.

The SDGs are a very inspiring and concrete manifestation of what inclusivity at the very least entails: ending poverty and hunger, good health and health care and education for everybody, regardless of gender, decent jobs, and the reduction of inequality, to mention just a few.

Inclusivity has geopolitical and geoeconomic implications as well. Europe can no longer make economic decisions and engage in economic activities without taking into account the position and rights of non-European nations, regions, and peoples. In a postcolonial age, the global South has to become a real partner, not a business model or, worse, an opportunity for exploitation. It implies that a global ethics has to replace the former separationist ethics (some of the tough dilemmas that come with this are discussed in Part III on geopolitics).

Co-creativity refers to the ingenuity, the resourcefulness, needed to create an economy that is truly in line with the central values or ideals just identified. But it also has intrinsic value. Making our present economy truly regenerative requires immense creativity and is a real challenge for the present generation as well as for generations to come: a technological, legal, and business challenge. In this kind of 'man on the moon' project (referring to Mazzucato's idea of 'mission economy'), all available talent should be nurtured and challenged: we need to mobilize an entire generation. The project can hopefully provide work and perspective to millions and millions of young people who can become actively involved in making products truly circular, in cleaning up the current pollution and coming up with new technologies. For a younger generation, with all the very different types of education that are available and that they receive suited to their individual abilities from practical to theoretical, from craftmanship to academic research, this should be a task that is at the same time as urgent as it is hopeful. Here lies an ocean of intriguing challenges, problems to solve – and everybody is needed: we need all hands and all brains.

Co-creativity is closely tied to entrepreneurship as well. An entrepreneur is essentially someone who has an idea that creates a new entity, the enterprise. In recent decades, however, an individualist interpretation of creativity has entirely taken over the discourse. For example, while the entrepreneur is always someone who organizes cooperation between people, the liberal-ideological misinterpretation of entrepreneurship assumes that he is just the great, singular genius behind every successful enterprise. With the term 'co-creativity,' we emphasize that a singular human being is not a true human being; rather, in the felicitous phrase of Paul Collier, "the atoms of a real society are relationships,"[38] and this obtains as much for those parts of society that we call enterprises. What an entrepreneur does, in essence, is organize cooperation between people and create an environment of and for co-creativity. A good company is like a jazz band where structure given by the conductor goes hand in hand with improvisation by the individual players.[39]

When discussing human dignity as the first element of the European value package, we already listed cooperation as one of its central implications. By introducing now 'co-creativity,' we build on this earlier insights, but at the same time we fully acknowledge the significance of the discovery of individuality that – although with much older roots[40] – erupted in the late 1960s. Individualization is often viewed negatively by philosophers and cultural critics, and it is even seen as the root problem of some of the derailments of the market economy in recent decades – 'neoliberalism' as an outgrowth of late-modern individualization. In our view, individual freedom is not necessarily the same as isolated egoism, and the idea of *homo economicus* is much older than the 1960s. Being a developed individual entails acknowledging one's own strengths and developmental potential but also one's weaknesses and shortcomings – and hence the need for others to supplement each other's shortcomings and the need for mutual appreciation and recognition. Being a human person always implies responsibility (and again, attempts to skirt this responsibility by egoism and the lust for dominance are unfortunately much older than the 1960s). Healthy individualization and engaging in teamwork go together, hence co-creativity.[41] Individualization and cooperation are two sides of one coin.

Why Values? Tests for Policies, Processes, and Products

Values have value only when actors in society, and hence in the economy, do not refer to them as empty shells around established courses of action and established practices but apply them as tests for designing policies, processes, and even products. For example, regenerativity can be formulated as the 'being able to last forever' test: Can we perpetuate this activity and this pattern of activities into the long-term future? Or, to put it more strongly: Does this activity contribute to a renewal of resources for future generations, or does it deplete those resources and take what they will need to live well?

Similarly, co-creativity could be made into a test for operational processes of and within organizations. How can we involve, and not just inform, stakeholders in this process? Do we give creative space to employees and to teams of employees? Or do we subject them to our KPIs and check constantly whether they are doing what they are told, period? Formulated as a test, inclusivity could, for example, go like this: For this job or this initiative, do we look beyond the 'usual suspects' and try to involve those whom we don't think of at first, especially those who may be very different from us or have some so-called 'disabilities'?

As for human dignity, the key test has already been formulated by the 18th-century philosopher Immanuel Kant: Do I treat these human beings as an end in themselves or as a means to other – usually my own – ends? Or we can refer to the theologian-philosopher Augustine who speaks in a short book about those who 'seek their own glory through the subjection of others.[42] To formulate this somewhat more explicitly: Do I instrumentalize, or perhaps even manipulate, this person, this group of persons, these customers, this nation? If so, then human dignity is at stake.

So, values should not be lovely terms that we put in our mission statements on our websites, showing how good we are. Rather, they should be auditable tests for our decisions at all levels – macro, meso, and micro – and in all the different domains and taskforces, for policies, processes and products at these levels. This value orientation can and should guide us into – and is at the heart of – a new phase of capitalism: 'responsible capitalism.'

Chapter 7
The Third Pillar of Renewal: Ideas about Economics

Over the course of the past two centuries – roughly the age of the 'escape from poverty' – economic thinking, teaching, and research have played an immensely important role. This is still true today. Therefore, what happens in economics as a science is of great importance for a transition to what we call responsible capitalism. Fortunately, what we see here is remarkable. In recent years, the contours of an emerging 'paradigm shift' can be discerned in economic science. In the classic theory of paradigm shifts, this does not imply that the previous paradigm immediately becomes obsolete. Only when alternative theories and explanations arise that give a better take on reality does the core of an existing paradigm come under attack and is gradually replaced by the new paradigm, based on different assumptions.[1] We believe that this is actually happening right now. We can point here only to some of the most eye-catching developments and transitions, especially the recent ones.

It has become fashionable among intellectuals and public opinion makers to 'debunk' economics. The phrase 'dismal science' is often quoted.[2] We have to keep in mind that the public image of economists has been shaped by popularists and market ideologues as much as it has by anti-market ideologues. These ideological battles have often harmed the reputation of many academic economists who often are aware of the limitations of their expertise and the models used.[3] In the meantime, economists have done a truly impressive job of developing a field of knowledge that has helped greatly in our understanding of the modern world. Many otherwise opaque mechanisms and relationships have been clarified by economists. (For example, international trade is intuitively a zero-sum game: if one country wins, the other loses; but as the British economist David Ricardo already made clear around 1830, even when country A is less productive on all fronts than country B, international trade can be beneficial for both countries simultaneously, a 'win-win'). A great deal of ingenuity was also needed to produce reasonably reliable data such as the GDP of countries.

And yet, while acknowledging the great significance and achievements of economics, a renewal of ideas about economics as a science is needed and is already on its way. Our argument here partly implies a return to and, in a way, a rehabilitation of Adam Smith and hence a critique of some imbalances that have occurred especially since the 19th century. It also partly concerns an updating of economic thought to prepare it for the challenges of the 21st century. To elaborate on this agenda, we first describe what we consider to be five 'megatrends' in economic thought since the 19th century that later on impacted business studies as well.

Megatrends in Economic Thinking

Homo economicus. The first megatrend concerns the increasing dominance of the assumption of the *homo economicus*: human beings are rational beings who are to maximize the fulfillment of their individual preferences.[4] Often, this basic assumption has been attributed to Adam Smith – but wrongly so, we believe (and will briefly elaborate below). But we do find this view in the famous comedic poem "The Grumbling Hive: Or, Knaves Turn'd Honest" also known as "The Fable of the Bees: Of Private Vices, Publick Benefits" by the Dutch-English writer Bernard de Mandeville, published in 1705 and again in 1714.[5] The poem is about a beehive, in which all the bees relentlessly pursue their own self-interest: "So every part [of the beehive] was full of vice, yet the whole mass a paradise." Here, the point is very clear: a productive market economy runs on vices – greed, vanity, jealousy: "Greed is good." This assumption, which was rejected by

Adam Smith (see below), was introduced in a modified form later in economics during the so-called 'marginalist revolution.' People like Jevons, Menger, Walras, and Marshall tried to understand (and mathematically describe) consumer behavior along this line. Later, a specific 'theory of the firm' was developed that projects these motives to the aggregate level of corporations and hence portrays businesses as guided by 'profit maximization,' thus turning them into 'money-making machines' for the firm's owners, and in the case of the publicly listed companies (which attract the most attention of theorists), the shareholders.[6]

Mathematization. This ties in with a second megatrend, that started already in the 19th century but has expanded explosively in the 20th: the inclination to envy and imitate the natural sciences with their universally valid laws and the possibility of describing them in mathematical formulas and formal models. Perhaps the main reason for the popularity of the *homo economicus* was precisely this: the possibilities it opened up for (mathematical) modeling and hence for finding 'objective laws' for economic behavior. Political economy, John Stuart Mill wrote, should not be an 'art' but a 'science,' and this required clear basic assumptions to build the system, even if the assumptions were empirical nonsense.[7] Mill himself still clearly understood the limitations of this, but quite a few others after him did not and started to treat their theoretical assumptions as statements of fact, of empirical reality. The popularity of rational choice theory and of measures like GDP is certainly connected to this trend.

Equilibrium Bias. The third megatrend was the dominance of the idea that markets tend to equilibria that are unavoidable and can be considered 'right.' Markets have the inherent tendency to be 'perfect,' to approximate as much as possible what is called the Pareto optimum. Through an 'invisible hand,' supply and demand meet each other somewhere in the middle, where the price is established, in the market of goods as well as in the labor market or whatever market we can conceive of. Even when it is simply impossible for a laborer to live on the market wage, economic theory may still, strictly speaking, use the term 'optimal price' and 'equilibrium,' as no one is willing, apparently, to offer a higher wage. This mentality has become a fixture of economics. Looking back at the financial crisis, Paul Krugman argued in an alarming essay, "How Did Economists Get It So Wrong?" that "economists, as a group, mistook beauty, clad in impressive-looking mathematics, for truth."[8] They had come to believe that markets are inherently stable, that stock prices are always priced right, that is, reflect all available information, and that markets cannot go astray. Rodrik calls this the EMH, the Efficient Market Hypothesis, which may be true in an ideal world (would it be?) but certainly isn't true in the 'second-best world' that we as humans usually inhabit.[9]

Pro-Growth. A fourth megatrend in economic thinking has been the focus on the creation of wealth. This started already with Smith himself, as is clear from the title of his book on economics, *An Inquiry into the Nature and Causes of the Wealth of Nations.* For more than two centuries, this was the central question indeed. For millennia, humankind has been haunted by the specter of poverty and destitution. The question that was posed in Europe, already in some form in the late Middle Ages was how we can overcome poverty. Eventually, this became – and still is – the 'mission' of economists.[10] The basis for their analyses was the insight that wealth is not something to be distributed in a zero-sum game but can be produced by human activity. So, finding the triggers of growth was a central concern for economists, and since 1935, growth was increasingly expressed in terms of GDP.

Hidden Morality. A fifth megatrend has been the denial of a hidden morality in economic claims. Markets are portrayed as amoral in themselves, and whoever wants to talk about morality in markets is introducing an alien discourse into a world that is determined by facts alone. There is certainly much wisdom in maintaining some kind of distinction between 'is' and 'ought,' between facts and norms. But if one massively invests in collecting and studying 'facts,' it is easily forgotten that the selection of facts is always influenced by theoretical assumptions. This framework then acquires a kind of normative status: this is what the world looks like, this is how people behave in it; this is how people should behave in it if they want to be rational; this is how you should behave, you student of economics, if you want to be a rational person (and who doesn't want to be that?). So, *homo economicus* becomes a self-fulfilling prophecy and 'being economical' starts to refer less and less to anything like its original meaning of 'keeping one's house in order' but more and more to 'acting selfishly, like a rational computer, maximizing one's interests.' Amartya Sen concluded that economic theory tends to celebrate "social morons."[11]

This overall framework came together in what can be called 'neo-classical' thinking. But the first generations of neo-classical thinkers still were aware of 'market imperfections' and 'negative externalities' and they asked that markets be corrected and negative external effects be addressed. But in what can be called the later 'neoliberal' school, markets were indeed affirmed as intrinsically optimal and the attention for negative externalities evaporated.[12] A kind of 'market fundamentalism' trickled down into textbooks, especially during the last decades of the 20th century, reaching hundreds of thousands of economics and business students.

All this would have been rather innocuous if it were not for the tendency in academics to establish 'orthodox' or 'mainstream' approaches and therefore to somehow suppress plurality in economic thinking.[13] So the neoliberal approach became dominant in teaching, research, and the policies of Western nations and even in multilateral organizations.

The combined result of the megatrends and the way they have influenced economics up until Hayek and Friedman is that, in recent decades, students of economics have not been invited to engage as economists in the 'art' of improving the world (which Smith still intended, but Mill abandoned, for science is not art, is not action). Rather, they are invited to abandon the notion that humans have some responsibility to evaluate whether an economy is doing well in terms of these ideals – for an economy is just a "spontaneous order" that eludes all human intervention, as Hayek and Friedman would say.[14] The only thing left is to become a player in this field of spontaneous interaction, pursuing one's private goals as much as possible and not worrying about the consequences for other human beings nor consequences in general. 'Social justice' is, as Hayek would call it, a "mirage."[15] Morality is useless; greed will do the trick. (This greed is of course to be employed within the limits of the law, but why actually obey the law if it does not further one's interests?)

This lack of pluralism creates the risk for an entire domain to develop a tunnel vision of reality and also to miss opportunities for serendipity and creativity. Part of the paradigm shift that we see occurring right now is that the field is opening up to plurality.[16]

Heralds of a New Paradigm

As we said earlier, these are exciting times for economists! It looks like the field is in the middle of yet another paradigm shift. In retrospect, it can be said that the change was triggered by the credit crisis. Critical questions that had been asked earlier about the assumptions and outcomes of 'mainstream economics' are now receiving a new urgency. We already referred to Krugman's *New York Times* article, "Why Economists Got It So Wrong," which was followed by many more detailed analyses of the financial crisis, both books and documentaries (such as the excellent *Inside Job*). If we are not mistaken, the heyday of neoclassical economics is over. In Chapter 3 above, we already referred to the fact that even Alan Greenspan, a staunch defender of the spontaneous, self-regulating order, showed himself in 2008 to be in a kind of shock, as the economic ideology that had guided him for more than 40 years failed him now. "I have found a flaw ... and I have been very distressed by that fact." And Greenspan didn't even mention the distress caused among the larger public and the breach of institutional trust that was going to have severe political consequences in the not-too-distant future.

In addition to the credit crisis, the ecological crises are also demanding that economics be rethought. Nor should we forget the deepening inequality and growing economic insecurity, which are reasons for concern, especially for younger people.

Last but not least, a fresh look at the actual outcomes of capitalism has given rise to second thoughts about the wonderful results of free market capitalism. 'Trickle-down economics,' the idea that the results of free market capitalism will automatically lead to wellbeing for everybody, is no longer credible. At the macro-level, inequality is indeed decreasing worldwide due to the strong development of former 'underdeveloped' nations in the South, particularly China and India. But inequality is increasing *within* almost all nations, together with the actual decline in living standards of considerable groups of citizens.[17] This led Angus Deaton, the winner of the 2015 Nobel Memorial Prize in Economics, to a remarkable conversion: in 2013 he had written a resounding eulogy for capitalism, whereas in 2020, together with his wife, the economist Anne Case, he penned a book reflecting an entirely different mindset, darkly called *Deaths of Despair and the Future of Capitalism*. In this book, they analyzed the physical and mental distress of those who are left out somehow by the system.[18]

Partly as a response to these developments, remarkable innovations are taking place in economics that may herald a new paradigm emerging alongside the neoclassical approach. Four developments stand out.

An empirical turn. For a long time, economic science had followed a path in which the available methodological tools, often of a mathematical nature, increasingly determined which 'facts' could be analyzed in the scientific models. The dynamics here are somewhat comparable to the man who lost his keys in the dark and was searching for them under a streetlight, even though he knew he couldn't possibly have lost them there. But at least there he had some light for searching. The research methods used by economists in recent years have expanded significantly, however. At least one result is that a number of subfields in economics have become more empirical and less reliant on theoretical model building.[19] Perhaps a start, at least an early indicator, of this movement can be seen in the project the World Bank started in the 1990s, Voices of the Poor, in which viewpoints and experiences were collected from tens of thousands of people in several dozen countries. Another clear sign of this empirical turn is the work of Banerjee and Duflo: they use 'randomized control trials' to see what the real-life effects of certain economic measures are. In 2019, their work was awarded the Sveriges Riksbank/Nobel Prize in Economic Sciences.[20] The empirical turn goes hand in hand with acknowledging that economists want to change something in reality, want to make the world a better place and are therefore interested in 'what works and what doesn't.' Economics as an 'art' is back. The above-mentioned work by Case and Deaton is another example.

A behavioral turn. Closely related to this empirical turn is the rise of what is called 'behavioral economics,' which is reflected by six other Sveriges Riksbank/Nobel Prizes in Economics. Behavioral economics focuses on what people actually do in reality, how they come to decisions, what they value in specific circumstances and what not. Are they always *homo economicus*, maximisers of individual material preferences? Do they behave 'rationally' in the sense that this was assumed earlier, maximizing quantified preferences, or is their rationality 'bounded' (Herbert Simon), or are all kind of psychological and neurological mechanisms interfering with their 'rational' decisions (Daniel Kahneman)?[21] One of the – in itself not surprising, yet almost revolutionary – outcomes is that, although there sure are people who behave selfishly, there are many others who display what have come to be called 'pro-social preferences' and ideas of fairness.[22] People may well prefer to cooperate with each other, even if their personal gains are not clear.[23]

An important element in the behavioral turn is the rise of game theory, and the concomitant game experiments. These confirm that it is impossible to put people into one behavioral straitjacket as the *homo economicus* approach tended to do. In game settings, people display a whole range of behavioral patterns, sometimes selfish indeed but more often pro-social, sometimes as initiator and sometimes as follower. And it is very interesting that they have and often act out of a sense of fairness that may override their calculated self-interest. This can be seen in ultimatum games in which one player may be given a certain amount of money provided he shares some of it with somebody else, and if it is not shared, the entire amount will be forfeited. It is very interesting here that people may reject an offer they deem too low, even when they know that this may mean that they lose everything. Game theory thus confirms Amartya Sen's theoretical insight regarding 'sets of preferences.'[24] People may have ethical convictions that are simply not 'for sale.' Or they may have social preferences or a sense of solidarity, and they don't want to trade these for material goods, and so on.

Multidimensionality. A third intriguing development is the emergence of what can be called multidimensional thinking and multidimensional assessment tools. In short, in macroeconomics a multidimensional approach is quickly complementing the monodimensional measure of the GDP, and at the meso level we are seeing the emergence of multidimensional, 'integrated' reporting complementing mere financial reporting. The measurable indicators are no longer taken as ultimate goals. New ideas and concepts are being developed, both conceptually and statistically, about more encompassing goals for our economies, like 'happiness' at first and later on concepts like 'wellbeing' or 'human flourishing' that are more sophisticated and thoroughly examined. Moreover, much energy is being invested in identifying the various dimensions, the central 'capabilities,' that are the key ingredients for these richer goals. The UN Millennium Goals first and more recently the UN SDGs play an important role here. We pointed to this development in chapter 5 above and will come back to it in chapter 8.

Interdisciplinarity. The trends just indicated are also a sign of a growing openness to interdisciplinarity within the field. Behavioral economics draws heavily on psychology; the empirical turn entails using research techniques (especially interviews) from other social sciences. We also see highly interesting and enriching exchanges with evolutionary biology ('evonomics') and neurosciences ('neuro-economics'). There are even growing signs of interaction with the humanities, literary studies, history, theology, and philosophy.[25] Gradually, after decades of (rather mathematical) specialization, economics (including business studies, though the situation was always a bit different here) seems to be moving closer to Keynes's requirements (as stated in his obituary for Alfred Marshall) for the "master-economist with the rare combination of gifts" – mathematician, historian, statesman, and philosopher in one – who studies "the present in the light of the past for the purposes of the future."[26]

Cautious plurality. Although there is still much to be gained here, we seem to discern a slowly growing sense of openness in economics and business schools for alternative approaches. There is, all too slowly, a growing plurality in curricula and research programs. But there is still a long way to go. When the Dutch chapter of the international student movement Rethinking Economics in 2018 did a review of all Dutch academic curricula of economics, they found that around 86% of the mandatory materials and classes were neoclassical in approach.[27] The orthodox/heterodox distinction still has strong institutional backing. Some theories say that true changes always require a full generation of scholars. We hope that we won't have to wait that long.

A New Paradigm: The *Homo Cooperans* within Planetary Boundaries

For Adam Smith, and even more explicitly for one of the other great shapers of economics, the aforementioned Alfred Marshall, economics had a clear moral and social goal: reducing and even eliminating poverty. There is nothing wrong indeed with positioning an academic field within the context of societal challenges. We are in a situation today in which, in the Northern countries, the goal of reducing poverty through the creation of wealth has been reached to a substantial extent. To be sure, there is still concern about the distribution of wealth. But Rostow's final stage of economic development, "mass consumption," has been reached by billions of people even to the degree that we now are confronted with overconsumption.

Globally, we now face quite new challenges alongside the older ones, and there is no objection at all to seeing a future role for economics as a discipline in meeting those challenges. Next to the continuing task of creating a necessary social threshold for all human beings, we are now confronted with the planetary boundaries for humanity and we have to find ways to stay in what Kate Raworth has called the 'doughnut': the safe space for humanity between the ecological ceiling and the social foundation.[28] Therefore we may redefine the task of economics quite differently from the old one of just creating wealth. An alternative definition of economics could now well be: *the science that investigates how humans create and distribute wealth fairly within planetary boundaries.*

But this definition in itself could still presuppose something like *homo economicus* as its basic assumption. The question is therefore whether this will not simply perpetuate the problems of our modern economy in some ways. Some of the intimations of behavioral economics and game theory and recent findings of evolutionary theory, as well as an overwhelming amount of philosophical and religious literature, point to other ways of thinking about humans: not primarily as *homo economicus* but as *homo cooperans* or even *homo amans*.[29] As indicated above, economic theory does not, perhaps, create the societal 'acting out' of *homo economicus*, but it certainly stimulates it. Please note: a concept of human beings as a basic assumption for a science is not a matter of 'realism' vs. 'idealism' or 'fact' vs. 'value.' Recent developments in various sciences are not merely a matter of engaging in wishful thinking about people as cooperative beings with social preferences – they are simply registering that humans *are* such. It may well be that the person solely focused on his (yes

– often male) own interests represents a deviant pattern, which is an indication of a particular social environment and social conditioning. As a species, human beings tend to be cooperative and relational – this is the claim. A paradigm shift along these empirical lines might imply that economics and business studies start to study interhuman cooperation instead. In line as well with the values we identified earlier in this book – human dignity, regenerativity, inclusivity, and co-creativity – our alternative definition of economics for the 21st century could then read as follows: *the science that investigates how humans cooperate in order to create and distribute wealth fairly within planetary boundaries.*

One further renewal was indicated already in several places in this book. The 'goal' or *telos* of economics – the answer to the question: 'What is the economy good for?'; 'Why do we as humans have an economy?' – has become a matter of extensive discussion, leading to new concepts like 'wellbeing' or 'human flourishing' instead of mere wealth. Taking this into account, the new science of economics would be defined somewhat along these lines: *the science that investigates how humans cooperate in order to ensure and increase mutual wellbeing within planetary boundaries.* Summarizing these steps: planetary boundaries instead of continuing the myth of unlimited resources, *homo cooperans* instead of *homo economicus* and human flourishing instead of material wealth.

There are already quite some initiatives that try to think along these lines, and that need further academic attention and elaboration, going by names like "relational economics" (Bovenberg, Schluter, Wieland), "economics of mutuality" (Roche), "economy of communion" and "civil economy" (Bruni), "economy for the common good" (Felber), "doughnut economics" (Raworth), "economics of arrival" (Trebeck), and so on.[30] Each one of these has different angels and emphases, but there is a lot of common ground in the overall assumptions and goals. Together, they certainly sketch the contours of a new paradigm. The student's movement 'Rethinking Economics' has already produced good survey literature of these new developments.[31] Worth mentioning is also the 'Core Curriculum' that aims to teach economics starting from real life problems, such as sustainability and inequality, not from abstract equilibrium models.[32]

We call upon academic institutions to become a real hub for these attempts to 'rethink economics' and to create incubators for this new paradigm to develop and to find academic expression and a context for critical dialogue.[33]

Rediscovering the 'Wealth' of Adam Smith

Just as the 'neoclassical' return to the basic principles of classical economics was presented as a return to Adam Smith, this new paradigm is a return to Adam Smith as well – the man who, according to Kenneth Boulding, has a rightful claim to be "both the Adam and the Smith of systematic economics."[34] In recent years, a true rediscovery of Smith has taken place, led not by economists but by ethicists and historians of ideas (although economists have certainly participated in this endeavor).[35] They have pointed out that the 'father of economics' wrote much more than just the one book, *The Wealth of Nations* (1776), and among his many other works was one called *The Theory of Moral Sentiments* (1759). Although the assumption was viable in the 19th century, especially among German scholars, that there are two different 'Smiths' – referred to as "das Adam Smith Problem" – recent scholarship agrees that Smith was working on one coherent "science of human nature."[36] This clearly indicates that *Moral Sentiments* and *The Wealth of Nations* belong to one project and there is no contradiction between what Smith is saying in the earlier book on morality where he wrote about the role of 'mutual sympathy' and 'benevolence' among humans, and his work on economics that allegedly focuses on 'self-interest.'

Of course, in his book on economics we do find the infamous statement: "It is not from the benevolence of the butcher, the brewer and the baker that we expect our dinner, but from their concern for their self-interest. We address ourselves, not to their humanity, but to their self-love."[37] But close reading in the context reveals what Smith really means: trade deals can only occur when I, as seller, address myself to the self-love of someone else, the self-love *of another person*. "I have something here that may be of interest for you." I have to put myself in the shoes of the other in order to understand what this other person needs or finds interesting. So, I do not refer to my own self-love but to the self-love of the other. Smith therefore states somewhere else in *The Wealth of Nations* that "commerce ought naturally to be, among nations as among individuals, a bond of union and friendship."[38] Economics and markets are ideally not about selfishness and greed but about mutually understanding the needs of others and about making deals on this basis of mutual understanding, deals from which both the seller and the buyer profit.

The entire *Wealth of Nations* itself provides ample evidence that, for Smith, a market economy is a moral enterprise through and through. A recent study, using a quite innovative quantitative reading method, found more than 200 statements in *The Wealth of Nations* that express the intricate relation between morality, markets and human flourishing, either positively affirming the crucial role of virtues or denouncing certain vices as frustrating human flourishing.[39]

Something similar can be said about that other famous phrase from Smith: the "invisible hand." If Smith had held that markets presuppose the vice of greed, he would have needed the idea of the invisible hand to turn this evil into a greater good. He would have given extensive treatment to the idea. But he doesn't, not even once. The only occasion where the metaphor of the invisible hand occurs in *The Wealth of Nations* is where he wants to assure the reader that international trade will never lead to a destitute situation at home, for entrepreneurs always tend to organize production close to where they have a better overview of what happens to their money, so they will always provide more employment at home than abroad.[40]

So, the result of revisiting Adam Smith is a view of the market economy as one in which people freely cooperate and overcome poverty together by starting to work (and specialize, the 'division of labor') and to exchange the products of these efforts on the market. Wealth is thus created, poverty is overcome, the humiliation of begging is no longer necessary, and human dignity is established.

Smith didn't hide his ideals behind quasi-objective natural laws, nor did Marshall, for that matter. They were clear about their 'mission,' and there is no reason why economists today shouldn't follow suit. Of course, these ideals, this mission, will be different from Smith's. Economics has been rather successful in the age of the 'Great Enrichment;' so, let us make sure that it will be just as successful in the age of creating responsible capitalism, of redirecting the economic activity of humans in line with human dignity, ecological regenerativity, social inclusivity, and interhuman co-creativity: not a 'dismal science' but a humanitarian and ecological science through and through.

In Conclusion: Education is Essential

There is quite a body of research showing that students of economics and business are more selfish than other students, and during their education this is enforced not mitigated.[41] And then we send them out into the world, hundreds of thousands year after year worldwide. In a famous speech on education in the British House of Lords, the late Rabbi Jonathan Sacks said, "To defend a country, you need an army; to defend a civilization, you need schools." And then he proceeded to say "Never has the world changed so fast, and it's getting faster each year. We have no idea what patterns of employment will look like twenty years from now, what skills will be valued, and which done instead by artificially intelligent, preternaturally polite robots. We need to give our children an internalized moral Satellite Navigation System so that they can find their way across the undiscovered country called the future."[42]

The alleged 'knock-down' argument against what we have been arguing in this chapter is that we have to teach students 'reality,' not lofty ideals; show them the world as it empirically is, not as we want it to be; facts, not values. This is a highly curious argument. It is like teaching students of politics that Stalin and Hitler are 'real' but Churchill and Roosevelt, Gandhi, Martin Luther King, and Mandela are not; that shareholders are 'real' but human rights and ecological movements are not. We have to teach them that avoiding taxes is 'real' but that the rule of law is a fantasy, that selfishness is 'real' but cooperation an illusion. There is simply no empirical basis for selling this highly truncated view of reality as being 'the real world.' Let's stop injecting hundreds of thousands of students each year with an unrealistic ideology of selfishness, after which we inject them into the real world, only to find out that for millions of other people real life is also about prosocial values, cooperation, morality, fairness, purpose, and long-term wellbeing. Let's no longer make generations of students victims of our defunct theories and let's no longer make the world a victim of these indoctrinated victims.

Chapter 8
The Fourth Pillar of Renewal: Indicators

How do we make sure that ideals and values do not remain idle talk? The proof of the pudding is in the eating. Do people, do nations, do companies 'walk the talk'? Do they live up to their 'purpose'? We would like to be able to keep track some-how, of how we are doing in this regard – if only to prevent 'greenwashing.' Although there are all kinds of risks in figures, numbers, data, and statistics, they have nonetheless played an irreplaceable role in improving the lot of humankind. The causes of diseases, for example, are often identified by statistical records.[1] While it is certainly true – to paraphrase a famous book title – that people can 'lie with statistics,' nations without statistics are blind; companies that do not have their accounting well organized are destined to fail. That puts heavy emphasis on the quality of statistics and accounting and a huge responsibility on those who design the sets of indicators on which data will be collected and presented. "Accountants will save the world," as Peter Bakker, president of the World Business Council for Sustainable Development, claimed in front of the United Nations Conference on Sustainable Development, the RIO+20 conference in 2012.[2] And rightly so: the renewal of ideals – moving away from 'greed is good' and 'maximizing financial gains' – has to be accompanied by clear, transparent accountability. As the saying goes, the road to hell is paved with good intentions. That is also why we need to develop good indicators, as one way – though not the only one! – to make intentions, values, and ideals tangible and our commitments measurable and hence manageable.

As indicated earlier, in chapter 5, an eye-catching development in recent years has been what can be called 'multidimensional thinking' in economics and increasingly among policy makers and in policy institutions. And this multidimensional thinking goes hand in hand with the development of increasingly sophisticated multidimensional sets of indicators for measuring as precisely as possible how we are doing.

From this angle as well, the third decade of the 21st century is an exciting time for economists. The paradigm shift the field is going through incorporates a transition from single performance indicators to complex, integrated ones, from mono-indication toward multiple indication, which is also a transition from GDP to quality of life at the national level and from profit to true value (and true pricing) at the company level. We observe strong movements in three domains, whereby the 'mono-indicator tyranny' is being broken at various levels:

1. Macro: *beyond GDP,* enlarging the GDP measure and complementing – or even replacing – it with many other dimensions to get a much clearer view of the development of the quality of life and hence of how economies are really doing.

2. Meso: *integrated reporting, due diligence, true value.* We see companies breaking out of narrow numerical cages in in similar fashion: here 'integrated reporting' complements and supplements financial reporting. We are thus getting a better view of how companies are really doing and whether or not they are incurring hidden costs and hence parasitizing human, social and ecological resources.

3. Micro (though with major meso and macro implications): *true pricing.* We notice an increasing call to internalize external effects of (the production of) products in the prices of the products and hence to make prices more realistic, richer in information, and truer in allocating responsibilities, gains, and losses.

Macro: Beyond GDP, Multidimensional Approaches and the SDG's

We noticed that the GDP focus of recent decades created a 'mono-indicator tyranny,' relegating the responsibility for evaluating how we are doing economically to one formal, abstract indicator. This is changing as we speak. Economists are moving away from the tunnel of the GDP growth paradigm toward a science of wellbeing based on much more realistic assumptions about human beings and about what a good life for all of us is. Although the construction of the GDP measure was an important achievement as such, the 'inventor' of the GDP measure himself, Simon Kuznets, already warned against the abuse of this very abstract indicator as a 'catch-all' for the true wellbeing of a nation. It looks like this warning has finally been heeded. What we see is a rapid development of multi-dimensional sets of indicators complementing the GDP and thus revealing how a country is doing in terms of wellbeing, human flourishing, 'better life,' or whatever term one wishes to use.

Pioneers of multidimensional thinking include Amartya Sen, Martha Nussbaum, and Manfred Max-Neef. But there have been earlier advocates as well, such as the philosopher Herman Dooyeweerd in the Netherlands and, inspired by him, the economist T.P. van der Kooy. The latter called for a "simultaneous realization of multiple norms," not just the maximalization of growth and profit – both at the level of the economy as a macro-entity as well as at the corporate level. Around 1990, the Chilian economist Max-Neef worked on a conceptually very well-thought-out account of *Human Scale Development* in which he identified nine basic human needs (subsistence, protection, affection, understanding, participation, idleness, creation, identity, and freedom), combining these with both 'satisfiers,' that is, the factors and circumstances that could bring about the realization of these needs, and 'violators' or 'destroyers,' the factors and circumstances that could hinder them.[3] Unfortunately, Max-Neef's innovative approach did not receive the attention it deserved, if we are seeing it correctly. A comparable attempt was launched around the same time by the economist Herman Daly, in cooperation with the theologian John Cobb, called the Index of Sustainable Economic Welfare (ISEW) and later developed further as the Genuine Progress Indicator (GPI).[4] Fortunately, Amartya Sen was much more influential in the early efforts to overcome the GDP bias in monitoring international economic development. In the early 1990s he advised the UNDP to develop more inclusive standards that would take into account such factors as the level of education and the level of health care as indicators for how a country is doing. It was an important step toward the widely used multidimensional Human Development Index. Together with Martha Nussbaum, Sen subsequently focused on the development of the "capabilities approach," shifting the focus to the conditions for the wellbeing of individual citizens, things that citizens should be able to do or acquire such as health, education, relationships, a stable political environment, ecological safety, and so on.[5]

A very important step forward in this development toward a broader set of indicators for assessing a country's economic performance was the publication in 2009 of the Stiglitz–Fitoussi Report, written at the behest of then French President Sarkozy. It was officially called the Commission on the Measurement of Economic Performance and Social Progress. It is certainly remarkable that the commission wasn't dissolved after it delivered its report, as happens so often with committees, but also continued to observe the progress made in the implementation of their recommendations. Unfortunately, in 2018, the committee noted that there was still a lot of work to be done with respect to developing better metrics for assessing inequality between various groups and for assessing sustainability and other issues.[6]

A further milestone on this route was the formulation of the UN SDGs, the Sustainable Development Goals (mentioned in the introductory chapter). The SDGs are the successors to the Millennial Development Goals that were drafted under the auspices of then UN Secretary General Kofi Annan. They have been remarkably successful: in 2015, the conclusion was that by far most of the MDGs had been realized.[7] This encouraged the formulation of new goals, focused less exclusively on the 'underdeveloped' global South but also targeted at the 'overdeveloped' North, which has created so many imbalances in the global economy. The intention behind these goals is to achieve together, as a global effort, a much more balanced, integral notion – and reality – of global development. In this new, more encompassing formulation, a multidimensional approach to development was made tangible in 17 goals, already listed in the introductory chapter of this book.

The SDGs are concretized into 169 goals that are made measurable through 247 indicators in total.[8] It is clear from these efforts that the SDGs do indeed have a clear intention to move beyond idle talk and good intentions and to provide a framework that can really track how we are doing globally. Moreover, compared to many other multidimensional approaches to economic development, the UN-led efforts to formulate development goals (first the MDGs in 2000 and the SDGs in 2015) stand out both for their impressive international legitimacy and support as well as their increasing specificity.

The need to be able to have much more sophisticated, multidimensional sets of indicators was felt so acutely that – especially during the last two decades – an entire cottage industry has developed in providing alternatives to GDP.[9] In addition to the efforts already mentioned above, the well-known Bhutan Gross National Happiness measure as well as the OECD Better Life Index (comprising housing, income, jobs, community, education, environment, civic engagement, health, life satisfaction, safety, and work–life balance) are worth looking at. The term 'wellbeing' is increasingly being used as an overarching term for what the broader sets of indicators are designed to measure.[10]

As promising as all these attempts are, there still is a lot of work to be done before there are some standardized and broadly applicable sets of indicators.[11] But perhaps we shouldn't want just one universal set of indicators (such a desire may be a hangover from the seeming but deceptive clarity of the GDP) as conceptions of human and societal flourishing may have both some universal elements as well as contextual, cultural differences. What is needed is basic: that the new sets of measures acquire real authority and relevance for policy making so that they give governments the opportunity to really move 'beyond GDP.' For while the myth of GDP growth = happiness or GDP growth = human flourishing or GDP growth = wellbeing is still with us, its force seems to be spent.

But what is still sorely lacking is policies fully geared toward the new multidimensional standards. Even this is slowly starting to change, however. The new sets of indicators are making inroads into local and national government policies, such as with the so-called 'Wellbeing of Future Generations Act' (2015) in Wales and, more recently, the 'Wellbeing Budget' (2019) introduced by the New Zealand government. In the Wellbeing Economy Alliance, experiences are combined and experiments reported on how a wellbeing approach may affect policies.[12]

So much is clear: the future belongs to the multidimensional indicators, with respect to both *a posteriori* accountability and *a priori* future-oriented policy design. There still is a long way to go, but more and more, the multidimensional sets of indicators will serve not only as indicators of how 'we' (as the world, as a nation, or as a region or city) are doing but also as goal-setting indicators of what we should do in the future. And they are just as important as indicators of what we should no longer do: violate the many dimensions of sustainable human flourishing in the name of that exclusive but deceptive indicator – GDP growth.

Meso: Integrated Reporting, Due Diligence and True Value

The farewell to what are essentially simplistic models – notwithstanding the sometimes-astonishing mathematical complexities – is also evident in the move away from single indicators to more multidimensional indicators of performance at the corporate level. When is a company doing well – when it maximizes financial profits but destroys the natural environment in which its factories are located? Is a company doing well when people – either on its premises or somewhere in the value chain – start becoming sick? Is a company doing well when its products are made through the exploitation of human beings? Is a company doing well when it – using smart, underpriced web applications – destroys local businesses in a long-term attempt to acquire monopolies (and then raise prices after all)?

Indeed, human beings and companies – and human beings in companies – have to make choices regarding scarce resources, but the basis on which they make these choices simply isn't always the maximalization of their short-term financial self-interest. It turns out that people, including entrepreneurs and business-people, have many other goals and preferences, such as 'social preferences' and commitments, long-term orientations, and a sense of purpose. The single indicator – 'how much bang for your buck' – doesn't do any justice at all to the complex decision processes humans engage in and to what they really value. So, both entrepreneurs and employees often have much deeper and broader motivations for what they are doing than can be expressed in profit alone. As Edward Freeman, one of the pioneers of the stakeholder approach in the US states: "Saying that profits are the only important thing to a company is like saying, 'Red blood cells are life.' You need red blood cells to have life, but you need so much more."[13]

It is important for all of us, however, that the 'non-profit motivations' be recognized by others, that they can somehow be seen and taken into account. If there is no publicly recognized and recognizable way of bringing these motivations into play, it becomes very hard to sustain them and make them truly relevant. Fortunately, in recent years, at the corporate level, new methods have been developed to get a much clearer picture of this 'more' and to sever it from earlier connotations of vagueness. 'Purpose' has become tangible, and this greatly enhances the opportunities to inspire each other and hold each other accountable according to a much broader set of indicators than mere profit.

What has been called 'integrated reporting' has developed into an essential part of the shift towards a new phase in the market economy. This movement, which first started on the outskirts of the business world (with pioneers like Robert Eccles and others), has gained momentum in recent years and is now a truly global movement.[14] This enables purpose-driven companies to report to their shareholders not just on their financial performance but also on their tangible social and ecological performance. More importantly, it makes it possible to publicly reward purpose-driven companies and helps them realize their ideals in concrete practices. Three things are needed to do this: first of all, to measure non-financial factors as well as financial ones; second, to make decisions accordingly; and third, to report the facts and decisions to all stakeholders.

As is the case with the macro indicators, there is a wide range of methods for integrated reporting at this level as well, which makes it hard for shareholders and stakeholders to objectively compare companies' performances. Companies themselves have to find a balance between limiting their administrative burdens, providing shareholders and stakeholders with the right information and complying with legal standards.[15]

But important steps are being made here. The international non-profit organizations Value Reporting Foundation and the International Financial Reporting Standards Foundation (IFRS) are making progress in providing tools for measuring, deciding on, and reporting non-financial information. The Value Reporting Foundation was officially formed in June 2021, merging the Sustainability Accounting Standards Board (SASB) and the International Integrated Reporting Council (IIRC). The Value Reporting Foundation offers SASB standards for measuring. The SASB has published standards for as many as 77 distinguished industries (e.g., health care, infrastructure, food and beverage) for disclosing ESG information to investors.[16] Additionally, the Value Reporting Foundation provides integrated thinking principles, a holistic management approach. Third, they offer an integrated reporting framework. The formerly independent non-profit organization IIRC published their first international IR framework in 2013[17] and issued an updated framework in 2021, which superseded the former one.[18] These inspiring examples are already used by many (multinational) companies, enabling them to (1) measure, (2) think, and (3) communicate about doing business comprehensively and above all (4) learn how to improve their performance in the various dimensions.

Of course, there is the danger that companies will artificially inflate their ratings to gain financial and PR advantages, so-called 'greenwashing'[19] as was the case earlier with the credit ratings of financial firms by rating agencies – an alarming possibility. Independent auditing is essential for the credibility of integrated reporting.

Even more far-reaching methods are being developed by other business associations and in civil society, such as B corporations/B-Corps and the 'Common Good Balance Sheet,' which is offered by the 'Economy for the Common Good Movement.'[20] The trend seems irreversible – that much may be clear. It is part of a larger movement of assigning integral responsibility to companies for their entire value chain.[21]

While the movements just discussed have primarily the character of civil society movements, depending on the voluntary participation of companies, government enforced standards are being implemented in the EU as we write. The term 'due diligence' was used at first primarily in the context of mergers and financial transactions, but in recent years it has come to refer as well to the integral, increasingly legal, responsibility of companies for their entire value chain. In March 2021, the European Parliament adopted a resolution on 'Corporate Due Diligence and Corporate Accountability' that enlarged the scope of due diligence toward full legal responsibility for breaches of sustainability and human rights standards. As a consequence of this resolution and other initiatives of the European Council, the *EU Corporate Sustainability Due Diligence Directive* (CSDDD) was issued in 2022, complemented by the *Corporate Sustainability Reporting Directive* (CSRD) issued in January 2023, which asked companies that are either located in Europe or do business there (with more than 250 employees, €40 million in turnover and/ or €20 million in assets) to report on their social and environmental impact, the full ESG range (Environmental, Social, and Governance aspects).[22]

Although the intended legal binding power of the EU regulations may be a new element, the resolution builds on many earlier declarations and initiatives with respect to content, notably the *UN Guiding Principles on Business and Human Rights* of 2011.[23] Here the three elements of 'protect, respect, and remedy' are the leading principles, both for governments and business, although the document assigns and acknowledges their different responsibilities. But the legal status of the CSRP issued by the EU can indeed be considered a 'landslide change' for companies.[24]

This movement toward integrated reporting and due diligence will impact how companies are evaluated both by stakeholders and shareholders. It is to be expected that especially investors with a long-term perspective will appreciate companies that are doing well in terms of ESG, SDGs, on so on, particularly when they can show that they walk the talk and really contribute to society and to sustainability as 'net positive.' The 'net positive' concept refers to the true value calculation of companies in which the financial, social, and ecological gains of a company are compared to the social and ecological losses, that were earlier identified as nothing more than 'externalities.' In that way, the damage that a company – or a project of a company – does to its neighborhood or the ecosystems is made immediately visible in one report.[25] And the external effects can be accounted for internally, within the company, that now takes responsibility.

The movement toward legislation and juridification of responsible business certainly contains risks. The phenomenon of 'crowding out' is discussed in moral literature: as soon as codes and laws are in place, the result may be that the moral inspiration of 'good' entrepreneurs evaporates and the lawyers take over, trying to find ways to avoid full implementation of the regulations – legal minimalism crowding out moral inspiration. Or the engineers take over, trying to find technological loopholes to avoid compliance, as was the case with Volkswagen and its diesel engines. There is also another possibility, which Johan Graafland calls "crowding in."[26] External pressure may also enhance the inspiration and intrinsic commitment to do the right thing, to comply with the legal requirements, and to use them as an opportunity to bring doing well and doing good together. Moreover, as the Volkswagen diesel case illustrates, while trying to minimalize or avoid compliance may seem advantageous in the short run, in the long run it can be disastrous and hugely expensive (not to mention the actual damage done that the regulations intended to avoid in the first place, in this case pollution). Viewed from this angle, companies may do well to not only wholeheartedly comply with legislation but also to call for regulation, to create a level playing field at a higher level. Moral inspiration and government regulations therefore shouldn't be seen as mutually exclusive but as working in tandem – both are needed at various phases of development.[27]

True Pricing

The final development that is highly interesting concerns the level of actual transactions between producers and consumers. Here, prices play a central role. In standard economic theory, the prices that result from the exchange are always the optimal price, containing all relevant information. For Friedrich Hayek, this has even become a cornerstone of his reflection on the economy: the myriad of interactions between millions and millions of consumers and producers form such a complex reality that it is inconceivable that any superbrain could ever come up with any legitimate judgment of the outcomes of the process. The free market is an expression of the wisdom of the crowd, and asking questions beyond this in the name of something like 'social justice' is a 'mirage.'[28]

But another perspective is possible, which is inspired by the rather simple observation that some prices are really disproportionate and that there are some obvious imbalances in prices. A flight from Amsterdam to Paris, which is known to be quite polluting, is much cheaper than going by train. Why? And a dead tree in the rain forest suddenly has financial worth and a price, whereas the same tree alive is just 'worthless' or, better, 'priceless,' in the literal sense of 'without a financial price attached to it' while indeed it may be priceless in the metaphorical sense. We see this with cigarettes as well: even though taxes have raised the price of cigarettes much higher than they would have been otherwise, the total cost of smoking in terms of the costs of health care for cancer patients, the loss of working years of those who become ill because of it – and one could even think of compensation for next of kin in the event of early death – is still not reflected in the price. The entire revenue model behind the industry might collapse, and the world would be a better place for it: true economic growth? A similar argument can be made for products with excessive sugar and calories that are designed to constantly tempt the consumer to buy and buy again but are a direct onslaught on their long-term health.

As Robert Reich has pointed out, however, there is also the internal dividedness human beings experience.[29] Reich distinguishes between various roles that people have. As consumers, they may do certain things – for example, buy consumer goods that are bad for the environment – that they would reject as citizens. So, they may still take an inexpensive flight between Amsterdam and Paris, knowing that taking the train would be better for the environment. But the awareness that others will take the flight might cause them to 'fear missing out' or just being silly when paying a higher price for a train ticket while others go almost for free by plane.

In medieval times, there was an attempt to somehow give objective value to some elements of the pricing process outside of the influence of individual market transactions. This was called the 'just price' (*iustum pretium*): when something can be considered a real necessity for human beings, then both the producer should get a fair price for producing it and the consumer should not have to pay too much for acquiring it: it should be within the range of what one can reasonably be expected to pay. For example, as a basic necessity, bread should be profitable to produce as well as affordable to buy.[30] Now, the typical reaction of later economists has been to view this idea of a just price as an entirely dysfunctional moral intervention in a free market. But the question as to whether this response has been too easy and avoids real problems with prices is a pertinent one.

'True pricing' attempts to remedy some of the deficiencies of market prices.[31] It is observed that quite a few real costs are 'externalized' and are made without being paid for by either the producer or the consumer of certain goods. This is a problem, particularly in cases of negative externalities, such as social or ecological costs, that actually are paid for but not by those who profit from the transaction. These costs are paid for by individuals and groups or even societies somewhere else in the value chain, such as underpaid workers who have to live in poverty, taxpayers, sick citizens, or future generations. In a way, we could even speak in some cases of slavery in a new form, of exploitation in value chains.

At least one remedy for externalization is the 'internalization of all costs.' For this, at least three things have to happen. First of all, costs should be made transparent. What, if this can be calculated, is the true cost of one tonne of CO_2? And does this match the current price? According to a 2019 calculation, the cost is about €110, while the actual price at the time was set at €27.50.[32] Other recent calculations even calculate the real cost at €185.[33] Due to the Ukraine crisis, the actual market price soared to around €90, thus moving in the direction of the real cost. Making this cost transparent is the first step toward internalization. But internalization alone is not enough – that will just raise prices (or the VAT). Thus, as a second element, the extra money raised by internalization should be used for remedying the problem. A third element of true pricing is to create, through government action, a level playing field for entire sectors.

True pricing often should not just be an issue between producers and consumers since this could create free rider problems and will easily result, in the end, in a race to the bottom. For example, a general kerosene tax is urgently needed to create a level playing field for all airline companies and to create a level playing field with other, less environmentally damaging ways of travel, thus ending hidden subsidies for air travel. But if some raise prices voluntarily while others refuse to do so, the 'good ones' may soon be out of business, and the extra money wouldn't be used for the reduction of emissions anyway. Obviously, government action is needed here.

There certainly are problems with the idea of true pricing. One problem is that it may be quite difficult to quantify and monetize the negative externalities. As Debra Satz, Michael Sandel, and others have pointed out, not everything that has value can be put up for sale or can be expressed in or compensated by money.[34] Another problem is that true pricing may encourage pollution and unjust production, providing moral coverage: "I paid for it, didn't I?" This relies on the very mechanism it criticizes, the disciplinary force of pricing. And consumers may not even notice the slightly higher price and continue buying polluting products. In spite of these shortcomings, however, the movement to make prices more adequately reflect the entire costs in the value chain and to distribute the profits along these chains is an urgent one and an integral part of the paradigm shift that can be witnessed in today's economic thinking.

In Conclusion

The fourth pillar of renewal, as we call it, that of indicators, is becoming established and is irreversible. At all levels, especially at the macro and meso levels, we see what sometimes looks like an avalanche of new sets of indicators for measuring the non-financial aspects of countries and companies. This may easily create confusion and uncertainty, especially for businesses. So, further standardization and clear, unequivocal legislation and guidelines are the order of the day.

This is not to claim that everything that is of value can be reduced to numbers and formulas, but the big gain of the almost revolutionary renewal of indicators at various levels is that countries and companies can start to track their own performance, can compare it to past performance – and sometimes to other countries or companies as well – and in that way can embark on continuous learning and innovation processes. It all contributes to remedying one of the most harmful effects of unfettered capitalism, as indicated earlier in this book, the externalization of negative effects of production and consumption. What was easily externalized can be increasingly internalized again. This 'idealistic' movement makes our sense of value creation much more realistic – a true gain.[35]

Chapter 9

The Fifth Pillar of Renewal: Institutions and the Multiactor Approach

Beyond the State–Market Dichotomy

The debate on organizing the economy has focused for decades on the 'state vs. market dilemma.' The 'right-wing' approach acts on the assumption that society is so complex that no overall coordinating mechanism will ever be able to come up with better outcomes than the spontaneous process itself. States exist only to set rules and enforce compliance, but it is not their task to provide long-term direction for society or the economy nor to create the conditions for human dignity and participation. In contrast, from the 19th century on, the 'left-wing' approach has focused on the state as the only institution that protects the wellbeing of its citizens and the environment.

We believe that both perspectives have severe shortcomings.[1] The European 'solution' to its search for a good society eventually turned out to consist not of One Big Recipe – either state or market, either freedom or solidarity – but of bringing different values together into a dynamic mix, with respect to both principles (liberty *and* equality *and* solidarity) and institutions in order to have a dynamic mix of free markets, well-developed governments/public sectors, and civil society/community. The great European discovery was that a modern society is best suited for promoting human flourishing and institutionalizing human dignity when it consists of various more or less independent spheres that recognize each other's existence without trying to dominate or usurp the others and at the same time aligning their different responsibilities with each other. This in no way implies that life will be perfect, but at least some important preconditions for a reasonable, shared level of human flourishing are in place. This constitutes the "narrow corridor" (to use a recent metaphor posed in Acemoglu and Robinson[2]) not only toward a free society but toward a free and just society.

Recently, economists have given explicit recognition to the insight that, for a healthy society – and a healthy economy for that matter – it is essential to move beyond the state-market dichotomy and to recognize the importance of a 'third sphere' in society or, to use Rajan's term, a "Third Pillar." Similarly, Paul Collier argues in his *The Future of Capitalism* that the significance of non-economic spheres for a good society, such as families and neighborhoods, needs to be recognized. These insights are also at the very heart of the 'European Economic Approach' that we identified earlier as the 'Third Way' or 'the Rhine model' (Northwestern Europe) or as the idea of a 'civil economy' (Italy). A healthy economy in a healthy society requires a full recognition of the distinct responsibilities of the state, the business sector, and civil society/community.

A Multiactor Approach

Although we find the intuition behind the community-oriented approach very valuable, talking about 'three spheres' or 'three pillars' in late modern society may turn out to be somewhat romantic and not really geared to the societal realities of today. There are many more spheres and actors than just these three that together comprise modern society. Moreover, the countervailing power over against either state or market often is not exercised by communities but by other actors such as academic, religious, or media institutions. We would like, therefore, to identify a number of societal actors and spheres that have crucial roles to play in a healthy society and a healthy economy. They also have to play crucial roles in the current task of the renewal of capitalism. Talking about 'three pillars' might let a couple of key players 'off the hook' while others who might have already developed worthwhile alternative perspectives are not taken into account. We thus propose ten actors and illustrate this by means of a figure called the 'Economic Decagon.'

Very much in line with what was earlier called the 'Rhine model' or the 'Third Way,' we propose a 'multi-stakeholder' or 'multiactor approach.' This approach assumes that markets or economies are dynamic platforms where a number of actors meet and each actor has its own role to play while at the same time coordinating their own actions with those of the other actors. We identify at least ten key actors or, better, clusters of actors, each of whom can be seen as a 'stakeholder' in the actions of the others. For an economy to function well – and contribute to human dignity, inclusivity, regenerativity, and co-creativity – it is vital that each of these actors plays its own role, but always in coordination with the other actors. So, each actor is a 'stakeholder' in the actions of the others. The ten actor clusters that we identify are governments (including local governments), businesses, financial institutions, civil society organizations and initiatives, communities, science/research and education, media, consumers, 'imaginative reflection,' and, last but not least, nature. For us, it is a crucial insight that, strangely enough, is almost never explained in textbooks on economics: in every economy many actors are actively involved, not just producers and consumers. And hence: for economic renewal many actors have to be mobilized.

In our concept of 'responsible capitalism,' these ten actors are responsible together for realizing the key values of human dignity, regenerativity, inclusivity, and co-creativity. This can be rendered as follows in the figure below:

The various actors in this graphic can be clustered into three groups corresponding to the colors given: Makers, Embedders, and Innovators of the economy. In short, the three sectors refer to 'making,' 'making it possible,' and 'making it good.'

In the black group, business, finance, and consumers together form the sphere of *practicing the economy* and therefore can be called the 'Makers' of the economy.

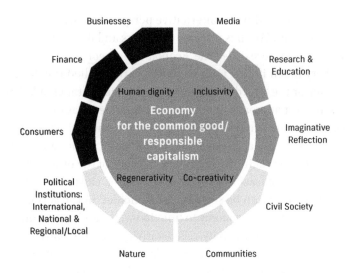

Figure 3: *The 'Economic Decagon': the Institutional Platform of Responsible Capitalism*

Light grey includes four actors that play roles in simultaneously *enabling and limiting the economy* (Dutch: *inkaderen*; French: *encadrer*): political institutions, communities, nature and civil society. We call them the 'Embedders' of the economy.[3]

Dark grey covers the other three spheres or actors concerned with *analyzing and giving orientation* to the economy. They can be identified as the 'Critical Innovators' of the economy. Civil society operates very much at the boundary of 'enabling/limiting/embedding' and giving orientation to/revitalizing the economy (and therefore could have been placed in the blue category as well).

The key idea behind the figure is that a free market can function properly only if each of the actors:
- has a clear sense of the specific nature of its own role: *role-consciousness*;
- allows the other actors to play their roles, without manipulation: *mutual respect of the other roles;*
- is willing to enter into meaningful dialogue with the other actors about how their actions impact them and how the alignment of goals can be achieved: *multiactor dialogues.*

The Heart of the Multiactor Approach: Cooperative and Co-creative Problem Solving

We call this a 'multiactor approach.' It has emerged in recent years in EU projects regarding agricultural innovation and has played a major role in the Horizon 2020 research agenda.[4] The multiactor approach invites – in the case of agriculture – farmers, scientists, policy advisors, consumers, and NGOs to come together to co-create shared knowledge and develop innovative practices. The heart of the approach is not to solve problems in a rather abstract way, either by government regulation or the free market, but to engage different stakeholders in solving problems, including consumers. Of course, this may also imply a specific role for government regulation, but this is certainly not the exclusive focus. Neither is the exclusive focus on the business sector, the market, in isolation from other sectors.

A multiactor approach acknowledges that entirely different types of knowledge are of crucial importance in a production process: scientific knowledge (of various types, liberal arts, natural sciences, social sciences), professional knowledge, commercial insights, and practical wisdom of those who work on the shop floor or on the farmland.

Such an approach focuses on the formation of meaningful coalitions around urgent societal challenges in which the stand-alone actions of one actor are doomed to fail. This approach is certainly inspired by what is often called the move 'from shareholder to stakeholder capitalism.' But it is not always clear what the stakeholder approach entails. In a recent publication by the Dutch chapter of the Global Compact Network, an attempt is made to clarify this by distinguishing between four 'gears,' referring to how businesses can deal with stakeholders:

1st gear: Legal minimum (financially driven);

2nd gear: Because (*and, we may add, in as far as*) it pays off; what's in it for me?

3rd gear: Opportunity driven: The 'you and I'-perspective

4th gear: For everybody: How can we solve this together?

Elsewhere, the document distinguishes, in parallel fashion, four stages of stakeholder involvement: information, consultation, involvement, partnership.

For us, the multiactor approach – in line with the core value of co-creativity as identified above – implies a 4th-gear type of relationship between companies and stakeholders: 'How can we solve this together?' and 'partnership.' Entrepreneurship and businesses are not there to manipulate other actors but, as stakeholder theory has emphasized for decades, to treat others as responsible, dignified actors in themselves.[5] Moreover, it is based on the idea of a social covenant as mentioned before (end of chapter 3 and in chapter 6): the sense that, in society, we are in this together, each in different circumstances and with different capabilities, and yet, cooperating for mutual benefit – the value of co-creativity that we referred to earlier as well. Last but not least, the value of cooperation and co-creativity is fully in line with the SDG17, 'partnership for the goals.'

But apart from this value basis, there are also very pragmatic reasons for a multiactor approach. One of these is the awareness that most problems cannot be solved by one actor alone. Nor can truly creative ideas be developed in isolation by one actor. As is becoming increasingly clear, today's problems are complex, and the external effects of one action or one product on many other actors and elements are difficult to keep track of and be managed well. Another reason is that companies may become aware that, to use the phrase from Feike Sijbesma that we quoted in the introductory chapter, "Nobody can be successful in a world that fails." So, engaging with one's social and ecological surroundings can just be part of wisdom.

Moreover, a multiactor approach can also lead to a much clearer 'license to operate' for all partners, especially for businesses. In the European Economic Model, the license to operate is related primarily not to the shareholders (as in the USA) nor to the state (as in China) but to the value that a company creates for all stakeholders, consumers, employees, the community, without infringing on but contributing to social and environmental capital. Again, it may be just smart to be aware of this.

Last but not least, a multiactor approach as proposed here is also a natural way to realize 'chain responsibility' for companies. 'Due diligence' (see chapter 8) is no longer primarily a matter of paperwork and auditing but of organizing the active involvement of partners within the chain. The reason why we – in addition to the well-known term 'stakeholder-approach' – emphasize the term 'multiactor approach' is precisely its emphasis on common action. It is not about informing other parties at a late stage in processes but about common action from the start. Thus, 'common-action-in-networks.'

The 'Problem of Many Hands' and the 'Power of Initiative'

There is a clear danger in a multiactor approach that has to be addressed and that ethicists have been referring to in recent years as the 'problem of many hands.' If there are many actors involved in a particular context, it is all too easy for each of them to escape responsibility, lean back, take a free ride, and wait for others to take action. This may even go as far as engaging in hidden subversion and obstruction. If many actors are responsible, no one is responsible. It could just be seen as a collective problem that occurs but is not attributable to any one actor and for which no actor can reasonably be expected to take responsibility.[6] Why should I solve all the problems of the world? This question of avoiding responsibility may be asked by an individual or it may be asked by a company or a government, a government agency, or a civil servant. So, a multiactor approach may end up as the Great Deferral and as simply another way to the Great Refusal of responsibility.

But, as with many problems, no one actor can be held responsible for having caused the problem in the first place ('backward responsibility'), and since no one actor can be held responsible for fully solving the problem, *every actor can be held responsible for taking the initiative.* Each actor can take the first step ('forward responsibility'), the initiative: 'Let's get together to see what can be done about it.'[7] The power of initiative, about which the philosopher Hannah Arendt has written so insightfully, belongs to all of us, regardless of our actual power.[8] The power of initiative ranges from a Swedish school girl to an American or Chinese president, from a small NGO to a big corporation like Unilever, from a small micro-finance initiative to the largest investment fund in the world like Blackrock, from local governments to multilateral political actors like the EU or the UN. The power of initiative, as we see it, is radically different from enclosing oneself in one's own bubble, either as a consumer, as a corporation, or as an NGO. On the contrary, it is about addressing issues at the public level. It is stepping up in the awareness that you yourself have to be the change you hope for – but not just on your own.

It may be clear as well that, in a multiactor approach, there ultimately have to be actors who can break through apathy and deadlock. At a societal level, this may in certain cases be a local or national government or an international body like the EU. Governments may provide the 'level playing field' or a framework for the parties involved. Or such an actor may be the good example, the first adapter, who starts doing and making things differently, in spite of the odds.

In the background of the approach that we propose here, there are also theories about 'system change' and 'complexity-theory.' In complex systems, and economies certainly are highly complex systems, it is impossible to orchestrate change from one central point, but change may occur anywhere in the system, and in some cases may gain traction, after which a tipping point may occur and the entire system goes through a change. This is also why it is not advisable to put all one's eggs in one basket, such as government regulations, for system-relevant changes can occur in all parts of the system. Everybody's contribution and innovation are relevant, and some may turn out, as a kind of multiplier, to have a much larger effect for the economy as a whole, bringing it into a new phase.[9]

Structures of Meaningful Encounter and Coalitions for a Better Economy

For us, the stakeholder-approach or multiactor approach is not about creating neutral platforms. On the contrary, the networks will have to address and respond to the key values we identified above right from the start: human dignity, inclusivity, regenerativity, and co-creativity. So, the approach implies that key actors in a certain economic domain or production chain form networks of meaningful dialogue around these values. What does each actor do and how can it establish supportive relationships with other actors to help them achieve these values? How do we bring our production processes, our neighborhood, our society, our schools, our financial institutions more in line with human dignity, inclusivity, regenerativity, and co-creativity? What is needed for that? And how can one actor assist the others in achieving this? And what is required from other actors to achieve this? If a company wants to be more regenerative or more inclusive, what is then required from financial institutions and investors? What role can schools and education play? What should a local government do? The list goes on.

The 'power of initiative' therefore is first of all 'invitational power': starting action-oriented networks and asking key actors to join in a co-creative process. So, we see the free market as an arena, a platform, literally an 'agora,' a meeting place, where all kind of actors encounter each other and relate to each other, address common issues and are motivated by common values, each in their own way.[10]

We can sketch a 'ladder of social and economic innovation':
- take an initiative, start to do it yourself, develop new expertise
- look for partners within the own sector, a coalition of the willing, scaling up
- involve actors from other sectors/actors, to more adequately address issues and perhaps as well to create public pressure
- if necessary: involve governments, lobby for regulation, creating a new level playing field at a higher level than before.

In the following three chapters we will present a somewhat sketchy assessment of the roles of various actors and of their interaction within the context of a European Economic Model: the 'Makers,' the 'Embedders,' and the 'Critical Innovators' of the economy of the future.

Resistance: Pessimism, Lethargy, Vested Interests

When we talk about the power of initiative found in every actor, it may be clear at the same time that actors can deny their responsibility and become lethargic. Or they may actively resist or frustrate the initiatives of other actors. There may be very different reasons for this. We just point to three types of reasons for resisting initiatives aiming at a reorientation of the economy toward human dignity, regenerativity, inclusivity and co-creativity.

The first type may have to do with a lack of knowledge, either a lack of awareness about the seriousness and urgency of the need for reorientation, or a lack of perspective on whether and how alternatives are viable. With this book we hope to contribute to both a sense of urgency and a view of possible alternative ways for doing business, and thus provide concrete hope.[11]

The second type has to do with the power of vested interests. Every change, every transition that affects the status quo also affects vested interests, especially short-term interests, such as those of investors, of banks, of large businesses. They can often mobilize strong resistance. This type of resistance is tough. Dialogues may fail. Here only using countervailing power can have some effect: the power of public opinion, or shareholders who have developed a different perspective, and/or government regulation.

The third type may have to do with weak or unwilling governments that do not provide a clear sense of direction – 'mission' – for the business and financial sector and may refuse to regulate or create level playing fields. If governments refuse to act as countervailing power – perhaps the lobby power of vested interests is just too big – then, in the long run an economy is truly in jeopardy. What we said in chapter 3 about 'regulatory capture' may apply here. In all three cases, resistance is something to expect and to reckon with when the power of initiative is utilized.

How to Start a Movement...

There is a video on YouTube called "How to start a movement?"[12] It begins with a lonely dancer on a crowded beach. It looks silly: What in the world is this figure doing there? But then, all of a sudden, another person joins the first – and now there are two dancers. This 'first follower' is crucial. It doesn't look so silly anymore: they are having fun. But still... Then something odd starts to occur. Apparently, what the two are doing looks so inviting to others on the beach that more and more people join the dance until we are watching what looks like a true dance party.

This scene can be a symbol for the multiactor approach that we are presenting in this book. The heart of the approach is what we called the 'power of initiative,' the first, and often lonely, dancer. But just as important as taking innovative initiatives is the 'art of coalition making' – the second dancer and the third. This is the ability to see which other partners are needed to give the first initiative a 'multiplier effect' – until an entire crowd starts to dance. Isolation is the enemy of innovation.

Chapter 10

The Flying Wheel of Responsible Innovation (A): The 'Makers' of a New Economy (Business, Finance, Consumers)

A Movement of Responsible Innovation

In the last chapter, we introduced the multiactor approach as a further step in the development of what is called stakeholder capitalism. We presented an illustration or figure of the actors involved in running an economy. This in itself provides a distinct idea of what an economy is, which may be different from how the economy is often portrayed: it is not just a market that is operating with businesses and consumers as the main actors, with or without government regulations; rather, it is a multitude of actors in constant interaction. In this chapter and in the next two, we will focus on this dynamic so that we bring movement to the figure in the last chapter. Therefore, the figure will here be presented as a flying wheel, the 'flying wheel of responsible innovation', innovation leading toward responsible capitalism. How can the various actors play their roles in such a way that the overall outcome builds toward responsible capitalism and are hence realizations of the common good, of sustainable human flourishing? How can a market be organized in such a way that it can be a force for good, directing the creativity, courage, and innovative flow of entrepreneurship toward sustainability and inclusivity? And who can start the wheel moving? Or, to use the metaphor that we used at the end of the last chapter: Who will start to dance in such an inviting way that others join in?

In our view, responsible innovation requires both awareness of the specific role of the various actors as well as awareness of which coalitions are essential for starting a movement leading to responsible capitalism. It is in that spirit that we will discuss the role of the various actors: their specific role or, one can say, their 'identity' or 'self-image,' and the key coalitions that they can establish, to set the wheel in motion. As we said in the last chapter, isolation is the enemy of innovation. Research shows that technological innovation is only one part of innovation, the social processes around technological innovation make up 75% of the effectiveness of innovations.[1] Co-creativity is key.

The fundamental idea that underlies this approach is that an economy is not a platform for some people to extract human, sociopolitical, and ecological resources for private gain. Rather, it is a common endeavor in which people and institutions with very different talents and roles work together to enhance long-term human flourishing or sustainable wellbeing. In this chapter, we discuss the various actors identified in the previous one: first, those that enact or 'make' the economy (businesses, consumers, financiers): the 'Makers.' In the next chapter we discuss those actors that 'make the economy possible' (political institutions, nature, communities, and civil society): the 'Embedders.' The final chapter in this part will be devoted to those institutional spheres that critically analyze and give direction to the economy (imaginative reflection, research and education, and media): the 'Critical Innovators.' But we will first look at enterprises, finance, and consumers – can they already start the innovative dance together?

Actor 1 – Responsible Entrepreneurship: Business for the Common Good

A crucial role in the European economy for future generations will of course be played by businesses. What is rather unique about businesses is how they can identify certain problems, come up with solutions that no one else has thought of before, and turn these solutions into reality. That capacity allowed

Rebecca Henderson to formulate her slogan: "Business can save the world."[2] To be more precise: without good businesses, the transition to responsible capitalism will be impossible. The creativity and 'realization power' of business is essential. Not only can businesses with the right mindset survive disruptive changes, they can even play a leading role in the transition to a new inclusive and sustainable economy.[3] So there is no point in 'bashing business,' which happens too often when the need for a reorientation of capitalism comes up.

If business is to play this leading role, we need to have a clear sense of what a business is about. According to the 'old school' of neoliberalism, a business is a private initiative for maximizing individual profits, even while it parasitizes social, political, and ecological resources.[4] In this school of thought, businesses are not at all concerned – and shouldn't have to be – with what are conveniently called 'externalities' or 'external effects.' A business is simply a money-making machine for shareholders, to summarize Friedman's view. It is only the law of the land that may put constraints on business; business itself doesn't have moral agency. In the new school of responsible capitalism, which we envisage in this book, a business is a cooperative hub of innovation and service to solve problems society and consumers experience. A creative entrepreneur or enterprise brings together people and means of production with the specific purpose of serving others. It is not exploitation but service, solving problems, that is the heart, the purpose, of business. Business is there, as Oxford professor Colin Mayer has argued, to profitably solve the problems of people and the planet and not to profit from producing or perpetuating problems.[5] Paul Polman has summarized this in stating that the purpose of business is to be 'net positive,' really contributing to a better world.[6] Simply reducing harmful external effects is not good enough. As Polman says, "Given that we are living well beyond planetary boundaries, the only long term viable business model is one that is restorative, reparative, regenerative. Most companies at best are still in the CSR or less bad mode. Reducing carbon emission, deforestation or plastics in the ocean. But we require a mindset change as less bad is still bad. To overcome an exponential challenge leading companies increasingly apply Net Positive thinking and getting rewarded for it."[7] It is the positive contribution that really counts, that really adds value.

Businesses should be able to make a profit while solving problems. People work there, and they have to make a living, and the company should be able to do business. But it is appropriate to recall Freeman's (not Friedman's) adage that profits are like red blood cells: they are necessary for life, but creating as many red blood cells as possible should never be the goal of an organism – it can even lead to the subject's death. The goal is to create inherent value for others and not at the expense of other stakeholders.[8]

Businesses bring various types of capital together – financial, natural, technological, human, and social – and transform this innovatively to create new products. And they do so while not depleting these types but allowing them to renew themselves. For a business to do otherwise would, in the end, undermine that business.[9]

A crucial precondition for good businesses is that they see themselves as real *citizens*.[10] Of course, in a formal sense, they are 'artificial,' legal persons, but this does not prevent them from being citizens, just as all natural persons are: you live in a country, you contribute to that country by 'giving back' or 'paying forward' what you receive, shouldering the burden of maintaining a common world. This conception of corporate citizenship requires what is expected from all citizens: paying taxes, not harming other citizens (therefore reducing negative externalities), and, together with other citizens – both natural and artificial persons – contributing to the common good, maintaining a common world in which all can live and live well. Corporate citizenship involves much more than and is even clearly to be distinguished from corporate philanthropy. Citizenship implies working actively with all relevant stakeholders to make society better at local, national, and international levels (if relevant), in creative partnership. It implies working on maintaining and fulfilling the ecological and social preconditions for society and the economy. The old opposition between 'public' and 'private,' with the implication that companies can make private gains at public expense, no longer holds water. Profit should be decent profit as a reward for created real value, not a premium on extraction or exploitation.

A fast-growing group of companies understand this and are taking on these public responsibilities. They are beginning to unite themselves in new associations, like the B corporations, as mentioned in chapter 8, which bring together almost 7,000 companies in 90 countries. They are setting a new standard for what the role of business in the future should be. There are other comparable initiatives, such as 'Economy for the Common Good Companies' and 'Economy of Communion,' or 'Economics of Mutuality,' and there are certainly other initiatives as well.[11]

It is very encouraging to see a real change in 'mainstream' business associations as well. The Dutch Employer Association VNO/NCW–MKB has recently published a new long-term Vision Paper called *Agenda NL 2030: Creating Broad Welfare through Enterprise – Towards a New Rhine Model* in which they officially adopt a new perspective on the role of business in society, inspired by what was earlier called 'Rhineland thinking.' This placed heavy emphasis on what is called *brede welvaart*, so 'wellbeing' in a much broader sense than GDP alone.[12] A similar move can be observed in the confederation of European business associations, Business Europe, whose policy document for the European Union, titled *Prosperity – People – Planet*, is clearly in line with the new insights regarding the social and ecological responsibility of business.[13]

This view of businesses as what we could call 'cooperative hubs of innovation and service to sustainably solve problems of society and of consumers' has several implications regarding – as a slight variation on 'triple-P' – seven P's: *purpose, people, products, profits, processes, partnerships, and polis/citizenship.*

– **Purpose.** For responsible businesses, it is essential to clearly formulate their purpose. The purpose differs from measurable short-term goals. Purpose refers to the long-term contribution to society and the planet that a company wants to make. To have a purpose implies having a long-term orientation. A well-formulated, and lived, purpose can motivate all those cooperating in and with the business, giving them a sense of direction, of standing shoulder to shoulder to achieve something worthwhile. When results are there, it gives a sense of pride and satisfaction too. A purpose also indicates that one is willing to make sacrifices and overcome hardships in realizing that purpose. As we know from many battlefields, troop morale is essential for results. A well-functioning purpose, as distinct from pre-ordered KPIs, stimulates creativity and innovation in all the layers of an organization.

If a company's leadership really has the courage to take its long-term purpose seriously, it can consider turning itself around and turning the company into what in the US is called a 'Public Benefit Corporation.'[14] Patagonia and Danone have done so in the US. In this way, social and ecological purposes become the legal heart of the corporation. This can truly be called 'commitment.' The European equivalent would be called a 'social enterprise.' But even without aiming for the champions' league of social responsibility, corporations can still turn their 'purpose' into a solid commitment to themselves and to the public.

– **People.** In a true economy for the common good or responsible capitalism (the European Economic Model as formulated here), workers are not 'means of production' (as they are sometimes described in standard economic theory) but coworkers in a common endeavor. They are part of a team, guided by the entrepreneur/CEO. Regardless of its legal form, every firm is a community, a cooperative.

Therefore, it makes sense to consider employees as stakeholders and give them a voice in management. Of course, this implies both shared responsibility and shared risk.[15] Some form of democracy (*Mitbestimmung* in German, *medezeggenschap* in Dutch, employee participation) in firms is by no means a utopian ideal since a great many firms already practice it. Some go quite far in this respect, such as the Brazilian multinational Semco Partners or the Dutch Breman Company. But there are many different ways of organizing this.[16]

In this line of thinking about firms as communities, excessive differences in payment between the 'top' and the 'bottom' are simply out of the question: each worker, from the 'lowest' to the 'highest,' contributes according to their abilities and is entitled to a fair share, well enough to live decently, including cases where people have responsibilities for families. In the US, the CEO–worker pay gap (the difference between the income of CEOs and that of the average worker in a company) has increased from 20:1 in 1960, via 42:1 in 1980 to 300:1 in 2019. This is, to put it bluntly, ridiculous.[17] Such a gap is destructive for companies themselves *and* for society at large, for it undermines any sense of shared purpose.

The future of the economy depends to a large extent on the resourcefulness and creativity of entrepreneurs *and their employees*, which makes it vitally important to promote co-creativity. Aligning the organizational culture throughout the entire chain with the overall goals of an enterprise is the crucial task of leadership.[18]

– **Products.** During the last 250 years, during what we earlier called the 'escape from poverty,' the basic paradigm of production was 'take – make – waste': take raw materials, make a product (often with a great deal of energy), and then say goodbye to the product and leave it to the consumer who will eventually discard it. This approach is clearly outdated now. To design products is now a different ball game altogether. Various terms are used for this innovative design of products, such as 'cradle to cradle' or 'integral chain responsibility.' This requires a new view of design, of technology, and of the marketability of products and services. 'Embedded aging' can no longer be part of product design. Can parts of a product be replaced and/or repaired easily? Can it be recycled? And can you make a profit on this (for this, see below as well, under 'consumers')? There are very interesting technological and commercial challenges here – and we already see teams of highly engaged and motivated engineers and product designers, working together in labs and hubs, to immerse themselves in what will become an entirely new phase of product design.[19]

– **Profits.** We have already emphasized several times throughout this book that profit and purpose can go together very well, and defining a clear socially engaged purpose can have a positive impact on profitability.[20] The purpose should be to become 'net positive' and profitable.[21] And, as the Mars company did quite a few years ago, it can be very helpful, and even liberating, to ask what should be the 'right' (as distinct from the 'maximum') level of profit.[22] Of course, it helps if a company can build on a relationship with its investors that allows for a long-term horizon. If shareholders put pressure on for increased profitability every three months, this may destroy companies in the long term. We recall here Edward Freeman's comparison of profit with red blood cells in a body: they are indeed needed, but there is much more to health than having enough of them.

– **Processes.** The way the processes within a company are organized is key to its success. In responsible capitalism, there is a preference for 'bottom up' organization, based on 'assignments,' not 'orders' (in German: *Auftrag* vs. *Befehl*).[23] Neither the idea of class struggle nor a 'principle-agent theory' does justice to what a company is.[24] The 'stewardship' approach is much more fitting.[25] In this approach, it is crucial for a company to develop a shared long-term focus on common goals (the 'purpose' mentioned above) among all coworkers, both at the management level and on the shop floor. Each member of the company sees him or herself as contributing to the common goals and is hence stimulated to look for ways to better achieve these goals, instead of just scoring the contractually agreed upon targets.[26]

Seeing a business as a community means that the management should not just control its employees but respect them, trust them, and give them dignity. Even in the 19th century, which can be described in general as an age of capitalist aberration, this view was applied by some 'enlightened capitalists.'[27]

Although all companies are 'cooperatives' by nature, it is good to point specifically to the potential for cooperatives in a legal sense. This form has centuries-old roots, and in 19th-century Europe, cooperatives became a very important shelter from the icy winds of unrestricted capitalism. Today, cooperatives are again leading the way worldwide and have started to actively adopt the UN SDGs, which fits their nature as organizations that are not taken hostage by short-term shareholder value.[28] They are proof that profitability and a long-term focus on social and ecological value are not contradictions. There are very large and highly successful cooperatives.[29] Earlier, we have seen cooperatives changing toward shareholder companies, it would be good to explore and facilitate the reverse route as well.

– **Partnerships.** No man is an island – that holds true for companies as well. SDG 17 calls for 'Partnerships for the Goals.' That is vital (and relates to what we above called the 'power of initiative'): companies can engage with all kinds of partners to realize their purpose. Often, knowledge and technology need to be developed, so teaming up with schools and universities can create great innovative opportunities. But active partnerships with other businesses in a production chain can also be very effective in furthering a more sustainable and inclusive production process. And, last but not least, public–private partnerships will be a key ingredient of responsible capitalism (see below).

– **Polis.** Companies are citizens too, members of a sociopolitical community, a polis. Their 'social responsibility' is not an optional add-on but lies at the heart of the company. That has implications for the interaction with the world 'outside,' the sociopolitical community and communities that that business operates in.

First of all, it implies paying taxes and not doing everything possible to avoid them. If it is honorable for a company to reward its shareholders, it is certainly just as honorable to pay its taxes. It is sad that a global tax threshold was and is urgently necessary. In addition, citizenship implies being transparent about what one is doing, and hence integrated reporting (as we discussed earlier) is needed. Stakeholders and society at large have a right to know what and how companies are doing and what their results are, be it net positive or still having many negative externalities. 'Due diligence' is the phrase that is used to challenge businesses to assess the (potential) impact of their business operations (see above, chapter 8). In the long run, integrated reporting also makes companies themselves much stronger – and therefore less vulnerable – if they see this reporting as a constant learning opportunity (again, chapter 8). Where can we improve? What is the knowledge and technology that we lack right now but can really help us make things better?

For a company to be a citizen also implies trying to get good laws and regulations that promote long-term sustainability and inclusiveness in the marketplace; it means lobbying for the common good. "Regulate us!" Mark Zuckerberg once cried to legislators in Brussels. There is a point here. The transition to a new economy often needs new regulations so that new level playing fields can be created. For this, companies in a certain sector may well team up and lobby for regulations in their sectors.[30]

The 'polis' is represented within the company as well via the supervisory board. To give real substance to stakeholder involvement, the composition of supervisory boards is of great importance. Supervisory boards tend to be old boys' networks. A supervisory board in which stakeholders, including nature itself, are truly represented, can create a new embeddedness of firms in the social and ecological environment.[31]

While the shareholders in the current economy are a clear, well-defined group, defining stakeholders is more complex. What and who are the legitimate stakeholders, how can they be identified, represented, and informed? This makes it important to structurally classify different kinds of stakeholders such as employees, governments, consumers, and NGOs. Stakeholders should be subsequently informed, consulted, and then involved, and their collaboration sought.[32]

In conclusion: From shareholder to stakeholder capitalism/responsible capitalism. Businesses face great challenges. The field in which they operate is changing fast.[33] Businesses cannot afford to be blind to these challenges: they have to develop long-term antennae for developments in society and nature. This entails organizing stakeholder dialogues and also staging dialogues with the public and with visionary transition scientists and following (social) media. For socially sensitive businesses, however, there are plenty of opportunities to become frontrunners for the economy of the future. The short-term focus on maximizing profit and shareholder value, which still often predominates, is giving way to a long-term focus on true value, on creatively contributing to a better world for all, within ecological limits. Strengthening this movement will require creativity, cooperation, and innovative thinking. But that is what business is all about anyway.

Actor 2 – Finance for the Common Good[34]

The financial sector is central to today's economy. Without it, normal day-to-day economic activity, from shopping and paying taxes to taking out business loans and trading stocks, would come to a halt. Nonetheless, it seems that the financial sector has increasingly put itself first in recent decades. The 2007 credit crisis revealed structural imbalances and derailments in a sector that used to be known for its solidity and trustworthiness. Since then, the sector has begun to engage in soul-searching and restructuring, but one can wonder whether this goes far enough and is directed at the right problems.

Financialization. Earlier in this book we already pointed to 'financialization' as one of the key characteristics of late capitalism, the fourth stage of the 'Great Enrichment.'[35] Financialization refers to how the financial sector and financial considerations have started to dominate the real economy as well as government policies, and money has increasingly become an end in itself, instead of being a means to other goals and values such as human dignity, regenerativity, and inclusivity. In short, financialization means that there is an abundance of money that is geared toward its own increase instead of toward the common good – "financial value over wellbeing."[36] The question of the allocation of money has therefore become an urgent matter.[37]

Financialization comes with certain so-called 'wicked problems.' First of all, finance has become 'footloose,' disembedded, disconnected from society.[38] Today's financial markets have been cut loose from the real economy, and money tends to become primarily an asset for making more money: capitalism in *optima forma*. As a result, financial markets have expanded enormously. Global stock market capitalization is up from $2.5 trillion in 1980 and $31 trillion in 2000 to $93.7 trillion in 2021. The amount of global (corporate + household + government) debt is up from $64 trillion in 2000 to $289 trillion in 2021 (360% of global GDP). The ECB's balance has expanded from $800 billion in 2000, to around $2 trillion in 2008 and to over $7 trillion in 2021. Much of this money goes into financing investment in other money, wherever opportunities for short-term profit occur.

This implies misallocation of money: the real economy risks missing out. A strange paradox has arisen: there is more than enough money in the world, yet it is hard for the real economy, especially small and medium-sized enterprises (SMEs) to obtain loans for the necessary investment in, for example, becoming more sustainable – simply because the money owner sees more return on investment (ROI) in finance itself than in the real economy. And it is proving to be very hard to change this, as there are hardly any countervailing powers that are able to influence the course of the big financial players. There is no democratic or 'relational' control on their decisions. These problems are aggravated by the rise of what is called 'fintech.'[39]

The (Re)allocation of Capital: Stakeholders in the Financial Sector in Europe. The most pressing challenge therefore is: How can we ensure that savings (wealth, capital) are allocated to organizations and companies that can contribute to the common good (climate, inequality, innovation, infrastructure, etc.), the common good that is hopefully realized through the real economy (and not destroyed by it) since it concerns our concrete everyday life? How can the investors be persuaded to stop investing their money exclusively via anonymous markets and to switch from financial speculation to targeted, productive long-term investments? We call this the change from transactional (short-term, anonymous, footloose) to relational finance (long-term, relational, participatory, shared risks).

In Dutch, it is possible to make a distinction between trading shares and financial assets in the abstract – *beleggen* – and really taking a financial part in actual projects, sharing the risks with the entrepreneurs – *investeren*. In English we could perhaps distinguish between 'footloose investment' (transactional) and 'participatory investment' (relational). With participatory investment there is some form of 'relational control' and shared responsibility over the allocation of money.

There is no reason to be naive about the possibilities of redirecting the financial sector and its relation to the real economy and society at large. Only a combination of policies and interventions can be expected to yield results. Here, the multiactor approach that we are outlining in this book may be of help. Redirecting finance is a matter for the financial sector itself, government regulation, and civil society (a societal domain that we will analyze in one of the following sections).[40]

The Challenge: From Transactional to Relational Finance. If we want capital investments to contribute to the flourishing of the real economy, it matters where capital is allocated. Research shows that there is a strong causal relationship between capital investments in non-financial firms (regular businesses) and the subsequent innovation capacity and productivity growth in the real economy. Conversely, capital investments in consumer credit, mortgages, or other financial products have a limited, zero, or even negative effect on innovation and productivity levels. The key question then becomes: How can the allocation of (patient) capital for productive uses, for good causes, be stimulated in the real economy? Here the multiactor approach is very relevant. Only a smart mix of various responsibilities of various actors has a chance of achieving the desired outcomes.

– **The 'normalization' of finance.** First of all, all businesses in the financial sector should start to view themselves as 'normal' businesses in the way we have shown that is characteristic for the European idea of the free market, that is, as companies that publicly define their purpose, build relations with a plurality of stakeholders, not only the shareholders, and are willing to report integrally on their impact. This holds for banks and pension funds as well as for private equity funds. Moreover, paying taxes (which may well include a financial transaction tax, tax on dividends and on shares) like every other company should not be seen as despicable costs but as investments in the quality of the society in which one is based. This implies as well that financial institutions give much more systematic attention to the moral standards that they want to uphold.

– **Long-term perspective.** Second, if we want the real economy to flourish, we need economic actors that understand the wishes of capital owners, capital controllers, and capital users and can bring them together in a sustainable relationship. We need economic actors that are not only accountable for the speed and quantity of investment but also for its quality and durability. There may well be a new role here for banks. Europe still has a predominantly bank-based financial system, which is fundamentally different from the Anglo-Saxon market-based system. European banks are in principle better equipped to build relations and come up with tailor-made solutions, sensitive to the specific context and with more of a long-term focus rather than a short term 'return on investment.[41] The long-term trend in Europe nowadays is less banking, more market. Perhaps this trend needs a countertrend.

This is also where those financial institutions that have a long-term perspective, especially pension funds, come into play. By their very nature, these are 'socially embedded firms' because they look after the pensions of large amounts of people in the very society where they are located. It is therefore not hard to imagine a kind of 'social contract' between these long-term institutional investors and society at large that will ensure that a substantial part of this money is reinvested in the long-term transition and innovation of the European economy itself. In that way, long-term perspectives are created for those who need a loan for long-term investments. Banks, with their local branches, can play a much-needed intermediary role here. For pension funds themselves, this may give long-term stability to a large part of their portfolios.

– **Diversification.** In quite a few countries, we see that different types of financial institutions can coexist side by side: large and small, cooperative, publicly traded, government owned. This can be turned into a policy in itself: ensuring diversity in the financial system.[42] It is noteworthy that some banks have become so large that they virtually form, if not a monopoly (control by one) in a strict sense, then at least a kind of 'oligopoly' (control by a few). This is where another actor comes in: government as the regulators of markets (for a more extensive discussion of this task, see the section below on governments). Governments have to make sure that markets are sufficiently diverse both to allow for competition as well as to prevent risks that may occur when there virtually is only one financial ecosystem, a monosystem.

A particular form of diversification that is most suitable to the approach that we outline in this book is the formation of new cooperative financial arrangements like crowd funding, new mutuals (in the Netherlands, for example, the so-called *broodfondsen* or 'bread funds'), credit unions, and peer-to-peer lending. Such types of financial institutions have existed widely in Europe already at least since the 19th century and still do.[43] We have the feeling that there is still a great deal of unused potential here for bringing about a new connectedness between finance and society.

– **Societal dialogue.** In addition to a well-equipped government supervision, a constant dialogue between financial institutions and civil society is needed to see what the actual and potential effects of financial arrangements for consumers and for society at large are. If financial institutions do not handle their stakeholder management well, civil society can take the initiative for meaningful dialogue and structures of encounter between financial institutions – especially those that have a long-term, more or less public, perspective, such as banks, pension funds, insurance companies – to see where common ground can be found between the goals of the financial institutions and the long-term interests of businesses, consumers, and society at large. Several pension funds in the Netherlands have already started this kind of dialogue with their participants. Moreover, civil society can also work to find alternatives to the current financial system, such as working in local currencies, that stimulate people to spend money in the local economy before the money becomes global.

In conclusion. Finance makes it possible to realize things that have not yet become reality. Without an active financial sector, the real economy would freeze. But a hyperactive financial sector could end up freezing the real economy as well. The key problem in responsible capitalism is how to reconnect the financial sector with the real economy. Although financial institutions are extremely large in terms of the amount of money they deal with in global markets and give the impression of being 'footloose,' this should not lure us into a sense of powerlessness. After all, the financial players are still located somewhere and can therefore be held accountable, legally, morally, and socially, by national and international political communities and sometimes even by civil society actors. They can be nudged, challenged, or, if needed, forced to (re)connect with the real economy and to contribute to the common good.

Actor 3 – Consumers as Drivers of Sustainable Innovation

Products are made and services designed – facilitated by finance – ultimately for consumers. This is what the economy is all about – or so it seems. In the transformation toward a sustainable and just economy, consumers certainly have a role to play. We should be very careful here, however. Is business there for consumers? Or are consumers there for business? A frequent argument on the role of consumers in the current crises of capitalism is that consumers are ultimately to blame. Many business actors (like supermarkets) claim that consumers are not willing to pay a fair price for their products. From consuming meat to buying clothes or airline tickets, at prices that don't come close to representing the actual ecological and social costs, the keys to a better (or a worse) world seem to be in the hands of the consumer – so the argument goes. The role of the consumer is, however, much more complicated than this, and a fair assessment of the role of the consumer is therefore important.

In classical liberal thinking, it is the government that is to be distrusted for its asymmetrical power: a strong government over against weak individuals. Hence, citizens have to be empowered by political (freedom) rights. But what is often overlooked in liberal political theory is that commercial parties can also turn into powerful and even oppressive entities. If we follow the crucial European intuition of human dignity, we have to empower consumers as much as we previously empowered citizens. Having left the old feudalism behind through the rise of the bourgeoisie, there are now analyses that speak of a 'neo-feudalism' that ordinary people have to liberate themselves from.[44] The 'lords' of feudalism now have become businesses that dominate people's lives.

Autonomy and consumption. The reason why we are starting on this cautionary note is that the freedom of consumers is quite relative. Consumption patterns are created somewhere in the twilight between freedom and being subject to influence or even manipulation. If we look at the marketing budgets in the private sector, it is clear that marketeers believe less in human freedom than they do in the power of influencing (and of – well-paid – 'influencers'!). While consumers may seem powerful in their potential to make free, sovereign, choices about what to buy and what not to buy or to buy at a fair price, this is mostly a myth. The scandal of Purdue Pharma's marketing of OxyContin for example, shows how vulnerable consumers can be to destructive, manipulative marketing. The same applies to the effective marketing of unhealthy, sometimes even lethal, products like soft drinks, fast food, and cigarettes. Very often, the temptation to buy the product again and again is built into the very design of a product.[45]

The same holds for the digital world, for example, in the way people are strongly pushed to accept cookies and consent to other use of their data so they can get access to information. There is a growing body of literature exposing the extent to which 'Big Tech' companies, as the great "attention merchants," are able to "get inside our heads," to quote the title of a book by Tim Wu.[46] The term 'surveillance capitalism' has even emerged.[47]

So, yes, consumers have a responsibility. But it's unfair to emphasize this responsibility while ignoring the highly subtle ways – often based on multimillion dollar marketing research and marketing techniques – in which consumers are lured into buying certain products. Making consumers exclusively responsible for market behavior and market outcomes is a distortion of reality. Moreover, it undermines the real responsibility of businesses to come up with better, healthier, more sustainable products (see what we said above when we discussed the business sector).

And yet: consumer responsibility

And yet, the other side of the coin also applies: a more sustainable economy will not be realized without a change in consumption patterns. The degree to which waste-generating consumption patterns, especially in the North, have become the standard of normal life – in just a couple of decades – is astonishing. Moreover, this level of consumption tends to acquire the status of a human right, not to be tampered with. But the truth should not be denied: a sustainable economy also requires sustainable consumption and sustainable consumers. And yes, this may imply changes in the consumer culture we have been building up since the 1960s. This doesn't have to be a doom scenario and can even entail a growth in the quality of life.[48] There are several ways in which consumers can play a role on the way to a regenerative economy.

– **Recycling, buying, leasing.** An area where consumers can be involved, even though the main initiative remains with producers, is that of waste and pollution. Of course, consumers can try to stop using plastic bags only once and stop drinking from plastic bottles. They can separate various types of waste if governments have arranged to make this possible and worthwhile.

But there are also other ways in which consumption can change and will have to change. One can think of the standardization of all kinds of products which would make parts of them interchangeable (such as chargers for electronic equipment to be used across different brands and devices). Replaceable modules would allow products to be repaired instead of having to throw the entire device away (see above under business: product design).

Of course, this may affect the profitability of businesses. Right now, it is still the case that the more 'stuff' a company can sell, the more profit it makes – and the waste continues to accumulate. These incentives will have to be reversed, for example by lease contracts that include the responsibility as well of the producer to take the product back after its life span and recycle it. So, 'buying' may change from just one momentary act into something like entering into a relationship with a producer who remains responsible for the proper functioning of the product until the end of its life cycle, and is then responsible as well for taking the product back in order to recycle it. This business model for companies would then cover the entire life cycle of a product, and the companies would receive a fee for the longevity of their product. (Something along these lines has already been developed by Philips/Signify, which leases 'light' to Schiphol Airport. This example deserves to be copied widely.)[49] Consumption in these cases would then entail leasing instead of buying, renting instead of owning.

A central area where consumers can have a real impact is that of *food*. In today's world, completely different from anytime previously in human history and very different from what could reasonably be expected, there is an abundance of food – to such an extent that, since 2010, obesity is an even bigger public health threat than hunger in terms of the number of people affected.[50] But the ecological burden of food, especially meat, is severe. Obesity is growing into a global pandemic, but even aside from this, how we produce our calories worldwide is unsustainable. Thanks to the 'Green Revolution' of Nobel Peace Prize winner Norman Borlaug, food production has multiplied ever since the late 1960s. But so has the consumption of animals, which is a very 'inefficient' way to grow calories. Technological breakthroughs in food production have greatly increased our options for replacing meat, for example, but consumers have to buy these alternatives.

The same applies to new materials that have become highly popular in recent decades but are totally unsustainable, such as plastics, which results in, for example, the 'plastic soup' in the world's oceans. Consumers and businesses can play a crucial role here in turning around a trend that has insidiously infiltrated our everyday life.

– **From consumer to prosumer.** The second way in which consumers can be involved in the renewal of the economy is the empowerment of consumers as prosumers. The coming decades will likely see the rise of the phenomenon of the 'prosumer.'[51] This will play an especially big role in the energy transition, with an increasing number of households that are able to provide their own energy through solar panels. Consumers have an active role in this process, reducing their carbon footprint and being able to obtain renewable energy for free.[52] In addition to solar panels, consumers can influence their carbon reduction by installing heat pumps and isolating their homes. The rise of the prosumer means an increasing autonomy of the consumer.

The danger here is that this will be possible only for the higher income groups since they have the resources to make the necessary initial investments, such as buying solar panels. Thus, without collective assistance, either as cooperatives and/or by government financing, this can be a source of growing inequality.

– **True pricing as a consumer's movement.** Consumers have buying power. They can buy Fair Trade products, if available. There are consumers' initiatives seeking to pay the 'true price' for products, the market price plus the social and environmental price in the whole value chain of a product.

It is difficult, however, for consumers to always be 'ethical consumers.' The time it takes for a consumer to do the necessary research into whether companies are asking a 'true price' makes it virtually impossible to always act according to principle. Yet the symbolic significance of these movements is considerable, as they signal a new concept of consumption that may stimulate change, both in other consumers as well as in producers. Citizens also have to 'dance' with governments on this topic (see below), asking for example for heavier taxation on unsustainable products, while lifting taxes on sustainable ones.

– **Consumers as citizens; consumer education.** Consumers have to be empowered in the same way as citizens have been empowered in the past, that is, with consumer rights (and European nations and the European Union have understood this). Similarly, how society judges consumers should be closer to how we look at citizens. The latter are expected to have values and to behave according to them. So, consumer rights go together with consumer responsibilities.

In the capitalist market, however, consumers are expected to act as *homo economicus* in their own interest, free of values like empathy or care. But is this really what consumers want to be? There is a growing movement of consumers who are aware that, as consumers, they are also citizens. At the end of the day, buying is not all that different from voting. We pay a great deal of attention to citizenship education in democracies (and perhaps should do more on that score), but there is also an important role for consumer education in making people aware of how marketing works and of consumers' rights and responsibilities.

Conclusion: scale up! The derailment of the economy cannot be fully attributed to consumers. Consumers are not autonomous actors in a free market but are often subjected to unhealthy and even destructive marketing and, recently, in the digital domain as well. Business treating consumers as dignified human beings instead of seeing them as exploitable resources is vital in moving toward a new economy.[53] This means both protecting them in the market as well as empowering them and involving them in this transition. Although the position of consumers has been strengthened, especially in Europe, there is still a long way to go. Consumers are not yet in the position to act as a counterbalance to the power of producers. So, it is necessary to explore how consumers can strengthen their position, perhaps by new forms of collective action and new types of consumers' associations. To really give leverage to consumer power, they need to organize themselves in civil society initiatives (see below).

But we do, of course, also have to state the obvious: as long as we define our identity and wellbeing in terms of ever-increasing consumption, a sustainable economy is never going to become a reality. The Jevons paradox is constantly chasing and overtaking any movement towards a sustainable economy: when something is produced more efficiently and hence more sustainably as well, the use of that product appears to go up, counteracting the gain in sustainability. Sooner rather than later, therefore, we need to start a true societal dialogue on what long-term sustainable consumption is.[54] When is it 'enough'?[55] When have we 'arrived' in our pursuit of overcoming poverty and have grown up and become liberated from the constant longing to have more?[56]

Chapter 11

The Flying Wheel of Responsible Innovation (B): The 'Embedders' of a New Economy (Government, Nature, Community, Civil Society)

Economies need embedding if they are to truly contribute to the wellbeing of all. That is an old lesson that apparently needs to be relearned by every generation. Economies are not just autonomous systems, like the weather, but are human products and are there to fulfill human purposes. So, we have to formulate these purposes clearly so that we will be able to judge – we used the term 'evaluate' earlier – whether we are really doing well. The initial purpose of the economy was, as we explained above, the great escape from poverty; but now it is the creation of a long-term sustainable and inclusive economy. For this "mission," as economist Mariana Mazzucato would call it,[1] it is essential to embed the economy in the political, natural, and social environment. Only if they are properly embedded, 'reconnected,' can the innovative 'makers' of an economy fulfill their role properly.

Actor 4 – Public Goalsetting: Bringing Government Back In

That a free market cannot function without well-functioning governments is an almost uncontroversial statement. Even the most radical free market thinkers hold that minimal government is necessary for national defense and for organizing a legal system that can hold people accountable for crimes as well as for settling disputes between market parties. Almost all economists – though there are already exceptions here – agree as well that governments should provide public infrastructure like roads and dikes and are therefore entitled to levy taxes. But beyond this is where the controversy starts. In this chapter, we will argue for active governments that give direction to markets by 'public goal setting' or formulating a 'mission' in Mazzucato's sense.

In recent decades, the dogmatic mainstream position among influential policy makers, inspired by free market, 'neoliberal' economists, has been: the smaller the government, the better it is for the economy. Governments – by definition – do not create economic value. Their expenses are to be characterized as expenditures, not as investments. In the European tradition, this strong anti-government rhetoric of the last few decades is rather new. It probably signals the fashionable dominance of certain American schools of economic thinking in Europe more than a self-conscious reflection of European insights and experiences. In European thinking, the right limits of each sphere and the right balance between them is the real issue, not the dilemma of either government or the market.

Reality is much more nuanced anyway. The US was the birthplace of the New Deal under Roosevelt (when many European countries were struggling with this idea), and the 'European' idea of a welfare state originated in a report by the very British, hence 'Anglo-Saxon,' Lord Beveridge. This report, among other things, led to the NHS, a national health service, free for all, which in the UK still is a matter of national pride (as became clear during the Covid pandemic). Indeed, in reality, governments have played an enormous role in all modern countries in directing and enabling the economy. Moreover, the astonishing economic growth in recent decades in countries with a rather authoritarian grip on their economies, like Taiwan, China, Korea, and Singapore, gives some cause for rethinking whether any role for governments in an economy is always bound – as a matter of iron law – to lead to a Soviet Union type of economic stagnation.

Reality is much more flexible, nuanced, and pragmatic than theory – probably a reflection of wisdom. But reality is much grimmer as well. It has even been claimed that, as the country that prides itself on being the champion of free markets, the US has given up on them, having made itself vulnerable to the power of big business and lobby groups, and is hence running the risk of becoming a plutocracy.[2] The anti-government rhetoric obscures the reality of new power concentrations in the market, the 'neo-feudalism' referred to above.

What does this imply for a European perspective on the role of government in a free market, with an eye to the central values of human dignity, inclusivity, regenerativity, and co-creativity? Today's challenges, including that of protecting a viable market economy itself, demand an active 'missionary' state, in addition to the private sector and civil society. We believe that there are five – not one or at most two, as Anglo-Saxon theory has it – essential tasks for governments in the European economic approach, going well beyond Anglo-Saxon minimalism.

– Creating a responsive and trustworthy political and legal environment for all, people and businesses alike. Governments throughout history have very often been exclusive, extractive and engaged in outright oppression.[3] So, the first task of government from a European perspective is to be, remain, and become a truly 'responsive institution' and to organize itself in such a way that fair access is given to all interests and viewpoints and a fair public deliberation process, free from business interference, is assured, with clear democratic control and the rule of law as the highest authority. The public good or the common good is its focus, not private interests.

There is a very clear but sometimes thin line between a multiactor approach needed to deal with societal challenges and cronyism where political and private parties make arrangements to secure their private interests, often at the expense of dealing with real societal challenges. This requires constant vigilance.

Thus, the rule of law at all levels is essential. Regulatory institutions that cannot be trusted to be truly independent and just form a major challenge for any society and constitute a tremendous obstacle for any functioning market economy. The same applies to situations in which the law becomes opaque, complex, and divided among different, sometimes outright contradictory, jurisdictions. This is a risk that is currently threatening the European economies especially, given the simultaneity of national and European jurisdictions.

– Ensuring a fair and secure distribution of (basic?) income and work. As we know from more than 200 years of experience with free markets, these markets have a strong tendency to create inequality of income and wealth. This has often been ideologically justified by invoking the idea of 'meritocracy': what you get is nothing more than the result of your own individual efforts. But both the basic idea of human dignity and the idea of co-creativity suggest another way of thinking.[4] People can all contribute to the economy, and hence to our common welfare, using their own talents. And these talents can be highly diverse. But all are needed in their own way. So, in a way the contribution of a garbage collector to society is different but just as worthy as that of the CEO of a large company (and depending on one's point of view, perhaps even greater).[5] This requires a certain measure of income security and income equality and at least a decent wage for the lowest paid. The flexibilization of late capitalism can be real threat to workers.[6]

Given this uncertainty about one of the basic necessities of life, one could ask whether a further general provision will not be required from governments. Should that be a universal basic income (UBI)? This provision has been proposed quite often In recent years,. One of the early proponents of this was – please note! – Milton Friedman, who favored a 'negative income tax.' The idea is worth fresh investigation.

We believe, however, that a UBI would make it too easy to lay people off – for 'Aren't they taken care of'?[7] We would rather go for a system of basic jobs, and require all companies above a certain size to employ a certain percentage of people who face some structural obstacles in finding jobs or pay the equivalent in taxes as they do not hire persons in this category, which is much less attractive. This system already works quite well in Slovenia, and all of Europe can and should learn from that. This creates a level playing field, and each company really participates in solving problems instead of buying it off financially via taxes. But it may be clear that new forms of basic social security are on the table and worth further investigation.

– Creating, directing, regulating markets: Smart taxation, standardization, 'top runner' identification. Although people have been exchanging goods and have developed trade relations since time immemorial, markets as the primary way to organize economies are often deliberately created. Modern markets are therefore not 'natural' phenomena but are organized. This implies that they fall under human responsibility. Therefore we have to reflect constantly on the outcome of markets in terms of the goals that we deem important as essential ingredients of human flourishing: human dignity, inclusivity, regenerativity, and co-creativity. There are various ways in which governments can and should responsibly relate to markets to ensure that the common good is promoted by, for example, (1) creating, outlawing, or directing markets, especially by taxation; (2) standardization; and (3) by a Japanese style 'top runner program.'

(1) From what has already been said above, it may be clear that governments can *allow, suspend/outlaw, or create markets* (such as outlawing the free trade of firearms or drugs or granting the right to privately exploit a formerly publicly run railway). Much more frequent is the role of government in *directing and regulating markets*, with *taxation* as a key instrument. Through taxation, governments can encourage or discourage certain market transactions, such as tobacco or gasoline. A substantial push can thus be made toward a circular, regenerative, and inclusive economy by, for example, taxing consumption instead of labor.[8] This instrument should be taken much more seriously, we believe, especially regarding what we mentioned earlier as the need for 'true pricing.' In cases where 'externalities' – both negative and

positive – are not sufficiently reflected in prices, the government can use sales taxes to redress this (kerosene tax, meat tax) which can be compensated by lower income taxes. Conversely, labor for repairing goods – as distinguished from replacing them with new ones – is taxed at a much lower rate in Sweden (reduced from 25% to 12%), and consumers can deduct costs for repair work.[9] There has to be constant evaluation as to whether the structure of taxes – and import and export duties – are still just and serve the long-term common good.

Something comparable can be observed regarding income taxes. We appreciate labor and good jobs, but at the same time we tax them heavily compared to the capital invested, for example, in robots. One can ask if a certain change from taxing labor to taxing capital shouldn't be recommended. Specifically, given how 'capital' has been granted almost free space to produce negative external effects whereas jobs are seen as very desirable, it just stands to reason to shift taxation away from labor to the negative externalities of capital, pollution, excessive energy use, and so on.[10] So, in a capitalist economy, in which capital is the most powerful force in the economy, taxing capital and having it bear its fair share of the common good is just the logical thing to do.

In short, taxation is one of the key instruments for giving direction to an economy. Therefore, it should be smart and stimulate those activities that are desirable from the perspective of the 'mission,' the long-term direction of the economy, and should discourage those activities that are undesirable or destructive for the planet and humans.

(2) A hugely important second element of governments directing markets is the role of *standardization*. When consumers buy a certain product, they shouldn't have to worry about the basic quality of the product nor about the way it has been produced. When I buy chocolate, do I in reality benefit from, and assist in the continuation of slave labor or other forms of outright exploitation? And how much waste is produced unnecessarily in the production process? Are personal data protected in the marketing of the product? Here, basic thresholds for market parties are needed.

Fortunately, the European Union has understood this very well: standardization has become one of its core competencies. What has been called the 'Brussels effect' is a remarkable achievement affecting not only the European economic region itself but far beyond it as well.[11] For producers, it is usually very unattractive to develop their products with an eye to different levels of standardization. They tend to go for the higher standards, given that the products that comply to the higher standard can also be sold elsewhere, but not the other way around.

(3) A third instrument of governments directing markets has not been frequently used in Europe yet, but it is highly relevant since it does combine doing justice in a unique way to the creativity of the markets with a concern for the long-term common good. We are referring here to the Japanese 'top runner program,' a program that goes back to the late 1970s. It creates a kind of competitive market in energy efficiency: as soon as a more energy efficient solution has been developed in a specific industrial sector, the government imposes this as the new standard that the entire sector is to adopt within a couple of years. This implies that those that achieved the new standards first by inventing them are already fulfilling their new legal requirements. But even more, this also means that, when other companies in the same sector are not able to meet the new standards on time, they have to buy the specific technology from the first developer, which then is able to earn back its R&D investments.[12]

A milder form of the top runner program is when governments give tax advantages to companies that have significantly reduced their negative external effects and are (close to) being ' positive.' In the US for example, 35 states have already legislated special rights and duties for Public Benefit Corporations that uphold the strictest social and environmental standards and are usually created from the start to be net positive, or have been fundamentally reorganized to achieve this standard.[13]

– Stimulating inclusive and regenerative innovation by public goal setting and coalition building. Markets are not actors but platforms for initiatives, competition, and cooperation. This implies that the overall outcome of market processes may or may not be desirable – there is no higher instance in the market to decide that. Making sure that the overall outcome of a free market is sustainable, for example, is not automatically guaranteed by the market itself. On the contrary, many incentives within the market may work against that desired outcome. Or certain projects may never come up because no entrepreneur or company sees future business prospects in it. This is the situation in which government can launch 'missions,' i.e, larger projects that are worthwhile or even necessary from the long-term public interest perspective and yet are not automatically produced by markets as they are.[14]

There is no reason whatsoever to be apologetic about this role. It is often used as a matter of common sense, such as during war ('wartime economies'), national disasters (the Dutch Delta project after the February flood in 1953) or pandemics (the search for vaccines during the Covid 19 crisis). It played a decisive role in the German *Wirtschaftswunder* after the destruction caused by World War II, by what later came to be known as *konzertiere Aktion* (coordinated action) between public and private parties.[15] It played a major role in the growth of the 'Asian tigers' and the BRICS countries. Another very telling example of public goal setting was the creation of Airbus, a project of European cooperation. Here, market forces were combined and bundled for a new, huge project, establishing an entirely new industry whose absence would have left Europe totally dependent on the US. Recent EU initiatives in creating a chip industry are going in this same direction.

Governments have the task of identifying long-term risks and challenges. On this basis, they can – and must – launch national or even international long-term projects or missions. The EU is leading the way in this respect with its 'Green Deal,' setting clear goals and hence creating a stable environment for the business sector to launch long-term R&D projects and to embark on innovation for sustainability. What missions require is the creation of coalitions – and often governments are uniquely placed to bring potential partners together and provide initial funds to start new R&D projects aimed at creating innovative solutions to urgent problems (sometimes) but even more to long-term challenges that are not yet seen as urgent.

For urgent reasons, government can become investors themselves (think again of the analogy with wartime economies). The 'EU Green Deal' is now using primarily regulations and standardizations as instruments, but an investment plan is attached to it, the Sustainable Europe Investment Plan, which is in line with the role governments can take in times of need.[16]

In conclusion: localization and globalization. 'Government' is a broad term that has many different layers: from local government via national government to intergovernmental organizations at the international level. Each layer has its own unique opportunities and tasks.

A hallmark of a healthy economy is the extent to which co-creative problem solving truly takes place on all these different levels. Even with global problems, the local level remains of the utmost importance. But what should be done where? Where should we look for the drivers of the economic reorientation, for which we advocate in this book? Some are pitting an 'elite reset' (wrong) over against a 'bottom-up reset' (right). We consider this to be a romantic approach. Both directions are needed and complement each other. As long as a global elite preaches a 'reset' without actually changing the macro behavior and rules of the game (which is happening to a certain extent, for example, in the prospect of setting a global tax minimum, but note how difficult this is proving to be), nothing can really change. Changes at the global level are essential. But without local and regional initiatives that give concrete proof that things can be done differently, there is neither public support for nor credibility regarding global changes. Two questions always need to be answered: What is the scale of a problem that we are facing? And, at what level can we organize a healthy balance of power and countervailing power? Here the famous 'subsidiarity principle' applies: organize matters and solve problems at the lowest level possible, hence involve citizens in cooperation at a concrete level but without any 'small-scale romanticism.' Problems that need to be addressed at a higher level should certainly be addressed there. In a world of Big Tech, Big Pharma, Big Oil, and whatever else is operating at a global level, we have no choice but to organize matters at a level where real power and countervailing power are present, if necessary, at the global level.

Actor 5 – Nature at the Table: Reconciling Anthropology, Economy, and Ecology

Reconciling anthropology, the economy, and ecology is without a doubt the most comprehensive contemporary challenge. We are the first generation to have a more or less comprehensive view of the entire earth as one ecosystem and also the first generation that – by the sheer volume of its emissions – threatens to knowingly destroy this ecosystem. It has become increasingly and alarmingly apparent in recent decades that nature is not a passive backdrop external to our economic activities. Rather, it is an entity that responds to humans. Nature is not an object; it is better to see it as an agent – and we humans are not its principal. Humans, and hence their economies, are embedded in a larger ecology that responds and poses limits to what humans can and cannot do. In practice, however, it remains difficult to treat it accordingly. The challenge of the coming decades is to refrain from treating ecology and the economy as different domains: we need to realize that our economy operates only within ecological limits.

The fact that the boundaries of the natural world are challenged by the (industrial) economy has been addressed for many decades, starting with Rachel Carson's alarming 1962 book *Silent Spring*, which addressed the pollution problem caused by pesticides, and subsequently most famously in 1972 by the Club of Rome, which addressed the exhaustion of natural resources. Since then, pollution and exhaustion are now accompanied by global warming as the third ecological problem cluster of the modern economy. To be clear: just reducing CO_2 emissions is not nearly enough. Our entire means of production and consumption are affecting nature. Earlier in this book we referred to Johan Rockström and his team, who identified nine 'planetary boundaries': climate change, ocean acidification, stratospheric ozone depletion, interference with the global phosphorus and nitrogen cycles, rate of biodiversity loss, global freshwater use, land system change, and aerosol loading.[17] And the reservoir of natural resources isn't inexhaustible either.[18]

Even if we succeed as humanity in containing climate change within the 1.5°C as agreed upon in Paris, there still will be, and already are, severe consequences in some areas of the world, areas that often have already more than enough problems to deal with. So, although we would like to see all efforts directed toward prevention (of global warning, for example), climate adaptation requires much investment as well. A famous and influential new conceptualization of the boundaries of the natural world has been the 'doughnut model' by the Oxford economist Kate Raworth. This model shows that a safe space for humanity is a regenerative and distributive economy situated between the minimum of a social foundation and the ecological ceiling.[19]

Growth or degrowth. There are roughly two paradigms addressing a reorientation of the economy towards ecological sustainability: 'deep ecology' and 'shallow ecology.'[20] The first is nature- or eco-centered and focuses on a new, holistic relationship between humans and nature in which the primacy of nature is acknowledged. The second is more anthropocentric and focuses on the planetary limits for human survival. Echoes of this debate are to be found today in the debate on growth. The 'post-growth' or 'degrowth' movement corresponds to deep ecology; shallow ecology can be found in the 'green growth' movement. The degrowth movement attributes our ecological problems to a distorted relation with nature that is manifested in the unbridled materialism and short-termism of our modern growth-oriented economy, which creates consumers by structurally overproducing material goods. Therefore, the path to a sustainable planet will have to be entirely different from the path to modernization. Meanwhile, the green growth movement emphasizes the need for economic growth to achieve sustainability goals and offers a more optimistic paradigm.

Without preferring one and disregarding the other, we advocate following a pragmatic approach to the reconciliation of anthropology, the economy, and ecology in the short term. A focus on growth forgets that growth – or shrinkage – of an economy is not a goal in itself, as was clear from what was said earlier about the GDP monomania. Growth is an *a posteriori* ('after the fact') outcome of those activities that we as a society deem important. When faced with collective challenges, such as war, a country gets down to work, and the question whether this implies growth or not is less important: it is a matter of meeting the challenge. In the next decades, the transformation toward a green economy will probably require many new activities, the reallocation of resources and the development of new technologies. This may or may not add up to what we can designate as growth (in the sense of 'GDP growth') 'after the fact.' The new technologies have trade value; they have to be bought and sold at home and abroad. So, it may well be that growth will occur, but that should no longer be the point of our activities. Rather, it is the nature of growth, the type of growth, that matters.

That being said, it is clear that in the long run – but actually not too long of a run – it is impossible to talk about 'perpetual growth' on a finite planet. So, our fundamental concepts of what an economy is will certainly have to be transformed from 'ways to overcome poverty by producing more goods and services' into 'how to live as humans in balance with nature.'[21] And we should start today – or should have started yesterday – to develop post-growth concepts and mechanisms, addressing questions like what 'profit' means in a post-growth economy and debunking distorted images that claim that a steady-state economy implies a technological and creative standstill.[22] Human nature is such that there will always be development, innovation, creativity. But the greatest part of human creativity throughout history has been largely immaterial – philosophy, art, music, and science usually do not require immense material resources. And it is fully conceivable that many technological innovations in the future will be designed to use less material or reuse older materials much more efficiently. Rethinking growth, and rethinking circularity, will be an urgent task. So, being 'growth-agnostic' seems the best way to go, opting for a pragmatic approach in the short run, with the long-term horizon of 'degrowth' or dematerialization.[23] Getting to work on the task ahead is more important than the question whether our necessary efforts add up to growth or not. Our argument at this stage is therefore for combining selective growth, new sustainable product design ('cradle to cradle,' etc.; see chapter 10 above on business), technological innovation, consumer action, true pricing (e.g., carbon price), dematerialization of the economy, taxation, and eventually an eco-neutral, or even regenerative economy. A smart mix of all these options is necessary to embark on the journey toward a fully regenerative economy. This may well turn out to be an alternative to both 'deep ecology' and 'shallow ecology,' as it fully acknowledges the unsustainability of our current relationship with nature (in the 'Anthropocene') and yet also acknowledges that we cannot simply abandon technology but have to use and redirect it in order to embed technology in nature and use all the creativity and innovative potential we can mobilize.[24]

Profit and planet? One of the ways in which ecological exhaustion by economic activity can be limited is if business goals are aligned with environmental goals (which was mentioned also in the section above on businesses). Eventually, 'cradle to cradle,' or full circularity or regenerativity, is the end goal for a long-term sustainable economy. Being more sustainable can certainly be more profitable as well.[25]

In the development toward full 'cradle to cradle,' more attention is often paid to the end product (which can also be subject to taxes and regulations). But it is also necessary to take an input-oriented approach.[26] The result of focusing on the input rather than the output is innovation that enables companies to create a more efficient production chain instead of only trying to comply with regulations after the fact, which might cause a loss of profit. This is in line with a very basic drive that every company already has, and it therefore offers an attractive, profitable incentive to be more sustainable. Stressing the power of innovation might unlock the necessary co-creativity to find new ways to be resource efficient.

As 'input' often comes from the global South, it is crucial for companies to take responsibility for the entire production chain. The 'waterbed effect' is a real danger: 'we' in the North feel good about ourselves by having a clean production process while elsewhere in the world the production of the half-products we use contributes greatly to pollution. What certainly will not work – and may even backfire in the long run by causing resentment – is to just impose standards on countries in the South. To have chain responsibility implies really participating in the improvement of production processes elsewhere, sharing clean technology, investing in improvement. (Carbon) emissions are a true global problem. Just shifting the pollution around will not be of any help in reducing global emissions but will only make some countries feel good while others get the blame. But, often, those that are blamed do not have any choice, for their people have to be fed as well. This raises the broader issue of climate justice.

Towards a broader discourse: Climate justice and representation of nature. One of the core issues that makes the question of ecology complex is its inseparable connection to the distribution of wealth. As Pope Francis argued in *Laudato Si'*, ecological and social crises are not separate issues; the current ecological crisis is at the same time a social crisis because it creates new ways in which the most vulnerable will suffer. The ecological crisis is therefore an ethical challenge; it shows the need for responsibility to future generations and people who are affected by (human-induced) natural disasters. The International Red Cross and Red Crescent, which monitors the expected humanitarian impacts of climate change, also argues this.[27]

While disasters can be a direct effect of climate change, ecology and inequality are connected in other ways as well. If countries, for instance, introduce carbon taxes, this will be yet another burden for the economically most vulnerable. One possible way to overcome this is by a carbon dividend. This means that the revenue of a tax is redistributed among those who are most severely affected by it.[28]

The examples show that ecology is a matter of economy and politics, not merely one of finding technical fixes for a material problem. If climate change discourse only leaves room for the quantification of problems and challenges, then climate policy becomes a question of technocracy. This means that scientists make political and moral choices that should be subjected to a broader debate.

Because of the social and moral dimensions of climate change, the borders between politics, science, the humanities, and the economy will have to be redrawn (see also what was said in chapter 7 on economics as an academic discipline). Climate policies should be designed and supervised by scientists as well as by philosophers, politicians, and economists, a true multiactor endeavor. The mixing of these fields can be organized in a very practical way by, for example, having specifically appointed/ elected parliamentarians and ministers represent 'nature' and by having ecological expertise in the supervisory boards of companies.[29] The above-mentioned Dasgupta Review, for example, has argued for an international supervisor of important ecosystems like oceans and rainforests. But this needs to be complemented by national and local representatives of nature. We need nature at the table somehow, for our tables are filled by nature.

A problem of many hands; but remember 'the power of initiative.' One of the main reasons why the climate crisis is so complex is the fact that it is a classic example of a 'problem of many hands.' The actions of many individual actors are not in themselves outright wrong; rather, it is the totality of all these actions that creates the problem. That's why it's hard to make one actor responsible and even harder to get all actors to cooperate. The complexity of 'a problem of many hands' is exemplified in the economy by the worry about a level playing field. Countries or companies might be willing to take action to reduce their carbon emissions or their impact on biodiversity, but they are only willing to lose profit if other companies take similar measures. The result is deadlock. This problem makes collaborative agreements crucial. The Paris Agreement during the COP in 2015 was a hopeful milestone, as was the COP in 2021 in Glasgow, where additional commitments were made. In the section on 'Business for the Common Good,' we already listed actions that businesses can take, such as cleaning up their own house, making their own production process as green as possible and aiming to become 'net positive.' Second, they can work on 'self-regulation,' working together across the sector. And they can indeed 'lobby for regulation' to create a level playing field for their entire sector. A top runner program, as explained above, can be a very helpful tool in this respect.

A new role for political actors. Here – if anywhere – it is certainly the case that the problem cannot be solved without clear government action in creating legal level playing fields, setting standards, what we previously called 'public goal setting.' The risk of one stalemate situation after another, while nothing really happens, can only be avoided when governments at all levels formulate the direction and the long-term policy framework. The European Green Deal, pushing for a 55% reduction of greenhouse gas emissions in 2030 and setting 2050 as the year in which Europe can be the first carbon-free continent is a typical example of this 'mission'-formulating role of, in this case, a cooperation of states, the EU. It is exactly this clear mission that is creating the space for businesses and other actors to act and innovate. Governments should not and cannot be the only actor, but without governments, ecological innovation will not take place on the necessary scale.

Conclusion: On the way toward regenerativity. Though the ecological problems are urgent, they are at the same time often still quite remote from the everyday concerns of people. It is like the degradation of Easter Island (Rapa Nui) – a disaster drawn out over several generations which at no point in time was viewed as acute. Easter Island, where the well-known huge statues were produced, had an economy that could not be sustained by its own resources (e.g., more trees were needed for transporting the statues than grew on the island). Every generation inherited a still livable island but left it to the next generation just a bit worse – until habitation became very difficult.[30] Fortunately, we now have overwhelming evidence of the degradation of our planet – it is not just a future prospect. And we can act as responsible human beings.

The future economy can no longer afford to act like it is operating in a physical void; our economy is grounded in and depends on a healthy ecology. For a sustainable economy we will need creative ways to reconcile business goals like efficiency with ecological ones. To make sure that companies operate in a level playing field, governments and organizations like the EU have a special task to invest and provide clarity and stability.

Finally, it is essential to move towards a discourse in which the borders between ecology, politics, economics, and philosophy are crossed. There is always the danger of what has been called the 'Jevons paradox.' This paradox states that any progress in combating the pollution of (the making of) products is often outdone by the growth in the consumption volume of that same product. For example, car engines are cleaner now than in the 1950s, but there are many more cars now and they are heavier, so the overall emission from cars has increased substantially.[31] Therefore, the prevention of pollution should always have precedence in the product design, but we shouldn't avoid the 'elephant in the room' and should thus start a broad dialogue about the long-term sustainability of our consumerist lifestyles as they have developed over the last 50 years (a very recent period!). We have to find a new relation with nature – which in a sense is also a new relation with ourselves, as participating in nature. As we said earlier, perpetual growth on a finite planet, with 8 billion people or, a few decades from now, 10 billion people, is simply impossible. As Paul Hawken has stated: regeneration is the task for this generation, a radical change in the relation between humans and nature, and "we need the involvement of every sector of society, top to bottom, and everything between."[32]

Actor 6 – Resilient Communities: Key to Economic Flourishing

We live in a digital, globalized, delocalized age, each of us behind our own screens – so it seems. And yet, we also live in houses, which are connected to streets, and we still go shopping in our neighborhood at least to get groceries (or it has to be delivered to us by a real person). We are still physical human beings. People live in communities, families, neighborhoods, villages, city quarters, cities, nations, and they are ultimately all part of the human community. In addition to localized communities, people do participate nowadays in virtual communities, sometimes anonymous networks but sometimes communities in which real encounters do take place. And a third type of community that often means a lot to people has already been mentioned earlier: the community of work, professional communities, often organized in companies. So, community matters – in a huge way, for people. And this also has bearing economically: some analyses attribute Brexit and Trump's rise to a lack of economic belonging or to the dominance of the 'anywheres' looking down upon the 'somewheres.'[33] And we should remember also that the two most destructive ideologies of the 20th century in Europe were based on the promise to restore a sense of community and both called themselves 'socialist.' Today, populism feeds off the same feelings. In the European Economic Model, as we see it, this needs to be fully recognized. An economy can flourish only if it is based on well-functioning communities, and an economy can only contribute to human flourishing when it preserves and enhances these communities – a reciprocal relationship that should not be turned into a parasitical one.

What do communities 'do' for people? First of all, they create and maintain a sense of solidarity and hence *protection*. Moreover, they involve people in common action and hence have an *empowering* role, both individually and collectively, by providing a base from which people can act and contribute to the common world. Third, communities can function as a platform for coalitions of the willing, for bringing actors together to address and deal with problems together, *collaborative networks*. When these three elements are present, people can develop a justified sense of belonging – the sociopsychological side of communities, which is often connected as well to a sense of identity.

The rediscovery of community: Commons, trust, social capital, relational goods. Communities and markets may have been a good match historically – in the Middle Ages, as Braudel points out, the organization of a market, the annual fair, was a festive occasion for an entire city – but in economic theory they do not fit well together.[34] While in economic theory markets tend to define consumers as individuals who make their private choices, communities count on them as members of a larger whole, as citizens. While markets tend to assume that maximizing individual preferences is the thing that really matters, communities assume that people will exert 'enlightened self-interest' at least or even act to achieve goods beyond self-interest, some form of the common good. While markets tend to define interactions primarily as cost-effective transactions, in communities the exchange of gifts, free reciprocity, cooperativity, and 'paying it forward' play a crucial role. And about other types of ownership than private ownership, such as the ancient and medieval 'commons'? Their story was only a tragedy – that is what every student of economics hears on many occasions.[35]

In the meantime, a great deal of new research has pointed out the crucial role of trust in societies, and the level of trust has substantial implications for the economy as well.[36] In 'high trust societies,' the transaction costs are much lower and form an excellent seedbed as well for large companies to emerge.[37] Partly overlapping with the literature on trust, the closely related concept of 'social capital' was coined, and later 'civic capital' as well.[38] Social capital concerns the number and quality of relationships outside the family that can result in common activities, cooperation and voluntary non-profit associations and initiatives. A high level of social capital makes it possible for civil society to flourish in a society. And, as we have argued before, this is an important precondition for a healthy economy that respects human dignity. When social capital is present in societies, people tend to be more satisfied with life, but the economy also does better: transaction costs are lower, collective action can be better organized (e.g., to fight monopolies and power concentrations), and platforms emerge for mutual learning processes and learning spillovers.[39]

The insights above invite us as well to break through the binary division between private and public goods. Communities are 'relational goods.'[40] Relational goods emerge in the very act of creating and contributing to them. A soccer game does not exist unless it is played and several people are engaged in it at the same time. For the rest, the game does not exist. Communities are neither private goods for which one can compete ('rival goods') nor institutionally provided goods ('non-rival goods') that one can just freely make use of. Rather, they are goods that need constant cooperative work or, to use the famous German phrase, they need constant *konzertierte Aktion*. Community is action.[41]

Community involvement. One of the most intriguing aspects of an economic order is that it manifests itself at once at the local level and the global level and at all levels in between. It is dangerous to lose sight of this. It is very easy – especially for intellectuals and 'news consumers' – to only focus on the global level (e.g., China, Russia, USA, Google, Amazon, Apple, Alibaba, Big Pharma, Big Oil) and assume that the local level is irrelevant among the 'Big Powers.' On the other hand, there is a tendency sometimes among those who advocate a transition to a more sustainable economy to just close their eyes to the global level and resort to 'small-scale romanticism' in which the renewal of the economy is expected from people working together in small communities at the neighborhood level. There is no use in pitting one level against another. The crucial issue is alignment between various levels, between the local and the global. There is a key role here for SMEs, which still constitute the largest sector economically in most economies and are a vital element in the web between the local and the global.

This also implies involving people not just in elections once every four or five years, but also by actively creating consultation opportunities that are truly meaningful. In recent years, a great deal of experience has been building up with these new forms of democratic engagement via citizen's panels. They can complement (not replace!) parliamentary democracy. In the Netherlands and Belgium, for instance, quite a few 'G1000' meetings were organized (analogous to G7 or G20 but now involving citizens at the local level). After the 'Yellow Vests' protests, President Macron of France did something similar, organizing a 'Convention Citoyenne pour le Climat,' in which 150 citizens who had been randomly selected were asked to come up with proposals for making the French economy more sustainable and for reaching the Paris 2015 climate goals.[42] In the summer of 2020, President Macron announced that he would adopt 146 of the total of 149 recommendations made by the Council.

Local communities. The local (and regional) context can be a very good platform for dealing with concrete problems.[43] The challenge in finding employment for people who have employability problems due to, for example, physical impairments or

215

mental health conditions is a problem in which local cooperation between government, educational institutions, businesses, and civil society can achieve great results.

A great deal of attention has been paid in recent years to the 'Triple Helix model,' that is, cooperative networks of knowledge institutions like universities, the business sector, and government to stimulate and facilitate new initiatives, often in connection with types of business, experience, and technology that was already present in a certain region. This can be expanded into what has been called a 'Quadruple Helix,' in which civil society is added as the fourth actor and even – in line with what we propose in this book – a 'Quintuple Helix,' where nature is included as a partner in the local or regional development. Right now, the Helix-model still focuses too much on the 'knowledge economy,' while it should be important to involve the blue-collar level as well. If this is done well, a sense of community – protection, empowerment, and collaboration – is promoted that can in turn create a 'yes, we can' atmosphere.

Nation states as communities. Nation states are crucial in providing a sense of belonging. They have the task of ensuring that the overall 'design' of an economy is diverse enough to be inclusive for all types of people. A one-sided emphasis on a 'knowledge-based economy' or a pure 'service-economy,' let alone a rentier economy or an economy that is disproportionately based on the financial industry, should not be allowed. A balance between 'blue collar' and 'white collar' is important to make sure that the economy allows a diversity of talents – heads, hands, and hearts – to flourish.[44]

This is closely connected to that other key role of communities: protection. When the only message at the national level is 'We can't protect you,' referring either to globalization or to corporate powers that have their own way, cynicism, despair, anger, and/or resentment may grow, and politicians who know how to address and exploit this will have a field day. Nation states have to act as conscious 'countervailing powers' to globalization and to corporate power in order to protect their people.

The European Community. In Europe, a specific community level has emerged that has not yet emerged in other parts of the world (although there are some comparable networks emerging in Africa) that can mediate between the local/national and the global in a unique way. The European Union is not a 'superstate' but an entity *sui generis* and, as such, new in the history of the world. It is a community that cannot and should not define itself over against the nation state but as a unique form of intensive cooperation between nation states within the context of shared values, a shared history, and a shared mission for the future. This specific level has very important potential – geopolitically and geoeconomically – but also specific risks. We will deal with the potential and the risks of the EU in the following part of this book.

The community of humankind. Ultimately, the largest community – in a way the most abstract and yet very real community – is the community of humankind, living on a finite earth, "our common home" (as Pope Francis calls it in the encyclical *Laudato Si'*). Or, to use another metaphor expressed by the first Dutch astronaut Wubbo Ockels on the basis of his personal experience, "We are all astronauts on Spaceship Earth." There is indeed a growing awareness of the interconnectedness of all people on this planet, and even an awareness of a broader and deeper interconnectedness with everything that lives on this vulnerable planet. This awareness is probably a factor in stimulating a unique type of political goal setting that has emerged in recent decades at the UN level: first the Millennium Development Goals and now the Sustainable Development Goals. We all participate and have to participate in the community of humankind to protect and empower ourselves and each other and form coalitions of the willing to actually take the necessary steps. Being part of local, national, and international communities doesn't have to prevent us from being part of the human community and seeking the connection between the global and the local.

In conclusion: togetherness in face of challenges. The road to a long-term sustainable and social economy cannot be traveled without well-functioning, resilient communities at all levels, from the local to the global. It is crucial that no one be left behind. Transitions, regardless of how urgent they are in their own right, should not undermine – or further undermine – a sense of solidarity among the very different strata of society. People should feel protected, empowered, and there should be cooperation in coalitions. It is a great danger when, for example, sustainability – or, as we have called it, 'regenerativity' – becomes a matter of the local or global elite, without any real involvement by and support for the poorer strata of society, locally and globally. For a 'green transition,' we need all the creativity that can be mobilized, from both 'blue collar' and 'white collar' employees, from local energy cooperatives and SMEs as much as from large international corporations, in order to have a sense of 'being in this together.'

Actor 7 – Civil Society: Creative and Countervailing Power

There is a long tradition in Europe, going back at least until the medieval 'cooperative revolution' we identified above, of what today would be called 'NGOs': initiatives and organizations that are non-governmental, do not distribute profits among their participants and exist outside family structures – thus, 'non-governmental,' 'non-profit,' and 'non-familial.' This threefold 'non-' raises the question, of course, of what the positive identification of this sphere is. As a preliminary indication, we could talk about 'private organizations for the common good.' They have great economic significance, but not primarily because their economic size and financial contribution is considerable – which it actually is, and civil society organizations employ millions of people in Europe and elsewhere.[45] They are economically significant because they are an essential part of a constellation of social actors that surround the market economy, interacting with it in all kinds of ways and in a way sustaining its proper functioning, primarily by limiting its scope. Civil society protects market economies by preventing excessive marketization and the emergence of market societies (as distinct from market economies).[46] A market economy can function sustainably only if it is accompanied by countervailing powers, otherwise it will eventually self-destruct, due to overconfidence and social overstretch.

'Civil society,' as we understand it here, is not just the community but refers primarily to the institutional field in which people organize themselves within their communities. Communities may often lack the institutional power in themselves to really protect themselves, and it is civil society that can mobilize the resources needed to act as a countervailing power. In the last decades of the 20th century, this old invention gained new momentum entirely. Today, the field has become highly diverse and may include philanthropic organizations, neighborhood schools, senior homes, hospitals, labor unions, the social work of churches, mosques and sanghas, environmental activist groups, human rights advocates, the MeToo movement, and so on. NGOs are everywhere now, from the local and neighborhood level to the global level. It is estimated that in the last five decades alone, the number of NGOs in the world has grown to tens and tens of thousands. The diversity of types of organizations and initiatives that we can see making up civil society today is immense.

A well-functioning civil society has very important 'positive externalities' that both governments and businesses may 'profit' from. This was observed already in the first half of the 19th century by the French aristocrat Alexis de Tocqueville. He traveled to the US and discovered that if people have their own associations in which they learn to negotiate, to lose some and win some in their cooperative endeavors, they foster a 'public spirit' that spills over into other spheres of life, including politics and business.[47] Others have built on De Tocqueville's observations and found that a well-functioning democratic order is, in turn, a key ingredient of a 'high trust society,' which is itself a key precondition for a well-functioning economy.[48]

In our judgment, civil society is indispensable for a healthy society and a healthy economy. It is vital for walking what Acemoglu and Robinson have called "the narrow corridor" between unprotected freedom and state oppression – and they could have given more attention to it.[49] Rooting out civil society would be a huge mistake, both from the viewpoint of social justice – an argument on principle – as well as from a more utilitarian perspective – arguments about the unique role and function of civil society in a modern society and a modern economy.

The function and 'utility' of civil society in the economy. An important theory about civil society holds that civil society is the result of 'government failure' and 'market failure.'[50] This implies that if governments and markets operated perfectly, civil society would not exist. But the phenomenon of people acting together to achieve some common goals is much older than both formal states and what can be called markets! Unforced and unprofitable mutual assistance is a state- and market-independent type of human action, and it creates its own organizational structures, free associations, which are neither bureaucracies nor businesses. So civil society is not the result of the failure of others: it has its own intrinsic significance. We see three key roles for civil society (which often may be intertwined in reality): social exchange, advocacy, and alternative practices.

– **Free social exchange/doing things together.** Life would be simply unbearable if all common actions were either political, directed toward or involving political authority, or took place in the form of formal market transactions. Caring commonality, from very informal and passing forms to more formal, institutional and lasting ones, is the 'oil' that 'greases' social interactions, which contributes considerably to an atmosphere of 'high trust' in society. Sports clubs, churches, cooperative insurance companies, and school associations often play a vital role in societies, without too much red tape and rather efficiently. There is no reason – it is, in fact, outright dangerous – to state that all these initiatives are somehow handicapped market initiatives or should ideally be provided by states.

– **Advocacy.** The second role of civil society is that it is a sphere in which people may become aware of and concerned about the nature of certain 'asymmetries' that are caused either by governments or market parties. This awareness may result in active advocacy. This phenomenon was present already in the 19th century when the first labor unions were founded to fight for the wellbeing – often the mere survival – of workers, livable wages, decent work.

Of course, advocacy organizations may be troubling for both governments and businesses (labor unions were forbidden during the 19th century in many countries!). And yet, in the long run, a society only gains from the criticism that is expressed by civil society. Civil society in this second role is certainly a force to be reckoned with, as the formerly Dutch–British oil company Shell found out, both in 1995 when it clashed with Greenpeace over the Brent Spart Oil Platform and in 2020 when Milieudefensie, a Dutch NGO, sued Shell over its climate policies and won.

But suing companies in court certainly is not the most preferable option for civil society organizations (although sometimes they may not have much choice). Seeing each other in court often creates an entirely different dynamic. When lawyers are getting involved, parties have an interest in emphasizing their compliance with the legal minimum and putting on their best face, not dealing innovatively with solving problems (that is why in other domains alternatives like 'mediation' or 'truth and reconciliation' can be more fruitful than a full legal procedure). Timely, meaningful dialogue with civil society partners is the much more recommended way to go for businesses and governments than ignoring them until they go to court.[51] And for civil society organizations going to court should really be a last resort.

– **Alternative practices.** Civil society can be a laboratory for social innovation. In the Netherlands, for example, the role of 'private initiative for the common good' is very substantial in the fields of education, broadcasting, and social housing (and historically has been literally life-saving for many people especially in the vulnerable classes). More recently, there have been some interesting attempts to develop local currencies and a 'sharing economy' that aim at preventing the siphoning away of local money toward globally operating mega-companies with their shareholders. The development of Wikipedia and Linux are examples of civil society initiatives in the digital world.

Earlier, in the section on business, we pointed already to the potential of cooperatives, which can be seen as 'hybrids' between civil society and the market. A different example of the innovative potential of civil society is also another 'hybrid': the social enterprise and social venturing entrepreneurship. Social enterprises are initiatives that position themselves in the market economy and hence intend to become financially independent by making a profit. But their explicit goal is to contribute to solving a social problem. Social venturing entrepreneurship can best be seen as a specific form of social enterprise targeted at 'wicked problems.'[52] Greyston Bakery wants to bake the best brownies in the world, but its explicit goal is to provide jobs for people who, for one reason or another – physical handicaps or a criminal record – have difficulty finding jobs elsewhere: "not hiring people to bake brownies, but baking brownies to hire people." Similar initiatives can be seen for people who have some form of autism.[53] Various countries within and outside Europe have special policies for social enterprises or, as they are called in the US, 'Public Benefit Corporations.'[54]

It is crucial for both governments and businesses to have a clear awareness of the presence and importance of civil society.[55] Governments should be keen on providing adequate legal (and sometimes physical) space for civil society initiatives.[56] Profit-oriented businesses are not the only game in town. Businesses can consider civil society initiatives as partners for cooperation or as critical dialogue partners (and also as potential goals for sponsoring – an opportunity to 'pay forward' to society what has been received from society, but beware: not to buy influence!).

Risks of and for civil society. The civil society sphere has inherent risks as well. Civil society is often associated with 'civility' and 'virtue' – often portraying itself in this respect as different from both the power-driven state and the greed-driven market. But this can lead to moral arrogance. Civil society organizations may easily become 'bubbles' of people sharing their own perspective on the world, who congratulate themselves in engaging in 'goodness' whereas others are seen as either adversaries or pathetic 'objects of compassion' who are out there to be helped by 'us.' Another risk is radicalization, claiming an ultimate moral superiority. Civil society initiatives may also undermine state legitimacy by claiming that they are doing a much better job than governments, while they may actually be involved in 'cherry-picking,' without much public accountability, whereas states have to deal with everybody indiscriminately.[57] There are risks involved as well in funding civil society initiatives, which can become a vehicle for private money to buy public influence without public transparency (for example, pharmaceutical companies paying the costs of patients' organizations, threatening their independence). So larger donors should be aware that sponsoring does not imply buying influence; 'civil society capture' is as much a risk as the well-known 'regulatory capture' mentioned earlier. Civil society is not holy but, just like states and markets, needs constant critical (self-)reflection as well.

In conclusion: A strong civil society. The presence of a well-functioning civil society is a key ingredient of the European model of Responsible Capitalism. Our argument in this section has not been that civil society embodies different values to those that are prevalent in the market. We do find this argument often: civil society is about trust and cooperation; the market is about greed and selfishness. To argue this way would continue and reaffirm a mistaken view of the market and too romantic a view of civil society. We believe that, according to European economic thinking in both the market and civil society, values like trust and cooperation are crucial for wellbeing in all spheres – market and non-market. And yet it is clear that markets have shown a tendency to derail in recent decades. A strong civil society should constantly remind market parties about the key values that are essential both for good business and for a good society.

Chapter 12

The Flying Wheel of Responsible Innovation (C): The 'Critical Innovators' of a New Economy (Media, Research and Education, Imaginative Reflection)

Europe has been the site of a cognitive-reflective revolution, as we argued earlier. This revolution has given rise to three different institutional spheres, of which the media and what can be called 'education and research' are the most clearly visible (more on this below). But part of this revolution has also been and still is the crucial role of critical thinking and the formulation of new, creative ideas. Like perhaps never before in history, the formulation of new ideas, often combined with the criticism of old ideas and practices, has become a highly valued and valuable practice in Europe – although new ideas and insights often clash with older practices and vested interests. All kinds of defining elements of modern society, technological innovations like electricity, automobiles and vaccines, and societal innovations like human rights, democracy, and an economy for all have been formulated as new, deviant ideas. Many businesses, when they start, are also based on an imaginative idea about a problem that needs to be solved or a product or service that exists only in the imagination of the entrepreneur and will fill some needs in a new way. And this emphasis on the 'new' can of course become a cultural addiction in itself, leading to an empty 'innovationalism' in which the new is always seen as better than the old simply by virtue of its newness and not by virtue of it actually being better than the old. But still, this practice of thinking 'outside the box' is crucial for the flourishing of a society as it increases the collective potential to be adaptive to new circumstances and challenges.

In this chapter, we first discuss media as critical inspectors of economic actors – no criticism, no innovation. We will then discuss the sphere of research and education, closing with a sphere that is almost never discussed in any textbook on economics and yet is of crucial significance: the sphere of what we call 'imaginative reflection' where we meet, among others, artists, spiritual leaders, and philosophers – they, too, are an indispensable part of an economy of wellbeing, of responsible capitalism (although, again, never discussed in any textbook on economics, poor students).

Actor 8 – Media: Critical (and Hopefully Independent) Inspectors

Historically, independent media (journalism, the free press, and public broadcasting) have been regarded as an important pillar in the protection and regulation of a free society, embodied in democracies. But the media have a crucial role as well in a healthy economy! Reporting about shortcomings and abuses, 'speaking truth to power,' is essential for the innovation of the economy, especially when the goal is to make it more inclusive and sustainable. There is too much fraud and greenwashing in the world than to allow us to dispense of critical media. Without journalist Bethany McLean, who wrote her alarming *Fortune* article, "Is Enron Overpriced?" in 2001, Enron would perhaps have continued its pyramid game for many more years and would have gotten away even with the practice of causing power shortages in certain areas of the US to drive up energy prices.[1] Without Patrick Keefe, we wouldn't have known about the genocidal practices of the Sackler family via their pharmaceutical firm Purdue.[2] Without the International Consortium of Investigative Journalists (ICIJ), the Panama Papers, the Paradise Papers, and the Pandora Papers would have remained a vast unexplored territory and we would never have known how quite a few of the world's richest avoid taxes, even though they can easily afford them. How can we make sure that this work of investigative journalism can continue in the future? No power, political or economic, should or can do without a countervailing power. Although our argument in this book is for a reorientation of business toward the common good, human and institutional weakness calls for critical investigators at the same time.

Both political leaders/institutions and business leaders/companies understand the great importance of media. This is shown not only in efforts to surround themselves with PR officers and entire PR departments but also in outright attempts to control the media. In the case of governments, for example, this is done by nationalizing them, by restrictive legislation, or, in case of business, by buying media – 'media capture' should become a theoretical term in economics just like 'regulatory capture' (and 'civil society capture,' as explained in the last chapter). So the freedom of the media is under constant threat of being 'colonialized' (as one of the most important contemporary philosophers of free speech, Jürgen Habermas, would call it).[3] We believe that it is in accordance with the principle of human dignity for people to have the right to not be manipulated and hence receive correct and true information and thus have a basic right to independent media, free from government and business influence.

This complex intertwining of politics, media, and markets requires structural rethinking. It is not only political freedom and limited government that require a free press, but a well-functioning free market needs it as well. So it is a crucial challenge for media today to maintain financial sustainability without compromising their independence and their commitment to truth. A fresh debate about this is urgently needed. Can new forms of public funding be developed for some media?

The disparate roles and shapes of media. Although people have always been telling stories to each other and have exchanged news, the media as we know it in the West today – first of all newspapers, then the second wave of mass media like radio and TV, and more recently the third wave, the so-called 'social media' – have their background both in the political-institutional and the cognitive-reflective revolutions we identified earlier. The general populace became gradually involved in public affairs, in politics, through the first revolutions. And, to be politically active, this new category of citizens needed to have information and held debates on it. Even when they didn't have the formal right to vote, groups of citizens started to meet in salons and at tea parties, and they started to exchange news and viewpoints in newspapers. It was on this basis that something like 'public opinion' arose and those in power increasingly were forced to take this public opinion into consideration in one way or another.

With the increasing democratization of society, the role of media changed as well. In many European countries over the course of the 19th century, they became part of what can be called the 'mobilization' of people.[4] We now see political mass movements arising, notably socialism, as a protest movement against elite liberalism and later Christian democratic parties as well. Media became 'mass media,' and this concept acquired an entirely new meaning when technological innovations like radio and, some decades later, TV also appeared. As is well known, some political leaders were very aware of the potential of these new media: Hitler's dark success in Germany would have been unthinkable without his monopolistic use of the radio orchestrated by his Reich Minister of Propaganda Joseph Goebbels.

A new technological breakthrough, the internet, gave rise to yet another new class of media, so-called social media, crystallized for now around Facebook/Instagram, Twitter, and TikTok. They form a highly intriguing new branch in this development in the sense that they complete in some way the movement toward the increasing democratization that was present from the beginning: now every single citizen can immediately air his or her viewpoint, spread information, participate personally in the work of the media. And again, some politicians have understood the significance of these media much better than others. The presidency of Donald Trump would have been unthinkable without the actual combination of 'second-wave media' (especially Fox News) and 'third-wave media,' including the targeted data-based campaigning that was possible because of how big tech companies were now able to profile individual voters and reach them with targeted, individualized messages, with the help of specialized data companies such as Cambridge Analytica – a very notable mix of commercial and political innovation.

During these two centuries, the media have taken on several roles. These roles are (1) a platform for exchange of information; (2) a 'speaker's corner' for opinions and viewpoints; (3) a sieve for separating truth from untruth, fact from fiction; (4) a signaling role regarding societal problems, challenges, shortcomings, and wrongdoings; (5) an expressivist megaphone for channeling individual messages and emotions, especially anger and indignation (this role seems closely connected to third-wave media) and finally, as well, (6) entertaining people, being a source of fun. These various roles are hard to combine, and therefore we often see confusion about and between the various roles. Recently, it has been especially the expressivist role that can easily influence and overshadow the other roles, certainly in the perception of the public. The fifth function is contagious in a way: it feeds the perception that media are nothing more but the individualistic expression of emotions, without any reference to truth, or else that they are channels of vested interests with an agenda to hide the truth, rather than publishing it. The case – eventually settled for well over $750 million – of voting machine producer Dominion against Fox News is a clear illustration. But the entertainment role, for example, may affect the information role as well: fun trumps facts.

What emerges here is a dangerous constellation in which commercial interests and 'post-truth' ideas undermine the critical role of media.[5] We see the consequences in, for example, the rise of climate skepticism or in the Covid-19 crisis where people, sometimes even influential political leaders, do not seem to be able to distinguish between facts that are 'beyond reasonable doubt' and personal opinions or even fact-free personal pipe dreams about a world in which nothing serious, for example a pandemic, is happening of can happen.

Rethinking the institutional landscape: maintaining independence by plurality. When people look back at the world of the early 21st century from a distant future, it may well be that they will be astonished about the extent to which we have put institutions that are crucial for a free and open society, both politically and economically, in private hands, and often in just a very few private hands. In recent decades, we have seen the rise of 'media tycoons,' people or holdings with great financial power buying or even setting up media organizations like newspaper and TV stations: people like Robert Maxwell in the UK, Rupert Murdoch in the UK and the US, Sylvio Berlusconi in Italy, and recently Vincent Bolloré in France. In several cases, they have acted out a very clear political agenda and used their media on its behalf, private money with public power. The situation regarding social media is not much better. Facebook, still the world's largest social network, is owned – and controlled – by just one man (as we noted earlier, Mark Zuckerberg). Twitter is now owned by a man with a clear political agenda (Elon Musk). Just as we don't want government control of media (censorship!), this should not be allowed to occur in the private sector either. It is obvious that ensuring plurality again and again is the least that can and should be done here.

– Institutional plurality. A healthy media landscape can be enhanced by having different types of media organizations, at least three different types. One type can be an official media outlet that falls under the responsibility of a government: thus, public media under a clear legal framework that ensures independence (comparable to an independent judiciary). It is good to give this type of media organization an independent financial base as well, just like the judiciary is paid for by taxes and yet is autonomous in its decisions. For media, it is advisable not to work with an ordinary tax rate but have a special media contribution to be paid by all citizens but not mediated by the state. In addition, there is room for privately owned commercial media. Often, their role will be different, with relatively more emphasis on the entertainment function. As long as this is clear, their presence does not constitute a problem. But what should always be present in any healthy media landscape are third-sector types of media organizations, organized more or less as cooperatives. As we stated earlier, cooperatives have been quite powerful vehicles for creating free spaces in contexts where an aggressive type of capitalism threatened human dignity and wellbeing. Cooperatives made it possible for people to join forces and create a free space, free from market forces and from the state. Given our present media landscape, cooperatives are of great significance in maintaining a kind of 'public commons.' This can take the specific form of media membership associations as in the Netherlands ('De Correspondent' or 'Follow the Money'). Outlets and stations could also be required in their self-presentation to make their financial structure known every time: "This is the public network {name}; this is your commercial network {name}; this is your cooperative network {name}."

– **Plurality of ownership**. It can simply be forbidden for any one person in one holding to own more than one public media outlet. This is classical market theory, which ensures competition and prevents cartels. One can even consider the possibility of breaking up stations, when their market share becomes disproportionately large. The era of 'media tycoons' should be over.

This holds as well for third-wave media, 'social media.' It is amazing to see the speed and extent to which an originally government-led invention like internet has become a totally private matter and a source of huge private profits that are not adequately taxed either. And on top of that, their contribution in terms of jobs is very small, compared to their financial size and profits. Here as well the recipe is to bring institutional diversity, first within the market sector itself by breaking up companies that have become too large and too powerful in the market – "move fast and break things."[6] This is in line with long established antitrust policies and there is no reason why they shouldn't be applied now as well. But one can also think about plurality in the way the internet itself is organized. This can also be done in a mix of public, private for profit, and civil society/ cooperatives.[7]

– **Plurality of genres.** A third type of plurality has been achieved to a certain extent but can be made clearer: the plurality of media *genres*. The six roles that we identified above are often so different that it should be clarified which genre one is engaging in as reader or viewer: What is being claimed? What can the reader or viewer expect? A talk show that claims to do investigative journalism should be clearly recognizable as such and should not be a vehicle for the personal opinions of the anchor, and so on. And those genres that concentrate on factual information should always have a 'fact check' department to openly correct the journalist if something turns out to be wrong, and so on.

By way of conclusion: Pluralistic reporting about the economy. Not only do the media themselves need to be institutionally enabled to do their work independently, they also have to train themselves in preventing blinkered thinking and tunnel vision. In the context of this book, we would like to draw attention to how newspapers, and financial media especially, often tend to, intentionally or unintentionally, uncritically continue ways of thinking about the economy that are still fully based on neoclassical ideas and the centrality of GDP growth. In much financial news, it is still simply assumed that a company is doing well when its turnover and profits are up compared to the previous year. It would be good if the media reports include elements of 'integrated reporting' as well. Is a company really doing well when its operations are harmful to society or to the environment? Does it have plans to do better next year? How robust are these plans? A balanced view on how a company or how an economy is doing is very much part of the information that both shareholders and the public at large are entitled to.

And why not report systematically on what we identified in this book as the '5 I's': the renewal of Ideals, Inspiration, Ideas, Indicators, and Institutions? This may give a much more complete sense of how the economy, and larger, our societies, are really doing.

When media are indeed committed to truth (and not to sensationalism), the corresponding attitude on the side of business should be transparency. If the media are to perform their role as critical observers that are able to see whether things are going right and are going well, they need information and the opportunity to check this.

Actor 9 – Research, Knowledge, and Education: The Laboratories of Innovation

Arguably, the most momentous manifestation of the cognitive-reflective revolution in Europe is the growth and societal impact of scientific and technological knowledge, as most significantly developed in scientific and technological research and educational institutions. Although universities have their roots deep in the medieval period (in chapter 6 we noted already that the first was founded in Europe in Bologna in 1088 as part of the cooperative revolution, organized as a cooperative of law students), their focus at first was on the categorization of existing knowledge.[8] The active pursuit of new knowledge by the use of empirical methods is of much later date. And it is only after the European Enlightenment that science increasingly became the most authoritative source of knowledge, trumping all other sources of knowledge, such as practical knowledge and religious knowledge. Since the end of the 18th century, science has also dovetailed more and more with technology, but it was only in the 20th century that this became a real marriage: businesses and governments (and other societal actors) are becoming increasingly aware of the huge potential of scientific research, in both the natural sciences and the social sciences (including economics) and the humanities. More and more companies are fully science-based (e.g., in pharmaceutics, AI, aviation, etc.) and there is even a separate 'technology sector index' on NASDAQ.

This makes research and education a key actor in the formation and reformation of the economy. Economies are becoming increasingly knowledge-based, and this also affects the reorientation to a more sustainable and inclusive economy. Other geopolitical/geoeconomic players understand this very well and invest heavily in science and technology. In recent decades, Europe has been hindered by what can be called a kind of 'techno-nationalism.' The structure of independent nation states was a real problem compared to other global players. Scaling up new technologies is difficult if there is no more or less unified market where the new technologies can be sold.[9] The EU has attempted to counter this situation by the formulation of increasingly larger Europe-wide research programs, of which Horizon 2020 is the most recent. It was realized as well that just developing new lines of research and technology is not sufficient to make a country or region a true global player. Businesses that can actually apply new technologies and bring them to the (global) market are also needed. So, next to the development of technology, attention was increasingly given to its (potential) use. That in turn led to the question whether this use is desirable in terms of the overall outcomes we want to see in an economy. The value dimension of research and technology was now fully acknowledged, leading to the idea of Responsible Research and Innovation (RRI).[10] This idea has become one of the leading ideas in Europe's innovation policy and is very much in line with the multiactor approach that we advocate in this book. Some key ingredients of RRI are stakeholder involvement and assessing the outcomes of innovation in broad terms, that is, human wellbeing and deliberately directing research and technological innovation toward solving urgent societal issues. RRI is "a strategy of stakeholders to become mutually responsive to each other and anticipate research and innovation outcomes underpinning the 'grand challenges' of our time for which they share responsibility."[11]

In an influential policy paper, Mariana Mazzucato has argued that innovation cannot just be guided by an expectation of a future financial 'return on investment.' It also needs to be guided by its potential to deal with social, political, and environmental problems.[12] Moreover, political actors can and should play a direction-giving role, defining 'missions.' We already referred to the idea of 'public goal setting' in our section on the role of political actors in the European Economic Model, a role that has been assumed by the US government as well – if not in theory, certainly in practice.

It seems that the Von der Leyen European Commission has adopted this point of view, as has already become clear in Ursula von der Leyen's 'presentation bid' as president of the European Commission.[13] She clearly sets a long-term agenda for Europe, including items that require intense knowledge innovation, such as the 'Green Deal' and 'Europe fit for the Digital Age.' An urgent range of challenges has been added to the list in recent years under the heading of 'Strategic Autonomy' (as will be discussed further in the next part of this book on geopolitical challenges).

In an earlier chapter, we already discussed the more specific topic of the renewal of economic ideas and economic education while touching upon economic research as well. Here we will make some observations regarding the role of research, knowledge, and education in general.

Moon problems and ghetto problems. In 1974, the American economist R.R. Nelson asked an intriguing question: "If we can land a man on the moon, why can't we solve the problems of the ghetto?"[14] This question led to a typology between 'moon problems' and 'ghetto problems.' The former are complex but exist within a well-traceable environment in which they can be solved technologically. They are 'tame' problems. But improving life in a ghetto is a so-called 'wicked problem' that involves several issues simultaneously: solving one may often affect the options for solving other problems, or even create new problems. That may well offer a warning against too-high expectations of 'mission-oriented innovation.' It is also a plea for research and innovation that involves different stakeholders, different types of knowledge, and different disciplines. It involves different stakeholders because the most important are those who are directly involved (i.e., those living in the ghetto), next to businesses, research institutions, educational institutions, and government agencies. It involves different types of knowledge because, apart from 'evidence-based' scientific knowledge, professional knowledge and wisdom may be just as valuable in concrete contexts[15] as 'common sense' and the knowledge of those directly involved themselves. It involves different disciplines because wicked problems always require going beyond one specific discipline, drawing from economics as well as from psychology, natural science, medicine, and so on.

– Use **science and innovation for connecting generations**. There is the risk today that an entire generation may fall prey to despair. Young people may have the feeling that they're arriving after the nicest party of world history, that of unlimited mass consumption, is over – and in a sense this is correct. The consumerist world that the present generation has built is not sustainable. But this doesn't mean that life in the future will be worse. There are all kinds of highly interesting challenges that can really stimulate the creativity of young students. So there should be an infrastructure in which all those who have an appetite for complex problems are truly challenged to give it their best. Why not complement the present Nobel Prize system with a European system of prizes for the most creative ideas regarding sustainability, social inclusivity, and perhaps even 'strategic autonomy' as well as for ideas that bring the fruits of new insights to bear on solving problems in the global South? There could be national competitions at the elementary school level, the high school level, and the level of vocational schools and academic institutions, complemented with a European prize in these four categories. The urgent challenges of the future could thus also be presented as problems that something can be done about, as occasions for creativity, even as ways of having fun.

In the Netherlands all universities for (higher) professional education (HBOs) have made, or have promised to make, the UN SDGs part of their curriculum. Universities and other educational institutions are considering doing the same. This can give ample opportunities for organizing exciting projects that can involve many partners from different societal sectors.

– **Speeding up the 'Knowledge Filter.'** Research shows that it may sometimes take a generation before new knowledge becomes part of the university curricula, let alone high school curricula or its application in new technologies. The knowledge filter is very often a slow hourglass through which new knowledge trickles down only slowly. The same holds true for the digestion of knowledge in many businesses. More intense interaction between educational institutions and research institutions and opportunities for upgrading knowledge during one's career are urgently needed.[16]

This should always involve broader questions as well, referring to the normative and value dimensions of new insights and new technologies. Speeding up the 'knowledge filter' should not be done at the expense of 'imaginative reflection' (see below).

– **Leaving the 'ivory tower' of monodisciplinary science.** It may be time to revise how academic research is organized nowadays. Universities run the risk of being and remaining an isolated world where everybody is involved in a 'publish or perish' struggle for life and therefore far too often take the safe route: publishing more of what we know already instead of exploring truly new approaches to new economic, social, and ecological problems. Moreover, in many high-level institutions, specialized research, reviewed by 'peers,' is valued much higher than interdisciplinary work aimed at solving concrete problems with other actors. Solving 'moon problems' is valued incomparably higher than dealing with 'ghetto problems.' We are not advocating an 'either/or' strategy but more of an 'both/and' division of labor. In each institution – or, even more broadly, in each domain – a combination of skills should be present and should be valued: specialized disciplinary work, educational skills for involving the next generation, skills in working in interdisciplinary and multiactor contexts, and skills in involving the larger public. Some people are able to combine everything as true 'universal humans,' but this should not be a requirement. Division of labor, team cooperation, coupled with equal financial and career opportunities, should be the standard in academic and research institutions.

– **Bridging the gap between knowledge and business.** Another persistent problem is the gap between science and scientific discoveries and the application of the results in actual products and services. This is partly due to the fact that it is often overlooked how much innovation actually depends on social innovation, apart from technological innovation.[17] There is often simply a lack of communication between scientific and educational institutions and business (and government agencies for that matter). So it is crucial to organize an intensive exchange between the various actors that feel responsible for giving answers to today's challenges. 'Clusters,' 'hubs,' 'incubators,' 'science parks,' or whatever form this may take (digitally as well) – it is crucial that that there be dialogue and exchange platforms where the 'partnerships for meeting today's challenges' (in line with SDG 17) can actually take shape. Everybody has the power of initiative, but perhaps governments – from the local to the EU level (and even the UN level) – have a special responsibility in this regard to use their 'convening power.'

– **Toward a global 'ECSC' 2.0 for sustainable technology.** In 1951, the European Coal and Steel Community (ECSC) was created, a first step toward what would later become the European Union. Given the urgent challenges of today, especially regarding the future of our planet Earth, it seems advisable to create a worldwide organization in which sustainable technology is shared. Regarding the problem of sustainability – perhaps as part of the reparations that are now agreed on in principle during COP 27 in Sharm Al-Sheikh – such a global fund can help countries in the global South to partly skip the fossil fuel stage of human (i.e., Western) development (just as quite a few countries went from no communication networks to mobile phones, skipping the cable phone system). For this truly globally shared interest, countries in the global North should generously share new technologies that make production cleaner, while respecting the need of countries in the South to develop themselves. So a Global Community of Sustainable Technology (GCST) could be a worthy successor of the 1951 ECSC.

In conclusion: Science certainly (but not science only). Although we have to acknowledge that the cognitive-reflective revolution has had many downsides, for example in the rise of some harmful political ideologies, the rise of some dismal economic theories, or the manipulative-exploitative attitude toward nature, it is clear at the same time that we will not be able to deal with the current challenges without the creativity and innovation that research and educational institutions foster. This certainly does not mean a technocracy or an expertocracy. Society needs broader reflection on the many aspects of our challenges than can be provided by science alone. Scientists and scientific knowledge do not have a monopoly on truth, let alone on wisdom. But, as a highly significant source of knowledge and innovation, they are indispensable, and they should be active participants in all contexts in which people are trying to find answers to today's challenges. And together they can establish true laboratories of sustainable and inclusive innovation.

Actor 10 – Nurturing Creative and Critical Thinking: Imaginative Reflection

The term 'imaginative reflection' includes all those people and institutions that critically think – or feel or have intuitions – about current problems and at the same time imagine future alternatives. Therefore, they often issue a call for action. It may be artists, imagining what may happen when we do something (or do nothing: think of the climate), or it may be philosophers, thinking through the hidden assumptions of our economic thinking and at the same time imagining other assumptions. Or it may be spiritual leaders, such as Pope Francis, whom we have mentioned already several times in this book and who, in addition to his encyclical on climate problems (*Laudato Si'*, 2015) also published one on the significance of community in human lives (*Fratelli Tutti*, 2020). It may also concern activist scientists who, alarmed by their empirical findings, take action to change the course of the economy. Those who are involved in the sphere of imaginative reflection often formulate criticism of existing practices. And they may articulate old or new values and moral insights that are relevant for businesses, for governments, for leaders and managers, and so on. A healthy economy needs critics and continuous reflection on current practices. There is age-old wisdom involved here. Kings often had court jesters whose task was just to say anything they wanted to say, to be critical, to make jokes, to contradict – everything to keep the minds of those who were in power open and prevent the blindness of arrogance and the arrogance of blindness. We have to invest in keeping our minds open, as people, as companies, as societies. Perhaps it would be a good idea to include 'jesters' in the supervisory boards of companies and in various political platforms.[18]

Institutionally, we may find imaginative reflectors in informal networks, in think tanks, in religious institutions, in some academic institutions (though universities, including their economics and business departments, are often conspicuously absent here), in NGOs, in artistic hubs, and so on. Although this is a highly disparate sphere with many different types of actors, it is still helpful to identify it as a separate sphere, as a distinct 'actor' in a multiactor approach. We would urge both business leaders and policy makers to invite these people to the table. Or we would urge them to take courses or lectures, to learn to think 'outside the box' and acquire a broader perspective on the problems our societies and economies are facing. This doesn't imply that one has to agree with them. But certainly, the interaction with 'imaginative reflection' is one of the sources that can help broaden and deepen one's mind and give substance to acknowledging and taking responsibility for the wider impact of one's actions in the market economy.

We have recently seen 'captains of business' eager to play this role themselves and acquire almost 'guru-like' status, as saviors of mankind. Steve Jobs had a tendency to present himself as a Messiah-like figure, as did Peter Thiel later, and recently Elon Musk. They are free to do so, as long as they recognize that their perspective is just what it is: a perspective subject to critical debate; they are not 'prophets of last resort.' Often, their success in business is related to a certain monodimensional focus, which is certainly a great strength in certain circumstances and often makes real innovation possible. But, at the same time, it has clear weaknesses as well, especially when it comes to a critical alignment of their vision with the interests and views of other stakeholders. Therefore – to quote Mao Zedong just once in this book – "Let a hundred flowers bloom; and a hundred schools of thought contend."

The functions of imaginative reflection. Broadly speaking, the sphere of imaginative reflection has at least five important roles in a healthy economy that wants to maintain its health and resourcefulness.

– **Exposing hidden assumptions.** Imaginative reflection can make us aware of the *hidden assumptions* of our established ways of thinking and acting. Artists, philosophers, religious thinkers, and others may break the spell of the obvious, the 'matter of course' character of our engrained patterns. Does our economy really have to be the way it is? Are we doomed to adhere to Margaret Thatcher's dictum "There Is No Alternative"? And do we have to base our theories and practices on the idea of the individualized consumer, bypassing the need for community and belonging that is (also) characteristic of human beings? Why can't businesses be community builders? Do we choose *homo economicus* as the lead star for our policies, and why? Or do we start from an idea of *homo cooperans*? Cultural and historical research may us make aware of very different ways in which human economic relations can be organized outside markets via reciprocity, gift exchanges, and mutual assistance.[19] The reservoir of human social possibilities is much larger than what was actualized in the first decades of the 21st century – and we can learn from that.[20]

This awareness of hidden assumptions may also concern our anthropocentric way of thinking as if we human beings are 'masters of the universe.' Carl Sagan's picture of the Pale Blue Dot in 1990 opened up the imaginative power to reflect upon our position on a tiny vulnerable Earth: "Look again at that dot. That's here. That's home. That's us."[21] We'd better be careful here – this is an imaginative wake-up call for 'earthlings.'

– **Uncovering unintended or hidden consequences of economic activities.** Sociocritical novels like Charles Dickens's *Hard Times* or Harriet Beecher Stowe's *Uncle Tom's Cabin* have had a great expository impact. Certain futuristic movies or novels may us make aware of new, exciting possibilities but may also make us aware of the futures we want to steer away from. Think of dystopic novels like Aldous Huxley's *Brave New World* and George Orwell's *1984*. They give the image of a type of society that is technically possible, and perhaps economically profitable, but is an affront to human dignity. More recently, Dave Eggers's *The Circle* may have a somewhat similar effect for businesses. Novels like these have played and are still playing an important role in the discussion on how to organize our personal data, for example, and how to avoid a Chinese-type social credit system. A movie like Ken Loach's *Sorry We Missed You* (2019) exposes a social reality of our developing 'platform economy' that we may or may not like – but it addresses central problems that we need to face, in a way that no economic statistics could ever do. Imaginative reflection may induce a sense of empathy as well as a sense of indignation sometimes and an urge to act, to do something – to incite the 'power of initiative.'

– **Pointing out the normative or moral dimensions of economics.** Those involved in imaginative reflection often point to the *normative or moral dimensions* of our economic system, the value dimension that is always present, even when it is vehemently denied. What is the type of world we want to build together? What are the standards that we use, implicitly or explicitly, when we say that our economy is 'doing well' or even 'doing great'? What do politicians mean when they ask: "Are you better off today than you were four years ago?" Are we then referring to GDP growth – and if so, is that our conscious or unconscious definition of 'the good'? Or are we referring to values (as in this book: human dignity, inclusivity, regenerativity, and co-creativity)? The critical reflectors are constantly asking the 'why' questions alongside the 'what' and 'how' questions and often argue that the latter two should follow the first, not the other way around. Therefore, closely connected to the question of values is indeed the question of 'purpose': What is our role, my role, the role of the company that I am working for or that I am leading, in making this world a better place? What is of true 'value'?

– **Exploring alternatives.** Fourth, imaginative reflection may be the source of *alternative lines of thinking and the development of new ideas, new practices,* 'outside the box' solutions. They provide the possibility of opening up new moral horizons from a plurality of sources: artistic, spiritual, moral, and historical. Also crucial in this regard is the formulation of new images and metaphors for what we are doing. To describe the world we live in as a storehouse of raw materials gives a very different perspective than a description of it as 'our common home.'

– **Giving a sense of the cultural plurality of today's world.** Fifth, those engaging in philosophy, theology, art, and the humanities in general are also able to give an acute sense of the plurality

and diversity of our modern society in terms of cultures, traditions, and worldview perspectives. Societies at large as well as
businesses need to be well aware of this. Cultural backgrounds,
customs and (religious) beliefs make up an important part of
people's identity and therefore their claim for recognition. This
awareness may well prevent an easy globalist universalization
of our Western economic models.[22]

Conclusion: the strength of soft power. One of the most unwise
things for all those who are engaged in the business sector or
in politics, especially those who have a leading role is to ignore
imaginative reflection or downplay its significance. Both the
spread of 'neoliberal' ideas right from the foundation of the Mont
Pèlerin Society in 1947 and the development of critical economic
thinking takes place primarily in networks and think tanks
(the pro-unfettered capitalism think tanks, in particular, are
extremely well funded). All those involved understand the power
of ideas and visions. John Maynard Keynes was very much aware
of this also, given his famous quote from 1935:

> The ideas of economists and political philosophers, both when
> they are right and when they are wrong, are more powerful
> than is commonly understood. Indeed, the world is ruled by
> little else. Practical men, who believe themselves to be quite
> exempt from any intellectual influence, are usually the slaves
> of some defunct economist. Madmen in authority, who hear
> voices in the air, are distilling their frenzy from some academic
> scribbler of a few years back. I am sure that the power of vested
> interests is vastly exaggerated compared with the gradual
> encroachment of ideas.[23]

Often, the confrontation with representatives of this sphere
of imaginative reflection can be painful and irritating at first.
People and institutions at all levels of economics, politics, and
society at large have a predilection for entrenched patterns and
display path dependency. But it is good to remember John Stuart

Mill's argument: that is, that truth is not a matter of a majority, for a single person can later on turn out to have represented the truth, against all odds.[24] We shouldn't deprive ourselves of the possibility that the dissenting view is right after all. Often, new ideas emerge on the margins and can be found in what historian Arnold Toynbee used to call "creative minorities," from where they start to move 'from the margin to the mainstream.'

The relevance of imaginative reflection for our society raises concerns about our education as well, especially our economics and business education. How does this stimulate values like creativity and empathy? Does it invite moral reflection? We see a growing movement toward 'business humanities' or 'humanomics.'[25] In light of what we are arguing in this book, these developments are as promising as they are necessary.

Part III

Europe's New Position:

A Global Player for the Common Good

In Part III we discuss the attitude and strategy that Europe can adopt in the geoeconomic and geopolitical context of the 21st century, as a self-conscious actor that is at the same time aware of the implications of the condition of a multipolar world order. In today's world, Europe is not an island. Formulating new ideals and nurturing new practices can hardly succeed if it is a 'stand-alone' exercise. We have entered an age of globalization, and there is no way back. Attempts to reorient the market economy must reckon with this new reality of living in a multipolar world.

Part III

Europe's New Positions:

A Global Player for the Common Good

Chapter 13
A New World Order is Emerging

In this book, we have looked back at the last 250 years in which Western societies embarked on the project of escaping from poverty by organizing an economy in which real material growth could occur. Labor, material resources, technological innovation, entrepreneurship, and trade, together with having colonies, made an unprecedented jump in living standards for large groups of people possible. We pointed, however, to severe downsides of this project as well: inequality and exploitation inside the launching countries of the project themselves (proletarization, the 'social question') and on a global level (colonialization). Moreover, in recent decades, people have gradually become aware that this entire project rests on a hidden assumption: that of unlimited natural resources and a stable and unshakable ecological environment – an assumption that isn't borne out by reality. The project is impacting nature in a way that is unprecedented in its damaging effects. So, the correction and embedding of the project that was urgently needed in the 19th and the 20th centuries is still needed, but now not only sociopolitically but ecologically as well.

Strangely enough, however, a different route has been chosen in recent decades. The world has increasingly become aware of the ecological preconditions for economic growth and of the potential damages that economic growth can cause, and the world knows about the risks of unfettered capitalism. Despite all this, a kind of world-historical replay of 19th-century capitalism has begun, led by the USA and boosted now as well by the collapse of potential rivals. We called it 'triumphant capitalism' (significantly enough the prefix 'neo' was often used: neoliberal, neoclassical).

Against this background, we argued that the world should now embark on a new mission, a new project of reorienting capitalism in the direction of a responsible capitalism that is regenerative and inclusive, a new project of embedding. But humankind doesn't have another 250 years to complete this immense task; it doesn't even have a hundred years. Kate Raworth has aptly summarized the urgency by saying that this present generation may be the first that can really see what is happening while at the same time it may be the last that can turn matters around. And if we make a united effort, crucial steps can be taken, even in one generation.[1] We have also argued that Europe should play a leading role in this project or at least be a frontrunner and make its own economies socially and ecologically sustainable while stimulating this worldwide as well.

This may all sound fair enough, but what are the real opportunities and chances for a project like this in today's geopolitical and geoeconomic constellation? What does today's world look like? How can European nations, apart and together, work together to further this agenda? Is there any real room for maneuver here? And what are the threats to Europe, internally and externally? Hasn't Europe become too weak, too dependent on others, to play a role in a global reorientation of the economy? And shouldn't it put its own short-term interests, the interests of its own people, first?

Such questions about the political, geopolitical, and geoeconomic dilemmas are often absent in the literature on the renewal of our economy. This omission gives this literature a bit of a utopian flavor sometimes. For us, it is important that innovative ideals and the harsh realities of everyday power politics have to come together somehow. In this chapter, we therefore intend to give an assessment of the contours of a new geopolitical and geoeconomic constellation that is emerging in the wake of the crisis of 'triumphant capitalism' and the war in Ukraine that somehow seems to prefigure this new constellation.[2] This can only be a sketch, for it would require a separate book (although the present geopolitical turmoil probably is too severe and unpredictable to capture in a book yet). In the next chapter we will zoom specifically in on Europe's position and potential.

The Larger Significance of Russia's Invasion of Ukraine

These geopolitical and geoeconomic questions are of the highest urgency because Europe is facing severe challenges right now. In the introductory chapter, we pointed to the likely watershed significance of Russia's invasion of Ukraine in 2022, unleashing a terrible tragedy with many casualties on both sides. It was a human disaster in itself by any standard. But at a different level, the impact of this invasion is potentially much larger than this initial tragedy. Most likely, it is a carefully deliberated move in a geopolitical chess match. And Europe would be wise not to underestimate its long-term significance.

There is a serious danger that Europe especially, more than the US, will be hit so hard by the consequences of the war (energy shortages, cost of living crisis, etc.) that it may lose a long-term perspective altogether and fall back on shortsighted policies that may seem to safeguard its standard of living for one or two winters, while ignoring the much more extensive consequences afterwards. The transition to responsible capitalism may simply be blocked, and the greening agenda obstructed. Or other countries, especially in the global South, will be saddled with the nasty consequences of some of the European measures to manage the implications of the crisis in the form of energy or food shortages elsewhere in the world, harming Europe's reputation. Europeans are given the impression that they can and have to make a choice between supporting Ukraine on the one hand and being warm in the winter and thus continuing a well-entrenched lifestyle on the other. This may gradually undermine support for Ukraine. But it may also undermine the support for a reorientation of our economies, as we have argued in this book. The 2015 agenda has to reckon with the realities of 2022, but 2022 should not be allowed to trump 2015. The following considerations are to be kept in mind to get a sense of the situation.

First Observation: The End of a Monopolar World and the Risk of 'Winner Takes All'

Though this was already occurring in previous years, the year 2022 symbolizes the probable end of a period in world history that can be called the age of American hegemony. One can argue when this age began, but 1948 seems to be a good pick. Thanks to America (and to the Soviet Union, by the way, though it had only been able to fight thanks to massive American shipments of military equipment), World War II ended, both in Europe and in the Asian Pacific. Japan was transformed into a more or less Western-style democracy. Under American leadership, the United Nations was founded with a clear charter, the Universal Declaration of Human Rights, and the sovereignty of nations was confirmed. Europe received massive American support to rebuild its economies under the Marshall Plan, and NATO was established.

Of course, during the first 30 years after 1948, American hegemony was contested by primarily the Soviet Union in the Cold War, during which the two superpowers engaged in a very threatening nuclear arms race in a 'bipolar world.'[3] And quite a few 'hot wars' were conducted as 'proxy wars' where the two superpowers played a role in the background. In the meantime, there was this other sleeping giant, China, where, in relative isolation, a communist regime under the leadership of Mao Zedong totally transformed a still largely traditional, agricultural society.

Halfway through the 1970s, it became increasingly clearer that the Soviet Union wasn't able to maintain its status as a superpower. Its weaknesses and failures, both economically and militarily, could no longer be concealed. This was symbolized most clearly by its failed invasion of Afghanistan (1979). The collapse of the Soviet Union was completed in 1991 with the creation of the Commonwealth of Independent States, formally ending the USSR. After this, a kind of unfettered capitalist economy was introduced in Russia, and, in the meantime, Deng Xiaoping established himself as the new leader of China in 1978, inaugurating pro-market reforms and becoming the architect of an emerging modern China.

The age of American political hegemony, with its zenith years between 1980 (the Reagan presidency) and 2007 (the credit crisis) was also a period of the new prominence of free market capitalism. Earlier in this book, we called this the 'age of triumphant capitalism' with the US as the political, economic, *and* ideological leader of the world, strongly supported here by the UK and other Western countries. The first Iraq War was a clear sign of this new power constellation: with almost worldwide support, the US expelled Saddam Hussein from Kuwait, which he had invaded months before. In Washington, the think tank Project for the New American Century (PNAC) tried to draw the policy implications of this new situation and sketch the contours of American global leadership, with a strong emphasis on military power with the agenda in the background of spreading democracy and global free market capitalism in one package deal. Especially after the 9/11 attacks on the World Trade Center and the Pentagon, the moment appeared to have arrived to really implement the New American Century, starting with regime change in the Middle East, in Iraq and Afghanistan (and who could say which country would be next?). Both democracy and free market capitalism were going to be the hallmarks of the 21st century led by the US. And every country that wouldn't fall in line would have to fear for its security and its prosperity. For the US, the vintage American idea of 'winner takes all' seemed to have become the lodestar of geopolitics and geoeconomics.

The justification for this dominant position in the world and the way it was used to create the twins of universal democracy and a globalized economy was the universalist idea that democracy and the free market are the best options for every human being, everywhere and always. Universal interests and the special interests of the US and, more broadly, the global North seemed to coincide, at least theoretically. Via a global 'trickle-down' effect, the monopolar dominance of the North would be universally beneficial. Not only was it a matter of making the world 'safe for democracy,' as Woodrow Wilson once called it, but also making it 'safe for capitalism.' In the global South, this is increasingly seen as nothing more than a neocolonial project: making sure the energy, raw materials, and consumption goods go where the money (still) is, which is the global North (see below).

In retrospect, we can now say that this moment inaugurated a phase for the US that historian Paul Kennedy famously warned against as "imperial overstretch."[4] The invasions didn't result in Western-style democracies and economies. Even the Arab Spring, which started more or less spontaneously, wasn't able to expand the free world either. A new phase in history – let alone what Fukuyama had announced earlier as the "end of history" – wasn't going to happen. Moreover, the credit crisis of 2007 and subsequent years cast serious doubts about the performance and moral integrity of capitalism.[5] Is this indeed the system that will benefit us all, if it already creates havoc, inequality, and cronyism in its own heartland?

It's not going too far to interpret Donald Trump's rise to power as a late result of the disappointment and frustration about this darker side of capitalism: powerful economic elites who were able to astronomically increase their wealth for decades by, among other things, embarking on a process of unchecked globalization while ordinary people didn't experience any progress but often saw their economic position regressing and becoming less and less secure.[6] Ironically enough, Trump's first priority was a big tax cut for the wealthiest upper class. All of this seems to mark a new era in which even the faith in the beneficial outcomes of democracy and capitalism has waned in the US itself and given way to outright cynicism: just special interests defending themselves, internally and globally: no longer the 'city on a hill' but an empire-as-usual for which the continuation of its own lifestyle has become the highest goal.

Since Trump, we have seen the emergence of two Americas that stand for entirely different values. There is an America that champions crony capitalism and an unfettered shareholder-oriented economy, regardless of the social or ecological consequences and regardless of the outcomes of democratic procedures. This is a US in which inequality is rising, the position of the middle class is deteriorating, and the poor remain stuck where they are, in "despair" (as Case and Deaton call it[7]). This is a US that – in one generation – is pumping every drop of oil that can be found by whatever chemical means to protect a consumerist lifestyle for parts of the population. And it will do so until the earth is so hot that people can only survive by air conditioning, creating energy bills that are beyond the capacity of anyone to pay. This US resists what it now condescendingly calls 'woke capitalism,' when investors at least try to do something about the negative effects of capitalism by implementing ESG criteria (Environmental, Social, Governance) in their investments. It is a US in which more and more people will desperately cling to conspiracy theories and become spellbound by hopeless political leaders who refuse to face reality.

And there is another America that realistically faces the challenges of today socially, ecologically, and politically and wants to work together in multilateral fashion with as many other nations as possible on these challenges. But even this second US seems to suffer from a nostalgia for a bygone world and still uses a superficial universalism to further a monopolar agenda. And one has to wonder how realistic this is in today's world (see below).

The geopolitical impact of the Trump era (which formally ended in January 2021 but may or may not continue for a few years in some form) is severe. On the one hand, Trump doubled down on the demise of the era of American hegemony by consciously pursuing an 'America First' policy and downplaying and sometimes withdrawing outright from America's international and multilateral role and responsibilities. Most notable was his decision to pull out of the Paris Climate Agreement. But his general attitude – and the support he was able to galvanize for it on his home front – toward age-old allies in Europe and elsewhere and his attempts to distance the US from NATO have radically altered the geopolitical scene, especially for Europe.

On the other hand, Trump embarked on a kind of new 'Cold War' with China. China was identified as the major rival of the US, and Trump recognized that the US – and the West in general – had been making China stronger and stronger for decades by outsourcing great parts of its manufacturing industries. Trump wanted this to end, but this obviously wasn't received well in China, which – precisely at that very moment – was increasingly manifesting itself on the world stage as the self-conscious leader of the future.

The Biden administration immediately started with a different tone – and more than that: after the Russian invasion of Ukraine, the US assumed a leading role from the start in organizing countermeasures and providing Ukraine with weapons to defend itself. But Biden doubled down on Trump's China policy, and the US seems to be en route toward a new global contest with China, perhaps hoping that it may prevail in the long run, as it once seemed to have prevailed during the collapse of the Soviet Union. And yes, Biden rejoined the Paris Agreement but at the same time combined ecological investment with a continuing 'America First' policy, as can be gathered from the Inflation Reduction Act.

For Europe, the outcome of the Trump era is a sobering reality check. The US can change its policies overnight, according to political whim and can therefore no longer simply be the 'big brother' to whom Europe can automatically – and almost parasitically – turn. After Trump – even if his presidency turns out to be a one-time intermezzo – all European nations have to rethink their geopolitical and geoeconomic position and 'grow up' by taking on a more self-conscious, independent role.

Moreover, a key point on the agenda will be the question whether it will make sense to continue this project of monopolar dominance, with the entanglement of democracy and human rights on the one hand and unfettered capitalism and globalization – 'winner takes all' on the other. Can this indeed be a viable agenda, or should Europe instead become a global champion of, for example, the SDGs and international cooperation rather than competition? This is both a moral question and a matter of long-term self-interest. Is the kind of neocolonial dominance of the global North – 'winner takes all' – sustainable in the long run, or even in the short run? 'Win-lose' or 'win-win' – what is the most likely scenario?

Second Observation – The Rise of the Non-Western World: Toward a Multipolar World of Empires

This question brings us to our second observation. In this first quarter of the 21st century, the geopolitical map of the world is changing forever. We are entering a new phase, which can be characterized as a multipolar world. This statement, which has been uttered time and again by the Russian president Vladimir Putin as well, is nonetheless certainly true – and it may be the better part of wisdom to acknowledge this truth.

The most significant manifestation of this emerging new world order is indeed the rise of China. Since the reforms of Deng Xiaoping, China has – almost under the radar – carefully built up first its economic power and now, under Xi Jinping, its political and military power. In 2010, China overtook Japan as the second largest economy in the world. In itself, this is a laudable development since China, with its 1.4 billion inhabitants, has every right to take its place in today's world as a superpower and economic giant. With the work it has done, it has vastly contributed to meeting first the Millennium Development Goals and contributes now very substantially to meeting some of the SDGs. Because of China's successes, the West should not underestimate the support that the Chinese Communist Party has among China's own population and can no longer count on its imminent collapse, based on theories of a supposed natural inclination of world history toward democracy and human rights.[8] Autocracy will most likely be among us for a considerable time – unless miracles happen, and though they do sometimes, it would not be wise to count on that.

Two years after achieving this second place in the world order, Xi Jinping came to power. Under his leadership, China almost immediately started to assume a much more self-conscious geopolitical and geoeconomic role. Earlier, we pointed to the great significance of the narrative about the 'Age of Humiliation' in this respect and of the year 2049 as a temporal horizon.[9] The clearest sign of this is the Belt and Road Initiative, China's effort to create a unified economic zone throughout central Asia, connecting China via the Middle East region to both Europe and Africa, directly involving about 150 countries, two thirds of the world population, and about half of the world GDP.[10] Moreover, China has, in a couple of years, become one of the largest if not the largest bilateral lender in the world, investing in infrastructure in many countries often requiring as collateral rights to raw materials or the ownership of ports (and acquiring some of these when repayment fails, so-called 'debt trap diplomacy').[11] Perhaps even more impressive is China's technological and scientific prowess: according to the 'Critical Technology Tracker' of the Australian Strategic Policy Institute, China is now leading in 37 out of 44 cutting-edge technologies, such as defense, space, robotics, energy, AI, advanced materials and quantum technology. For some of these technologies, the world's top ten research institutes (in terms of high-impact research papers) are Chinese.[12] At the same time, it became clear that this new role as a geoeconomic and geopolitical superpower will not be accompanied by a gradual adaptation to values that are often considered – certainly by China – as 'Western,' such as pluralism, democracy, and the rule of law, but also are reflected in the Universal Declaration of Human Rights. The crackdown on the Uyghurs, the handling of Hong Kong, and the increasingly threatening rhetoric against Taiwan doesn't bode well for the future of a world in which human rights are more and more respected. Moreover, China has made it one of the cornerstones of its economic policy that everyone who has or enters into economic relations with China will have to give up the right to criticize China in any way, especially regarding human rights and how it deals with what it calls its 'internal affairs.'

Regarding some of today's big challenges, China is sending out mixed messages. On the one hand, for example, it tries to convey the impression that it is clearly committed to achieving the SDGs and has adopted and even added the idea of an 'ecological civilization' to its constitution in 2018. At the same time, however, its use of fossil fuels, including coal as a key ingredient, is growing fast. China opens new coal-fired power plants every year.[13] And it is building other ones around the world that are often even worse than those it is building in China itself as far as emissions are concerned.[14]

The second major manifestation of the emergence of a multipolar world is the rise of India. In 2023 India overtook China as the country with the world's largest population. It has already been the world's largest democracy for decades. Its economy is currently growing at a faster rate than China's. The pattern of its growth follows that of China: first there was a boom in its production of goods, and this was followed in recent decades by rapid growth in the 'knowledge intensive' sectors, notably the IT sector.[15]

If we recall here the well-known acronym BRICS, it is immediately clear that the rise of China and India are not isolated phenomena: Brazil, Russia, India, China and South Africa together are proof that the world has changed beyond recognition within a few decades – and it is well past time for the West to take that into account.

Although itself part of BRICS, the reentry of Russia onto the world stage as a global superpower is worth singling out as the third major manifestation of the emergence of a multipolar world. Although economically small, with a GDP of 7% of that of the US, 10% of that of China, and with a military budget that is less than 10% of that of the US – a budget that puts Russia formally on the same level as the UK or Saudi Arabia – it still is a technologically very advanced nuclear superpower.[16] In recent years, it has been working consistently to enhance its global network, most notably in the Middle East and in Africa. After the collapse of the Soviet Union, Russia first chose to follow Western-oriented policy lines. But this changed after 2007, when Putin gave his (in)famous Munich speech on a multipolar international order, partly as a response to the American invasion of Afghanistan and Iraq. A clear sign of this repositioning was the expansion of Russian influence in the Middle East, most clearly visible by its backing of the Syrian regime, and in Africa as well. Russia seems to have started to play an active role as well in intermingling with the digital infrastructure of Western countries and thus sometimes interferes in this way in elections, especially via social media, in the supply of public information.

This multipolar world that is arising is not a particularly friendly world. Huge interests are at stake for each 'pole': raw materials, energy, water, economic growth, sheer military power, digital power, power in outer space, having global networks for production and trade, and the room to follow one's own cultural path – all that is now on the table for each of them. Political scientists have started to talk about this new phase in history as a new 'Great Power Competition.' The 'poles' will behave more and more like entities that we have known throughout the last 3,500 years of history: empires. Empires are large political units comprising many peoples, nations, and even civilizations that organize full-scale economic systems, from food and raw materials to luxury goods around an established center. They exert almost unlimited power internally and a strong defense externally. Empires do not count in days or years but centuries, and they do not count individual people but legions and strategic areas. Violence and war are part of the normal way of operating for empires, without many moral scruples. Their morality is geared toward the safe continuation and, if possible, expansion of the empire. In a multipolar world, one may well speak of the relationships between the various poles as characterized by 'weaponized interdependence,' a situation in which all the poles are simultaneously connected to each other, especially economically and technologically, but at the same time are trying to contain and sometimes control the other.[17]

A final word on China, the most prominent proof of the emergence of a new world order. Despite China's impressive growth during recent decades and in spite of its clear ambitions for the future, Europe shouldn't feel intimidated by this but count on its own strengths, as outlined earlier. Given its enormous population, there is a rightful place for China in today's world. But the 'system' China chose is a very risky one in the long run. Of course, democracy has inherent risks also, but it has one unsurpassable strength, as quite a few people have pointed out: it is always possible to get rid of bad leadership in a peaceful way.[18] In totalitarian and autocratic systems, a country is stuck with its leadership, even when it is failing. Autocratic leaders can start as wise leaders with a justifiable agenda, but the arrival of – parallel to Paul Kennedy's analysis of empires – 'autocratic overstretch' is almost inevitable. At some point (and no one knows when exactly) a leader becomes blind to his own mistakes and weaknesses, silencing opposing viewpoints and starting to live between 'walls of mirrors,' with nobody daring to give non-desirable – but nevertheless true – information anymore. In the case of China, this was already evident from the start of the Covid crisis: the doctor who gave an early warning, when the outbreak could have been easily contained, was silenced – and eventually died from the disease he tried so hard to prevent. The same mechanism was repeated in that other would-be autocratic regime, the Trump administration. The denial of unwelcome evidence is the Achilles heel of autocracies throughout the ages. And it may be a strong trigger for outward violence: saving one's skin by projecting an enemy against which a country can be united by rallying around the leader. Just as it triggered the failed attempt at a coup in Washington, and played a role in Russia's invasion of Ukraine, it could trigger an invasion of Taiwan by China as well with highly unpredictable consequences.

Third Observation – Active Weakening of Western Hegemony: Europe as a Key

An entirely new phase in this return of the Great Power Competition began with the invasion of Ukraine. Although its exact moment may have been triggered partly by cunning calculations about perceived American uncertainty after the withdrawal from Afghanistan and the change of power (a new chancellor) in Germany, this is most probably a carefully deliberate move in a geopolitical chess game with a much longer timeframe and wider horizon, as we indicated earlier. And, most likely, the central target isn't Ukraine but Europe. We shouldn't let ourselves be deceived by the initial military clumsiness of the invasion.

What is remarkable first of all about this invasion is that Russia had carefully secured Chinese support. China and Russia share the view that the age of Western hegemony is over and should be over. Steps toward truly ending it are politically and morally justified, given that the historical track record of Western domination isn't all that impressive – Europe had its chance for centuries and blew it. Moreover, its present role is often a nuisance for many (autocratic) leaders in the world – in an issue like, for example, human rights. For China and Russia, and most probably openly or secretly supported in this respect by quite a few countries, the world could be a better, and certainly a more convenient, place without Western domination.

The second remarkable thing is that Putin has thought through a clear narrative about the past, present, and future of the Russian empire, and the areas and peoples that belong to it (as we indicated above, developing grand narratives is a common feature of active civilizations). In the background, there is most likely a still grander narrative about a Eurasian civilizational space that should be brought together into one economic space as a complement to the Chinese Belt and Road Initiative and as a counterweight to the European Union and the economic, political, and cultural power of the US and the West.[19] This story, which has elements like "The Historical Unity of the Russians and Ukrainians" – the title of the ominous essay Putin wrote in the summer of 2021 – and the historical greatness of the Russian empire, serves as the legitimation of and inspiration for his long-term political goals.[20] A strong independent Europe, or one that is closely connected to the US and functions as a vanguard of American influence on the Eurasian continent, doesn't fit this picture.

The third thing we should note is the most probable geopolitical calculation that is behind it, one that both Russia and China share. Western hegemony was initially Europe-based for several centuries (the age of trade empires and colonization) and then US-based in the 20th century, though with Europe's strong support. Now, if Europe is weakened or even cut loose from the US somewhat, the US would be considerably isolated. In that case, the former hegemonic power in the world would be on the way to becoming isolated, lonely, and American power would hence be severely curtailed. Therefore, Europe is a key 'battlefield' in the long-term geopolitical scheme for Russia and China as well as for the US itself. Given that the US is still rather untouchable, targeting its key allies is a major goal. Taking Europe out of the geopolitical equation would be a major step toward a multipolar world, in which China and Russia would have a very different role from those they have had in the last decades. Both Russia and China do realize this, as does the US, and it is certainly part of the US's vehement response to the invasion of Ukraine and, for example, America's long-term opposition to the Nord Stream gas pipelines.

Against this background, the sudden Trump presidency was a real gift to both China and Russia. He did exactly what they were hoping to achieve: minimizing American involvement in Europe ('America First') and loosening the bonds with its former allies, leaving Europe hanging. The Ukraine war is also a culmination of earlier attempts, both by China and especially by Russia, to have close economic relations with Europe on the one hand by delivering energy and consumer goods on a mass scale. On the other hand, these attempts were also aimed at undermining European unity by a *divide et impera* policy, giving different deals to different countries (as analyzed recently in a very realist fashion by the Dutch analyst of international relations, Rob de Wijk).[21] And, of course, this massive dependence weakens Europe's ability to act sovereignly in the international arena. The way Europe is organized, as an association of sovereign nations, also lends itself particularly well to this means of strangulation.

Against this background, the sudden reunification of Europe in the wake of the Russian invasion of Ukraine is most probably an outright surprise for all parties involved, including the European nations themselves. All of a sudden, they have been roughly awakened from their geopolitical slumber.[22] But beyond the immediate resistance to the Russian invasion, what is the long-term geopolitical and geoeconomical agenda of Europe? In 2019, Fons Stoelinga, the former Dutch ambassador to India, sketched a future in which there will be two 'hard power superpowers,' the US and China, and two 'soft power superpowers,' India and the EU.[23] In light of the return of Russia, the picture has to be adjusted, for Russia will most probably continue to aspire to the position of 'hard power superpower' as well, based on its huge nuclear arsenal and its growing political-military network in the global South. And will Europe continue to have the luxury of remaining a 'soft power'? Or should it develop its 'hard power' too? And if it wants to pursue 'soft power,' what could then be a viable long-term agenda?

Fourth Observation: Growing Anti-European/Anti-Western Sentiments

Clearly, the Russian invasion of Ukraine was a flagrant violation of international law. But it is telling that many countries were very hesitant to condemn it outright, let alone act on a possible condemnation. Yes, no fewer than 141 countries condemned the invasion at the UN General Meeting on March 4, 2022 (and it was repeated in February 2023), while Russia received support from only four 'pariah states.' But the many abstentions were very striking, including of course China as well as important countries like India and South Africa. And actual sanctions against Russia were supported only by Australia, New Zealand, South Korea, Japan, Taiwan, and Singapore, in addition to Europe and North America. In short, the real support that 'the West' was able to mobilize in the world was limited. Countries may have the feeling that it is a kind of historical justice that Europe is now confronted by a non-Western power instead of the other way around.

This has to be seen in conjunction with a growing resentment against the West and hence also against Europe, sometimes particularly against Europe. A global atmosphere is growing in which the 'West,' the 'North' (Europe) is increasingly being held responsible for its colonial past and its aftermath. We saw this already earlier when we pointed to China's leader Xi Jinping's reference to the 'Age of Humiliation,' when European countries launched the Opium Wars against China (already back then under the pretext of 'free trade'). Among African intellectuals, 'postcolonialism' is a key topic, often drawing on the work of Franz Fanon. This is reinforced by many Western intellectuals who ferociously attack what we above called 'Europe-I' (in chapter 6), often without acknowledging 'Europe-II' or conflating this with 'Europe-I' but providing a great deal of revealing evidence.[24]

Kishore Mahbubani, former Singapore ambassador to the UN and former President of the UN Security Council, states very provocatively that "the West has lost its way" because it refuses to acknowledge the new geopolitical and geoeconomic realities.[25] Therefore, it constantly provokes its own backlash and is constantly disappointed by the opposition it meets in the world.

Even a quick glance at the global economic map shows how unequal the world still is and how risky this is for Europe in the long run. Although the colonial past is behind us, it seems that the current organization of the world is still very 'neocolonial': countries in the South are there to provide energy in the form of fossil fuels, raw materials, and consumer goods to the North, which is not (or no longer) able or willing to produce these goods itself. One container ship stuck in the Suez Chanel – the Ever Given, in 2021 – gives a sense of the geoeconomic constellation: it is like an intravenous drip from South to North.

This implies as well that the biggest share of global pollution and emissions, although not necessarily actually taking place in the North, still happens on behalf and in favor of those countries. Moreover, serious consequences of the Ukraine war were felt in the global South: food shortages in Africa along with liquid gas shortages. And while Europe was able to buy this off (to be sure: at the cost of rising prices and inflation), countries in the South did not have this escape route, with real shortages as a consequence.

The same can be said about the consequences of climate change. While the global North is directly or indirectly responsible for about 70% of global emissions, the consequences of climate change will hit countries in the South most: directly in terms of unbearable heat, drought, and floods, but also indirectly, for the technological options and economic reserves to adapt to climate change are less available and more costly. Waves of climate migration may occur, with consequences for the North as well. But the entire constellation is morally untenable and therefore, in the long run, politically as well. We can see the dim contours of a Marxist type of revolution against the privileged classes, which may in the long run result in what we earlier referred to, using a phrase coined by Manuel Castells, as "excluding the excluders." A moment may come when countries in the South start to refuse being part of the Northern economic system and form a Southern coalition (in which China will no doubt play the leading role). The moment may come when they have the resources, the technology, the people and the will. The global North may do well to heed Machiavelli's old warning: you may be loved, or you may be feared, but make sure you are not hated.[26]

Conclusion: Curiously and Tirelessly Tracking World History

In 1989, the Western world was lulled asleep by Francis Fukuyama's phrase "the end of history." Of course, at no time did he mean to imply that nothing was going to happen anymore and that everything in the world would come to a standstill. But he did imply that the struggle over ideas on how to organize a good society had come to an end, for from now on we all would know that only equal recognition before the law, individual freedom, and democracy are the bases of a just political order. And from now on, history would somehow follow that path, the path of freedom and democracy, no longer the millennia-old way of autocracy, dictatorship, or totalitarian rule.

Fukuyama's insight should not be given up lightly or condescendingly. The idea of human dignity as a universal standard runs deep in Europe, and Europe can't be Europe without, for example, defending the Universal Declaration of Human Rights in theory and practice. But we have to learn and argue other insights too, such as the fact that a good society cannot survive without some kind of balance with nature. In that respect, history hasn't gone upwards, as Fukuyama suggested, but may even have gone downwards.

The idea that history would somehow 'automatically' curve in one or any direction is therefore highly deceptive, let alone the idea that it would do so automatically in the direction of the good, as if history is something that simply occurs without humans defending or fighting for key values that can be found but can also be lost. Any 'automatized' view of history may cause us to lose interest in what is actually going on. We – that is, all those involved in national and international politics and economics, policy makers, civil servants, business leaders – have to constantly study world history vigilantly and with curiosity, to see what is actually happening in a certain period of time and to be open to new, unexpected developments so that we can respond with wisdom and acumen.

It is certainly possible that we may discern some regularities and returning patterns in world history – it remains the same old "crooked timber of humanity" (as Immanuel Kant called it) that is at work after all in all ages.[27] So there is plenty to learn for everyone who is involved in international relations, from people like Oswald Spengler, Arnold Toynbee, or Paul Kennedy pointing to the rise and fall of civilizations, people like Eric Voegelin, Hans Morgenthau, or Samuel Huntington pointing to nation states or civilizations as identifiable 'entities' that have had their own patterns of interaction developed over centuries, or the recent work of Ray Dalio on the 'cycles' of empires and the resultant constantly changing world order.[28]

This constant study may teach us at least three things: (1) the world is in constant flux, but (2) in that flux we may well encounter repeating patterns that may help us to evaluate and design our responses, and (3) no political constellation will last forever, and even 'eternal empires' have their day. Therefore, we should never bet on the mere continuation of yesterday's world but be open to an ever-changing future – and perhaps try to shape it.

Chapter 14

Europe's Contribution to Tomorrow's World

Europe's Response: Becoming a Non-Imperial Empire

Where does this all leave Europe? The time to be geopolitically and geoeconomically naive is over now. No longer can the European nations just rely on the US to defend their geopolitical and geoeconomic interests and values *ad infinitum*. Although the US will remain Europe's primary partner in today's world, in some respects their interests may differ, and this should be duly acknowledged. On some key values especially, there is a potential gap between the US and Europe as we envisage it. Above, we spoke of two Americas: 'America First' and 'Global America.' From the viewpoint of a reorientation of the (global) economy toward regenerativity and inclusivity, the second is certainly more promising, but even here the 'winner takes all' mentality may create a strong long-term backlash. Given the long-term uncertainty about which America (if either: a constant wobbling between the two and a stalemate remains an option as well) will prevail, Europe has to take its own position as one pole in the multipolar world in cooperation with the US, as its preferred partner, based on shared values like human dignity and freedom. But Europe has to take some distance as well as long as the US asserts itself as the cornerstone of an economic system that is unsustainable and untenable in the long run and as long as it aspires to play a role that doesn't fully acknowledge the new realities of a multipolar world.

The other option for Europe is to let itself be gradually divided between the other two superpowers and become a fragmented relic of a distant past. For inherent reasons, this option is not particularly attractive, but even less so, given the topic of this book, for the future of another type of market economy. A world dominated by the Beijing–Moscow axis doesn't bode well for the development of a sustainable and just economy. Nor does unfettered capitalism under US guidance. Europe has to step up and articulate its own long-term mission in line with what we earlier called the '2015 agenda,' a 'Third Way.'

This 2015 agenda, however, has to reckon with the realities of the seven years that followed it up until 2022 and beyond. This implies two important roles for Europe, one 'external,' the other 'internal.'

Externally, we see no other option than that Europe, here the EU, will have to play a new role in the world of tomorrow; it will have to combine a sober realism with regard to safeguarding its own basic necessities (energy, food, raw materials, essential technology, etc.) and thus protecting its own people in the short- and medium-term, with a long-term view of the future of the planet as a whole. It should be a strong driver for the transition toward responsible capitalism, a market economy that works for all people, within ecological boundaries, for generations to come. Europe has to combine the role of a superpower, an 'empire,' alongside the three or four other superpowers – which will require participating in today's economic system – with that of an advocate of a different type of economy, an economy of the future, a 'non-empire.' It is not 'Great Power Competition' that Europe should be the advocate of to deal with the global challenges but 'Great Power Cooperation' – and to mobilize other countries in the world for this. At the same time, it has to make sure that it doesn't fall behind economically, technologically, or militarily, for when the rubber hits the road, these are the bases on which it will be taken seriously in the international arena (regardless of how much one would like the world to be different). So, yes, given the current debate, Europe should develop its 'hard power.' But it should do so not as an end in itself but in order to be able to become more of an independent partner, a friendly counterweight to the US (perhaps restraining the US sometimes) on the one hand and to give substance to its higher goal of engaging in 'soft power' and cooperation on the other.

The second role is that Europe, the EU, will also have to act as a shield for its own citizens against the consequences of unfettered capitalism and unlimited globalization. Although national governments have often tried to frame the EU as a swamp of bureaucracy and secret lobbying processes and consistently blame domestic problems on the EU, this is entirely out of sync with the geopolitical reality that, without the EU, no European country would have any shield against the geopolitical and geoeconomic vicissitudes of the 21st century. The EU is certainly not perfect, but it is an indispensable player between (national) localization and unshielded globalization. And Europe is already delivering on its promises. Of all the global powers, only Europe has set out to, for example, protect its citizens and their data against the exploitative and monopolistic practices of Big Tech companies, imposing fines for violating privacy – the so-called General Data Protection Regulation (GDPR). Only Europe has thus far been able to start to protect its citizens against the consequences of ecological degradation by formulating and enacting an ambitious Green Deal on a scale that really matters. But it is clear as well that for this second role to play well, Europe needs to renew its relationship with its own members and their populations and come to a new type of 'covenantal relationship,' a promise to protect the dignity of European citizens in all respects.

These roles fit Europe and Europe's story very well. As a whole, Europe has quite a story to tell (and we tried to briefly reconstruct this in chapter 6): that of a continent torn apart by strife and war ('Europe-I') that created the concepts, visions and practices in the margins of its own history of an alternative future ('Europe-II'), which it has been and is still gradually implementing. The latter is concerned with ending the senseless striving for exclusive domination of the entire continent by one nation (always prevented by the others); it has now started a difficult but promising practice of cooperation between equals.[1] This is a 'powerful' story indeed and may even make Europe a laboratory for the future as humankind has to live with deep differences on one planet Earth. Although critics can easily and often rightfully point to shortcomings, a new mode of operation has emerged in the international arena via Europe, which can be characterized as "leading diversity by dialogue."[2]

Implications for Europe's Global Positioning

Does this not mean that Europe should punch way above its weight? We don't think so. On the contrary, there is no reason to speak in a condescending way about Europe, neither economically nor politically. Depending on how and when one makes the exact calculations, Europe has become the largest, or second largest, economic zone in the world in recent decades. Moreover, if one wants to include this in the equation, at around $290 billion, the military expenditures of the European nations combined out-perform Russia by seven times ($42 billion) and they still spend 1.5 times more than China ($178 billion).[3] To be sure, Europe's military expenditures are fragmented and not well coordinated compared to the 'single country armies,' but still. Europe is home as well to two of the world's nine nuclear powers. So, Europe is a global power, whether it wants to be or not. And with that comes responsibility, a truly global responsibility. Nonetheless, recognizing global responsibility is quite different from striving after unipolar dominance. The time of European dominance is over, and Europe should be very clear about that for itself and for all other nations. But that doesn't mean that Europe shouldn't play a crucial role in today's world.

From our perspective, Europe should become the geopolitical and geoeconomic advocate of a 'wellbeing economy,' 'responsible capitalism,' or whatever term one likes to use: the champion of the SDGs and hence of a socially and ecologically sustainable economy while remaining committed to democracy and human rights. The European nations have to establish themselves as a joint geoeconomic power with a clear common goal to protect the dignity of all human beings and therefore their own citizens as well, those who are alive now and those who are yet to be born. But this 'idealistic' goal should be combined with a very realistic analysis of the new multipolar world and a growing ability to play the complex game of international relations in such a world. We will substantiate this claim with further considerations.

A. European Actorship

1. Treasuring and nurturing unity. Europe has an inherent weakness in that it is not one nation, with one command structure, that can act overnight. It seems to combine a first-rate geoeconomic position with a politically fragmented structure. In 1991, the then Belgian Minister of Foreign Affairs Eyskens famously characterized Europe as "an economic giant, a political dwarf and a military worm."[4] There have certainly been developments since, but in essence this statement still holds.

Therefore, there is a great danger that other major geopolitical players in today's world have a kind of common interest in taking Europe out of the geopolitical and geoeconomic equation somehow, if only to reduce geopolitical complexity. Because of its seemingly weak political structure, Europe appears to be an easy target for other superpowers to start a game of *divide et impera* by fanning internal divisions through, for example, giving some nations preferential treatment. China and Russia have already been very active, each in their own way, in this game, even trying to somehow divide Europe into several spheres of influence.[5] Within Europe itself, this implies that all European nations should recognize the danger of becoming puppets in the hands of one of the other superpowers or being played off against each other by them. In the short term, some offers on behalf of China, for example, may be very tempting, but in the long run, such offers may weaken Europe as a whole and therefore weaken the very countries that accepted them. While it is clear that all European nations have much more in common than what separates them, there will be a constant danger of wanting to cash in on short-term advantages and privileges, with short-term gains causing long-term losses.

A new recognition of the geopolitical and geoeconomic significance of Europe also implies that, within Europe, politicians should resist the easy temptation to blame other European nations and especially the European Union for any problem that comes up internally. That is how we ended up with Brexit, which, as has been argued, was a very complex and expensive way to solve some internal problems in the British Tory party (and ended up not solving them!). The European blame game is an easy one to play for national politicians, but in the long run it is a dangerous game for all European nations.

2. *Geopolitical and geoeconomic actorship.* The urgency of the problem has become only more apparent in Russia's invasion of Ukraine. Europe has responded with unprecedented – and probably for Russia highly unexpected – swiftness, unity, and strength. But at the same time, this was all improvised, and if someone else had been Head of the European Commission, the response could have been very different.

So, the European nations and the European Union need to rethink the organization of their actorship in a multipolar world of Great Power Competition. Shouldn't the Chair of the European Commission have stronger executive powers in some areas, especially in foreign policy?

This regards military cooperation as well. As stated above, the total military expenditure of European nations combined is considerable and considerably larger than that of Russia or China. But its military is still fragmented, both technologically and with respect to command structure. Why not take steps toward forming one European army to which all member states contribute or at least have more intensive coordination of military investments among all European states? This implies having a military industry that is advanced and able to scale up its production when necessary.

B. Treasuring and Strengthening Internal Subsidiarity

3. *Creating a new sense of community by recalibrating centralization and decentralization.* Although it may at first sight contradict what we just said, for a strong European Union, it is essential that a new division of labor be found between what should be done together and what can be left to the nation states. Recalibrating the respective roles of centralization and decentralization, or in other words, recalibrating the principle of 'subsidiarity' ('leave matters that can be dealt with at a smaller scale and at a lower level, at that level, and only do things collectively at a higher level when necessary'), is an urgent matter.[6] Cooperation doesn't imply uniformity. If Europe stresses uniformity too much, it may backfire and in the long run weaken Europe.[7]

We see a great deal of tension in Europe: economic tensions between the North of Europe and the South, cultural tensions between Western Europe and countries in the Eastern part, tensions between the nation state level and the city level. We see tensions between Europe's divided past and the resistance to truly embarking on a common future, tensions between what the different European countries have in common and what is unique to each of them (let alone separate regions within countries). There are tensions between the interests of an increasingly older population and the younger generations. And yet, despite all these tensions, Europe is a community that does what a community is supposed to do (as we argued above in the section on communities, chapter 11): it offers protection, gives empowerment and is a platform for collaborative action. But Europe has not yet been able to create the concomitant sociopsychological sense of belonging and shared identity to a sufficient degree. There is a huge harvest waiting here. For this, it is crucial that people see the most important relevance of Europe now: to be a shield for its citizens in a globalized and increasingly grim world.

But internally, within Europe, we should perhaps try to endure and live with some deep differences, also regarding (some) values. In each context, the key actors should carefully consider which values they want to emphasize or even declare 'non-negotiable,' and which not. Should the rule of law, democracy, and sustainability have the same priority as LHBTQ+ rights – to mention just one dilemma (which is a dilemma for European nations while dealing with each other, but it is also a dilemma when dealing with for example countries in Africa)? What differences should be allowed or at least endured?

4. *Treasuring smaller nations.* Europe is unique as a cooperative structure between nations, large and small. It is understandable that a great deal of attention is given to the large nations, especially Germany and France. A recent, intriguing book, however, draws attention to the unique role, the innovative potential, of small nations in particular like Finland, Denmark, Ireland (and, more broadly, Singapore and Israel). James Breiding argues that small nations are leading the world in important respects – in innovation, for example, or in education, health care and ecological cities.[8] He could have but does not discuss Estonia and its innovative digital infrastructure. It is a new argument for what was earlier known as "Small is Beautiful" (E.F. Schumacher). The European structure of intensive cooperation between nation states provides it as well with a richness of 'hubs' where new ideas can be tried from which all can learn. If an attitude of mutual learning is fostered between the European nation states, this can greatly contribute to a sense of the legitimacy of European cooperation. This is a new, more dynamic application of the principle of 'subsidiarity' that is mentioned in the European Treaty (Art. 5.3): "the Union shall act only if and in so far as the objectives of an action cannot be sufficiently achieved by the Member States" (in matters that are not its exclusive competence). We should view (small) member states as spaces for experiments and innovation. Again, acknowledging diversity makes Europe as a whole stronger.

This treasuring and protection of internal diversity – and thus furthering a sense of community of equals while at the same time emphasizing unity in dealing with external threats – may be the core of a new covenant between the EU, the European nations and the populations in these nations. The 'story of Europe' as we have tried to sketch this in chapter 6, together with the four future-oriented key values we identified there (human dignity, regenerativity, inclusivity and co-creativity) may be of help here.

C. Multiple Alliances

5. The US: the preferred partner. Although Europe will always have a strong tendency to look to the other side of the Atlantic Ocean, it is clear that the Transatlantic axis should no longer be the only geopolitical refuge for Europe. Given the very fragile political situation in the US, Europe should stand on its own two feet. The Trump era has shown beyond any reasonable doubt that there is a risk that the US will abandon Europe when the internal political tensions in the US become unmanageable for moderate leaders, be they Democrat or Republican.

'Standing on one's own two feet' as a geopolitical player does not imply that there are no preferred partnerships. It is clear that the US will remain the primary ally in today's world in many respects, and the same holds for all other nations that are committed to human rights, the rule of law, democracy, and pluralism, such as Canada, South-Korea, Japan, Australia, and New Zealand.

But from this point on we need to propose a mental caveat. It is now conceivable that the US itself may depart from these very principles, in spite of the fact that 'making the world safe for democracy' has been one of its long-term and most important goals. It is no longer beyond imagination that the US will prefer to make deals with autocratic leaders rather than deals with free democracies. It may be that, from now on, it is Europe on whom the historical task falls that was once formulated by Abraham Lincoln in his Gettysburg Address of 1863, to make sure that – at least in one region – "government of the people, by the people, for the people shall not perish from the earth." And this should be complemented by an 'economy of the people, by the people, for the people.' But as long as this scenario doesn't materialize, the US will in many respects remain the preferred, and badly needed, primary partner.

6. *A diversity of coalitions.* With respect to the agenda of building a more social and sustainable economy, Europe and the European nations need to have the courage to choose and go their own way, inspired by and based on their own unique history, their own value traditions and value innovations. Given the urgency of ecological and social problems, there is no time to wait for others to act. Standing on one's own two feet implies as well that, regarding various key issues, European nations will sometimes have to look beyond the US and pursue partnerships and coalitions with other countries. Regarding sustainability, for example, it is conceivable that Europe can have much closer alliances with other nations – and perhaps it should even pursue this actively, sharing green technology, for example, and making sure that pollution is reduced globally, with or without the US (and helping to reduce pollution elsewhere may be very effective overall, as we are dealing with a truly global problem). It may well be that at one point China is a better partner in this. Standing on one's own two feet also entails making one's own deals and coalitions. In a multipolar world, it is conceivable that a rather complex constellation emerges in which various poles have coalitions on one issue while being opposed to each other on other issues.

7. *Africa.* Since the geopolitical scene now seems to be dominated by the Washington–Brussels vs. Beijing–Moscow axes, another continent is on the rise that may well turn out to be a major player in tomorrow's world: Africa. Africa has by far the youngest population of all continents, and its population is still growing strongly. An active and generous Africa policy by European nations is needed for several reasons. Africa is a relatively close neighbor; its population is growing quickly, and if new generations do not have any prospects in Africa itself, the pressure to migrate will be substantial. Geopolitically, China may succeed in making

Africa almost a kind of satellite continent, though a substantial immigration from Africa to China is not conceivable. Europe should consider deeply what its response is going to be. What is its Africa policy? How can Europe best cooperate with African nations out of true respect? The vaccine diplomacy during the Covid crisis doesn't bode well for a sound Africa policy, denying as it did the common, interconnected fate of Europe and Africa. Instead, it is advisable to build strong relations with at least all more or less democratic/rule of law-abiding countries in Africa and give them preferred status as EU partners.

8. India (and the UN). We already mentioned India above as one of the emerging 'poles' in the world and the largest functioning democracy. Moreover, India is not particularly befriended by China (more so by Russia). For all kind of reasons, a generous and open India policy by the EU is crucial for the balance of power in tomorrow's world, both politically and economically. India seems to be increasingly aware of its place in the world as potential mediator between West and East.[9] A closer alignment with India can be very important for Europe as they together can play a role as 'soft power,' as stated above in chapter 13 (with the qualifications given there).

In general, Europe has to actively anticipate the new world order by not clinging to the past. Rather, it needs to try to win sympathy by, for example, proposing that the French seat in the UN Security Council become a European seat, while Britain's seat be transferred to India.[10] This would be a clear sign that Europe is sincere in recognizing the multipolarity of today's world and really wants to truly leave the colonial era behind.

D. Strong Awareness of Values (and their Diversity)

9. Consciously held values. What operating in a multipolar world requires is not a thorough prior assessment of one's economic and security interests but a new, vigilant consciousness of the key values that are at stake. The values that have emerged in Europe – in a painful history in which precisely these very same values were often trampled upon, as we briefly sketched in Part I – should be articulated and defended clearly in the international arena. The fact, after all, that some essential values have historically been articulated in Europe does not imply that they don't have universal significance – as is clear from the broad support, on paper, for the Universal Declaration of Human Rights. (And this may also be clear from the fierce opposition they have elicited in Europe itself as well: Europe cannot claim them for itself, nor boast of its own compliance.) The same holds for the broad global support for the SDGs. To be a geopolitical and geoeconomic actor requires a strong sense of the values one wants to uphold and a determination to build broad coalitions around them. And clear commonalities and common interests with others may emerge in the process.

10. *Recognizing value plurality.* In a multipolar world with "multiple modernities" (as the Israeli sociologist Eisenstadt called it[11]) we nonetheless have to reckon with the idea that there will not be an easy global convergence of values and practices. Historically, the European nations have had ample experience with multipolar international arenas. In a way, this goes back to the 1648 Westphalian system of sovereign states living together on one continent, without one being able to dominate the others. Despite very disastrous exceptions (Napoleon, two world wars), this system has more or less held its ground (the defeat of both Napoleon and Hitler, as well as the end of World War I can be attributed to this very system). But especially after the European disasters of World Wars I and II, European nations have developed an entirely new way of living together as independent nations and yet constantly aligning their interests, often through tough negotiations, in a common union. In a way, this relatively small multipolar world may be a model for the global multipolar world we described earlier in this part. Europe shows that it is possible for nations and peoples to work together in certain areas, while being separate or different in others. The European Union is proof of this. Viewed

from this angle, it is certainly fitting that the EU was awarded the Nobel Peace Prize in 2012. But this has something to say for how Europe operates in the world: cooperation doesn't require uniformity. That brings us to our next point.

E. Strategy and Tone of Voice

11. *Respectful suspicion.* Being the champion of a new type of economy does not imply that we envisage Europe going around the world, lecturing all other 'poles' about their shortcomings according to 'our' standards. That would be – for both historical and pragmatic reasons – totally inappropriate. And it would contradict what was just said, that is, that it is not to be expected that a wholesale value convergence will take place in today's global world.

Therefore, the appropriate general attitude to other poles in a multipolar world can be characterized as 'respectful suspicion' or 'suspicious respect' or, to put it in a friendlier way, 'cautious respect.' This attitude is particularly fitting in the case of Europe, for there is no reason to have rosy illusions about the geopolitical ambitions and interests of others and the way Europe is viewed.

This attitude of careful or suspicious or reserved respect is a difficult one when dealing with, for example, dictators and autocrats who violate important human rights principles. It requires that each party have a strong set of basic principles and be firmly rooted in its own traditions and values. And yet, it is the better part of wisdom to always stick to one of the key principles of international relations after 1648, the basis of the entire 'craft' of diplomacy: 'Do not humiliate others.' As Europe learned the hard way after World War I, humiliation breeds resentment, and resentment can easily explode in unexpected ways.

There are ways in which Europeans can operate in the international arena that allow them to more or less keep their integrity as European nations (although the concrete decisions will often be tough) and are probably quite effective even in a grim international arena. These are as follows.

- as a *'committed pioneer'* who walks the talk for itself, even when standing alone. Europe should be committed to the New Economy, to 'responsible capitalism' as we have tried to outline it in this book, even when others do not follow the example. Europe has intrinsic reasons for doing so because this fits its values and seems to be the best way to promote the long-term wellbeing of its own citizens.
- as a *'guardian'* over its own internal market, applying ecological and social production standards more and more not only internally but also externally. When countries or businesses want to trade with Europe, their entire production chain, and not only the end product, should adhere to certain minimum standards regarding, for example, no child labor or slavery, the reusability of raw materials, the repairability of products, and so on. This is the very important 'standardization power' that has been called the 'Brussels effect' (see below as well).
- as a *'broker'* between the various other superpowers to achieve parts of a global sustainability and/or social agenda, particularly as formulated in the SDGs (and therefore with global legitimacy).
- as a *builder of coalitions.* Even in dark times, it turns out to be possible to build coalitions to deal with very concrete problems, as proven by the Paris agreement of 2015 and the recent High Seas Treaty (2023), agreed upon after almost 20 years of negotiations. One can imagine many more 'coalitions of the willing' that Europe can broker with ever-changing partners. The crucial question is whether Europe itself will be willing, as the financially and economically strong partner, to really invest in these coalitions. Below, we will propose a Global Community of Sustainable Technology as a worthy successor of what was once the European Coal and Steel Community.
- as a *'conscious receiver of criticism'* from other nations regarding its own performance in terms of justice and sustainability, with respect to its SDG compliance, and so on. Europe should have the courage to receive criticism and try to learn from it, thus adding humility to its self-assertion.

– as a *'loyal friend'* of all countries that have some measure of democracy and rule of law. Countries in Africa that are part of the world order as Europe would like it to become, for example, should be granted special partnerships and very advantageous trade conditions, even if this could hurt some internal markets in Europe. In the long run, it is highly important to have friends in the world that are given the opportunity to do well economically.[12]

F. 'Strategic Autonomy' Without Isolation – Globalization and De-globalization

12. *Moderate or 'open' strategic autonomy.* The attitude of 'careful/ suspicious respect' also implies rethinking the balance between globalization and 'de-globalization' and hence a new balance between geoeconomic and geopolitical considerations. The economic theory regarding international trade provided a very clear recipe (and it was sometimes almost naively followed in the 'age of triumphant capitalism'): remove all boundaries, let trade have its way, and – via Ricardo's law of 'comparative advantages' – a global division of labor will take place in which one country specializes in one type of product, the other in another. So, even the vital infrastructure of countries can be part of this global division of labor. We have witnessed this in recent decades. China has become the manufacturer of the world, whereas countries in the North have more and more become service providers. This results in China manufacturing essential medical supplies, for example, and, given China's incredible technological development, now full communications networks as well, such as the 5G system. For political reasons, however, this may not be the optimal solution. There are good reasons for any country, or at least any geopolitical region, to ensure that it has control over its own critical infrastructure when, for instance, global logistical networks break down or, worse, when the essential supplies become weapons in a kind of 'cold war' between the superpowers. That is one element of the condition

of 'weaponized interdependence' mentioned in the last chapter, which certainly justifies the element of 'suspicion' in our phrase 'respectful suspicion.'

In addition to medical supplies and network technology, this may also apply to energy. Sustainable energy, produced in Europe, is not only an ecological necessity but also a geopolitical requirement. Reducing Europe's energy dependence on other countries is of utmost importance. The recent Russian invasion of Ukraine has driven this point home – if not for the first time (it happened earlier in the 1970s with the Arab Oil Crisis), but now certainly with much greater urgency than before.

This plea for "strategic autonomy," as the French president Macron called it, should not be exaggerated, however. It should be decided case by case: What products need to be produced in Europe that can still be part of the global market? There are pragmatic reasons for caution, but also more principle-related points: (fair) international trade is a source of wealth for many countries in the global South, much more effective than what used to be called 'development cooperation.' So 'trade, not aid' should remain an important geopolitical and geoeconomic principle.

Of course, there is a trade-off here with ecological requirements, for international trade relations themselves contribute very much to pollution: worldwide transportation requires a great amount of fossil fuels. And yet, having trade relations is vital for many countries in the world. So, Europe should try to make the production processes, in the South especially, as clean as possible (another reason for a Global Community of Sustainable Technology; see below).

In addition to fuels from Russia, the idea of 'strategic autonomy' concerns primarily China of course. China is formidable and should be treated as such, but the principle of 'suspicious respect' should certainly apply here. All European nations, separately and combined, should work on a well-deliberated long-term geopolitical strategy in which the question of how to deal with China should be central.[13] And a thorough revision of what sectors of the economy can have Chinese influence and what should be firmly within European jurisdiction should be a top priority, and Europe should take a united stance on this. Respect for China should not imply free access to key elements of European infrastructure. A new balance between globalization and localization is needed, and hence this plea for moderate strategic autonomy, for which recently the term 'open strategic autonomy' has become viable as well.

G. Contributing to Tomorrow's World Order

13. *The 'Brussels Effect.'* One of the core instruments that Europe – in particular the European Union – has is the power of standardization, which Anu Bradford has called the 'Brussels effect.'[14] The ability to set production standards and enforce these standards within its own market is a legitimate competence of each market zone. But given the size of the European market, the global effect of this turns out to be huge. Usually, manufacturers are not keen on producing two versions of the same product, one with high standards and another with lower ones. They want to engage in business all over the world. So, the highest standards tend to become global standards. Being one of the largest markets zones in the world, Europe has a very strong 'soft power' weapon here. All globally operating companies and countries desire access to the European market. So, creating a level playing field inside and outside Europe, at a high level of sustainability and human dignity, is key to improving the lives of people not only inside Europe but globally.

In this respect, it is crucial that these standards are not just imposed on others in the supply chain but are seen as a shared responsibility of the end users as well. Companies in Europe should actively engage in joining producers outside Europe to enhance the sustainability and inclusivity of the production processes together – and pay a fair price for the product.

14. *Due diligence.* A very important further development of this global responsibility requirement is the EU policy on 'Corporate

Due Diligence and Corporate Accountability' and the ensuing directives that we discussed in chapter 8. This policy requires all corporations active in the EU to make sure that their supply chain meets the international Human Rights Standards as well as worldwide agreed upon sustainability standards.[15]

This is in line with the earlier legislation on digital privacy, the General Data Protection Regulation (GDPR), regulating the collection and handling of data by companies active in Europe. It is a clear example of the moral framework that we identified as 'European' in which the principle of human dignity is key. Whereas data in the USA are primarily owned and can be exploited by commercial companies and in China privacy data are in principle owned by the state, the European approach is to protect the individual, ensuring freedom not only from the state but from market exploitation as well.

15. *Fighting Poverty Globally.* A lot of attention is given nowadays – including by us in this book, as well – to sustainability and geopolitical and geoeconomic security. But this shouldn't lull us into forgetfulness about an issue that is of much more imminent concern for billions of people elsewhere in the world, the issue of poverty. During the Dialogue Sessions on the Future of Capitalism that were held as preparation for this book, both Muhammed Yunus and Jeffrey Sachs made it emphatically clear that poverty is still the number one burning issue in the world. If we compare what the global North has been spending on wars and now on climate change with what has been really done in regard to poverty, there is no comparison, they told us. And they made similar arguments in their writings.[16]

Again, we find here the remarkable convergence of long-term self-interest and regard for others, in one globalized world. Without substantial new value creation in the global South, migration and political turmoil will threaten global stability and will therefore threaten long-term Northern security interests. So, if not out of moral considerations, then at least based on a clear calculation of long-term interests, the North, and therefore Europe, should really take the fight against global poverty seriously.

It is also in line with the due diligence discourse that we discussed above several times. This implies also a true commitment to fair trade regulations, especially for poor countries.[17]

16. A *Global Community of Sustainable Technology*. Another very important way in which Europe can contribute is its provision of low-cost clean technology for the production chains of products that enter Europe. This may greatly help in avoiding the 'waterbed effect' that occurs when production processes that become prohibited in Europe itself are used elsewhere with all their polluting and socially undesirable consequences. A well-designed policy of technology export and technological cooperation can be a good strategy for making the world cleaner. It may have the effect that other parts of the world do not have to go through the polluting stages of industrial development that Europe did. Compare this to how, for example, telecommunication technology in Africa has virtually skipped an entire stage of landline telephones, jumping immediately to mobile phones. In the same way, it is conceivable that new industrial enterprises don't need to go through a very polluting stage but can, with the help of clean technology, jump immediately to sustainable production methods. For the sake of the earth, Europe should be generous with 'green technology,' fully recognizing that the profit of this technology doesn't have to be financial but ecological in any case; green technology spread generously for a clean earth. Above, we called this a new version of the association with which modern Europe started: instead of a regional European Coal and Steel Community, Europe could now strive for a Global Community of Sustainable Technology (GCST).

Conclusion: The 'Third Europe' in the 'Third Europe'

A very rough 'Big History' sketch of the history of Europe could divide that history into three phases. At first, Europe was an area on the outskirts of the ancient world, largely inhabited by 'barbarians.' Much later than in the Ancient Near East, this area gave rise to an empire, the Roman Empire. But the Roman Empire didn't last, and the European part of the empire collapsed. Attempts to revive it – by Charlemagne, for example – were impressive but short-lived. Historians even refer to the period after his empire as the age of 'feudal violence.'[18]

It is only after this that Europe as we know it today came into existence, consisting of various parts that would eventually become nation states, the second phase of Europe. The specific culture, the European 'spirit,' if we may use this word, was formed mainly in monasteries and medieval cities (and it is mainly here that the ideas that we identified previously as 'Europe-II' took shape; see chapter 6). But in this phase the nation states did not really embody the humane ideas we described in chapter 6 but each gradually started to behave like global empires: conquering the world, competing with each other and fighting each other. This phase, which lasted roughly from 1200 to 1950, ended, or rather imploded, with two bloody world wars.

Now a third phase has started to emerge: a Europe of internal cooperation. The warring nation states somehow gave up some of their 'sovereignty' (historically a typical European term that includes the right to declare war on others) to find a new way of living together on one continent in line with its 'cooperative' tradition that was so much part of the civil societies within many European nations for centuries. This third phase of Europe has now lasted for about 70 years and is therefore still young (and fragile).

This 'Third Phase Europe,' Post-War Europe, has in turn gone through two main phases, and now a third phase of European cooperation can be discerned. The first phase was Europe as a peace project. To be sure, the ECSC, founded in 1951, was a vehicle for economic cooperation, but its founders, people like Robert Schuman and Jean Monnet, saw it as a way to ensure future peace on a war-ridden continent: *doux commerce* or *Wandel durch Handel*. In a second phase, the former means to an end (economy for peace) now became the end itself: a flourishing market economy seemed to increasingly become the main goal and justification of the European Union, perhaps with the euro as a symbolic culmination point. This phase coincided with and was deeply colored by the 'age of triumphant capitalism,' as we called it.

It seems that the post-war European project is now entering a third phase in which the redirection, the reorientation of the market economy is becoming the main goal and justification of European cooperation. To bring the market economy into balance with nature and to redirect it to human flourishing, not only in Europe itself but well beyond that continent, seems to be the brief of the 'Third Europe.'

Chapter 15

In Conclusion: Challenges and Recommendations for a Rejuvenated Europe

At the beginning of our journey in this book we pointed to the 'Rodrik trilemma' and adapted this to what we called the 'thorny triangle' facing Europe right now – and in a way not only Europe, but governments and businesses all over the world. It is quite obvious that a simple continuation of the way we have run our economies during the last 250 years, and especially again during the last half-century, is impossible in the long run. The results of the project to escape from poverty are impressive. But the time has come for a transition toward another type of economy in Europe as well as worldwide, an economy that is in balance with the regenerative potential of nature and that does justice to the equal dignity of humans. This implies a thorough reorientation of capitalism. This reorientation is propelled by and acquires its direction from a strong sense of the 'why,' a sense of the values that are at stake in our economies – the heart of the triangle.

But the transition can only be successful if as many people as possible can see the point of it and can participate in it and do not feel excluded or victimized by it. This is one of the corners. Difficult transitions require a sense of connectedness among the different layers of the population, being part of a community of partners who care for each other's well-being, no matter what. This is more a 'covenant' than a 'contract,' since a contract is always conditional. A covenant, however, stands for a bond-re-gardless-of-circumstances; it stands for belonging.

And to make matters even more complicated, the third corner of the triangle: this transition will have to be made in a world that is developing rapidly from a unipolar to a multipolar world and that has as a result become grimmer, harder, more competitive,

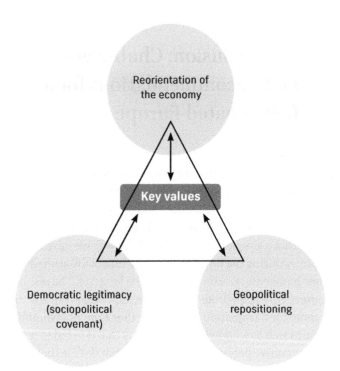

Figure 1: *Value-orientation within the Thorny Triangle of the Transition Towards a Sustainable, Inclusive and Innovative Economy*

with political and financial superpowers that are keen on pursuing their own interests, with almost no sense of shared interests or something like the common good, and in which the various 'poles' are progressing at very different speeds, if they are at all, regarding the proposed transition toward a more sustainable economy. What now looks like a rather peaceful intermezzo in the world after 1989 has come to an end.

As was indicated earlier in this book, Europe has experience with redirecting unfettered capitalism toward the common good. It is the continent of 'third ways,' and it should consciously strive to (again) become and be this. But the European nations, and Europe as a whole, have to 'play ball' in this new, multipolar world, protecting their own interests and their own people, but at the same time, as we have argued throughout this book, becoming a strong broker of international cooperation and an advocate of a global common good. There will be no easy solutions, and there will be many difficult trade-offs ahead. But many new opportunities emerge too.

Against the background just sketched, we see four types of challenges connected to the four elements of the 'thorny triangle': the three corners as well as the heart of the matter, values. We will discuss them in this final chapter and give a number of recommendations as to where to go from here.

Four Types of Key Challenges

Regarding the reorientation of the economy. The first type concerns the reorientation of the economy itself. A host of new ideas have been emerging in recent years, and we have tried to give an overview of these ideas in this book. And yes, Europe has been creative in the past in this regard, coming up with welfare states, social market economies, 'third ways,' civil economy, and so on. There are now many new concepts on the table, as we mentioned earlier: conscious capitalism, regenerative capitalism, progressive capitalism, moral capitalism, responsible capitalism, the doughnut economy, the economy for the common good, and so on. But while the earlier project of the reorientation of capitalism implied a distribution of the fruits of economic progress, making it available to what Adam Smith once called the "different ranks of the people," the new orientation may involve sacrifice and moving beyond what have come to be seen as established rights, such as unlimited consumption. This reorientation could be framed as not progress but regress. Psychologists often refer to the so-called 'endowment effect,' indicating that acquiring a new good gives less satisfaction compared to the sense of indignation when something you already have is taken away from you. You are moderately happy and surprised when someone gives you a present for your birthday. But if the giver has second thoughts and says "Well, I'm going to take the present with me again, after all," you will be outraged, and the party spoiled – even though you didn't have a clue about the existence and nature of the present an hour earlier. If the tone of voice and the content of the reorientation of the economy continually and primarily refers to 'less,' to going backwards, going down, it may become extremely difficult to engage people. On the other hand, not being honest about real changes in consumption patterns, investments, and jobs, for example, makes a transition untrustworthy and suspect. So it is essential to embed the reorientation of our economies in a discourse of realistic hope that doesn't plaster over difficulties, hardships, and challenges and yet gives a clear sense of moving toward a better future for both the present generation and (especially) the next generations, to which we want to bequeath a rejuvenated Europe.

It is in this line of thinking that we formulated the 'Five Pillars of Renewal' in this book: Ideals, Inspiration, Ideas, Indicators, and Institutions, each inspired by the core values of human dignity, generativity, inclusivity and co-creativity. And much of it is already going on, the air is full of new initiatives, of new creative solutions, of new entrepreneurship, of governments creating new frameworks, and so on. The flying wheel is moving, and we have to fuel it with new flows of energy that emerge from creative thinking in as many societal domains as possible, with multiple actors.

Regarding inclusivity / democratic legitimacy. The second type of challenges concerns the internal solidarity within European democracies. Recent socioeconomic developments are pointing in the direction of increasing inequality and a growing discrepancy between 'winners' and 'losers,' increasing anger about the 'elites' who take good care of themselves without protecting the 'ordinary people.' Almost all democracies in the world right now are haunted by the specter of 'populism' and the presence of identity movements. Most probably, this is no accident. It may have partly to do with disappointment about overblown expectations that have been fueled since the 1970s regarding ever-rising standards of living and ever-increasing democratic control by the people, which in a world dominated by social media is experienced more and more as 'control by me behind my screen.' And then disappointment is never far away.[1] But it certainly has to do also with the political and economic systems that are becoming more and more 'unresponsive,' complex, and opaque, not able to exercise authority,[2] fueling mysterious blame-games and outright conspiracy theories. If a transition toward a new type of economy isn't handled with great care, it may easily stimulate this anger and feed into a populist backlash. If the backlash is strong enough, the entire transition may come to a standstill – with serious long-term consequences.

We pointed above to the image of the 'covenant' as a symbol of a sense of shared fate and community. This is a point of attention especially at the European level. From a community point of view, what seems to be lacking in Europe, both at the European level and that of many nation states, is the engagement of citizens, a sense of bottom-up involvement. A 'mission' for a transition toward a new type of economy can be successful only if it is shared, involves everybody, and distributes both the advantages and the disadvantages fairly.

Regarding geopolitical and geoeconomic developments. The third type of challenge has to do with the geopolitical context. A new multipolar world is emerging in which those nations that are not able to act clearly as an independent 'pole' will be weak and cannot really be part of the agenda-setting for tomorrow. This may well be the fate of European nations if they are stuck in the memory of being a superpower once upon a time but are no longer. If they really want to have an impact, they need to act in unity and somehow make sure they are part of the new multipolar arena. The ball game has changed forever.

With the European Union and the other allied European nations, one of the largest integrated economic zones in the world has come into existence, which therefore can – and we say: must

– play its own role in the current geoeconomic constellation, with a distinct European idea about the relation between government and markets: with the courage to protect its citizens, the vision to engage in public goal setting, and the leverage to keep 'Big' economic powers in check (in a way that no national state within Europe would be able to do on its own, and neither the US or China are willing to), while maintaining and improving its democratic accountability. This 'Brussels effect,' to which we referred earlier, is of crucial geopolitical and geoeconomic significance.

In the new multipolar world, however, all the concerns that have been raised in the International Relations School of 'political realism' are becoming topical again. Think of the *si vis pacem, para bellum* paradigm ("if you want peace, prepare for war"). Formulated a bit more broadly, if you lack the economic, political, and military strength that is the superpower standard in tomorrow's world, you will be sidelined and have no influence at all. But how can this be squared with the value orientation that we are advocating as well? Here are a host of dilemmas that have to be faced directly, without taking refuge in moral purity or the cynicism of power politics. How are the many autocratic regimes in the world, that don't care about human rights nor ecological sustainability – especially when they are key providers of energy or other raw materials – to be dealt with? Whose agenda should prevail? An ethics of compromise is an urgent necessity, steering between the Scylla of utopian wishful thinking and the Charybdis of moral cynicism.

Values. Last but not least are the fourth type of challenges. These are not often discussed in policy documents and day-to-day politics because what they are about is often just assumed without much articulation: the dimension of values. In this book we have given extensive attention to it. Historically, Europe is a very ambivalent continent regarding values. We even made a distinction between 'Europe-I' and 'Europe-II.' There is a Europe of oppression and exploitation, of the social question and the class struggle internally and imperialism, colonialism, slavery externally. But there is also a

Europe of human dignity, the rule of law, cooperation, democracy, 'third way capitalism,' the abolition of slavery, and human rights. There is a clear risk that both internally and externally the legacy of 'Europe-I' is silencing the advocacy of 'Europe-II.' In this book, we have argued, however, that this second Europe should be the future of Europe and the Europe of the future. Added to this mix should be the value of regenerativity, with a view to the ecological embeddedness of human activities.

So in Europe a new, moderate, purified sense of value consciousness is needed that should be retained with as much moderation (because of the past) as determination (because of the future). A Europe that consciously defends values, human rights, global cooperation, and the SDGs cannot be missed in today's and tomorrow's world. Yes, European moral arrogance and dominance has in the past resulted in immense harm, but giving up on a values-driven agenda now will result in great harm as well. Europe should present itself, internally and externally, on the one hand as a continent that has learned and is continuing to learn and is willing to learn from its mistakes. But it also has to present itself as committed at the same time to values that it has itself discovered often through painful processes and has found them to be of the utmost importance for human wellbeing and now as well for the survival of the planet itself, or better: the possibility of humans living well on the planet.

The key risks seem to be cynicism and relativism, combined with and engendering short-termism both within and outside Europe. An attitude of *après nous le déluge* may abound. But still, Europe shouldn't give up on the universal appeal of these values (and the protests against autocratic regimes, in China itself or in Iran itself are a strong indication of this).

Recommendations

Against the background of the challenges just outlined, we give the following recommendations.

I. On the Reorientation of the Economy

– **Balance with nature.** At the present time, 'nature' isn't represented very well in our democracies. Concerns about the environment are too often relegated to small groups of idealists and activists. 'Nature ambassadors' should be brought into positions of influence and power in all types of governments and businesses.

Although the reduction of carbon emissions is one of the key assignments for the next decades, bringing our economy in balance with nature goes much further than that: biodiversity, waste-pollution, the 'chemistrification' of food and food production are problems that need to be addressed as well. Increasingly, regenerativity should be a fundamental design principle for all production processes – and that implies that the definitions of technology and technological progress are going to change.

– **Institutional architecture: Balance between markets, state, civil society/community.** A new, balanced relationship between market, states (including the EU), and civil society/community is key to the ecological and social embedding of the economy. Governments, at the local, regional, and national level, including the EU as an intergovernmental institution, should implement long-term policies ('public goal setting,' 'mission'), create level playing fields, and reward sustainable innovation. Civil society can be the constant source of critical and alternative ways of thinking and doing. Businesses play a major role in making things really happen through innovative and sustainable entrepreneurship.

– **Active governments.** As distinct from mainstream ideology during the last 50 years, there is an active role for governments in the European Economic Model of the future (at various levels, from the local to the EU level). Markets need embedding. Governments shouldn't be big overall planners but public goal setters, 'embedders' of markets, providing clear legislation whenever this is needed for a transition toward a regenerative, inclusive economy. Government action is needed as well to prevent markets from becoming socially divisive forces by, for example, providing safety nets. A Japanese-style 'top runner program' may well speed up the transition to a regenerative economy: reward the innovators.

Another key element is shifting the tax burden from an almost exclusive focus on labor to bringing it more into balance with desirable outcomes – thus to capital and non-regenerative consumption. 'Fair pricing' is part of this active role of governments in close cooperation with the business sector and with consumers.

Active governments, including the EU, are focused on visible results, on solving issues, not on endlessly postponing and avoiding. Herman van Rompuy used to speak about a 'Europe of Results.'

– **Multiactorship and the power of initiative.** Embedding the economy in society and nature, however, can in no way be a task only for governments. That would totally distort and perhaps even kill the needed reorientation of the market economy. It is at once a technological, financial, economic, political, intellectual, and a moral and even spiritual challenge. It is a shared 'mission' that requires cooperation by very different actors – and yet, no actor should wait for the others to take initiative. Each has the 'power of initiative' to start cooperative networks for developing and implementing the 'greening' of production and consumption.

– **Businesses as problem-solving communities.** Businesses in the European economic model are very important actors in solving problems for stakeholders and making a profit in doing that. Profits are a means for the continuation of the potential to solve problems, but not the ultimate goal of a company. The goal of a company should be to be a 'net positive' problem solver for key stakeholders without creating problems for other stakeholders. This implies that businesses should see themselves as creative and crafting communities in which people with very different talents and insights cooperate. Moreover, businesses are 'citizens' with public duties and responsibilities (of which paying taxes is a very basic, but certainly not the only, responsibility).

– **Finance for the common good.** Financial structure and financial agencies are also at the heart of the capitalist system. They have to recognize their substantial responsibility for the real value that is produced with their money. Therefore, financial institutions in Europe should reformulate their goals and make 'participatory investments' a substantial part of their activities and reduce the percentage of share investment (in Dutch: from *beleggen* to *investeren*). In that way, resources can be made available for the reorientation of the economy toward ecological and social innovation.

While a lot of attention is going to banks, not only banks, but also investors, like hedgefunds, should have a formal 'license to operate' in European economies, with rights and duties. The duties should also include the duty to comply with 'integrated reporting.' In a balanced economy, it is not consistent to require integrated reporting from corporations but not from those actors who have such a determining influence, even outright power, about the financial possibilities for companies.

II. On Internal Legitimacy

– **Connecting the 'different layers of the people.'** Embedding the economy in society requires social and democratic innovation. An 'elite-driven reset' should be avoided. The renewal of the economy should not derail into a 'feel-good' exercise for the elite. The focus should always be on how this can be a project in which all participate, in which all may have to bring sacrifices (especially those who are able to cope with sacrifices), and in which all can share in the advantages – a fair distribution of sacrifice and gains.

It is a very interesting phenomenon that recently for the first time a European political party ('Volt') has been able to organize itself in various countries. And the European Union is investing a great deal of effort in consulting civil society organizations on all kinds of issues. Recently, the first European Citizens' Consultations have been organized – in line with the G1000 initiatives, again at the initiative of the French president Macron – that are now being followed up by European Citizens' Panels on topics like democracy, climate change, and digital transformation. These initiatives – when they become better known among the European population – may turn out to be important tools for creating a sense of ownership, of belonging, at the European level, provided their outcomes are taken very seriously by the formal political institutions.

– **Starting with the least advantaged.** To ensure that the transition to a sustainable economy and sustainable life standard will not become a privilege of the rich (who can afford Teslas and solar panels), the plans for the transition from fossil energy to renewables should include an EU-wide plan to prioritize social housing. This even can be budget neutral: in the long run, the savings brought about by renewable energy will be such that the initial costs can be covered in any case. So institutional investors should be stimulated to take a leading role. Starting with the housing of those who are least well off, and then working upwards in society (a kind of reversed 'trickle-down' theory) may greatly increase the support for a transition to a green economy and a sense of solidarity.

– **A fairer top earnings/low earnings ratio**. A key token of solidarity between elites and 'common people' is the ratio of top earnings to low earnings within a company. The argument often goes like this: 'In order to really make sure we have the most competent persons at the top of the corporation, we need to pay them extraordinarily well and give high bonuses.' One can ask, however, whether the very desire to get rich beyond any measure at the cost of solidarity is not a disqualifier for any function in the business sector. Leadership is about bringing the various types of capital – financial, human, social, technological – together and let them all flourish in their own way. If a leader is motivated only by financial capital, he (indeed, usually 'he') is by definition not qualified as a leader.

– **Basic income or basic jobs.** To make sure that people do not feel excluded, proposals have been made by various parties that go in the direction of what is often called a 'basic income' (a 'Universal Basic Income,' 'participation income,' 'negative income tax,' etc.). For us, it seems more promising to investigate whether a system of basic jobs is conceivable to make sure that people can always participate in meaningful networks of production and cooperation. A basic income can easily lead to employers getting rid of personnel if they are 'taken care of' by the state. A system of basic jobs is therefore preferable. It is thus typically a multiactor endeavor: social security is neither an exclusive government responsibility (an 'externality' for business), nor can it be left to the market. It requires smart cooperation between governments, market actors, and civil society. The 'Slovenian model' may an interesting source of inspiration (see above, chapter 11, section 1).

– **New room for cooperatives.** To find new connections between people and businesses, including finance, much more generous and well-designed legal provisions should be put in place for establishing cooperatives and the equivalents of what are called 'Public Benefit Corporations' in the USA. The cooperative is a typical old European invention that still has great potential to align business and the common good. There are still large cooperatives in agriculture, in housing and in finance, to mention a few areas. But more room should be created not only for starting a cooperative, for example, but also for transforming existing companies into cooperatives (or public benefit corporations). When operating well, cooperatives are uniquely positioned to shield people from the negative effects of unfettered capitalism, creating long-term safety.

III. Geopolitical and Geoeconomic Challenges

– **Geopolitical and geoeconomic actorship**. European nations will have to reposition themselves as geoeconomic and geopolitical actors. Although the USA will remain the primary and preferred partner, the world as a whole needs advocates for a different type of economy than that of the USA. Europe should be the laboratory and advocate of a 'third way' between unfettered capitalism and state-led capitalism. Given the scale of globalized relationships, it is clear that no European nation can do this on its own. That's why it's essential to strengthen the EU and enable it to act on as a geopolitical entity on behalf of all European nations with a clear agenda to defend common interests of Europe and at the same time promote human dignity, sustainability, and inclusivity, as values that Europe itself has learned – and is still learning – to honor throughout its long and often difficult history.

– **Balanced globalization.** In recent decades, the relation between globalization and strategic autonomy has been out of balance. Globalization is very important because it gives great opportunities for wealth creation. But each economic zone should assess what a healthy regional economy should entail: What kinds of products and services are essential for that zone to produce itself? A more differentiated economy creates macroeconomic and geopolitical robustness. Moreover, a good balance between 'blue-collar' and 'white-collar' jobs is also a crucial requirement, given that it is not to be expected that an entire continent only has people who can flourish in one of these types of professions. The macro emphasis on a knowledge economy may threaten those whose main talents are not intellectual but more practical. A healthy economy, based on human dignity, has a plurality of types of jobs on offer for its population.

Moreover, to have a differentiated economy at a national or European scale also creates a macroeconomic and geopolitical robustness. If all the production is outsourced to other parts of the world, this creates a particular vulnerability, especially in times of geopolitical tension or disasters. This has the production of food in view as well. To pursue a more balanced, long-term globalization policy, is also one of the lessons of the Covid crisis.

Nonetheless, a more balanced approach to globalization should at the same time go together with an increased effort to stimulate the economic development of countries in the global South. The relation with Africa and India should especially be given new attention. Special task forces on raw materials and on sensitive technologies will have to further identify what is needed for Europe's long-term 'strategic autonomy.'

– **Global impact scan.** We argued above that in a way the present world situation is still very much continuing the old colonial situation. In that sense, the world economy can be called neo-colonial, instead of postcolonial. This is not sustainable in the long run. The North cannot take advantage of the need for jobs and prosperity in the South by avoiding the responsibility for pollution and exploitation of the products it is using. Therefore, European nations and/or the EU should do an honest scan about the global social and environmental impact of its own production and consumption. This could serve as a starting point for moving toward a more balanced world in which Europe takes responsibility for its own 'footprint' and can start to assist countries in the South to reduce this. A clean, zero-emission Europe in 2050 is an empty symbol if the pollution continues to be exported to other countries.

– **Green Technology Hub.** The ecological threats to today's world are such that the broadest possible coalitions in the world must be built. Europe should strive to become the Green Technology Hub of the world. A Global Community of Sustainable Technology (GCST) could be a worthy successor of the 1951 ECSC. When Europe is making deals with countries regarding raw materials, it should at the same time commit to working actively with those countries to organize the mining process in such a way that it is as regenerative as possible. For both moral reasons and long-term geopolitical reasons, Europe should be known in the world as the continent that does not live or no longer wants to live at the cost of other continents but really works with them. 'Waterbed effects' should be prevented.

IV. Regarding Values

– **Rethinking and re-presenting values.** European nations, separately and together, need to consciously rethink their leading values and work on a sense of shared mission based on that. This shared mission will have to acknowledge the darker sides of Europe's past as well as the plurality of European nations and the diversity of their histories. And yet, Europe's nations can find a new mission in line with some of their best traditions, centering around human dignity, inclusivity/solidarity, co-creativity, and ecological regenerativity. What is important is that these values be presented in the public sphere and not hidden in some obscure documents. Values can only function when they are talked about, including – in the best of European tradition – critical discussion.

– **The (limited) value of markets.** European nations have to develop a new perspective on the role the market economy has to play in their societies. Embedding the economy in society and in nature is the challenge of the 21st century. Market economies should not be allowed to develop into full-blown market societies in which the pursuit of material-financial self-interest is dominant in all spheres of life. Value is much more than financial value and encompasses social and ecological value – in general 'sustainable human wellbeing.' This implies a thorough reorientation of capitalism. The shareholder approach that has been dominant in the economy has to give way to a stakeholder approach or, better, a multiactor approach in which diverse actors, businesses, governments, communities, and civil society actors develop new partnerships to realize common purposes. The economy doesn't have people; people have economies to improve the quality of life and realize common goals.

– **A new 'art of measurement.'** A new 'art of measurement' is essential for assessing how the reorientation of the economy and how businesses are doing. The movement away from the dominance of GDP and financial profits and toward broader sets of measures at the national level (happiness, wellbeing, better life, etc.), the level of business (integrated reporting), and the level of market transactions (true pricing) should be stimulated not only as means for evaluation. This broader sets of measures should also be stimulated as prospective tools for designing new policies and business strategies (from redressing and compensation to prevention and innovation). Without measurement, values can easily remain non-committal.

Of course, we could get as many 'integrated standards' as there are countries or business sectors. Standardization is highly recommended and the EU can take further steps in this respect.[3]

– **New Economic Thinking.** The EU should organize a task force and annex a research project 'New Economic Thinking.' This project would be aimed at collecting and assessing new ideas about how to organize an ecologically regenerative and socially inclusive economy for future generations and come up with recommendations for implementing this at the EU level, with full regard for cultural and economic differences within the EU. The outcomes of this research project can also stimulate new educational materials that provide younger generations with a plurality of new economic insights.

– **Young Nobel Prizes for sustainability and inclusivity.** To stimulate the development of knowledge among the young generations regarding sustainability and inclusivity, one could think of instituting a new type of 'Nobel Prize' at the European level, especially for representatives of younger generations, who have come up with breakthrough solutions and innovative knowledge in these areas.

In Conclusion

We believe that the world of tomorrow cannot do without a Europe that is really prepared to act on behalf of the future of tomorrow's world. Europe should be prepared to reform its own economy and, as much as possible, the global economy in such a way that it contributes to human wellbeing and is fully sustainable.

It looks like self-interest and the common interest are coming together at this time in history in a way it never has before. In the 21st century, we are becoming aware that we are ultimately one human race living on one, finite planet. It is certainly possible that the future will see a great deal of self-interested infighting and competition regarding the limited resources. Wars, even worlds wars, are not inconceivable. But Europe should do all it can do to prevent this and hence be and become a force for just peace, for cooperation, for sustainability – and the entire world will reap the fruits. We should be the generation that chooses to shape our economy in such a way that we can pass it on to the next generation so they can live – and live well.

Epilogue

Towards an Economics of Hope

Hope is not the same as joy that things are going well, or willingness to invest in enterprises that are obviously heading for success, but rather an ability to work for something because it is good, not just because it stands a chance to succeed. Hope is definitely not the same thing as optimism. It is not the conviction that something will turn out well, but the certainty that something makes sense, regardless of how it turns out. It is also this hope which gives us the strength to live and continually to try new things.

Vaclav Havel[1]

In one of his poems, the English poet Matthew Arnold describes a mood in which he found himself "wandering between two worlds, one dead, the other powerless to be born."[2] This line was later almost literally repeated by the Marxist Antonio Gramsci, who spoke in his *Prison Notebook* about the crisis that he saw in interbellum Europe consisting "precisely in the fact that the old is dying and the new cannot be born; in this interregnum a great variety of morbid symptoms appear."[3]

It may be clear from this book that we share the sense of 'wandering between two worlds,' but we do not share the sense of the powerlessness of the new. On the contrary, economic thinkers, businesses, consumers, politicians – many are working on a new, more humane, and more sustainable regenerative economy. As we speak/write, the 'Flying wheel' we identified is running, with increasing speed.

And yet, the morbid symptoms loom large in our time, too. We indicated some of the dangerous dynamics in chapter 4. It has somewhat become fashionable to illustrate the looming dangers by referring to apocalyptic stories, 'inconvenient truths.' A strong apocalyptic mood pervades our present discourse. And of course, there is reason enough to tell stories of doom. It is certainly necessary to have the facts on the table, so the work of the IPCC (Intergovernmental Panel on Climate Change) is to be lauded.

And yet, there is a danger that all this is paralyzing, and paralysis and action do not go well together. Martin Luther King – in dire circumstances – mobilized us with his dream, not his nightmare.

That is why we call for 'hope' in this epilogue. Hope is – as the Czech anti-communist dissident, later post-communist president Vaclav Havel reminded us – not the same as optimism. Optimism can be described as the expectation that things will get better anyway, simply by extrapolating of some current trends that we like, often while turning a blind eye to other trends that we don't like. In the millennia-old tradition of virtue ethics, 'hope' is different in that it is a virtue, which is a character trait that is not inborn – neither is it always borne out by the current facts – but can be and has to be acquired and strengthened by practice, just like a muscle, especially in difficult circumstances. Hope is an act of courage in that it looks for a different future, that may or may not have started to emerge already.

But hope is not without foundation or reason. There is reason for hope, and this hope is based not in the extrapolation of current trends but in the ability of humans to adapt to new circumstances, the ability to 'rise to the occasion' or 'the challenge,' precisely in times when this is an urgent necessity. For hope as a viable path between utopian optimism and dystopian despair, three things are needed:[4] first, a realistic acknowledgement of facts, hence no hiding from the truth; second, an attitude of openness to new solutions; and third, intellectual humility, thus rejecting the assumption that we can technically shape reality as we see fit. To the contrary, there are degrees of uncontrollability, and, to state it in a positive way, surprises are possible. Poverty at once seemed to be ineradicable, and yet, in the course of the 19th century, the escape from poverty gradually became a reality, as we argued earlier. It was a surprise by any standards, but a surprise for which the ground had been prepared. We can and must do something similar now: redirect our economies toward long-term sustainability and social wellbeing/human flourishing. What we have been trying to outline in this book can ultimately be seen as the groundwork for an economics of hope.[5]

In one of his last books, the Dutch economist Bob Goudzwaard used three metaphors regarding hope.[6] Hope requires 'periscopes': people in a submarine need an enlarged vision, a bigger picture of where they are going, above the surface of short-term waves and tides. We have tried to give something like this periscope vision in this book. Hope also needs 'minesweepers': identifying the deeper threats and long-term dangers that my pop up any time, if they are not really addressed. We have tried to point out mistaken assumptions in both modern Western culture and in economics that we should get rid of, in order to sail safely toward a new future. And hope requires 'rope ladders': identifying opportunities to climb out of the problems by coordinated action, two hands, two feet: let's say, in our terms, a multiactor approach.

One issue that we have not discussed extensively in this book, but which is certainly critical, is that of leadership. We seem to have plenty of managers (involved in running business as usual) but we are in dire need of leaders who can break new ground, because they are able to bring together their values with an attitude of hope. And yet, we did discuss leadership in a way: we spoke of the 'power of initiative' that resides in each of us, in our own context. Everybody who takes initiatives for a more socially inclusive and ecologically sustainable world – from young children to pensioners, from practical artisans to theoretical scientists, from left to right, from the 'lowest ranks' in a company to the boardroom – is, by definition a leader and carves out a path others can follow, starts a dance in which others can join. As the 20th-century historian Arnold Toynbee stated, history is not made by those who follow the majority but by creative minorities who set the tone of a new era. As far as we are concerned, this era will be that of responsible capitalism, a market economy that contributes to human flourishing within ecological boundaries.

Overview of online dialogue sessions – Fall 2021

The Future of Capitalism in Europe
Evaluating and Transforming Market Economies

September 21 (18.30 – 20.00 CET) – First Dialogue: *Joseph Stiglitz and Herman van Rompuy*
- What Really Matters in Markets: The Long-Term Challenges for Europe

September 28 (18.30 – 20.00 CET) – Second Dialogue: *Rebecca Henderson and Colin Mayer*
- The Future Role of Business as a Force for Good

October 5 (18.30 – 20.00 CET) – Third Dialogue: *Raghuram Rajan and Paul Collier*
- Inside Markets, Outside Markets: The Role of Non-Market Actors and Spheres (Civil Society/Communities, the State)

October 12 (18.30 – 20.00 CET) – Fourth Dialogue: *Isabelle Ferreras and Josh Ryan-Collins*
- The Effects of Market Distortions on Everyday Life: The Precariousness of Work in a Digitalized Capitalism and the Precariousness of Housing

October 19 (18.30 – 20.00 CET) – Fifth Dialogue: *Elizabeth Anderson and François Bourguignon*
- Free Markets and Huge Inequality: An Inescapable Marriage?

<u>October 26 – Sixth Dialogue:</u> *__Mohammad Yunus and Jeffrey__*
__Sachs__
- **Aligning Economies Worldwide to Ending Poverty: The Role of Europe in the Global Economy**

<u>November 2 (18.30 – 20.00 CET) Seventh Dialogue:</u> *__Julia Stein-__*
__berger and Ann Pettifor__
- **How Can Markets Be Reconciled with Ecology?**

<u>November 9 (18.30 – 20.00 CET) Eight Dialogue:</u> *__Rana Foroohar__*
__and Jonathan Taplin__
- **The New Corporate Power Concentrations in Finance and Tech and the Possibilities for Checking Them**

<u>November 16 (18.30 – 20.00 CET) – Ninth Dialogue:</u> *__Christian__*
__Felber and Luigi Zingales__
- **Can a Different Market Economy Work in Practice?**

<u>November 23 (18.30 – 20.00 CET) – Tenth Dialogue:</u> *__Tito Boeri__*
__(Italy), Luis Garicano (Spain),__
    __Dalia Marin (Austria/Germany), and Geert Noels (Belgium)__
- **European Perspectives**

Endnotes

By way of introduction

1. "Europe. A Beautiful Idea?" See https://www.feelingeurope.eu/ Pages/europe%20a%20beautiful%20idea.pdf. Organized with the Nexus Institute.
2. See Appendix 1 for an overview of the Dialogue sessions, and for recordings (see https://dezwijger.nl/programmareeks/future-of-capitalism).
3. See https://www.moralmarkets.org/futuremarketsconsultation/activities/think-tank/.
4. In this section we will not provide the exact academic titles and/or credentials of the participants but simply their names.

Chapter 1

1. See below, chapter 8.
2. Thane Gustafson, *Klimat: Russia in the Age of Climate Change* (Cambridge, MA: Harvard University Press, 2021).
3. Dani Rodrik, *The Globalization Paradox: Democracy and the Future of the World Economy* (New York: Norton, 2011).
4. As argued by R. James Breiding, *Too Small to Fail: Why Some Small Nations Outperform Larger Ones and How They Are Reshaping the World* (New York: Harper Business, 2019).
5. Manuel Funke, Moritz Schularick, and Christoph Trebesch, "Going to Extremes: Politics after Financial Crises, 1870–2014," European Economic Review 88, issue C (2016): 227–60.
6. https://managementscope.nl/en/magazine/article/5187-feike-sijbesma-sustainability.
7. Jonathan Sacks, *The Home We Build Together: Recreating Society* (London: Continuum, 2007).
8. Ulrich Beck, Wolfgang Bonss, and Christoph Lau, "The Theory of Reflexive Modernization: Problematic, Hypotheses and Research Programme," *Theory, Culture & Society* 20, no. 20 (2003): 1–33.
9. To give some indications of who is using the various terms: "responsible capitalism" is found in a report by the Institut Montaigne (see *Responsible Capitalism: An Opportunity for Europe.* Paris, 2020); "moral capitalism" is used by Stephen Young

(2003, 2014); "conscious capitalism" by John Mackey and Raj Sisodia (see *Conscious Capitalism: Liberating the Heroic Spirit of Business*. Boston: Harvard Business Review Press, 2013); "regenerative capitalism" by John Fullerton (see *Regenerative Capitalism: How Universal Principles and Patterns Will Shape Our New Economy*. Greenwich, CT: Capital Institute, 2015); "progressive capitalism" comes from Joseph E. Stiglitz (see *People, Power, and Profits: Progressive Capitalism for an Age of Discontent*. London, Allen Lane, 2019); an "economy for the common good" by Christian Felber (see *Change Everything: Creating an Economy for the Common Good*. London: Zed Books, 2019) and in slightly different terms by Jean Tirole (see *Economics for the Common Good*, trans. Steven Rendall. Princeton: Princeton University Press, 2017); "doughnut economics" was introduced by Kate Raworth (see *Doughnut Economics: Seven Ways to Think Like a 21st-Century Economist*. London: Random House, 2017); "an economy of arrival" by Katherine Trebeck and Jeremy Williams (see *The Economics of Arrival: Ideas for a Grown-Up Economy*. Bristol: Policy Press, 2019); "complete capitalism" by Bruno Roche and Jay Jakub (see *Completing Capitalism: Heal Business to Heal the World*. Oakland, CA: Berrett-Koehler, 2017); "democratic capitalism" by Martin Wolf (see *The Crisis of Democratic Capitalism*. New York: Penguin, 2023). Rebecca Henderson has titled her book *Reimagining Capitalism: How Business Can Save the World* (London: Penguin, 2020), a title that is parallel to Dominic Barton, Dezsö Horváth, and Matthias Kipping, eds., *Re-Imagining Capitalism* (London: Oxford University Press, 2016), which again sounds quite close to Michael Jacobs and Mariana Mazzucato, eds., *Rethinking Capitalism: Economics and Policy for Sustainable and Inclusive Growth* (Nashville: John Wiley & Sons, 2016). Paul Mills and Michael Schluter search for the time "after capitalism" with a plea for "relational economics" (see *After Capitalism: Rethinking Economic Relationships*. Cambridge: Jubilee Centre, 2012). Others also envisage a "post-capitalist" era (see Paul Mason, *PostCapitalism: A Guide to Our Future*. London, Allen Lane, 2015; Wolfgang Streeck, *How Will Capitalism End?* London: Verso, 2016) or 'life after capitalism' (Tim Jackson, *Post Growth: Life after Capitalism*. Cambridge: Polity, 2021). This list is by no means exhaustive. For full bibliographical data see the References section at the end of this book.

10. Stiglitz argued this explicitly as well in his 2020 book *Rewriting the Rules of the European Economy: An Agenda for Growth and Shared Prosperity* (New York: Norton), especially in the final chapter on Europe and globalization. "Europe will have to take the lead. There is simply no other plausible candidate, at least until a period of reactionary politics eases in the United States' (p. 289). In a way our book is a modest attempt to respond to this call.

11. Geoffrey M. Hodgson, *Conceptualizing Capitalism: Institutions, Evolution, Future* (Chicago: University of Chicago Press, 2015).

12. Cf. Bas van Bavel, *The Invisible Hand? How Market Economies Have Emerged and Declined since AD 500* (Oxford: Oxford University Press, 2016), pp. 271ff.

13. Karl Marx, *Das Kapital: Kritik der politischen Ökonomie*, vol. 1 (Berlin: Dietz Verlag, 1975 [1867]), ch. 3 and 4, especially pp. 118–28 (ch. 3, sec. 2.a), 161–70 (ch. 4, sec. 2).

14. As Marx states very poignantly, "Akkumuliert! Akkumuliert! Das ist Moses und die Propheten!. ... Akkumulation um die Akkumulation, Produktion um der Produktion willen, in dieser Formel sprach die klassische Ökonomie den historische Beruf der Bourgeoisperiode aus." Ibid., p. 621.

15. This distinction between market economies and market societies is derived from Michael Sandel, *What Money Can't Buy: The Moral Limits of Markets* (New York: Farrar, Strauss and Giroux, 2012), p. 10.

16. This distinction goes back to Karl Polanyi, *The Great Transformation: The Political and Economic Origins of Our Time* (Boston: Beacon Press, 1944/1957), pp. 45–58.

17. For example, Raghuram Rajan, *The Third Pillar: How Markets and the State Are Leaving Communities Behind* (London: William Collins, 2019). The argument is often traced back to Alfred Hirschman, *Exit, Voice, and Loyalty: Responses to Decline in Firms, Organizations, and States* (Cambridge, MA: Harvard University Press, 1970). But it is also a rather consistent line of thinking in Christian social thought that can be traced back to the papal encyclical issued by Leo X, *Rerum Novarum* (1891), and in the Netherlands to the opening address of Abraham Kuyper at the first Christian Social Congress in 1891, entitled *Het sociale vraagstuk en de Christelijke religie*. Translated as "The Social Question and the Christian Religion," republished in *On Business and Economics: Collected Works of Abraham Kuyper in*

Public Theology, ed. Jordan J. Ballor, Melvin Flikkema, and Peter Heslam (Bellingham: Lexham Press, 2021), vol. 11, pp. 169–230.

18. In a sense one can speak here of an economic parallel to the famous 'Böckenförde Dilemma' in the political realm, which states that "Der freiheitliche, säkularisierte Staat lebt von Voraussetzungen die er selbst nicht garantieren kann" (The liberal, secularized state lives by prerequisites which it cannot guarantee itself). See Ernst-Wolfgang Böckenförde, *Staat, Gesellschaft, Freiheit: Studieren zur Staatstheorie und zum Verfassungsrecht* (Frankfurt: Suhrkamp, 1976), p. 60. An economic analogy seems to hold: a well-functioning economy, if it is to continue to function well (that is, in a way that contributes to human flourishing), is dependent on moral and social, perhaps even spiritual, preconditions that it cannot provide itself – non-market goods are essential for markets.

19. On the role of ideology, see Thomas Piketty, *Capital and Ideology*, trans. Arthur Goldhammer (Cambridge, MA: Harvard University Press, 2020).

20. Edmund Burke (1790), *Reflections on the Revolution in France*. (There are many extant editions, both online and in print, but all without further chapters or parts, the quote is to be found about two-fifths of the way into the text).

21. Thunberg has now brought together many scientists to further explore the state of the climate in Greta Thunberg, *The Climate Book* (London: Allen Lane/Penguin, 2022).

22. Manuel Castells, *The Rise of the Network Society*, vol. 1 of *The Information Age* trilogy (Oxford: Blackwell, 1996), p. 25, cf. vol. 2 of the trilogy: *The Power of Identity* (Oxford: Blackwell, 1997/2004); Wendy Brown, *Undoing the Demos: Neoliberalism's Stealth Revolution* (New York: Zone, 2015); Francis Fukuyama, *Liberalism and its Discontents* (London: Profile, 2022).

Chapter 2

1. Deirdre McCloskey, *Bourgeois Equality: How Ideas, Not Capital or Institutions Enriched the World* (Chicago: University of Chicago Press, 2016).

2. The explanation of why this project happened in Europe and not, for example, in China, which had been economically and technologically more advanced than Europe in prior centuries, has already occupied historians since the 19th century.

Some explanations are more in line with Marx, focusing on the material bases of economies, raw materials, energy, and above all cheap labor, both inside and outside Europe (proletarians, slaves), while others are more in agreement with Max Weber (see *The Protestant Ethic and the Spirit of Capitalism* (New York: Charles Scribner's Sons, 1905)), focusing on the 'spirit' of capitalism and/or the cultural characteristics of Europe. The literature on this is immense. To mention just a few more recent studies: David Landes, *Wealth and Poverty of Nations* (London: Little, Brown, 1998); Kenneth Pomeranz, *The Great Divergence: China, Europe, and the Making of the Modern World Economy* (Princeton: Princeton University Press, 2000), and also P.H.H. Vries "Are Coal and Colonies Really Crucial? Kenneth Pomeranz and the Great Divergence," *Journal of World History* 12, no. 2 (Fall 2001): 407–46, the works of Daron Acemoglu and James A. Robinson *Why Nations Fail: The Origins of Power, Prosperity, and Poverty* (New York: Crown, 2012), and idem, *The Narrow Corridor: States, Societies and the Fate of Liberty* (New York: Penguin, 2019); McCloskey's trilogy on bourgeois culture, *The Bourgeois Virtues: Ethics for an Age of Commerce* (Chicago: University of Chicago Press, 2006) *Bourgeois Dignity: Why Economics Can't Explain the Modern World* (Chicago: University of Chicago Press, 2010), *Bourgeois Equality: How Ideas, Not Capital or Institutions Enriched the World* (Chicago: University of Chicago Press, 2016); and Joel Mokyr, *A Culture of Growth: The Origins of the Modern Economy* (Princeton: Princeton University Press, 2016). There is no way we can go into this field here, let alone draw any conclusions. But the safest way would be to assume that a combination of exploitative extraction (since the 17th century) and a tradition of social and technological creativity and innovation since the High Middle Ages together form the background of the European *Sonderweg.*

3.   Adam Smith, *An Inquiry Into the Nature and Causes of the Wealth of Nations*, ed. Edwin Cannan (New York: The Modern Library, 1776), book I, ch. 1.

4.   For a readable account of this progress, see Hans Rosling, *Factfulness: Ten Reasons We're Wrong About the World – And Why Things Are Better than You Think* (London: Sceptre, 2018). Other books that – proudly – list the progress of humanity are Rutger Bregman, *De geschiedenis van de vooruitgang* (Amsterdam: De Bezig Bij, 2013); Steven Pinker, *Enlightenment Now: The Case for*

Reason, Science, Humanism, and Progress (New York: Penguin, 2018), and Maarten Boudry, *Waarom de wereld niet naar de knoppen gaat* (Kalmthout: Polis, 2019). Peter Diamandis and Steven Kotler, *Abundance: The Future is Better than You Think* (New York: Free Press, 2012), extrapolate these positive developments to the future. Pessimists have a lot to think about here.

5. And conversely, the belief in progress stimulated innovation and the acceptance of new technologies. Of the immense literature, let us merely point to some older studies, if only to save them from oblivion: J.B. Bury, *The Idea of Progress: An Inquiry Into its Origin and Growth* (New York: Dover, [1932] 1960); Carl L. Becker, *The Heavenly City of the Eighteenth Century Philosophers* (New Haven: Yale University Press, 1932); Bob Goudzwaard, *Capitalism and Progress. A Diagnosis of Western Society* (Grand Rapids: Eerdmans, 1979); Robert Nisbet, *History of the Idea of Progress* (London: Routledge, 1994).

6. Gøsta Esping-Anderson, *The Three Worlds of Welfare Capitalism* (Princeton: Princeton University Press, 1990).

7. Theo van de Klundert, *Kapitalisme: Over de dominantie van kapitaal en de lange uitzondering* (Utrecht: Eburon, 2019). Van de Klundert refers to Jeffrey Helgeson, "American Labor and Working-Class History, 1900–1945," *Oxford Research Encyclopedia of American History* (Oxford: Oxford University Press, 2016). But Helgeson himself refers to Jefferson Cowie and Nick Salvatore, "The Long Exception: Rethinking the Place of the New Deal in American History," *International Labor and Working-Class History* 74, no. 1 (2008): 3–32.

8. Thomas Piketty, *Capital in the Twenty-First Century* (Cambridge, MA: Belknap/Harvard University Press, 2014).

9. The influential books of the time were Friedrich Hayek (1944), *The Road to Serfdom* (reprinted in Bruce Caldwell, ed., *Collected Works of F.A. Hayek*, vol. 2 (Chicago: University of Chicago Press, 2007)) and his later work, *The Constitution of Liberty* (Chicago: University of Chicago Press, 1960), and Milton Friedman, *Capitalism and Freedom* (Chicago: University of Chicago Press, 1962). The intellectual background of this rise of 'neoliberalism' as it is often called, and the role of the Mt. Pèlerin Society, has become the object of extensive historical research. See, for example, Quinn Slobodian, *Globalists: The End of Empire and the Birth of Neoliberalism* (Cambridge, MA: Harvard University Press, 2018); and Dieter Plehwe, Quinn Slobodian, and Philip Mirowski, eds.,

The Nine Lives of Neoliberalism (London: Verso, 2020). In the
Dutch context we can refer to Gabriël van den Brink, *Ruw ontwaken uit een neoliberale droom en de eigenheid van het Europese
continent* [A rude awakening from a neoliberal slumber and
the specific character of the European continent] (Amsterdam:
Prometheus, 2020).

10. Shoshana Zuboff, *The Age of Surveillance Capitalism: The Fight
     for the Human Future at the New Frontier of Power* (Manchester:
     ProFile, 2019). Two of our dialogue participants, Jonathan Taplin
     and Rana Foroohar, have also done very interesting – and alarm-
     ing – work in this area. See Jonathan Taplin, *Move Fast and Break
     Things: How Facebook, Google, and Amazon Cornered Culture
     and Undermined Democracy* (New York: Little, Brown, 2017) and
     Rana Foroohar, *Don't Be Evil: How Big Tech Betrayed its Found-
     ing Principles – And All of Us* (New York: Currency, 2019). In the
     Netherlands, the work of Marleen Stikker (2019) stands out: *Het
     internet is stuk – Maar we kunnen het repareren* [The Internet is
     Broken – But We Can Fix It] (Amsterdam: De Geus, 2019).

11. There is an abundance of literature on the relation between
     markets, culture, values and morality. A very helpful typolo-
     gy is provided by Marion Fourcade and Kieran Healy, "Moral
     Views of Market Society," *Annual Review of Sociology* 33 (2007):
     285–311, building on Albert O. Hirschman, "Rival Interpretations
     of Market Society: Civilizing, Destructive, or Feeble?" *Journal
     of Economic Literature* 20, no. 4 (December 1982): 1463–84. See
     also Paul J. Zak, *Moral Markets: The Critical Role of Values in the
     Economy* (Princeton: Princeton University Press, 2008). Rather
     extensive, interesting work has been done recently as well on
     the relation between morality, markets, and theology: see, for
     instance, Paul van Geest, *Morality in the Marketplace: Reconcil-
     ing Theology and Economics* (Leiden: Brill, 2022). The relation
     of markets and virtues has received less attention but has
     been central to the research project on "What Good Markets
     Are Good For," led by Buijs and Graafland, mentioned in the
     introduction to this book. For a short introduction and over-
     view of results, see Johan Graafland, *Ethics and Economics: An
     Introduction to Free Markets, Equality and Happiness* (London:
     Routledge, 2022), especially part 3, pp. 125–98.

12. Just some literature for orientation will be mentioned here. Michel
     Albert, *Capitalism Against Capitalism* (London: Whurr, 1992) is
     indispensable. For the emergence and the intellectual roots (Wil-

helm Röpke, Walter Eucken, Alfred Müller-Armack, Alexander Rüstow, etc.) of the German *soziale Marktwirtschaft*, see Anthony Nicholls, *Freedom with Responsibility: The Social Market Economy in Germany 1918–1963* (Oxford: Clarendon Press, 1994) and James Van Hook, *Rebuilding Germany: The Creation of the Social Market Economy in Germany 1945–1957* (Cambridge: Cambridge University Press, 2004). For the various 'middle ways' of capitalism as well, see the recent volume by Eelke de Jong, ed., *Economic Ideas, Policy and National Culture* (London: Routledge, 2022). Visionary attempts in the British context are Philip Blond, *Red Tory: How Left and Right Have Broken Britain and How We Can Fix It* (London: Faber & Faber, 2010), and Maurice Glasman, *Blue Labour: The Politics of the Common Good* (Cambridge: Polity, 2022). Theoretical background is to be found in the 'Varieties of Capitalism'-literature, see Peter Hall and David Soskice, *Varieties of Capitalism* (Oxford: OUP, 2001).

13. A point made forcefully by Martin Wolf, *The Crisis of Democratic Capitalism* (New York: Penguin, 2023).

14. See the earlier mentioned works by Wendy Brown, *Undoing the Demos: Neoliberalism's Stealth Revolution* (New York: Zone Books, 2015) and Francis Fukuyama, *Liberalism and its Discontents* (London: Profile Books, 2022).

Chapter 3

1. Francis Fukuyama, first an article in 1989, then a book with the same title: see *The End of History and the Last Man* (New York: Free Press, 1992).

2. Mariana Mazzucato, *The Entrepreneurial State: Debunking Public vs. Private Sector Myths* (New York: PublicAffairs, 2015).

3. Jonathan Holslag, *Van muur tot muur: De wereldpolitiek sinds 1989* (Amsterdam: De Bezige Bij, 2021).

4. In a hearing before the 'Committee on Oversight and Government Reform' of the American 110th Congress, on October 23, 2008. Available at https://www.govinfo.gov/content/pkg/CHRG-110hhrg55764/html/CHRG-110hhrg55764.htm and 'live' https://www.youtube.com/watch?v=txw4GvEFGWs

5. It is remarkable that this deregulation took place under 'left-leaning' governments (Clinton, a Democrat in the US and Blair, of the Labour Party in the UK). It may well be a sign of the extent to which a new 'orthodoxy' had been able to enamor minds across the political spectrum.

6. Cf. Luigi Zingales, *A Capitalism for the People: Recapturing the Lost Genius of American Prosperity* (New York: Basic Books, 2012) and the earlier work written before the credit crisis and therefore somewhat outdated, but still relevant: Raghuram Rajan & Luigi Zingales, *Saving Capitalism from the Capitalists* (New York: Crown, 2003).

7. We referred earlier, in chapter 2, to Shoshana Zuboff, *The Age of Surveillance Capitalism: The Fight for the Human Future at the New Frontier Of Power* (Manchester: ProFile, 2019); Jonathan Taplin, *Move Fast and Break Things: How Facebook, Google, and Amazon Cornered Culture and Undermined Democracy* (New York: Little, Brown, 2017); and Rana Foroohar *Don't be Evil: How Big Tech Betrayed its Founding Principles – and All of Us* (New York: Currency, 2019). To their work should be added Timothy Wu, *The Master Switch: The Rise and Fall of Information Empires* (London: Atlantic Books, 2012) and idem, *The Attention Merchants: The Epic Scramble to Get Inside Our Heads* (New York: Vintage, 2017).

8. Geert Noels, *Gigantisme: Van too big to fail naar trager, kleiner en menselijker* (Tielt: Lannoo, 2019). Cf. idem, *Capitalism XXL: Why the Global Economy Became Gigantic and How to Fix It* (New York: McGill-Queen's University Press, 2023).

9. The 'capture theory' goes back to a seminal article by George J. Stigler, "The Theory of Economic Regulation," *Bell Journal of Economics and Management Science*, 2 (1971): 3–21. Robert Reich (2007), *Supercapitalism,* gives many examples of how it works and how the lobbying power of big companies can supersede democratic powers and procedures.

10. Mariana Mazzucato and Rosie Collington (2023), *The Big Con: How the Consultancy Industry Weakens our Businesses, Infantilizes our Governments, and Warps our Economies* (London: Allen Lane, 2023).

11. Milton Friedman, *Capitalism and Freedom* (Chicago: University of Chicago Press, 1962) and Milton and Rose Friedman, *Free to Choose: A Personal Statement* (Orlando: Harcourt Brace, 1980).

12. Joel Kotkin, *The Coming of Neo-Feudalism: A Warning to the Global Middle Class* (New York: Encounter Books, 2020).

13. Michael Sandel, *What Money Can't Buy: The Moral Limits of Markets* (New York: Farrar, Strauss and Giroux, 2012). Cf. Debra Satz, *Why Some Things Should Not Be for Sale: The Moral Limits of Markets* (Oxford: Oxford University Press, 2010).

14. Mariana Mazzucato, *The Value of Everything: Making and Taking in the Global Economy* (New Delhi: Allen Lane, 2018), passim.

15. Sander Heijne and Hendrik Noten, *Fantoomgroei: Waarom we steeds harder werken voor steeds minder* (Amsterdam and Antwerp: Atlas Contact, 2020). Cf. Dirk Bezemer, *Een land van kleine buffers: Er is genoeg geld, maar we gebruiken het verkeerd* (Amsterdam: Uitgeverij Pluim, 2020).

16. Joseph Stiglitz, J.-P. Fitoussi, and M. Durand, *Beyond GDP: Measuring What Counts for Economic and Social Performance* (Paris: OECD, 2018), p. 54: "It may well be the case that reliance on the wrong indicators, with governments announcing a recovery when large fraction of the population were not experiencing any improvement in their well-being, contributed, at least partly, to the distrust in public institutions and the rise in discontent and anti-globalization sentiments that we are witnessing today throughout the world."

17. See Walt W. Rostow (1960), *The Stages of Economic Growth: A Non-Communist Manifesto*.

18. Wendy Brown, *Undoing the Demos: Neoliberalism's Stealth Revolution* (New York: Zone Books, 2015), pp. 17–45.

19. Margaret Thatcher (1987), 'Interview for "Woman's Own" ("No Such Thing as Society"),' in *Margaret Thatcher: Speeches, Interviews and Other Statements*. Also available at Margaret Thatcher Foundation, https://www.margaretthatcher.org/document/106689.

20. Michael Sandel, *The Tyranny of Merit: What's Become of the Common Good?* (London: Allen Lane, 2020).

21. Joseph E. Stiglitz, *The Price of Inequality: How Today's Divided Society Endangers Our Future* (New York: W.W. Norton, 2013).

22. See, for example, Richard Wilkinson and Kate Picket, *The Spirit Level: Why Equality is Better for Everyone* (London: Penguin, 2010); Angus Deaton, *The Great Escape: Health, Wealth, and the Origins of Inequality* (Princeton: Princeton University Press, 2013); Jason Hickel, *The Divide: A Brief Guide to Global Inequality and its Solutions* (London: Penguin Random House, 2017); Keith Payne, *The Broken Ladder: How Inequality Affects the Way We Think, Live, and Die* (New York: Penguin, 2018); Richard Wilkinson and Kate Picket, *The Inner Level: How More Equal Societies Reduce Stress, Restore Sanity and Improve Everyone's Well-Being* (London: Penguin, 2018); Heather Boushey, *Unbound: How Inequality Constricts our Economy and What We Can Do About*

It (Cambridge, MA: Harvard University Press, 2019); Anne Case and Angus Deaton, *Deaths of Despair and the Future of Capitalism* (Princeton: Princeton University Press, 2020). A relevant Dutch study is Kees Vuyk (2017), *Oude en nieuwe ongelijkheid: Over het failliet van het verheffingsideaal* [Old and New Inequality: The Demise of 'Levelling Up'] (Utrecht: Uitgeverij Klement, 2017).

23. Henry Sanderson, *The Volt Rush: The Winners and Losers in the Race to Go Green* (London: One World, 2022).

24. See, e.g., David Goodhart, *The Road to Somewhere: The New Tribes Shaping British Politics* (London: Penguin, 2017).

25. See above, chapter 1.

26. Johan Rockström et al., "Planetary Boundaries: Exploring the Safe Operating Space for Humanity," *Ecology and Society* 14, no. 2. (2009), art. 32. Cf. Will Steffen et al., "Planetary Boundaries: Guiding Human Development on a Changing Planet," *Science* 347, no. 6223 (2015), and Johan Rockström and Owen Gaffney, *Breaking Boundaries: The Science of Our Planet* (London: DK, 2021).

27. Harald Sverdrup and Kristin Vala Ragnarsdottir, "Natural Resources in a Planetary Perspective," *Geochemical Perspectives* 3, no. 2 (2014): 129–341.

28. Brett Christophers, *Rentier Capitalism: Who Owns the Economy, and Who Pays for It?* (London: Verso, 2020); Martin Wolf, *The Crisis of Democratic Capitalism* (New York: Penguin, 2023), pp. 118–74.

29. An argument made by Paul Collier, *The Future of Capitalism: Facing the New Anxieties* (New Delhi: Allen Lane, 2018) and Martin Sandbu, *The Economics of Belonging: A Radical Plan to Win Back the Left Behind and Achieve Prosperity for All* (Princeton: Princeton University Press, 2020).

30. Cf. Maurice Glasman, *Blue Labour: The Politics of the Common Good* (Cambridge: Polity, 2022), ch. 3.

Chapter 4

1. Branco Milanovic, *Capitalism Alone: The Future of the System that Rules the World* (Cambridge, MA: Belknap/Harvard University Press, 2019), pp. 217ff.

2. This terminology is in line with ideas Jan Peter Balkenende developed in the 1990s, especially the inaugural lecture for

the Chair in Christian Social Thought at the Vrije Universiteit, J.P. Balkenende (1993), *Over verantwoordelijkheid en economie: Wat nu?* ('On Responsibility and Economics: The Challenges Ahead').

3. Michael Jacobs and Mariana Mazzucato, eds., *Rethinking Capitalism: Economics and Policy for Sustainable and Inclusive Growth* (Nashville: John Wiley, 2016); Bert de Vries, *Ontspoord kapitalisme: Hoe het kapitalisme ontspoorde en na de coronacrisis kan worden hervormd* (Amsterdam: Prometheus, 2020); Dominic Barton, Dezsö Horváth, and Matthias Kipping, eds., *Re-Imagining Capitalism* (London: Oxford University Press, 2016); Rebecca Henderson, *Reimagining Capitalism: How Business Can Save the World* (London: Penguin, 2020). In the introductory chapter we have already mentioned much more literature when we discussed the 'new intellectual resources.'

Chapter 5

1. As pointed out and discussed by Christian Felber, *Change Everything: Creating an Economy for the Common Good* (London: Zed Books, 2019), p. 15ff., who gave us the idea to look at and compare some constitutional documents, as we do here.

2. For an overview of different religious and spiritual traditions, see Karen Armstrong, *The Great Transformation: The Beginning of Our Religious Traditions* (New York: Anchor Books, 2006). A still relevant elaboration of the social and political implications of the 'Golden Rule' is given by Amitai Etzioni, *The New Golden Rule: Community and Morality in a Democratic Society* (New York: Basic Books, 1996).

3. An interesting recent example of a Protestant economist and a Catholic theologian working together on formulating a new 'relational' perspective on the economy is Lans Bovenberg and Paul van Geest, *Kruis en munt: De raakvlakken van economie en theologie* [Cross and Coin: The crossroads between economics and theology] (Utrecht: KokBoekencentrum, 2021).

4. As argued particularly in Friedrich Hayek, *The Constitution of Liberty* (Chicago: University of Chicago Press, 1960) and *Law, Legislation, Liberty* (London: Routledge, 1976), vol. 1, *Rules and Order.*

5. See Rudi Verburg's (forthcoming) study on the 'mission of economists,' which shows the sociomoral inspiration behind the

work of many influential economists in the 19th and 20th centuries. They wanted to make the world a better place with less poverty, less deprivation, and less suffering. Mariana Mazzucato is reviving this explicitly with her idea of a 'Mission Economy'; see *Mission Economy: A Moonshot Guide to Changing Capitalism* (New York: Allan Lane, 2021).

6. On the distinction between 'value-based' and 'values-based,' see Jan Peter Balkenende, "Over governance en maatschappelijke verantwoordelijkheid: hoe verder?" Inaugural Lecture Erasmus University Rotterdam (2011), p. 15, referring to Donald H. Chew and Stuart l. Gillan, *Corporate Governance at the Crossroads* (New York: McGraw-Hill/Irwin, 2004), p. 112. The terminology isn't always consistent with how it is used here, as is clear from Arjo Klamer, *Doing the Right Thing: A Value-Based Economy* (London: Uniquity Press, 2016), where 'value' actually refers to what Balkenende calls 'values.'

7. See Elizabeth Anderson, *Value in Ethics and Economics* (Cambridge, MA: Harvard University Press, 1993); Mariana Mazzucato, *The Value of Everything: Making and Taking in the Global Economy* (New Delhi: Allen Lane, 2018); Mark Carney, *Value(s): Building a Better World for All* (London: William Collins, 2021).

8. See Katherine Trebeck and Jeremy Williams, *The Economics of Arrival: Ideas for a Grown-Up Economy* (Bristol: Policy, 2019); Nicky Pouw, *Wellbeing Economics. How and Why Economics Needs to Change* (Amsterdam: Amsterdam University Press, 2020). Trebeck is founder of the Well Being Economy Alliance, an NGO that develops and builds coalitions to further the idea and practices of employing the idea of a Wellbeing Economy.

9. In 2022 the first official report on wellbeing in New Zealand was published by the New Zealand Treasury: *Te Tai Waiora: Wellbeing in Aotearoa New Zealand 2022*. See https://www.treasury. govt.nz/sites/default/files/2022-11/te-tai-waiora-2022.pdf

10. For information on this coalition see https://weall.org/wego.

11. James Coleman, *Foundations of Social Theory* (Cambridge, MA: Belknap/Harvard University Press, 1990); Robert D. Putnam, *Making Democracy Work: Civic Traditions in Modern Italy* (Princeton: Princeton University Press , 1993), and subsequent research; Francis Fukuyama, *Trust: The Social Virtues and the Creation of Prosperity* (New York: Free Press, 1995). The term 'moral capital' was used and explained by Piotr Sztompka in a keynote address at the Second International Modernization

Forum held in China in May 2016: "Moral Capital: An Important Prerequisite for Social Change and Successful Modernization," *China Academic Journal Electronic Publishing House.*

12.   Daron Acemoglu and James A. Robinson, *Why Nations Fail: The Origins of Power, Prosperity, and Poverty* (New York: Crown, 2012). Their work is partly inspired by Douglas North and B.R. Weingast, *Violence and Social Orders: Orders: A Conceptual Framework for Interpreting Recorded Human History* (Cambridge: Cambridge University Press, 2009), who make a similar argument.

13.   Milton Friedman (1970), "A Friedman Doctrine: The Social Responsibility of Business Is to Increase Its Profits," *The New York Times,* September 13, 1970, p. 17.

14.   Rebecca Henderson, *Reimagining Capitalism: How Business Can Save the World* (London: Penguin, 2020), p. 92.

15.   Sustainable Finance Lab–Utrecht, *De Purpose van Nederlandse financiële instellingen*, position paper (Utrecht: SFL, 2020). Cf. Colin Mayer, *Prosperity: Better Business Makes the Greater Good* (Oxford: Oxford University Press, 2018).

16.   Johan J. Graafland, *Ethics and Economics: An Introduction to Free Markets, Equality and Happiness* (London: Routledge, 2022), ch. 9 and 10. J.J. Graafland, *Corporate Social Responsibility and SMEs: Impact and Institutional Drivers* (London: Routledge, 2022), especially ch. 17.

17.   Harry Commandeur et al., *Agapè/caritas in bedrijf: Een praktisch raamwerk voor leidinggevenden* [Agape in business: A practical framework for leaders] (Amsterdam: Boom, 2021); Harry Hummels, 'An agenda for Agape' https://goldschmeding.foundation/wp-content/uploads/An-agenda-for-Agape-A-mandate-for-humanity-April-2021.pdf (2021); Muel Kaptein, "The Moral Duty to Love One's Stakeholders," *Journal of Business Ethics* 180 (2022): 813–27.

18.   Paul Polman and Andrew Winston, *Net Positive: How Courageous Companies Thrive by Giving More than They Take* (Boston: Harvard Business Review Press, 2021).

19.   Henk W. Volberda, Jatinder Sidhu, Pushpika Vishwanathan, and Kevin Heij (2022), *De winst van Purpose: Hoe ondernemingen het verschil kunnen maken* [The Profit of Purpose: How companies can make the difference] (Amsterdam: Mediawerf, 2022).

20.   For the idea of a 'common good balance sheet,' see Felber, *Change Everything*, pp. 21ff. and *passim*. For becoming 'net positive,' see Polman and Winston, *Net Positive.*

21. Aaron Hurst, *The Purpose Economy: How Your Desire for Impact, Personal Growth and Community is Changing the World* (Boise: Elevate, 2016).

22. Martijn Hendriks, Martijn Burger, Antoinette Rijsenbilt, Emma Pleeging, and Harry Commandeur, "Virtuous Leadership: A Source of Employee Well-Being and Trust," *Management Research Review* 43, no. 8 (2020): 951–70.

23. See the "Thought Leader Interview with Manfred Kets de Vries" by Art Kleiner, *Strategy+Business* 59 (Summer 2010), https://www.strategy-business.com/article/10209 and a range of books by Kets de Vries; see, among others, Kets de Vries, *The Leader on the Couch: A Clinical Approach to Changing People and Organizations* (New York: John Wiley, 2006).

24. James O'Toole, *The Enlightened Capitalists: Cautionary Tales of Business Pioneers Who Tried to Do Well by Doing Good* (New York: Harper Business, 2019).

25. Jeremy Rifkin, *The European Dream: How Europe's Vision of the Future is Quietly Eclipsing the American Dream* (New York: Tarcher/Penguin, 2004); Steven Hill, *Europe's Promise: Why the European Way Is the Best Hope in an Insecure Age* (Berkeley: University of California Press, 2010); Jonathan Holslag, *De kracht van het paradijs: Hoe Europa kan overleven in de Aziatische eeuw* [The Power of Paradise: How Europe Can Survive in the Age of Asia] (Antwerp: De Bezige Bij, 2014).

26. The story was retold right at the beginning of Xi Jinping's speech at the 100th anniversary of the Chinese Communist Party on July 1, 2021. See https://asia.nikkei.com/Politics/Full-text-of-Xi-Jinping-s-speech-on-the-CCP-s-100th-anniversary. That this is a recurrent and eminently important theme for Xi is clear from his works, *The Governance of China* (3 vols, 2014–2021). Xi's works have been officially declared as having the same authoritative status for the Communist Party of China as the works of Karl Marx and Mao Zedong (effectively relegating Deng Xiaoping to second rank, though Xi offers due praise to Deng as well).

27. For a lesser-known but beautifully researched overview of narratives on European identity, with a special reference to Christianity but broader in scope as well, see Mary Anne Perkins, *Christendom and European Identity: The Legacy of a Grand Narrative Since 1789* (Berlin: De Gruyter, 2004).

28. Our emphasis on 'stories' dovetails with the highly interesting body of literature on 'economics and culture' which received

a new boost around 2000 with the work by Fons Trompenaars and Charles Hampden-Turner, *Riding the Waves of Culture: Understanding Cultural Diversity in Business* (London: Nicholas Brealey, 1997); Lawrence E. Harrison and Samuel P. Huntington, eds., *Culture Matters: How Values Shape Human Progress* (New York: Basic Books, 2000); and the new, revised edition of Geert Hofstede's seminal 1980 book, *Culture's Consequences: Comparing Values, Behaviors, Institutions and Organizations Across Nations* (Thousand Oaks: Sage, 2003). Cf. Eelke de Jong, *Culture and Economics: On Values, Economics and International Business* (London: Routledge, 2009).

Chapter 6

1. Especially, but not exclusively! In their recent book *The Dawn of Everything: A New History of Humanity* (London: Allen Lane, 2021), David Graeber and David Wengrow point out that a diversity of ways to organize social hierarchy versus equality can probably be observed throughout the history of homo sapiens, so a clear-cut distinction in terms of hierarchy vs. equality between sedentary cultures and hunter gatherers can probably not be supported by the more recent archeological findings.

2. See John Keane, *The Life and Death of Democracy* (London: Simon & Schuster, 2009), pp. 107ff, referring to (among others, of course) Athens, but also to much earlier Syrian-Mesopotamian examples of assembly rule or advisory roles for assemblies, drawn from the higher classes, hemming in royal power.

3. There have been other attempts to analyze the history of Europe in terms of a struggle between opposing, unreconciled frameworks. Below we will point to the work of Von Gierke and Ullmann. We could point also to the psychoanalyst Karen Horney, *The Neurotic Personality of Our Time* (London: Routledge, [1937] 1999); and more recently Iain McGilchrist, *The Master and his Emissary: The Divided Brain and the Making of the Western World* (New Haven: Yale University Press, 2009; expanded edition 2018), attributing tensions within Western cultures to the division between the right and the left hemisphere in the brain, which have taken on a specific shape in Europe. If we follow Graeber and Winslow, mentioned in the footnote just above, we could perhaps say that a struggle between entirely different types of sociopolitical orders is characteristic for *homo*

sapiens, as far as the records go. Europe can then be said to be a place where this struggle has erupted very openly.

4. For example, see Frantz Fanon (1961), *Les damnés de la terre,* translated as *The Wretched of the Earth* (London: Penguin, 1965).

5. Referring to McCloskey, *The Bourgeois Virtues: Ethics for an Age of Commerce* (Chicago: University of Chicago Press, 2006), and later publications.

6. Some examples of more extensive accounts of the history that is referred to here are: Joshua Berman, *Created Equal: How the Bible Broke with Ancient Political Thought* (Oxford: Oxford University Press, 2008); Hans Joas (2013), *The Sacredness of the Person: A New Genealogy of Human Rights* (Washington DC: Georgetown University Press, 2013); Larry Siedentop, *Inventing the Individual: The Origins of Western Liberalism* (London: Allen Lane/Penguin, 2014).

7. Ulrich Meier, "Der falsche und der richtige Name der Freiheit: Zur Neuinterpretation eines Grundwertes der Florentiner Stadt-gesellschaft (13.-16. Jahrhundert)," in Klaus Schreiner and Ulrich Meier (1994), *Stadtregiment und Bürgerfreiheit*, vol. 7, *Bürgertum* (Göttingen: Vandenhoeck & Ruprecht, 1994).

8. The document refers to the biblical story of the creation of humans, in which they enjoyed a *pristina libertas,* an original liberty. This Latin phrase is not to be found in the biblical story but was used by Pope Gregory I in a letter, written around AD 592, in which he freed his slaves, having come to the insight that slavery was not the original design of God for humans.

9. See for the earliest formulations of this, in the context of medie-val canon law Brian Tierney, "Religion and Rights: A Medieval Perspective," *Journal of Law and Religion* 5, no. 1 (1987): 163–75.

10. John Witte, *The Reformation of Rights: Law, Religion, and Human Rights in Early Modern Calvinism* (Cambridge: Cambridge University Press, 2007).

11. See Otto von Gierke, *Das Deutsche Genossenschaftsrecht,* 4 vols (Berlin: Weidmannsche Buchhandlung, 1868–1913). The idea was later picked up by Walter Ullman, who spoke of an "ascend-ing" and a "descending" idea of authority. See Walter Ullmann, *Medieval Political Thought* (London: Penguin, 1975), pp. 12ff.

12. Charles Taylor, *A Secular Age* (Cambridge, MA: Belknap/Har-vard University Press, 2007), *passim.*

13. This is already apparent in Adam Smith, *An Inquiry Into the Nature and Causes of the Wealth of Nations,* ed. Edwin Cannan

(New York: The Modern Library, 1776), book III, ch. 3; and in
Karl Marx and Friedrich Engels, *Manifest der kommunistischen
Partei (Communist Manifesto)* (London: Hirschfield, 1848). Cf.
just some examples in the academic literature, with great time
intervals: Peter Kropotkin, *Mutual Aid: A Factor of Evolution*
(London: Freedom Press, [1902] 2006), ch. 5 and 6; Max Weber,
Wirtschaft und Gesellschaft (Tübingen: J.C.B. Mohr, [1920] 1972),
part. II, ch. 7, pp. 727–814, on cities; Antony Black, *Guild and
State: European Political Thought from the Twelfth Century to
the Present* (New Brunswick and London: Transaction, 2003);
Tine de Moor, "The Silent Revolution: A New Perspective on the
Emergence of Commons, Guilds, and Other Forms of Corporate
Collective Action in Western Europe," *International Review of
Social History* 53, supp. 16 (2008): 179–212; Tine de Moor, *Homo
Cooperans* Inaugural Lecture, Utrecht University (2013), https://
issuu.com/humanitiesuu/docs/gw_moor_tine_de_oratie_
nl_definitie; Maarten Prak, *Citizens without Nations. Urban
Citizenship in Europe and the World, c. 1000–1789* (Cambridge:
Cambridge University Press, 2018).

14.   For this, see Michel Mollat, *The Poor in the Middle Ages: An
Essay in Social History* (New Haven: Yale University Press, 1986;
originally published as *Les Pauvres au Moyen Age: Étude sociale*,
1978).

15.   Bernd Moeller (1971), "Piety in Germany around 1500," in S.E.
Ozment, ed., *The Reformation in Medieval Perspective* (Chicago:
Quadrangle Books, 1971), p. 66, n. 14, relates an interesting detail
about a councilor of Electoral Saxony, Pfeffinger (d. 1519), who
apparently was a 'typical 'joiner' and was simultaneously a
member of no less than 35 brotherhoods, perhaps in an effort to
reach the Guinness Book of Records well before it was established. To all brotherhoods he left bequests after his death.

16.   Sheilagh Ogilvie, *The European Guilds: An Economic Analysis*
(Princeton: Princeton University Press, 2019), makes the important qualifying observation that the actual membership of cities
and of guilds wasn't as open as it looked in principle. Guilds
were networks of exclusion as much as they were of inclusion.

17.   See Black, *Guild and State*, pp. 44–65. For the impressive influence of the idea of 'covenant' in European political and social
thought and practice, see the four-volume work by David Elazar,
The Covenant Tradition in Politics (New Brunswick: Transaction, 1995–1998); for the period of the 'cooperative revolution'

as mentioned in the text, see especially vol. 2, *Covenant and Commonwealth.*

18. Diana Wood, *Medieval Economic Thought* (Cambridge: Cambridge University Press, 2002), pp. 115–17; Deirdre McCloskey, *Bourgeois Dignity: Why Economics Can't Explain the Modern World* (Chicago: University of Chicago Press, 2010), pp. 40ff, and *passim.*

19. Hannah Arendt, *The Human Condition* (Chicago: Chicago University Press, 1958), pp. 248ff; Charles Taylor, *Sources of the Self: The Making of the Modern Identity* (Cambridge, MA: Harvard University Press, 1989), pp. 211ff.

20. Samuel Cohn, *Lust for Liberty: The Politics of Social Revolt in Medieval Europe, 1200–1425* (London: Harvard University Press, 2006).

21. Keane, *The Life and Death of Democracy*, pp. 171ff.

22. See Douglas North, J.J. Wallis, and B.R. Weingast (2009), *Violence and Social Orders: A Conceptual Framework for Interpreting Recorded Human History* (Cambridge: Cambridge University Press, 2009), pp. 148ff.

23. Ulrich Beck, Wolfgang Bonss, and Christoph Lau, "The Theory of Reflexive Modernization: Problematic, Hypotheses and Research Programme," *Theory, Culture & Society* 20, no. 20 (2003): 1–33. Beck applies the term 'reflexive' to 'late modernity' in particular, but it is also applicable to modern society as such.

24. A highly influential modern European philosopher who has analyzed the emergence and dynamic of the public sphere is of course Jürgen Habermas. See, among other works, *Strukturwandel der Öffentlichkeit* (1962), trans. as *The Structural Transformation of the Public Sphere: An Inquiry into a Category of Bourgeois Society* (Cambridge, MA: MIT Press, 1982) and "Religion in the Public Sphere," *European Journal of Philosophy* 14, no. 1 (2006): 1–25.

25. Luigino Bruni & Stefano Zamagni (2007). *Civil Economy: Efficiency, Equity, Public Happiness.*

26. Norman Cohn, *The Pursuit of the Millennium: Revolutionary Millenarians and Mystical Anarchists of the Middle Ages* (London: Paladin, [1957] 1984); Samuel Cohn, *Lust for Liberty.*

27. In her first Tanner Lecture "When the Market was Left," Elizabeth Anderson states regarding the market, in reference to both Smith and Marx (and to the egalitarian movement of the Levellers): "The parties each undertake the exchange with their dig-

nity, their standing, and their personal independence affirmed by the other." To be sure: in her judgment these ideals have run aground. See *Private Government: How Employers Rule Our Lives (and Why We Don't Talk about It)*, Tanner Lectures on Human Values (Princeton: Princeton University Press, 2017), p. 4.

28. Raghuram Rajan, *The Third Pillar: How Markets and the State Are Leaving Communities Behind* (London: William Collins, 2019). See below chapter 11 for our interpretation of the present-day significance of this sphere.

29. Wilhelm Röpke, *Civitas Humana: A Humane Order of Society* (London: William Hodge, 1948), p. 10, perhaps the first time the phrase 'third way' is used with this particular meaning; cf. idem, *A Humane Economy: The Social Framework of the Free Market* (Chicago: Henry Regnery, 1960).

30. Gøsta Esping-Anderson, *The Three Worlds of Welfare Capitalism* (Princeton: Princeton University Press, 1990).

31. Daron Acemoglu and James Robinson, *Why Nations Fail: The Origins of Power, Prosperity, and Poverty* (New York: Crown, 2012).

32. Daron Acemoglu and James Robinson, *The Narrow Corridor: States, Societies and the Fate of Liberty* (New York: Penguin, 2019).

33. We could refer here to the essay of Jürgen Habermas (1980), "Modernity – An Unfinished Project," reprinted in Craig J. Calhoun, ed., *Contemporary Sociological Theory* (Hoboken: Wiley Blackwell, 2022), pp. 395–400; however, the point we are making is with more depth analyzed in his *Theorie des kommunikativen Handels (Theory of Communicative Action* (Frankfurt am Main: Suhrkamp, 1981), where he makes the distinction between the actual development of Western modernity and the unrealized developmental potential of Western modernization. However, we do not share Habermas's stress on the Enlightenment but see the European development going through much more phases from the emergence of the medieval monasteries and cities, involving not just 'reason' but also new spiritual developments. Our analysis therefore seems closer to Habermas's later work where he recognizes the relevance of religion. For the idea of 'reflexive modernization' see Beck et al., "The Theory of Reflexive Modernization".

34. Max Weber, *The Protestant Ethic and the Spirit of Capitalism* (New York: Charles Scribner's Sons, [1905] 1958), p. 181.

35. Bob Goudzwaard, *Capitalism and Progress: A Diagnosis of Western Society* (Grand Rapids: Eerdmans, 1979).

36. Cf. Frieda Assmann, *Der europäische Traum: Vier Lehren aus der Geschichte* (Munich: Beck, 2018).

37. It would take us too far afield here to make further distinctions here between 'circular,' 'regenerative,' or 'restorative,' although this is often done in the literature. For an overview, see Piero Morseletto, "Restorative and Regenerative: Exploring the Concepts in the Circular Economy," *Journal of Industrial Ecology* (2020): 1–11. Cf. Paul Hawken, *Regeneration: Ending the Climate Crisis in One Generation* (New York: Penguin, 2021).

38. Paul Collier, *The Future of Capitalism: Facing the New Anxieties* (New Delhi: Allen Lane, 2018), p. 209.

39. Hans Boutellier, *De improvisatiemaatschappij: Over de sociale ordening van een begrensde wereld* (Amsterdam: Boom, 2011).

40. For a thorough history of the discovery of the individual before the 1960s, see Taylor, *Sources of the Self.* We also referred earlier to Siedentop, *Inventing the Individual: The Origins of Western Liberalism.*

41. Richard Sennett, *Together: The Rituals, Pleasures and Politics of Cooperation* (New Haven: Yale University Press, 2012).

42. St. Augustine (around 403), *De catechizandibus rudibus* [The first catechetical instruction], 19.31. Here a key theme is introduced that Augustine elaborates extensively in his later work 'De Civitate Dei' (413–426) [The City of God], that of two 'cities' in history, but this concise formulation of 'seeking one's own glory by subjecting others' is not repeated there, although materially this analysis permeates his later work too. The formulation that comes closest is right at the beginning of the later work (Book I, preface) where Augustine states that the 'earthly city aims at dominion, which holds nations in enslavement, but is itself dominated by that very lust of domination,' elaborated upon in Book XIV, 28 and Book XV.

Chapter 7

1. The seminal work on paradigm shifts is of course Thomas Kuhn, *The Structure of Scientific Revolutions* (Chicago: University of Chicago Press, 1962).

2. Actually, this characterization as 'dismal science' originated in the 19th century when some persons with racist leanings called economics 'dismal' because it didn't take 'race' into account, which today we would certainly ascribe to the economists' credit!

3. A point driven home by Dani Rodrik, *Economics Rules: Why Economics Works, When it Fails, and How to Tell the Difference* (Oxford: Oxford University Press, 2015).

4. This assumption was critically addressed in a seminal article by Amartya Sen, "Rational Fools: A Critique of the Behavioral Foundations of Economic Theory," *Philosophy & Public Affairs* 6, no. 4 (1977): 317–44. Cf. Rudi Verburg, *Greed, Self-Interest and the Shaping of Economics* (London: Routledge, 2018), and Joost Hengstmengel, *De homo economicus: een familiegeschiedenis* (Amsterdam: Boom, 2020).

5. The poem was first published anonymously in 1705, then republished in 1714 as the opening of a larger book, with a commentary on the poem and other essays. Only in the 1723 edition did De Mandeville publish it under his own name, constantly expanding the book until it consisted of two volumes. A recent edition is Bernard Mandeville, *The Fable of the Bees*, 2 vols (Indianapolis: Liberty Fund, 1988), a photographic reprint of the 1924 Oxford University Press edition. It is clear from the volumes that the poem is not only a satire but a serious interpretation of the modern economy as driven by immoral impulses and yet delivering advantageous results. On Adam Smith's position on this, see the end of this chapter.

6. Friedman's (in)famous 1970 *New York Times* article on "The Social Responsibility of Business Is to Increase Its Profits," can be seen as a late echo of this. Cf. Fritz Machlup, "Theories of the Firm: Marginalist, Behavioral, Managerial," *The American Economic Review* 57, no. 1 (1967): 1–33.

7. John Stuart Mill (1844), "On the Definition of Political Economics; and on the Method of Investigation Proper to It," in *Essays on Some Unsettled Questions of Political Economy* (Kitchener: Batoche Books 2000), pp. 86–114. A characteristic quote by Mill when considering the diversity of motives actual humans may have but which he wants to disregard when doing 'science': "Not that any political economist was ever so absurd as to suppose that mankind are really thus constituted, but because this is the mode in which science must necessarily proceed," p. 98. In science, we consciously and deliberately deal with unrealistic assumptions, such as the one that people are only motivated by "the mere desire of wealth," but we (should) know that this is not realistic or true.

8. Paul Krugman, "How Did Economists Get It So Wrong?" *New York Times*, September 6, 2009.

9. Rodrik, *Economics Rules,* pp. 156ff.
10. Rudi Verburg, *The Mission of Economists* (forthcoming).
11. Sen, "Rational Fools."
12. For the distinction between 'neoclassical' and 'neoliberal,' see Johan Graafland and Harmen Verbruggen, "Free-Market, Perfect Market and Welfare State Perspectives on 'Good' Markets: an Empirical Test," *Applied Research in Quality of Life* 17, no. 3 (2021): 1–24.
13. Irene van Staveren, *Economics after the Crisis: An Introduction to Economics from a Pluralist and Global Perspective* (London: Routledge, 2014).
14. Cf. what was said about this assumption above in chapter 5.
15. Friedrich A. Hayek, *Law, Legislation, Liberty,* 3 vols. (London: Routledge, 1976), vol. 2, *The Mirage of Social Justice.*
16. Cf. van Staveren, *Economics after the Crisis.* Restoring pluralism is a key element of the Rethinking Economics movement. See Sam de Muijnck and Joris Tieleman, *Economy Studies: A Guide to Rethinking Economics Education* (Amsterdam: Amsterdam University Press, 2021).
17. See as well above, chapter 3, when we discuss the *'There is No Such Thing as Society' Assumption* and the literature mentioned there. Of course, Thomas Piketty has done a great deal to expose this increasing inequality; see *Capital in the Twenty-First Century* (Cambridge, MA: Belknap/Harvard University Press, 2014). But we should also refer to the work of one of the conversation partners in the 'Future Markets Consultation,' the French economist François Bourguignon, *The Globalization of Inequality* (Princeton: Princeton University Press, 2015; originally published in French, 2012).
18. Angus Deaton, *The Great Escape: Health, Wealth, and the Origins of Inequality* (Princeton: Princeton University Press, 2013); Anne Case and Angus Deaton, *Deaths of Despair and the Future of Capitalism* (Princeton: Princeton University Press, 2020).
19. Rodrik, *Economics Rules*, pp. 201ff.
20. They applied their approach and insights to a number of economic fields and themes in Abhijit Banerjee and Esther Duflo, *Good Economics for Hard Times: Better Answers to Our Biggest Problems* (London: Penguin, 2020).
21. Herbert Simon, *Models of Man: Social and Rational* (New York: John Wiley, 1957); Daniel Kahneman, *Thinking: Fast and Slow* (New York: Farrar, Straus and Giroux, 2011). Both authors were

awarded the Sveriges Riksbank/Nobel Prizes in 1978 and 2002 respectively. Cf. George A. Akerlof and Robert J. Shiller, *Animal Spirits: How Human Psychology Drives the Economy, and Why It Matters for Global Capitalism* (Princeton: Princeton University Press, 2009).

22. As was shown in a seminal article by Ernst Fehr and Urs Fischbacher, "Why Social Preferences Matter: The Impact of Non-Selfish Motives on Competition, Cooperation and Incentives," *The Economic Journal* 112, no. 489 (2002): 1–33. For a brief overview see Johan Graafland, *Ethics and Economics: An Introduction to Free Markets, Equality and Happiness* (London: Routledge, 2022), pp. 181–86.

23. Luigi Bruni and Alessandra Smerilli, *De ongekende kant van de economie: Gratuïteit en markt* (Nieuwkuijk: De Nieuwe Stad, 2015; originally published as *L'altra metà dell'economia. Gratuità e mercati*, Rome, 2014), pp. 138–52.

24. Sen, "Rational Fools."

25. For the interaction between economics and theology see the recent publication of Lans Bovenberg and Paul van Geest, *Kruis en munt: De raakvlakken van economie en theologie* [Cross and Coin: The crossroads between economics and theology] (Utrecht: KokBoekencentrum , 2021), and Paul van Geest, *Morality in the Marketplace: Reconciling Theology and Economics* (Leiden: Brill, 2022).

26. John M. Keynes, "Alfred Marshall, 1842–1924," *The Economic Journal* 34, no. 135 (1924): 311–72.

27. See Joris Tieleman et al., *Thinking Like an Economist? A Quantitative Analysis of Economics Bachelor Curricula in the Netherlands*; Rethinking Economics NL (2018); https://www.rethinkingeconomics.nl/.

28. Kate Raworth, *Doughnut Economics: Seven Ways to Think Like a 21st-Century Economist* (London: Random House, 2017).

29. Just to give an impression of the wealth of recent books on the topic: Frans de Waal, *The Age of Empathy: Nature's Lessons for a Kinder Society* (London: Souvenir Press, 2010); Tom R. Tyler, *Why People Cooperate* (Princeton: Princeton University Press, 2011); Martin Nowak and Roger Hitfield, *Super Cooperators: Beyond the Survival of the Fittest* (New York: Free Press, 2012); Mark Pagel, *Wired for Culture: The Natural History of Human Cooper-ation* (London: Penguin, 2012); Matthieu Ricard, *Altruism: The Power of Compassion to Change Yourself and the World* (New

York: Little, Brown, 2013); Richard Sennett, *Together: The Rituals, Pleasures and Politics of Cooperation* (New Haven: Yale University Press, 2012). For an even larger perspective Jeremy Rifkin, *The Empathic Civilization: The Race to Global Consciousness in a World of Crisis* (Cambridge: Polity, 2009). This all relates to other descriptions of humans as 'social animals' (Aristotle's *zooion politikon*) or as *homo amans, homo florens*.

30. Book titles can be found in the "References" section at the end of this book.

31. See the above-mentioned work of Sam de Muijnck and Joris Tieleman, *Economy Studies*.

32. See https://www.core-econ.org/ A online freely available textbook has been published by the CORE team (Samuel Bowles, Wendy Carlin and Margaret Stevens) titled *The Economy. Economics for a changing world.* (Oxford: Oxford University Press/ CoreEcon, 2017).

33. An interesting indication of a new orientation in academic economics in the Netherlands was the 'Impact Forum' organized October 2022 by the joint deans of all economics departments of Dutch universities where the connection of academic economics with current societal challenges, and the earlier criticisms of 'heterodox' economists, were critically discussed in a very open, future-oriented atmosphere. A short report on this meeting is given by Peter Olsthoorn, "Behalve gelijk hebben, ook gelijk krijgen," *Economisch Statistische Berichten (ESB)* 107, no. 4816 (2022): 562–65. https://esb.nu/behalve-gelijk-heb-ben-ook-gelijk-krijgen/.

34. Kenneth Boulding, "Economics as a Moral Science," Presidential Address for the American Economic Association 1968, *The American Economic Review* 59, no. 1 (1969): 1–12.

35. Amartya Sen, "Adam Smith and the Contemporary World," *Erasmus Journal for Philosophy and Economics* 3, no. 1 (2010): 50–67. https://doi.org/10.23941/ejpe.v3i1.39.

36. Nicholas Phillipson, *Adam Smith: An Enlightened Life* (New Haven: Yale University Press, 2010), pp. 2ff. There is even a reconsideration of theological themes in Smith's work taking place: Jordan J. Ballor and Cornelis van der Kooi, eds., *Theology, Morality and Adam Smith* (London: Routledge, 2022).

37. Adam Smith (1776), *An Inquiry into the Nature and Causes of the Wealth of Nations*, ed. Edwin Cannan (New York: The Modern Library, 1776), book I, ch. 2.

38. Ibid., book IV, ch. 3, pt. 2.

39. Johan Graafland and Thomas R. Wells, "In Adam Smith's Own Words: The Role of Virtues in the Relationship between Free Market Economies and Societal Flourishing, A Semantic Data-Mining Approach," *Journal of Business Ethics* 172 (2021): 31–42.

40. Smith, *Wealth of Nations*, book IV, ch. 2.

41. See Jelle van Baardewijk, *The Moral Foundation of Business Students: A Philosophical and Empirical Investigation of the Business Student Ethos*, PhD dissertation, Vrije Universiteit Amsterdam, 2018. Just one recent example of empirical research into this John Ifcher and Homa Zarghamee, "The Rapid Evolution of Homo Economicus: Brief Exposure to Neoclassical Assumptions Increases Self-Interested Behavior," *Journal of Behavioral and Experimental Economics* 75, issue C (2018): 55–65.

42. https://www.youtube.com/watch?v=1yupkG7NB8w, retrieved March 13, 2023.

Chapter 8

1. At a very basic level sometimes: the famous case here is that of John Snow who discovered the source of, or at least the means of transmission of, cholera by tracing the movements of those who developed the symptoms of the disease to a particular water pump in Broad Street in Soho, London, in 1854.

2. He later rewrote his speech as a contribution for the *Harvard Business Review*, March 5, 2013.

3. Manfred A. Max-Neef, *Human Scale Development: Conception, Application and Further Reflections* (New York: Apex Press, 1991).

4. John Cobb and Herman Daly, *For the Common Good* (Boston: Beacon Press, 1989), another fine example of interdisciplinary cooperation.

5. In the case of Nussbaum and Sen, the origins of this approach can be found in their UN-sponsored project, which resulted in the volume: Martha C. Nussbaum and Amartya Sen, *The Quality of Life* (Oxford: Oxford University Press, 1993). In subsequent years, both developed their own ideas and published somewhat different versions of what has come to be called the "capabilities approach."

6. Joseph E. Stiglitz, Jean-Paul Fitoussi, and Martine Durand (2018a), *Beyond GDP: Measuring What Counts for Economic and Social Performance* (Paris: OECD, 2018); a more extensive and

technical companion volume was published as idem, *For Good Measure: Advancing Research on Well-being Metrics Beyond GDP* (Paris: OECD, 2018).

7. Although many challenges remained squarely on the agenda, the results were still impressive. See United Nations, *The Millennium Development Goals Report* (2015); available at file:///D:/Downloads/MDG%202015%20rev%20(July%201).pdf

8. For the more concrete goals, see https://sdgs.un.org/goals. For the tangible indicators, see https://unstats.un.org/sdgs/indicators/indicators-list/.

9. Rutger Hoekstra, *Replacing GDP by 2030: Towards a Common Language for the Well-Being and Sustainability Community* (Cambridge: Cambridge University Press, 2019).

10. For greater depth on this, see the report by the Think Tank of Young Economists connected with this project: Sam de Muijnck, Elisa Terragno Bogliaccini, and Jim Richard Surie, eds., *Towards the Wellbeing Economy: Implications for Public, Environmental and Financial Policy* (Amsterdam: Vrije Universiteit, 2021).

11. See Hoekstra, *Replacing GDP*; Nicky Pouw, *Wellbeing Economics: How and Why Economics Needs to Change* (Amsterdam: Amsterdam University Press, 2020).

12. See https://wellbeingeconomy.org/wp-content/uploads/WEAll-brochure_2021Update_FINAL_Feb17.pdf.

13. The particular quote is to be found in various places, e.g., https://www.smartsheet.com/what-stakeholder-theory-and-how-does-it-impact-organization; in this interview: https://www.forbesindia.com/article/third-anniversary-special/edward-freeman-businesses-should-be-driven-by-purpose/32934/1; and in the Ted Talk: https://www.youtube.com/watch?v=7dugfwJthBY

14. Robert Eccles and Michael Krzus, *One Report: Integrated Reporting for a Sustainable Strategy* (Hoboken: Wiley, 2010); idem, *The Integrated Reporting Movement: Meaning, Momentum, Motives, and Materiality* (Hoboken: Wiley, 2014).

15. Rob Bauer, Tereza Bauer, Mieke Olaerts, Constantijn van Aartsen, *Sustainability Embedding Practices in Dutch Listed Companies* (Maastricht: Maastricht University, 2021), pp. 9, 101, 112.

16. Value Reporting Foundation, SASB Standards, https://www.sasb.org/standards/download/

17. International Integrated Reporting Council (IIRC) (2013), *The International <IR> Framework*. https://www.integratedreport-

ing.org/wp-content/uploads/2013/12/13-12-08-THE-INTERNA-
TIONAL-IR-FRAMEWORK-2-1.pdf

18.   International Integrated Reporting Council (IIRC) (2021), *The
        International <IR> Framework.* https://www.integratedreport-
        ing.org/wp-content/uploads/2021/01/InternationalIntegrated-
        ReportingFramework.pdf

19.   Dennis Bams and Bram van der Kroft, *Tilting the Wrong Firms?
        How Inflated ESG Ratings Negate Socially Responsible Investing
        Under Information Asymmetries* (Boston: MIT Center for Real
        Estate Research, 2022): Paper No. 22/12, available at SSRN:
        https://ssrn.com/abstract=4271852.

20.   The B-Corp movement now includes almost 7000 companies
        in 161 sectors in 90 countries. See https://www.bcorporation.
        net/en-us/. For the 'common good balance sheet,' see Chris-
        tian Felber, *Change Everything: Creating an Economy for the
        Common Good* (London: Zed Books, 2019), p. 21ff and *passim.*
        The Gemeinwohl-Ökonomie/Economy for the Common Good
        movement brings together about 1200 companies, mainly in
        Germany and Austria. Both movements have active auditing
        procedures for companies to apply and comply with.

21.   For an overview of both discussions leading to new regulations
        as well as the present regulations themselves, see Leen Paape,
        *Maatschappelijke zorgplicht voor ondernemingen: Tien redenen
        waarom dat geen vraag zou moeten zijn* (Breukelen: Nyenrode
        Business University, 2022). Available at https://www.nyenrode.
        nl/docs/default-source/faculty/emeritaten/afscheidsre-
        de-leen-paape-8-december-2022.pdf?sfvrsn=7ae27813_1

22.   https://eur-lex.europa.eu/legal-content/EN/TXT/?uri=CELEX-
        :32022L2464

23.   https://www.ohchr.org/sites/default/files/documents/publica-
        tions/guidingprinciplesbusinesshr_en.pdf

24.   Leen Paape, *Maatschappelijke zorgplicht*, p. 45.

25.   For an example of this type of 'true value assessment, see the
        work of KPMG: https://assets.kpmg.com/content/dam/kpmg/
        xx/pdf/2019/01/valuing-your-impacts-on-society-how-kpmg-
        true-value-can-help-measure-and-manage-your-impacts.pdf
        and https://assets.kpmg.com/content/dam/kpmg/nl/pdf/2020/
        services/commonland-true-value-report.pdf

26.   Johan Graafland and Frank G.A. de Bakker, "Crowding In or
        Crowding Out? How Non-Governmental Organizations and
        Media Influence Intrinsic Motivations toward Corporate Social

and Environmental Responsibility," *Journal of Environmental Planning and Management* 64, no. 13 (2021), 2386–2409.

27. For this cycle from frontrunner to the institutionalization of a new level playing field, cf. Lucas Simons and André Nijhof, *Changing the Game: Sustainable Market Transformation Strategies to Understand and Tackle the Big and Complex Sustainability Challenges of Our Generation* (London: Routledge, 2021).

28. Friedrich A. Hayek, *Law, Legislation, Liberty* (London: Routledge, 1976), vol. 2, *The Mirage of Social Justice*.

29. Robert Reich, *Supercapitalism: The Battle for Democracy in an Age of Big Business* (London: Icon Books, 2007), p. 5: "Capitalism has become more responsive to what we want as individual purchasers of goods, but democracy has grown less responsive to what we want together as citizens."

30. Diana Wood, *Medieval Economic Thought* (Cambridge: Cambridge University Press, 2002), ch. 6; Rudi Verburg, *The Mission of Economists* (forthcoming).

31. See True Price Foundation, *A Roadmap for True Pricing: Vision Paper* (Amsterdam: True Price Foundation, 2019). Available at https://trueprice.org/wp-content/uploads/2022/09/2019-06-True-Price-A-roadmap-for-true-pricing-v1.0.pdf.

32. Ibid., p. 2.

33. Kevin Rennert et al., "Comprehensive Evidence Implies a Higher Social Cost of CO_2," *Nature* 610 (2022): 687–92.

34. Debra Satz, *Why Some Things Should Not Be for Sale: The Moral Limits of Markets* (Oxford: Oxford University Press, 2010). Michael Sandel, *What Money Can't Buy: The Moral Limits of Markets* (New York: Farrar, Strauss and Giroux, 2012).

35. Cf. Mariana Mazzucato, *The Value of Everything: Making and Taking in the Global Economy* (New Delhi: Allen Lane, 2018); Mark Carney, *Value(s): Building a Better World for All* (London: William Collins, 2021).<

Chapter 9

1. The approach developed here can be seen as a further step in the line of thought outlined already in J.P. Balkenende, *Overheidsregelgeving en maatschappelijke organisaties*, PhD dissertation, Vrije Universiteit, 1992; and in Balkenende's inaugural lecture, 'Over verantwoordelijkheid en economie: wat nu?' ('On Responsibility and Economics: The Challenges Ahead'), Vrije

Universiteit Amsterdam (1993) and in line with what the late 19th- and early 20th-century theologian and statesman Abraham Kuyper called an "architectonic critique" of societal structures. See Abraham Kuyper (1891), "The Social Question and the Christian Religion," republished in Jordan J. Ballor, Melvin Flikkema, and Peter Heslam, eds., *On Business and Economics: Collected Works of Abraham Kuyper in Public Theology* (Bellingham: Lexham Press 2021), vol 11, pp. 169–230.

2. Daron Acemoglu and James Robinson, *The Narrow Corridor: States, Societies and the Fate of Liberty* (New York: Penguin, 2019).

3. The background for the term 'embedding' is the famous study of Karl Polanyi, *The Great Transformation: The Political and Economic Origins of Our Time* (Boston: Beacon Press, [1944] 1957), in which he argued that the modern capitalist market economies have established themselves through a process of disembedding markets from society. We argue for a re-embedding of markets in society or for the idea of reconnecting markets and society.

4. For a brief exposition in this context, see https://h2020-demeter.eu/the-multi-actor-approach-in-demeter/.

5. See R. Edward Freeman, *Strategic Management: A Stakeholder Approach* (Boston: Pitman, 1984), and numerous subsequent publications. Particularly interesting is the 'libertarian defense' of stakeholder theory: ultra-liberals should be committed to a stakeholder approach rather than a shareholder approach, for non-interference in others private lives and paying them equal respect is central to libertarianism. See R. Edward Freeman and Robert A. Phillips, "Stakeholder Theory: A Libertarian Defense," *Business Ethics Quarterly* 12, no. 3 (July 2002): 331–49.

6. Ibo van de Poel, Jessica Nihlén Fahlquist, Neelke Doorn, Sjoerd Zwart, and Lambèr Royakkers, "The Problem of Many Hands: Climate Change as an Example," *Science and Engineering Ethics* 18, no. 1 (2021): 49–67.

7. The distinction between 'backward responsibility' and 'forward responsibility' is taken from Ibo van der Poel (2011), "The Relation Between Forward-Looking and Backward-Looking Responsibility," in Nicole A. Vincent, Ibo van der Poel, and Jeroen van den Hoven, eds., *Moral Responsibility: Beyond Free Will and Determinism* (Dordrecht: Springer, 2011), pp. 37–52.

8. Hannah Arendt, *The Human Condition* (Chicago: Chicago University Press, 1958). In the phrase 'power of initiative,' we here combine Arendt's notions of 'natality' and 'plurality,' which are

both constitutive of the 'human condition' as she sees it and determine the arena of 'action': with each human newborn a new perspective enters the world, and all these human perspectives are different. Only by giving room to these conditions can a political community be healthy. Conversely, all human beings are, by nature of their citizenship, called upon to act out this natality and plurality in the public sphere.

9. Cf. David Colander and Roland Kupers, *Complexity and the Art of Public Policy* (Princeton: Princeton University Press, 2014); Roland Kupers, *A Climate Policy Revolution: What the Science of Complexity Reveals About Saving Our Planet* (Cambridge, MA: Harvard University Press, 2020).

10. At the moment of writing this book, the Dutch 'Sociaal-Economische Raad,' the most important platform where the business sector meets labor unions, civil society organizations, and independent economic advisers, is developing this idea of 'meaningful dialogues' between business and a range of stakeholders, depending on the specific context, in the entire international value chain; working material is being prepared. See https://www.ser.nl/nl/thema/imvo/ser-en-imvo/betekenisvolle-dialoog.

11. Cf. Peter Diamandis and Steven Kotler, *Abundance: The Future is Better Than You Think* (New York: Free Press, 2012).

12. https://www.youtube.com/watch?v=r0872fKNtIw

Chapter 10

1. Henk W. Volberda, Justin Jansen, Michiel Tempelaar, and Kevin Heij, "Monitoren van sociale innovatie: Slimmer werken, dynamisch managen en flexibel organiseren," *Tijdschrift voor HRM* (2011) 1: 85–110.

2. Rebecca Henderson, *Reimagining Capitalism: How Business Can Save the World* (London: Penguin, 2020).

3. Jan Rotmans and Mischa Verheijden, *Omarm de chaos* (Amsterdam: De Geus, 2021), ch. 4. Cf. Harry Hummels and Erik Hilgers, *Anders groeien: Een medemenselijke aanpak van duurzaam en maatschappelijk ondernemen*. [Growing differently: A compassionate approach to sustainable and social entrepreneurship] (Culemborg: Van Duuren, 2022).

4. For more in-depth analysis see the extensive Preface of Colin Mayer, *Prosperity: Better Business Makes the Greater Good* (Oxford: Oxford University Press, 2018), pp. 1–12.

5. Mayer has been spearheading a large research and engagement program with the British Academy about the 'Future of the Corporation' that is practically built around the statement given here in the text. See https://www.thebritishacademy.ac.uk/programmes/future-of-the-corporation/ Besides the book just mentioned, see also the various reports resulting from this project, such as *Reforming Business for the 21st Century: A Framework for the Future of the Corporation* (2018) and its sequel *Principles for Purposeful Business: How to deliver the framework for the Future of the Corporation* (2019). See https://www.thebritishacademy.ac.uk/documents/76/Reforming-Business-for-21st-Century-British-Academy.pdf and https://www.thebritishacademy.ac.uk/documents/224/future-of-the-corporation-principles-purposeful-business.pdf

6. Paul Polman and Andrew Winston, *Net Positive: How Courageous Companies Thrive by Giving More Than They Take* (Boston, MA: Harvard Business Review Press, 2021).

7. Statement made during a public lecture at the Erasmus University Rotterdam, November 25, 2021.

8. As indicated earlier in chapter 8, the particular quote is to be found in various places, e.g., https://www.smartsheet.com/what-stakeholder-theory-and-how-does-it-impact-organization; in this interview https://www.forbesindia.com/article/third-anniversary-special/edward-freeman-businesses-should-be-driven-by-purpose/32934/1 and in the TedTalk: https://www.youtube.com/watch?v=7dugfwJthBY

9. Bruno Roche and Jay Jakub, *Completing Capitalism: Heal Business to Heal the World* (Oakland, CA: Berrett-Koehler, 2017).

10. The concept of 'corporate citizenship' gained currency through the work of the South African "King Committee" that, led by Judge Mervyn King, has produced several reports and codes on corporate governance since 1993. The term 'corporate citizenship' became a key term in King IV, published in 2016. See https://www.iodsa.co.za/page/king_iv_report — an impressive example of 'the South' leading the way for 'the North.'

11. See chapter 8 above. https://www.bcorporation.net/en-us/; https://www.ecogood.org/who-is-ecg/ecg-companies/; https://www.edc-online.org/en/imprese-alias/storie-di-imprese-edc.html; https://eom.foundation/.

12. https://www.vno-ncw.nl/sites/default/files/creating_broad_welfare_through_enterprise_-_vno-ncw_and_mkb-nederland.pdf

13. Business Europe (2019), *Prosperity – People – Planet. Three Pillars for the European Union Agenda 2019–2024*, http://euyour-business.eu/content/uploads/2019/11/2019-11-13-Prosperity-People-Planet_interactive.pdf.

14. To be distinguished from the B-Corps, mentioned in chapter 8. The B-Corps is a private initiative, whereas the Public Benefit Corporation is a specific legal entity, see below in chapter 11.

15. Christian Felber, *Change Everything: Creating an Economy for the Common Good* (London: Zed Books, 2019), pp. 86–87.

16. One of our dialogue partners, the Belgian sociologist Isabelle Ferreras even argues that firms should be seen as equivalent to political entities and should therefore be organized democratically. See Ferreras, *Firms as Political Entities: Saving Democracy Through Economic Bicameralism* (Cambridge: Cambridge University Press, 2017).

17. https://inequality.org/wp-content/uploads/2021/03/Anderson-Senate-Budget-Committee-WRITTEN-Testimony-final.pdf. Cf. Lawrence Mishel and Julia Wolf, "DEO Compensation Has Grown 940% Since 1978," Research Paper *Economic Policy Institute* (2019), https://files.epi.org/pdf/171191.pdf

18. See Polman and Winston, *Net Positive*, ch. 9, "Culture is the Glue," on "putting values into action, deep in the organization" (pp. 217–44).

19. To get a taste of how inspiring this can be, we recommend the book by Sabine Oberhuber and Thomas Rau, *Material Matters: Developing Business for a Circular Economy* (London: Routledge, 2022).

20. Henk W. Volberda, Jatinder Sidhu, Pushpika Vishwanathan, and Kevin Heij, *De winst van Purpose: Hoe ondernemingen het verschil kunnen maken* [The profit of purpose: How companies can make the difference] (Amsterdam: Mediawerf, 2022).

21. Polman and Winston, *Net Positive*.

22. This triggered a rethinking of the entire corporation, eventually leading to the idea of 'Economics of Mutuality.' See Roche and Jakub, *Completing Capitalism*.

23. Cf. Jan Jaap Brouwer and Piet Moerman, *Angelsaksen versus Rijnlanders: Zoektocht naar overeenkomsten en verschillen in Europees en Amerikaans denken* (Amsterdam: Garant, 2010).

24. Harry Commandeur et al., *Agape/caritas in bedrijf: Een praktisch raamwerk voor leidinggevenden* (Amsterdam: Boom, 2021), pp. 49ff.

25. James Davis, David Schoorman, and Lex Donaldson, "Toward a Stewardship Theory of Management," *Academy of Management Review* 22, no. 1 (1997): 20–47.

26. This view is – although couched in slightly different terms – also at the heart of the Moral Capitalism Approach of the Caux Round Table. See Steven Young, *Moral Capitalism: Reconciling Private Interest with the Public Good (A Guide to the Caux Round Table Principles for Business)* (San Francisco: Berrett-Koehler, 2003), pp. 109–24.

27. See the fascinating recent book by James O'Toole, *Enlightened Capitalists: Cautionary Tales of Business Pioneers Who Tried to Do Well by Doing Good* (New York: Harper Business, 2019). This book relates many stories from Robert Owen's New Lanark to Anita Roddick's Body Shop, but there are many more across the continent. For the Netherlands, see, for example, Jacques van Marken, Gerard & Anton Philips, the Stork brothers, and so on.

28. Data taken from the World Cooperative Monitor 2021, https://monitor.coop/sites/default/files/2021-11/WCM_2021%20spread%20FINAL.pdf.

29. To give an impression of this, Crédit Agricole (banking sector) in France had a turnover of $114 billion in 2019. If one takes into account the relative wealth in various countries (purchase power parity), IFFCO in India (agricultural sector) is even larger, with a turnover per capita of almost $4 million, Sistema in Brazil (education, health, social work) has a per capita turnover of almost $2 million. The phenomenon is not unknown in the US either: State Farm (insurance) has a turnover of $42 billion, and three agricultural cooperatives rank in the top ten globally in this sector (CHS, Dairy Farmers, and Land O'Lakes, with a turnover of $32 billion, $16 billion, and $14 billion respectively). European agricultural cooperatives include Friesland Campina (Netherlands, turnover $13 billion) and Arla (Denmark, $12 billion). Mondragon in Spain (turnover $14 billion) is a relatively young cooperative (founded in 1956) and is the world's largest cooperative in the industrial sector (both in absolute numbers as in the per capita adjusted list). Others are active in the wholesale and retail sectors.

30. See below as well for the "frontrunner program." In chapter 8, we referred in this respect to Lucas Simons and André Nijhof, *Changing the Game: Sustainable Market Transformation Strate-*

gies to Understand and Tackle the Big and Complex Sustainability Challenges of our Generation (London: Routledge, 2021).

31. Rob Bauer, Tereza Bauer, Mieke Olaerts, and Constantijn van Aartsen, *Sustainability Embedding Practices in Dutch Listed Companies* (Maastricht: Maastricht University, 2021), pp. 69–70.

32. Global Compact Network Netherlands, *Stakeholder Inclusion as an Accelerator for the Sustainable Development Goals. Inspiration from the Netherlands* (2020). https://ungc-communications-assets.s3.amazonaws.com/docs/publications/Global-compact-NL-Stakeholder-Inclusion.FINAL_.pdf

33. Cf. Rotmans and Verheijden, *Omarm de chaos* distinguishes ten 'transitions' taking place almost simultaneously, including energy, raw materials, circularity, financial, educational, social and democratic transitions, see ch. 5. Cf. Rob van Tulder and Eveline van Mill, *Principles of Sustainable Business: Frameworks for Corporate Action on the SDG's'* (London: Routledge, 2023); they refer to the VUCAworld, i.e., Volatile, Uncertain, Complex and Ambiguous.

34. This section is partly based on the report of the Think Tank of Young Economists connected to this project: Sam de Muijnck, Elisa Terragno Bogliaccini, and Jim Richard Surie, eds., *Towards the Wellbeing Economy: Implications for Public, Environmental and Financial Policy* (Amsterdam: Vrije Universiteit, 2021), https://www.moralmarkets.org/futuremarketsconsultation/activities/think-tank/ and partly on a contribution written for this book by Kees Buitendijk, project director of the Finance for the Common Good Project of the Dutch Think Tank Socires. See also Cor van Beuningen and Kees Buitendijk. *Finance and the Common Good* (Amsterdam: Amsterdam University Press, 2019).

35. See above, chapter 3. For a much more extensive treatment of some of these problems, see the 2016 report by the Dutch 'Wetenschappelijke Raad voor het Regeringsbeleid (WRR),' the 'Netherlands Scientific Council for Government Policy,' *Samenleving en financiële sector in evenwicht* [Finance and Society: Restoring the Balance] (The Hague: WRR, 2016).

36. Think Tank of Young Economists, *Towards a Wellbeing Economy*, p. 45.

37. See Institut Montaigne, *Responsible Capitalism: An Opportunity for Europe* (Paris, 2020), especially ch. 1.

38. Arnoud Boot, *De ontwortelde onderneming: Ondernemingen overgeleverd aan financiers?* (Assen: Koninklijke Van Gorkum, 2009).

39. Arnoud Boot, Peter Hoffmann, Luc Laeven, and Lev Ratnovski, 'Fintech: What's Old, What's New?' *Journal of Financial Stability* 53 (April 2021).

40. On this, see also the above-mentioned report by the Institut Montaigne, *Responsible Capitalism.*

41. De Nederlandsche Bank (May 3, 2021), *Trust in the Dutch financial sector has held up during the COVID-19 crisis.* https://www. dnb.nl/en/general-news/dnbulletins-2021/trust-in-the-dutch-financial-sector-has-held-up-during-the-covid-19-crisis/ Accessed August 18, 2023.

42. Cf. the above-mentioned report by the Think Tank of Young Economists, *Towards the Wellbeing Economy*, pp. 53ff.

43. Donal McKillop, Declan French, Barry Quinn, Anna L. Sobeich, John O.S. Wilson, "Cooperative Financial Institutions: A Review of the Literature," *International Review of Financial Analysis* 71 (October 2020).

44. See, e.g., Joel Kotkin, *The Coming of Neo-Feudalism: A Warning to the Global Middle Class* (New York: Encounter Books, 2020).

45. For shocking cases, see Nicholas Freudenberg, *Lethal but Legal: Corporations, Consumption, and Protecting Public Health* (Oxford: Oxford University Press, 2016).

46. Tim Wu, *The Attention Merchants: The Epic Scramble to Get Inside Our Heads* (New York: Knopf, 2016).

47. Soshana Zuboff, *The Age of Surveillance Capitalism: The Fight for the Human Future at the New Frontier of Power* (Manchester: ProFile, 2019).

48. Paul Schenderling, *Er is leven na de groei: Hoe we onze toekomst realistisch veiligstellen* (Voorschoten: Bot Uitgevers, 2022).

49. See the above-mentioned book by Oberhuber and Rau, *Material Matters: Developing Business for a Circular Economy,* ch. 5.

50. Global Burden of Disease (2010); https://www.who.int/newsroom/fact-sheets/detail/obesity-and-overweight.

51. Kirsi Kotilainen, *Perspectives on the Prosumer Role in the Sustainable Energy System*, PhD dissertation, Tampere University, 2020.

52. The investment that has to be made creates a new form of inequality, as not everyone will be able to invest and will thus be forced to keep buying energy. An inclusive economy should include compensation for this.

53. See the argument referred to earlier by R. Edward Freeman and Robert A. Phillips, "Stakeholder Theory: A Libertarian Defense," *Business Ethics Quarterly,* 12, no. 3 (July 2002): 331–49.

54. On the Jevons paradox in relation to consumption growth and the great obstacles to realizing something like 'green growth' or the 'decoupling' of consumption and use of raw materials, see Schenderling, *Er is leven na de groei*.
55. Robert Skidelsky and Edward Skidelsky, *How Much Is Enough? Money and the Good Life* (London: Other Press, 2012).
56. Katherine Trebeck and Jeremy Williams, *The Economics of Arrival: Ideas for a Grown-Up Economy* (Bristol: Policy, 2019).

Chapter 11

1. The term 'mission' has been introduced in economics by Mariana Mazzucato, *Mission Economy: A Moonshot Guide to Changing Capitalism* (New York: Allan Lane, 2021), developing an argument from her earlier book *The Entrepreneurial State: Debunking Public vs. Private Sector Myths.* (New York: PublicAffairs, 2015).
2. Thomas Philippon, *The Great Reversal: How America Gave Up on Free Markets* (Cambridge, MA: Belknap Press, 2019). As referred to already in chapter 4 above, the fear of the US becoming a plutocracy has been voiced by Branco Milanovic, *Capitalism Alone: The Future of the System that Rules the World* (Cambridge, MA: Belknap Press, 2019), pp. 217ff. Raghuram Rajan and Luigi Zingales had earlier already made their plea in *Saving Capitalism from the Capitalists* (New York: Crown, 2003).
3. Daron Acemoglu and James Robinson, *Why Nations Fail: The Origins of Power, Prosperity, and Poverty* (New York: Crown, 2012).
4. See Michael Sandel. *The Tyranny of Merit: What's Become of the Common Good?* (London: Allen Lane, 2020).
5. Rutger Bregman and Jesse Frederik, *Waarom vuilnismannen meer verdienen dan bankiers* [Why garbage collectors should earn more than bankers] (Amsterdam: De Correspondent, 2015).
6. Cf. Richard Sennett, *The Culture of New Capitalism* (New Haven: Yale University Press, 2006); Martin Sandbu, *The Economics of Belonging: A Radical Plan to Win Back the Left Behind and Achieve Prosperity for All* (Princeton: Princeton University Press, 2020); Paul Collier, *The Future of Capitalism: Facing the New Anxieties* (New Delhi: Allen Lane 2018).
7. See the report as well of the Think Tank of Young Economists participating in the Future Market Consultation: "Renewing the Welfare State: The Right Mix of Ensuring Jobs, Income and Services." Amsterdam: Vrije Universiteit.

8. See Femke Groothuis/Ex'tax Project, ed., *The Taxshift: A EU Fiscal Strategy to Support the Inclusive Circular Economy* (2022). The report by the Ex'tax Project, which provides a detailed road map toward a different taxation structure in Europe, away from taxing what is desirable, jobs, toward what is undesirable, pollution and wasting. See https://ex-tax.com/wp-content/uploads/2022/06/The-Taxshift_EU-Fiscal-Strategy_Extax-Project-2June22def.pdf. A plea for more taxation on consumption relative to that on labor is to be found in Paul Schenderling, *Er is leven na de groei: Hoe we onze toekomst realistisch veiligstellen* (Voorschoten: Bot Uitgevers, 2022), ch. 2 and 3.

9. For these and similar measures, see Rens van Tilburg, Elisa Achterberg, and Max van Son, "Financiële beleidsinterventies voor een circulaire economie," in Amsterdam Center for Corporate Finance, *Sustainable Finance and Government Policy,* Topics in Corporate Finance Series (issue 27), pp. 27–70.

10. Although, of course, a substantial tax base has to remain that is not connected to negative externalities, otherwise the eventual effect may be that there is no tax base left as soon as all the externalities have been dealt with, but this seems to be a concern for the long-term future.

11. Anu Bradford, *The Brussels Effect: How the European Union Rules the World* (Oxford: Oxford University Press, 2020).

12. https://www.futurepolicy.org/climate-stability/japans-top-runner-programme/.

13. It is worth repeating here what we said already in chapter 10: that a Public Benefit Corporation under US law is not the same as a B corporation company, although the standards come close. In the US, a PBC is an official legal status that may entail certain tax exemptions and other provisions, whereas a B corporation is a private initiative that is certified by the B corporation standards. In the US, Patagonia and Danone North America have acquired official PBC-status.

14. See above, footnote 1, about the concept of 'mission' and the work of Mariana Mazzucato.

15. Strictly speaking, the term *konzertierte Aktion* referred to the policies of the German SPD after 1976. But from a broader perspective, the term may well be applied to a longer tradition in Germany of mutual attunement between government policy and market parties.

16. This argument is made forcefully by one of the dialogue participants: Ann Pettifor, *The Case for the Green New Deal* (London: Verso, 2019), who starts her book with the assurance "we can afford what we can do," meaning that when matters are urgent and we take action, then this can always be financed. Finance follows plans, not the other way around.

17. See above, chapter 3: Johan Rockström et al., "Planetary Boundaries: Exploring the Safe Operating Space for Humanity," *Ecology and Society* 14, no. 2 (2009), art. 32.

18. Harald Sverdrup and Kristin Vala Ragnarsdottir, "Natural Resources in a Planetary Perspective," Geochemical Perspectives 3, no. 2 (2014): 129–341.

19. Kate Raworth *Doughnut Economics: Seven Ways to Think Like a 21st-Century Economist* (London: Random House, 2017). A recent, valuable, very research-based contribution to a more comprehensive reconciliation between the economy and ecology is *The Economics of Biodiversity: The Dasgupta Review* (London: HM Treasury, 2021) by Cambridge professor Partha Dasgupta. The review made a case for different measures than the GDP and measuring the negative ecological consequences of businesses.

20. A distinction made viable by Arne Naess, "The Shallow and the Deep, Long-Range Ecology Movement: A Summary," *Inquiry* 16, nos. 1–4 (1973): 95–100.

21. The literature on 'degrowth' has been growing quickly in recent years. Original inspiration, after the publication of *Limits to Growth* by the Club of Rome came E.F. Schumacher's *Small is Beautiful: Economics as If People Mattered* (London: Blond & Briggs, 1973), followed by Herman Daly, *The Steady State Economics*, 2nd ed. (Washington, DC: Island Press [1977] 1991). Some of the most influential recent publications include Jason Hickel, *Less Is More: How Degrowth Will Save the World* (London: William Heinemann, 2020); Giorgos Kallis, Susan Paulson, Giacomo D'Alisa, and Federico Demaria, *The Case for Degrowth* (Cambridge: Polity, 2020); Matthias Schmelzer, Aaron Vasintjan, and Andrea Vetter, eds., *The Future is Degrowth: A Guide to a World Beyond Capitalism* (London: Verso, 2020). Kallis and Hickel, together with one of our dialogue participants, Julia Steinberger, were awarded a large ERC grant for doing research in this area in December 2022.

22. For this, see the important but yet untranslated book by Paul Schenderling (2022), *Er is leven na de groei: Hoe we onze toekomst realistisch veiligstellen* [There is life beyond growth. How we can secure our future in a realistic way]. A first attempt at a major institutional level is made by the OECD-report *Beyond Growth. Towards a New Economic Approach* (Paris: OECD Publishing 2020).

23. See the report by the Think Tank of Young Economists connected to this project: Sam de Muijnck, Elisa Terragno Bogliaccini, and Jim Richard Surie, eds., *Towards the Wellbeing Economy: Implications for Public, Environmental and Financial Policy* (April 2021), pp. 32ff., on taking a 'growth-agnostic' stance.

24. For this 'anthropocentric' attitude, cf. Clive Hamilton, *Defiant Earth: The Fate of Humans in the Anthropocene* (Sydney: Allen & Unwin, 2017).

25. Henk W. Volberda, Jatinder Sidhu, Pushpika Vishwanathan, and Kevin Heij, *De winst van Purpose: Hoe ondernemingen het verschil kunnen maken* [The profit of purpose: How companies can make the difference] (Amsterdam: Mediawerf, 2022).

26. Bruno Roche and Jay Jakub, *Completing Capitalism: Heal Business to Heal the World* (Oakland (CA): Berrett-Koehler, 2017), pp. 87–98.

27. International Federation of Red Cross and Red Crescent Societies (IFRC) (2020), *World Disasters Report 2020: Come Heat or High Water: Tackling the Humanitarian Impacts of the Climate Crisis Together.*

28. This is suggested by the authors of the report of the Young Economists' Think Tank, which was part of the preparation phase for this book: Sam de Muijnck, Elisa Terragno Bogliaccini, and Jim R. Surie, *Towards the Wellbeing Economy: Implications for Public, Environmental and Financial Policy* (Amsterdam: Vrije Universiteit, 2021).

29. An inspirational example on the mixing of politics and nature is Bruno Latour's concept of a parliament of things. Bruno Latour, *Het Parlement der Dingen* (Amsterdam: Boom, 2020), which contains a translation of his earlier essay (1994, republished in 2018), "Esquisse du Parlement des choses," *Ecologie politique* 1, no. 56 (2018): 47–64.

30. Jan J. Boersema, *The Survival of Easter Island: Dwindling Resources and Cultural Resilience* (Cambridge: Cambridge University Press, 2015).

31. See Schenderling, *Er is leven na de groei,* passim.

32. Paul Hawken, *Regeneration: Ending the Climate Crisis in One Generation* (New York: Penguin, 2021), p. 10.

33. Martin Sandbu, *The Economics of Belonging*; Paul Collier, *The Future of Capitalism: Facing the New Anxieties* (New Delhi: Allen 2018); David Goodhart, *The Road to Somewhere: The New Tribes Shaping British Politics* (London: Penguin, 2017).

34. Ferdinand Braudel, *Beschaving, economie en kapitalisme (15de–18de eeuw)*, Part 2, *Het spel van de handel* (Amsterdam: Contact, 1989), pp. 69ff; Michael Storper, "Community and Economics," in Ash Amin and Joanne Roberts, eds., *Community, Economic Creativity, and Organization* (Oxford: Oxford University Press, 2008), pp. 37–68.

35. This in the wake of Garrett Hardin, "Tragedy of the Commons," *Science* 162, no. 3859 (1968): 1243–48. In 1990, Elinor Ostrom published her empirical study on 'commons' (something Hardin had never done), titled *Governing the Commons: The Evolution of Institutions for Collective Action* (Cambridge: Cambridge University Press, 1990), and found that communities often know well how to handle, create, maintain, and pass on their 'commons.' It took time, but gradually the significance of her findings started to become recognized, eventually bringing her the 2009 Sveriges Riksbank/Nobel Prize in Economic Sciences, making her the first woman to win the prize.

36. The book that can serve as kind of landmark for this literature is Francis Fukuyama (1995), *Trust: The Social Virtues and the Creation of Prosperity*. Intellectually, this literature can be broadly located in the movement of 'communitarianism' – not to be confused with communism! – which first started as a philosophical and social theoretical critique of individualist liberalism, first with the book *After Virtue* by Alasdair MacIntyre (Notre Dame: Notre Dame University Press, 1981) and was then introduced into sociology and at the same time into economics by Amitai Etzioni, *The Moral Dimension: Toward a New Economics* (New York: Free Press, 1988). In this section, research is introduced that does not often come under the heading 'communitarianism' but can be seen as part of the same overarching movement. The importance of healthy communities is often illustrated by reference to the difference between northern and southern Italy. In Edward Banfield's 1958 study of a southern village, *The Moral Basis of a Backward Society* (New York: Free

Press) all the possible negative potential of closed communities are brought out: enmity, bigotry, corruption. By contrast, Robert D. Putnam, *Making Democracy Work: Civic Traditions in Modern Italy* (Princeton: Princeton University Press, 1993), shows that in northern Italy there was a high level of trust and cooperativity, 'social capital,' between the citizens, harking back to what we identified earlier in this book as the medieval "cooperative revolution."

37. In the Netherlands, this literature was addressed in a volume edited by J.P. Balkenende, E. J. J. M. Kimman, and J. P. van den Toren, eds., *Vertrouwen in de economie: Het debat* [The role of trust in the economy: The current debate] (Assen: Van Gorcum, 1997).

38. James Coleman, *Foundations of Social Theory* (Cambridge, MA: Belknap/Harvard University Press, 1990); Putnam, *Making Democracy Work*.

39. Irene van Staveren and Peter Knorringa, "Unpacking Social Capital in Economic Development: How Social Relations Matter," Review of Social Economy 65, no. 1 (2007): 107–35; Tom Healy (2002), "The Measurement of Social Capital at International Level," OECD-paper. See https://www.oecd.org/innovation/research/2380281.pdf (accessed February 18, 2022).

40. A lucid discussion of "relational goods" is given in Luigino Bruni, *The Wound and the Blessing: Economics, Relationships and Happiness* (New York: New City Press, 2012), pp. 83–98.

41. This perspective is very much in line with the innovative theorizing on community by Paul Adler and Charles Heckscher, *The Firm as Collaborative Community* (Oxford: Oxford University Press, 2006), especially the substantial introduction "Towards Collaborative Community." They see a new type of community emerging between the traditional *Gemeinschaft* and the modern individualized *Gesellschaft*: "collaboratives" where people work together to solve commonly perceived problems, pulling their diverse skills together and inviting everyone who shares the same concerns.

42. For the outcomes, see: https://g1000.nu/wp-content/uploads/2020/07/Covention-Citoyenne-Climat.pdf.

43. Benjamin Barber, *If Majors Ruled the World: Dysfunctional Nations, Rising Cities* (New Haven: Yale University Press, 2013).

44. Cf. the interesting book by David Goodhart, *Head, Hand, Heart: The Struggle for Dignity and Status in the 21st Century* (Lon-

don: Penguin, 2020). For a similar argument, see Bregman and Frederik, *Waarom vuilnismannen meer verdienen dan bankiers.*

45. As was evident from the extensive cross-country research conducted by Lester Salamon and his team between 1987 and 2022 at the Johns Hopkins Center for Civil Society Studies. See https://ccss.jhu.edu/

46. As mentioned in the introductory chapter, we are borrowing the distinction between market economies and market societies from Michael Sandel, *What Money Can't Buy: The Moral Limits of Markets* (New York: Farrar, Strauss and Giroux, 2012), p. 10.

47. Alexis de Tocqueville, *De la démocratie en Amérique* (1830–1835); translated in English as *Democracy in America* (numerous editions, online and in print). Cf. Fukuyama, *Trust*; Putnam, *Making Democracy Work.*

48. See the above-mentioned books: Putnam, *Making Democracy Work* and Fukuyama, *Trust.*

49. Daron Acemoglu and James Robinson, *The Narrow Corridor: States, Societies and the Fate of Liberty* (New York: Penguin, 2019).

50. Burton A. Weisbrod, *The Voluntary Nonprofit Sector: An Economic Analysis* (Lexington: Lexington Books, 1977).

51. A very interesting analysis, from a very different context, of the different dynamics between social, future-oriented conflict resolutions and the often backward-oriented legal procedures is given by Martha Minow, *Between Vengeance and Forgiveness: Facing History After Genocide and Mass Violence* (Boston: Beacon Press, 1998).

52. Moulen Siame Siame, M. "A Practical and Theoretical Approach to Social Venturing Entrepreneurship," in Silvio Manuel Brito, ed., *Entrepreneurship – Trends and Challenges* (Rijeka: InTech 2018), pp. 83–104. Open access: https://www.intechopen.com/chapters/58202. DOI: 10.5772/intechopen.72011

53. For example, Swink is an internet company that only hires people with autism and makes a normal profit, like all other companies.

54. 'Internationaal beleid,' Social Enterprise NL. See https://www.social-enterprise.nl/beleid-en-onderzoek/internationaal-beleid (accessed January 10, 2021). See also chapter 10 section 1 and chapter 11 section 1, above.

55. For an argument for recognizing the importance of an independent civil society in the Dutch context see Paul Frissen, *De integrale staat.* (Amsterdam: Boom, 2023).

56. An impressive argument in favor of this statement within the French context, often characterized as 'statist,' is given by Pierre Rosanvallon, *The Demands of Liberty. Civil Society in France since the French Revolution* (Cambridge, MA: Harvard University Press, 2007).

57. On these types of critical questions, see Robert Reich, *Just Giving: Why Philanthropy is Failing Democracy and How It Can Do Better* (Princeton: Princeton University Press, 2018).

Chapter 12

1. Bethany McLean, "Is Enron Overpriced?" *Fortune Magazine* 143, no. 5 (March 5, 2001).

2. Patrick R. Keefe, *Empire of Pain: The Secret History of the Sackler Dynasty* (New York: Anchor Books, 2022). It is estimated that around 500,000 people died because of their addiction to the painkillers, which were said not to be addictive.

3. Habermas remains the authoritative philosopher who has uncovered the historical background of the public sphere and later reflected as well on the preconditions for a healthy public sphere in Jürgen Habermas (1962), *Strukturwandel der Öffentlichkeit*. This study drew a great deal of new attention through its translation in 1989 as *The Structural Transformation of the Public Sphere: An Inquiry into a Category of Bourgeois Society* (Cambridge, MA: MIT Press, 1989). His later *magnum opus* on the topic is *Theorie des kommunikativen Handels (Theory of Communicative Action)* (Frankfurt am Main: Suhrkamp, 1981).

4. Charles Taylor in *A Secular Age* (Cambridge, MA: Belknap/Harvard University Press, 2007), refers to the 19th century as "the Age of Mobilization" (pp. 423–72).

5. As explained for example in Michiko Kakutani, *The Death of Truth: Notes on Falsehood in the Age of Trump* (New York: Tim Duggan Books, 2018).

6. To apply the earlier internal slogan of Facebook against the company itself. Cf. Jonathan Taplin, *Move Fast and Break Things: How Facebook, Google, and Amazon Cornered Culture and Undermined Democracy* (New York: Little, Brown, 2017).

7. For further suggestions along these lines by an important Dutch internet pioneer, see Marleen Stikker (2019), *Het internet is stuk maar we kunnen het repareren* [The internet is broken, but we

can fix it] (Amsterdam: De Geus, 2019), especially pp. 236–45; no translation is available as of yet.

8. The oldest university in the world that has been in constant operation is Al Quaraouiyine in Morocco, founded in 859; it was then and is still now primarily devoted to the study of Islamic theology and Islamic law.

9. This section is partly based on a MA thesis by Bart Gulden, *Transformatieve Innovatie: Europees innovatiebeleid binnen een wereld van sociale waarden* [Transformative Innovation: European innovation policies within a framework of social values. MA program 'Philosophy of Culture and Governance], Vrije Universiteit, 2022.

10. René van Schomberg, "A Vision of Responsible Innovation," in R. Owen, M. Heintz, and J. Bessant, eds., *Responsible Innovation* (London: John Wiley, 2013), pp. 51–74.

11. Van Schomberg, "A Vision of Responsible Innovation," p. 51.

12. Mariana Mazzucato, *Mission-Oriented Research & Innovation in the European Union* (Brussels: European Commission, 2018).

13. Ursula von der Leyen, "A Union that Strives for More: My Agenda for Europe," *Political Guidelines for the Next European Commission* (2019). Brussels: European Parliament 2019. https://www.europarl.europa.eu/resources/library/media/20190716RES57231/20190716RES57231.pdf

14. Richard R. Nelson, "Intellectualizing about the Moon-Ghetto Metaphor: A Study of the Current Malaise of Rational Analysis of Social Problems," *Policy Sciences* 5 (1974): 375–414.

15. The still impressive advocates of the importance of this type of knowledge are Donald Schön, *The Reflective Practitioner: How Professionals Think in Action* (London: Routledge, 1983), and Michael Lipsky, *Street-Level Bureaucracy: Dilemmas of the Individual in Public Services* (New York: Russell Sage, 1980). We mention these here just to illustrate the fact that innovation involves very different types of knowledge and that academic institutions should not claim or have a monopoly on knowledge.

16. Edwin Koster. "Het Knowledge Filter: Leidt consensus tot betrouwbare kennis?" in E. Koster, ed., *Wat is wetenschap? Een filosofische inleiding voor levenswetenschappers en medici* (Amsterdam: VU University Press, 2019), pp. 183–207.

17. Henk W. Volberda, Justin Jansen, Michiel Tempelaar, and Kevin Heij, "Monitoren van sociale innovatie: slimmer werken, dyna-

misch managen en flexibel organiseren," *Tijdschrift voor HRM* (2011) 1: 85–110.

18.   When Roman emperors made their way through Rome, they were accompanied – while cheered by the enthusiastic crowds – by someone constantly whispering in their ear, "Remember Caesar, you are human." See Manfred Kets de Vries. "Thought Leader Interview by Art Kleiner." *Strategy+Business* 59 (Summer 2010). https://www.strategy-business.com/article/10209.

19.   Some 'classics' in this respect: Peter Kropotkin, *Mutual Aid: A Factor of Evolution* (London: Freedom Press, 1902); Marcel Mauss (1923), *Essai sur le don: Formes et raisons de l'échange dans les sociétés archaïques. L'Année Sociologique* [An Essay on the Gift: The Form and Reason of Exchange in Archaic Societies] (London: Routledge, 1950). A still intriguing, and very influential, history of capitalism, which portrays capitalism as a highly ambivalent departure from other, more community-oriented, ways to organize an economy is Karl Polanyi, *The Great Transformation: The Political and Economic Origins of Our Time* (Boston: Beacon Press, [1944] 1957).

20.   To give some examples, just two, of exercises along these lines see Arjo Klamer, *Doing the Right Thing: A Value Based Economy* (London: Uniquity Press, 2016); and Govert Buijs, *Waarom werken we zo hard? Op weg naar een economie van de vreugde* [Why are we working so hard? Towards an economy of joy] (Amsterdam: Boom, 2019).

21.   Carl Sagan, *Pale Blue Dot: A Vision of the Human Future in Space* (New York: Random House, 1994).

22.   For an analysis of the culturally very diverse ways in which in several parts of the world 'modernization' takes on different forms, see Haroon Sheikh, *Embedding Technopolis. Turning Modernity into a Home* (Amsterdam: Boom, 2017).

23.   John Maynard Keynes, *The General Theory of Employment, Interest and Money* (London: MacMillan, 1936), ch. 24, p. 383.

24.   John Stuart Mill (1859), *On Liberty*, ch. 2, the famous argument against censorship: the censored opinion may later turn out to be true. See John Stuart Mill, *Three Essays: On Liberty; Representative Government; The Subjection of Women* (Oxford: Oxford University Press, 1975).

25.   Just an example: Deirdre Nansen McCloskey, *Bettering Humanomics: A New, and Old, Approach to Economic Science* (Chicago: University of Chicago Press, 2021).

Chapter 13

1. As the upbeat title of Paul Hawken indicates: *Regeneration: Ending the Climate Crisis in One Generation* (New York: Penguin, 2021).

2. The term 'geoeconomics' isn't used today with the same frequency as geopolitics, but in substance it is very much on the table. The term was introduced by Edward N. Luttwack, "From Geopolitics to Geo-Economics: Logic of Conflict, Grammar of Commerce," *The National Interest* 20 (Summer 1990): 17–23. See also Haroon Sheikh, "Aanbevelingen voor een geo-economische wereld" [Recommendations for a geoeconomic world], *Economisch-Statistische Berichten* 106, no. 4801 (2021): 407–9. Although geopolitics and geoeconomics are different ball games, they are closely intertwined.

3. Paul Kennedy, *The Rise and Fall of the Great Powers* (New York: Vintage Books, 1987), pp. 347ff.

4. Kennedy, *The Rise and Fall of the Great Powers,* p. 515.

5. This is a general pattern after financial crises; see Manuel Funke, Moritz Schularick, and Christoph Trebesch, "Going to Extremes: Politics after Financial Crises, 1870–2014," European Economic Review 88, issue C (2016): 227–60.

6. See the data in Anne Case and Angus Deaton, *Deaths of Despair and the Future of Capitalism* (Princeton: Princeton University Press, 2020).

7. Case and Deaton, *Deaths of Despair and the Future of Capitalism.*

8. As the earlier work by Fukuyama strongly suggested, which was also one of the bases for the second invasion of Iraq. Cf. Kishore Mahbubani, *Has China Won? The Chinese Challenge to American Primacy* (New York: Public Affairs, 2020).

9. See above, ch. 5.

10. Christoph Nedopil, "Countries of the Belt and Road Initiative," in *China Belt and Road Initiative (BRI): Investment Report 2022* (Shanghai: Green Finance & Development Center, FISF Fudan University, 2022), p. 25. https://greenfdc.org/wp-content/uploads/2023/02/Nedopil-2023_China-Belt-and-Road-Initiative-BRI-Investment-Report-2022.pdf

11. It may be that the accusation of "debt trap diplomacy" is a Western response to its own loss of hegemony. The debts owed by countries in the global South China are a fraction of what they

owe to the West. See Janet Eom, Deborah Brautigam, and Lina Bedabdallah, "The Path Ahead: The 7th Forum on China-Africa Cooperation," SAIS-CARI Briefing Papers 01/2018, Johns Hopkins University, School of Advanced International Studies (SAIS), China Africa Research Initiative (CARI). https://www.econstor.eu/bitstream/10419/248242/1/sais-cari-bp01.pdf. Retrieved August 29, 2022. The overview article indicates that the amount of Chinese debt owed by most African countries is relatively small compared to other lenders (exceptions: Djibouti, the Congo Republic, and Zambia). In by far most countries, China still is just one of many multilateral creditors.

12. Jamie Gaida et al., *ASPI's Critical Technology Tracker: The Global Race for Future Power* (Canberra: ASPI, 2023), Policy Report no. 69.

13. Centre for Research on Energy and Clear Air (CREA). "China Dominates 2020 Coal Plant Development." *Global Energy Monitor – Briefing February 2021.* https://globalenergymonitor.org/wp-content/uploads/2021/02/China-Dominates-2020-Coal-Development.pdf. Retrieved 18 August 2023.

14. Henk Schulte Nordholt, *Is China nog te stoppen? Hoe een virus de wereldorde verandert* (Amsterdam: Querido, 2021), p. 63. In September 2021, however, China announced that it is going to terminate its program of building coal-fired power plants outside China, especially in Africa, but it is unclear as to when this will commence and what it implies for projects that have already been started.

15. Cf. Fons Stoelinga, *India: Land van de toekomst* (Amsterdam: De Kring, 2019).

16. The actual military spending of Russia in terms of PPP (purchasing power parity) is much more than this percentage suggests, however.

17. Henry Farrell and Abraham L. Newman, "Weaponized Interdependence: How Global Economic Networks Shape State Coercion," *International Security* 44, no. 1 (Summer 2019): 42–79.

18. Perhaps most famously by the philosopher Karl Popper, *The Open Society and Its Enemies* (London: Routledge & Kegan Paul, 1945).

19. Inspiration for this idea of a Eurasian civilizational space may well have been drawn from Alexander Dugin. See Victor Kal, *Alexander Doegin. Poetins filosoof* (Amsterdam: Prometheus, 2023).

20. Vladimir Putin has given his perspective in various speeches over the years, of which the so-called Munich Security Con-

ference speech of 2007 stands out: see http://en.kremlin.ru/events/president/transcripts/24034. His most recent views can be found, for example, on Ukraine: see http://en.kremlin.ru/events/president/news/66181 and the speeches given at the Duma on July 7, 2022, http://en.kremlin.ru/events/president/news/68836, and at the formal annexation ceremony of four Ukrainian regions, https://www.miragenews.com/full-text-of-putins-speech-at-annexation-866383/ and at the anniversary of the Ukraine invasion in the Duma, http://en.kremlin.ru/events/president/news/70565.

21. Rob de Wijk, *De slag om Europa: Hoe China en Rusland ons continent uit elkaar spelen* (Amsterdam: Balans, 2021).

22. Cf. Govert Buijs and Paul Bosman, *Ontwaken uit de geopolitieke sluimer: De herpositionering van Europa in een woelige wereld* (Utrecht: Eburon/Thijmgenootschap, 2023).

23. Stoelinga, *India*, pp. 219ff.

24. See, e.g., Kehinde Andrews, *The New Age of Empire: How Racism and Colonialism Still Rule the World* (London: Penguin, 2021).

25. Kishore Mahbubani, *Has the West Lost It? A Provocation* (London: Allen Lane, 2018).

26. Niccolò Machiavelli, *The Prince* (1513/1532), ch. 17 and 19.

27. "Out of the crooked timber of humanity not straight thing was ever made". In German: "Aus so krummem Holze, als woraus der Mensch gemacht ist, kann nichts ganz Gerades gezimmert werden." In Immanuel Kant, "Idee zu einer allgemeinen Geschichte in weltbürgerlicher Absicht," *Berlinische Monatsschrift* (November 1784): 385–411, quote to be found in the 'Sechster Satz.' The quote was famously used as book title by Isaiah Berlin, *The Crooked Timber of Humanity* (1959).

28. Ray Dalio, *The Changing World Order: Why Nations Succeed and Fail* (New York: Simon & Schuster, 2021).

Chapter 14

1. For a more elaborate version of this argument, see Govert Buijs, "De Oekraïne-oorlog als kanarie in de kolenmijn: Europa en de zoektocht naar een nieuwe wereldorde," in Govert Buijs and Paul Bosman, eds., *Ontwaken uit de geopolitieke sluimer: De herpositionering van Europa in een woelige wereld* (Utrecht: Eburon/Thijmgenootschap, 2022), pp. 123–38.

2.   Gerda van Dijk and Rens van Loon, "The European Commission: Leading Diversity by Dialogue," in Rob Koonce and Rens van Loon, eds., *The Dialogical Challenge of Leadership Development* (Charlotte, NC: Information Age Publishing), pp. 125–38.

3.   Data based on Globalfirepower.com.

4.   Statement made a few days before the outbreak of the First Gulf War, *New York Times*, January 25, 1991.

5.   Rob de Wijk, *De slag om Europa: Hoe China en Rusland ons continent uit elkaar spelen* (Amsterdam: Balans, 2021).

6.   For the importance of this principle in European history, see the recent dissertation of Herman Jozef Kaiser, *In Ordinata Concordia. Het Subsidiariteitsbeginsel en de Geordende Eendracht in de Politieke Economie* (Tilburg: Open Press Tilburg University 2023).

7.   René Cuperus, *7 Mythe über Europa: Plädoyer für ein vorsichtiges Europa* (Bonn: Dietz Verlag, 2022). Cuperus argues for a Europe that is strong outwardly and mild inwardly.

8.   R. James Breiding, *Too Small to Fail: Why Some Nations Outperform Larger Ones and How They Are Reshaping the World* (New York: Harper Business, 2019).

9.   See the book by India's Minister of External Affairs Subrahmanyam Jaishankar, *The India Way: Strategies for an Uncertain World.* (New Delhi: HarperCollins Publishers India, 2020).

10. A proposal by Kishore Mahbubani, *Has the West Lost It? A Provocation* (London: Allen Lane, 2018), p. 86.

11. S.N. Eisenstadt, "Multiple Modernities," *Daedalus* 129, no. 1 (Winter 2000): 1–29.

12. When a substantial group of African countries held a climate conference in the Dutch city of Rotterdam in September 2022, in preparation for COP 27 (discussing the consequences for their countries of climate change, which they didn't cause), no European leaders showed up, and the Dutch prime minister only gave a short late afternoon greeting. The 'Do not humiliate others' rule was certainly violated here and all this was incredibly shortsighted from a long-term geopolitical and geoeconomic point of view, not to mention irresponsible.

13. Cf. Henk Schulte Nordholt, *Is China nog te stoppen? Hoe een virus de wereldorde verandert* (Amsterdam: Querido, 2021), and de Wijk, *De slag om Europa* (2021); also the wake-up call issued by Mahbubani in *Has the West Lost It?* (2018) and in *Has China Won? The Chinese Challenge to American Primacy* (New York:

Public Affairs, 2020); Ray Dalio, *The Changing World Order: Why Nations Succeed and Fail* (New York: Simon & Schuster, 2021).

14. Anu Bradford, *The Brussels Effect: How the European Union Rules the World* (Oxford: Oxford University Press, 2020).

15. https://www.europarl.europa.eu/doceo/document/TA-9-2021-0073_EN.html. See above, chapter 8.

16. To mention just two of them: Muhammad Yunus, *A World of Three Zeros: The New Economics of Zero Poverty, Zero Unemployment, and Zero Net Carbon Emissions* (London: Hachette, 2017), and Jeffrey Sachs, *The End of Poverty: How We Can Make it Happen in Our Lifetime* (London: Penguin, 2005/2015).

17. Christian Felber, *Trading for Good: How Global Trade Can Be Made to Serve People Not Money* (London: Zed Books, 2019).

18. See, for example, Thomas N. Bisson, "The 'Feudal Revolution,'" *Past & Present* 142 (1994): 6–42 for a very grim view of the period. Of course, this view is not uncontested, but it still contains many elements on which there is large consensus among historians. A critical review of Bisson's work can be found in Hans Hummer, "Were the Lords Really All That Bad?" *Historical Methods* 43, no. 4 (2010): 165–70.

Chapter 15

1. Cf. Eric Sadin, *L'ère de l'individu tyran* (Paris: Grasset, 2020).

2. Cf. Ad Verbrugge, *De gezagscrisis. Filosofisch essay over een wankele orde* (Amsterdam: Boom, 2023).

3. Cf. Rutger Hoekstra, *Replacing GDP by 2030: Towards a Common Language for the Well-Being and Sustainability Community* (Cambridge: Cambridge University Press, 2019).

Epilogue

1. Václav Havel, *Disturbing the Peace: A Conversation with Karel Hvížďala*, trans. Paul Wilson (New York: Vintage, 1990), p. 181.

2. Matthew Arnold, "Stanzas from the Grande Chartreuse" (1852). To clarify, the poem deals with religious struggles, not with the development of society or the economy.

3. Antonio Gramsci, *Selections from the Prison Notebooks*, trans. Quintin Hoare and Geoffrey Nowell Smith (London: Lawrence and Wishart, [1971] 1999), p. 556. The quote is situated in a context in which Gramsci speaks about a 'ruling class' that no longer 'leads' but only is 'dominant,' exercising coercive force

alone. This gives a sense of lostness among the 'great masses.' Despite his Marxism, Gramsci did make sharp observations.

4. As argued by the Dutch philosopher/theologian, Patrick Nullens, in an as yet untranslated treatise on hope, *Hoop als kunst van verantwoord leiderschap* (Antwerp: Garant, 2021).

5. A phrase we borrow from Mariana Mazzucato, *The Value of Everything: Making and Taking in the Global Economy* (New Delhi: Allen Lane, 2018), final chapter, pp. 270–80.

6. Bob Goudzwaard, Mark Vander Vennen, and David van Heemst, *Hope in Troubled Times: A New Vision for Confronting Global Crises* (Grand Rapids: Baker Academic, 2007), pp. 180ff.

Bibliography[*]

Acemoglu, D., and J.A. Robinson. *Why Nations Fail: The Origins of Power, Prosperity, and Poverty.* New York: Crown Business, 2012.

Acemoglu, D., and J.A. Robinson. *The Narrow Corridor: States, Societies and the Fate of Liberty.* New York: Penguin Press, 2019.

Adler, P., and C. Heckscher. *The Firm as Collaborative Community.* Oxford: Oxford University Press, 2006.

Akerlof, G.A., and R.J. Shiller. *Animal Spirits: How Human Psychology Drives the Economy, and Why It Matters for Global Capitalism.* Princeton: Princeton University Press, 2009.

Albert, M. *Capitalism Against Capitalism.* London: Whurr, 1992.

Anderson, E. *Value in Ethics and Economics.* Cambridge, MA: Harvard University Press, 1993.

Anderson, E. *Private Government: How Employers Rule Our Lives (and Why We Don't Talk about It).* Tanner Lectures on Human Values. Princeton: Princeton University Press, 2017.

Andrews, K. *The New Age of Empire. How Racism and Colonialism Still Rule the World.* London: Penguin, 2021.

Arendt, H. *The Human Condition.* Chicago: Chicago University Press, 1958.

Armstrong, K. *The Great Transformation: The Beginning of Our Religious Traditions.* New York: Anchor Books, 2006.

Assmann, F. *Der europäische Traum: Vier Lehren aus der Geschichte.* Munich: Beck, 2018.

Augustine, St. A. *De catechizandibus rudibus* [The first catechetical instruction]. Circa 403 (multiple editions, online and in print).

Augustine, St. A. *De civitate Dei contra paganos* [The city of God against the pagans]. Circa 413–426 (multiple editions, online and in print).

Baardewijk, J. van. *The Moral Foundation of Business Students: A Philosophical and Empirical Investigation of the Business Student Ethos.* PhD dissertation, Vrije Universiteit Amsterdam, 2018.

Bakker, P. "Accountants will Save the World." *Harvard Business Review.* March 5, 2013.

Balkenende, J.P. *Overheidsregelgeving en maatschappelijke organisaties* (State regulations and civil society organizations). PhD dissertation, Vrije Universiteit Amsterdam, 1992.

---

[*]   English translations of Dutch and German titles are provided between brackets. Of older 'classical' works, there often exist many editions, both online and in print. When referring to these works in the footnotes, we have not provided page numbers, as they differ from one edition to the other, but as far as possible refer to the established table of content of the work.

Balkenende, J.P. et al. *Europa en maatschappelijke organisaties* (Europe and civil society organizations). The Hague: Wetenschappelijk Instituut voor het CDA, 1993.

Balkenende, J.P. *Over verantwoordelijkheid en economie: Wat nu?* (On responsibility and economics: The challenges ahead), Inaugural Lecture, Vrije Universiteit Amsterdam, 1993.

Balkenende, J.P., E.J.J.M. Kimman, and J.P. van den Toren. *Vertrouwen in de economie: Het debat.* (The role of trust in the economy: The current debate). Assen: Van Gorcum, 1997.

Balkenende, J.P. et al., eds. *Onderneming & Maatschappij: Op zoek naar vertrouwen,* (Corporations and society: Searching for trust). Assen: Van Gorcum, 2003.

Balkenende, J.P. *Shaping Europe's Future: Working Together on Prosperity, Security, and Respect.* The Hague: Government Information Service, Ministry of General Affairs, 2004.

Balkenende, J.P. *Het woord is aan de minister-president. Acht jaar premierschap in vijftig speeches.* (The Floor is given to the Prime Minister. Eight years of premiership in fifty speeches). Den Haag: Ministerie van Algemene Zaken, 2010.

Balkenende, J.P. "Over governance en maatschappelijke verantwoordelijkheid: hoe verder?" (About governance and societal responsibility: What is next?') Inaugural Lecture, Erasmus University Rotterdam, 2011.

Balkenende, J.P. "Integrated Reporting, Integrated Thinking en The Moral Code." In A. de Bos et al., eds., *De dynamische accountant,* pp. 191–204. Rotterdam: Erasmus Universiteit, 2016.

Balkenende, J.P. "De Europese Unie: van crisismanagement naar een duurzaam toekomstperspectief" (The European Union: From crisismanagement to a sustainable future). In B.J. van Ettekoven et al., eds., *Rechtsorde en bestuur* (Liber Amicorum aangeboden aan Piet Hein Donner), pp. 429–43. The Hague: Boom Juridisch, 2018.

Ballor, J.J., and C. van der Kooi, eds. *Theology, Morality and Adam Smith.* London: Routledge, 2022.

Bauer R., T. Bauer, M. Olaerts, and C. van Aartsen. *Sustainability Embedding Practices in Dutch Listed Companies,* Maastricht: Maastricht University, 2021.

Bams, D., and B. van der Kroft. *Tilting the Wrong Firms? How Inflated ESG Ratings Negate Socially Responsible Investing Under Information Asymmetries.* Paper No. 22/12. Boston: MIT Center for Real Estate Research, 2022.

Banerjee, A.V., and Duflo, E. *Good Economics for Hard Times: Better Answers to Our Biggest Problems.* London: Penguin Books, 2020.

Banfield, E. *The Moral Basis of a Backward Society.* New York: Free Press, 1958.

Barber, B. *If Majors Ruled the World: Dysfunctional Nations, Rising Cities.* New Haven: Yale University Press, 2013.

Barton, D., and Kipping, M., eds. *Re-Imagining Capitalism.* London: Oxford University Press, 2016.

Bavel, B. van. *The Invisible Hand? How Market Economies Have Emerged and Declined Since AD 500.* Oxford: Oxford University Press, 2016.

Beck, U., W. Bonss, and C. Lau. "The Theory of Reflexive Modernization: Problematic, Hypotheses and Research Programme." *Theory, Culture & Society* 20, no. 20 (2003): 1–33.

Becker, C.L. *The Heavenly City of the Eighteenth-Century Philosophers.* New Haven: Yale University Press, 1932.

Berman, J. *Created Equal: How the Bible Broke with Ancient Political Thought.* Oxford: Oxford University Press, 2008.

Beuningen, C. van, and K. Buitendijk. *Finance and the Common Good.* Amsterdam University Press, 2019.

Bezemer, D. *Een land van kleine buffers: Er is genoeg geld, maar we gebruiken het verkeerd.* (A country of small buffers: There is plenty of money, but we use it in the wrong way). Amsterdam: Uitgeverij Pluim, 2020.

Bisson, T.N. "The 'Feudal Revolution.'" *Past and Present* 142 (1994): 6–42.

Black, A. *Guild and State: European Political Thought from the Twelfth Century to the Present.* New Brunswick and London: Transaction Publishers, 2003.

Blond, P. *Red Tory: How Left and Right Have Broken Britain and How We Can Fix It.* London: Faber & Faber, 2010.

Böckenförde, E-W. *Staat, Gesellschaft, Freiheit: Studien zur Staatstheorie und zum Verfassungsrecht.* Frankfurt: Suhrkamp, 1976.

Boersema, J.J. *The Survival of Easter Island: Dwindling Resources and Cultural Resilience.* Cambridge: Cambridge University Press, 2015.

Boot, A.W. *De ontwortelde onderneming: Ondernemingen overgeleverd aan financiers?* (The disconnected enterprise: Enterprises in the hands of financiers?). Assen: Koninklijke Van Gorkum, 2009.

Boot, A.W., P. Hoffmann, L. Laeven, and L. Ratnovski, 'Fintech: What's Old, What's New?' *Journal of Financial Stability* 53 (April 2021). DOI: 10.1016/j.jfs.2020.100836

Bourguignon, F. *The Globalization of Inequality.* Translated by T. Scott-Railton. Princeton: Princeton University Press, 2015.

Boudry, M. *Waarom de wereld niet naar de knoppen gaat* (Why the world isn't going to pieces). Kalmthout: Polis, 2019.

Boulding, K. "Economics as a Moral Science': Presidential Address for the American Economic Association 1968." *The American Economic Review* 59, no. 1 (1969): 1–12.

Boushey, H. *Unbound: How Inequality Constricts Our Economy and What We Can Do About It.* Cambridge, MA: Harvard University Press, 2019.

Boutellier, H. *De improvisatiemaatschappij: Over de sociale ordening van een begrensde wereld* (The improvisation society: About the social coordination of a limited world). Amsterdam: Boom, 2011.

Bovenberg, L., and Paul van Geest. *Kruis en munt: De raakvlakken van economie en theologie* (Cross and Coin: The crossroads between economics and theology). Utrecht: KokBoekencentrum, 2021.

Bradford, A. *The Brussels Effect. How the European Union Rules the World.* Oxford: Oxford University Press, 2020.

Braudel, F. *Beschaving, economie en kapitalisme (15de–18de eeuw).* Deel 2, *Het spel van de handel.* Amsterdam: Contact, 1989 (originally published as *Civilisation materiélle. Economie et Capitalisme XVe–XVIIIe siècle. Tome 2: Les Jeux de l'échange,* 1979).

Bregman, R. *De geschiedenis van de vooruitgang* (The history of progress). Amsterdam: De Bezig Bij, 2013.

Bregman, R., and J. Frederik. *Waarom vuilnismannen meer verdienen dan bankiers* (Why garbage collectors deserve more than bankers). Amsterdam: De Correspondent, 2015.

Breiding, R.J. *Too Small to Fail: Why Some Small Nations Outperform Larger Ones and How They Are Reshaping the World.* New York: Harper Business, 2019.

Brink, G. van den. *Ruw ontwaken uit een neoliberale droom en de eigenheid van het Europese continent* (A rude awakening from a neoliberal slumber and the specific character of the European continent). Amsterdam: Prometheus, 2020.

British Academy. *Reforming Business for the 21st century. A Framework for the Future of the Corporation.* London: The British Academy, 2018. https://www.thebritishacademy.ac.uk/documents/76/Reforming-Business-for-21st-Century-British-Academy.pdf

British Academy. *Principles for Purposeful Business. How to deliver the framework for the Future of the Corporation.* London: The British Academy, 2019. https://www.thebritishacademy.ac.uk/documents/224/future-of-the-corporation-principles-purposeful-business.pdf

Brouwer, J.J., and P. Moerman. *Angelsaksen versus Rijnlanders: Zoektocht naar overeenkomsten en verschillen in Europees en Amerikaans denken* (Anglo-Saxons versus Rhinelanders: A search for parallels and differences between European and American thought). Amsterdam: Garant, 2010.

Brown, W. *Undoing the Demos: Neoliberalism's Stealth Revolution.* New York: Zone Books, 2015.

Bruni, L., and S. Zamagni. *Civil Economy: Efficiency, Equity, Public Happiness.* Oxford: Peter Lang, 2007.

Bruni, L. *The Wound and the Blessing: Economics, Relationships and Happiness.* New York: New City Press, 2012.

Bruni, L., and Smerilli, A. *De ongekende kant van de economie: Gratuïteit en markt.* Nieuwkuijk: De Nieuwe Stad, 2015 (originally published as *L'altra metà dell'economia: Gratuità e mercati,* Rome 2014).

Buijs, G.J. 'The Souls of Europe.' In *Limes: Cultural Regionalistics* 2, no. 2 (2009): 126–39.

Buijs, G.J., with A.M. Verbrugge and J.J. van Baardewijk. *Het goede leven en de vrije markt* (The good life and the free market). Rotterdam: Lemniscaat, 2018.

Buijs, G.J. *Waarom werken we zo hard? Op weg naar een economie van de vreugde* (Why are we working so hard? Towards an economy of joy). Amsterdam: Boom, 2019.

Buijs, G.J. and Paul Bosman, eds. *Ontwaken uit de geopolitieke sluimer. De herpositionering van Europa in een woelige wereld* (Waking up from geopolitical slumber: Repositioning Europe in a world adrift). Utrecht: Eburon/Thijmgenootschap, 2022.

Burke, E. *Reflections on the Revolution in France.* 1790 (multiple editions, online and in print).

Bury, J.B. *The Idea of Progress: An Inquiry Into its Origin and Growth.* New York: Dover, [1932] 1960.

Carney, M. *Value(s): Building a Better World for All.* London: William Collins, 2021.

Case, A., and A. Deaton. *Deaths of Despair and the Future of Capitalism.* Princeton: Princeton University Press, 2020.

Castells, M. *The Rise of the Network Society* (vol. 1 of *The Information Age* trilogy). Oxford: Blackwell, [1996] 2004.

Castells, M. *The Power of Identity* (vol. 2 of *The Information Age* trilogy). Oxford: Blackwell, [1997] 2004.

Centre for Research on Energy and Clear Air (CREA). "China Dominates 2020 Coal Plant Development." *Global Energy Monitor – Briefing February 2021.* https://globalenergymonitor.org/wp-content/uploads/2021/02/China-Dominates-2020-Coal-Development.pdf. Retrieved 18 August 2023.

Chew, D.H., and S. l. Gillan. *Corporate Governance at the Crossroads.* New York: McGraw-Hill/Irwin, 2004.

Christophers, B. *Rentier Capitalism: Who Owns the Economy, and Who Pays for It?* London: Verso, 2020.

Cobb, J., and H. Daly. *For the Common Good.* Boston: Beacon Press, 1989.

Cohn, N. *The Pursuit of the Millennium: Revolutionary Millenarians and Mystical Anarchists of the Middle Ages.* London: Paladin Books, [1957] 1984.

Cohn, S.K., Jr. *Lust for Liberty: The Politics of Social Revolt in Medieval Europe, 1200–1425.* London: Harvard University Press, 2006.

Colander, D., and Roland Kupers. *Complexity and the Art of Public Policy.* Princeton: Princeton University Press, 2014.

Coleman, J. *Foundations of Social Theory.* Cambridge, MA: Belknap/Harvard University Press, 1990.

Collier, P. *The Future of Capitalism: Facing the New Anxieties.* New Delhi: Allen Lane, 2018.

Commandeur, H. et al. *Agapè/caritas in bedrijf: Een praktisch raamwerk voor leidinggevenden* (Agape in business: A practical framework for leaders). Amsterdam: Boom, 2021.

Cools, K. "Naar een duurzaam economisch paradigma" (Toward a sustainable economic paradigm). In *Topics in Corporate Finance,* no. 30, pp. 17–46. Amsterdam: Amsterdam Centre for Corporate Finance, 2023.

CORE team (Samuel Bowles, Wendy Carlin and Margaret Stevens). *The Economy. Economics for a changing world.* Oxford: Oxford University Press/CoreEcon, 2017.

Cowie, J., and N. Salvatore. "The Long Exception: Rethinking the Place of the New Deal in American History." *International Labor and Working-Class History* 74, no. 1 (2008): 3–32.

Cuperus, R. *7 Mythe über Europa. Plädoyer für ein vorsichtiges Europa.* Bonn: Dietz Verlag, 2022.

Dalio, R. *The Changing World Order: Why Nations Succeed and Fail.* New York: Simon & Schuster, 2021.

Daly, H. *The Steady State Economics.* 2nd ed. Washington, DC: Island Press, [1977] 1991.

Dasgupta, P. *The Economics of Biodiversity: The Dasgupta Review,* London: HM Treasury, 2021.

Davis, J., D. Schoorman, and L. Donaldson, "Toward a Stewardship Theory of Management," *Academy of Management Review* 22, no. 1 (1997): 20–47.

Deaton, A. *The Great Escape: Health, Wealth, and the Origins of Inequality.* Princeton: Princeton University Press, 2013.

Diamandis, P.H., and S. Kotler. *Abundance: The Future is Better Than You Think.* New York: Free Press, 2012.

Dijk, G. van, and R. van Loon. "The European Commission: Leading Diversity by Dialogue." In R Koonce and R. van Loon, eds., *The Dialogical Challenge of Leadership Development,* pp. 125–38. Information Age Publishing, 2019. ,

Eccles, R.G., and M.P. Krzus. *One Report: Integrated Reporting for a Sustainable Strategy.* Hoboken: Wiley, 2010.

Eccles, R.G., and M.P. Krzus. *The Integrated Reporting Movement: Meaning, Momentum, Motives, and Materiality.* Hoboken: Wiley, 2014.

Eccles, R.G., M.P. Krzus, and C. Solano. "A Comparative Analysis of Integrated Reporting in Ten Countries." 2019. https://papers.ssrn.com/sol3/papers.cfm?abstract_id=3345590

Elazar, D. *The Covenant Tradition in Politics.* 4 vols. New Brunswick: Transaction, 1995–1998.

Eisenstadt, S.N. "Multiple Modernities." *Daedalus* 129, no. 1 (Winter 2000): 1–29.

Eom, J., D. Brautigam, and L. Bedabdallah. "The Path Ahead: The 7th Forum on China-Africa Cooperation," SAIS-CARI Briefing Papers 01/2018, Johns Hopkins University, School of Advanced International Studies (SAIS), China Africa Research Initiative (CARI). https://www.econstor.eu/bitstream/10419/248242/1/sais-cari-bp01.pdf. Retrieved August 29, 2022.

Esping-Anderson, G. *The Three Worlds of Welfare Capitalism.* Princeton: Princeton University Press, 1990.

Etzioni, A. *The Moral Dimension: Toward a New Economics.* New York: Free Press, 1988.

Etzioni, A. *The New Golden Rule: Community and Morality in a Democratic Society.* New York: Basic Books, 1996.

Fanon, F. *The Wretched of the Earth.* Translated by Constance Farrington. London: Penguin, 1963 (originally published as *Les damnés de la terre,* 1961).

Farrell, H., and A.L. Newman. "Weaponized Interdependence. How Global Economic Networks Shape State Coercion." *International Security* 44, no. 1 (Summer 2019): 42–79.

Fehr, E., and U. Fischbacher. "Why Social Preferences Matter:The Impact of Non-Selfish Motives on Competition, Cooperation and Incentives." *The Economic Journal* 112, no. 489 (2002): 1–33.

Felber, C. *Change Everything: Creating an Economy for the Common Good.* London: Zed Books, 2019 (originally published as *Die Gemeinwohl-Ökonomie,* 2012).

Felber, C. *Trading for Good: How Global Trade Can Be Made to Serve People Not Money*. London: Zed Books, 2019 (originally published as *Ethischer Welthandel. Alternativen zu TTIP, WTO & Co*, 2017).

Ferreras, I. *Firms as Political Entities: Saving Democracy through Economic Bicameralism*. Cambridge: Cambridge University Press, 2017.

Fourcade, M., and K. Healy. "Moral Views of Market Society." *Annual Review of Sociology* 33 (2007): 285–311.

Foroohar, R. *Makers and Takers*. New York: Crown Business, 2017.

Foroohar, R. *Don't be Evil: How Big Tech Betrayed its Founding Principles – and All of Us*. New York: Currency, 2019.

Freeman, R.E. *Strategic Management: A Stakeholder Approach*. Boston: Pitman, 1984.

Freeman, R.E., and R.A. Phillips. "Stakeholder Theory: A Libertarian Defense." *Business Ethics Quarterly* (2002): 331–49.

Freudenberg, N. *Lethal but Legal: Corporations, Consumption, and Protecting Public Health*. Oxford: Oxford University Press, 2016.

Friedman, M. "Neo-Liberalism and its Prospects," *Farmand* (February 1951): 89–93.

Friedman, M. *Capitalism and Freedom*. Chicago: University of Chicago Press, 1962.

Friedman, M. "A Friedman Doctrine: The Social Responsibility of Business Is to Increase Its Profits." *The New York Times*, September 13, 1970, p. 17.

Friedman, M., and Friedman, R. *Free to Choose: A Personal Statement*. Orlando: Harcourt Brace International, 1980.

Frissen, P. *De integrale staat*. Amsterdam: Boom, 2023.

Fukuyama, F. *The End of History and the Last Man*. New York: Free Press, 1992.

Fukuyama, F. *Trust: The Social Virtues and the Creation of Prosperity*. New York: Free Press, 1995.

Fukuyama, F. *Liberalism and its Discontents*. London: Profile Books, 2022.

Fullerton, J. *Regenerative Capitalism: How Universal Principles and Patterns Wil Shape Our New Economy*. Greenwich, CT: Capital Institute, 2015.

Funke, M., M. Schularick, and C. Trebesch. "Going to Extremes: Politics after Financial Crises, 1870–2014." European Economic Review 88, issue C (2016): 227–60.

Gaida, J. et al. *ASPI's Critical Technology Tracker: The Global Race for Future Power*. Policy Report 69. Canberra: ASPI, 2023.

Geest, P. van. *Morality in the Marketplace: Reconciling Theology and Economics*. Leiden: Brill, 2022.

Gierke, O. van. *Das Deutsche Genossenschaftsrecht* (The German Community Law), 4 vols. Berlin: Weidmannsche Buchhandlung, 1868–1913.

Glasman, M. *Blue Labour: The Politics of the Common Good*. Cambridge: Polity, 2022.

Global Compact Network Netherlands, *Stakeholder Inclusion as an Accelerator for the Sustainable Development Goals. Inspiration from the Netherlands* (2020). *https://ungc-communications-assets.s3.amazonaws.com/docs/publications/ Global-compact-NL-Stakeholder-Inclusion.FINAL_.pdf*

Goodhart, D. *The Road to Somewhere: The New Tribes Shaping British Politics*. London: Penguin, 2017.

Goodhart, D. *Head, Hand, Heart: The Struggle for Dignity and Status in the 21st Century.* London: Penguin, 2020.

Goudzwaard, B. *Capitalism and Progress: A Diagnosis of Western Society.* Grand Rapids: Wm. B. Eerdmans, 1979.

Goudzwaard, B., M.V. Vennen, and D. van Heemst. *Hope in Troubled Times: A New Vision for Confronting Global Crises.* Grand Rapids: Baker Academic, 2007.

Graafland, J.J., and T.R. Wells. "In Adam Smith's Own Words: The Role of Virtues in the Relationship Between Free Market Economies and Societal Flourishing. A Semantic Data-Mining Approach." *Journal of Business Ethics* 172 (2021): 31–42.

Graafland, J.J., and F.G.A. de Bakker. "Crowding In or Crowding Out? How Non-Governmental Organizations and Media Influence Intrinsic Motivations toward Corporate Social and Environmental Responsibility." *Journal of Environmental Planning and Management* 64, no. 13 (2021): 2386–2409.

Graafland, J.J., and H. Verbruggen. "Free-Market, Perfect Market and Welfare State Perspectives on "Good" Markets: an Empirical Test." *Applied Research in Quality of Life* 17, no. 3 (May 2021): 1–24.

Graafland, J.J. *Ethics and Economics: An Introduction to Free Markets, Equality and Happiness.* London: Routledge. 2022.

Graafland, J.J. *Corporate Social Responsibility and SMEs: Impact and Institutional Drivers.* London: Routledge, 2022.

Graeber, D., and D. Wengrow. *The Dawn of Everything: A New History of Humanity.* London: Allen Lane, 2021.

Gramsci, A. *Selections from the Prison Notebooks*, trans. Quintin Hoare and Geoffrey Nowell Smith. London: Lawrence and Wishart, [1971] 1999.

Groothuis, F., ed. *The Taxshift: A EU Fiscal Strategy to Support the Inclusive Circular Economy.* Amsterdam: Ex'tax Project, 2022.

Gulden, B. *Transformatieve Innovatie: Europees innovatiebeleid binnen een wereld van sociale waarden* (Transformative innovation: European innovation policies within a framework of social values). MA thesis, Vrije Universiteit Amsterdam, 2022.

Gustafson, T. *Klimat: Russia in the Age of Climate Change.* Cambridge, MA: Harvard University Press, 2021.

Habermas, J. *Strukturwandel der Öffentlichkeit* (1962) Translated as *The Structural Transformation of the Public Sphere: An Inquiry into a Category of Bourgeois Society.* Cambridge, MA: MIT Press, 1962.

Habermas, J. "Modernity: An Unfinished Project" (1980). In C.J. Calhoun, ed., Contemporary Sociological Theory, pp. 395–400. Hoboken: Wiley Blackwell, 2022.

Habermas, J. *Theorie des kommunikativen Handels* (*Theory of Communicative Action*). Frankfurt am Main: Suhrkamp, 1981.

Habermas, J. "Religion in the Public Sphere." *European Journal of Philosophy* 14, no. 1 (2006): 1–25.

Hall, P.A. and D. Soskice (eds.). *Varieties of Capitalism: The Institutional Foundation of Comparative Advantage.* Oxford: Oxford University Press, 2001.

Hamilton, C. *Defiant Earth. The Fate of Humans in the Anthropocene.* Sydney: Allen & Unwin, 2017.

Hardin, G. "Tragedy of the Commons." *Science* 162, no. 3859 (1968): 1243–48.

Harrison, L.E., and S.P. Huntington, eds. *Culture Matters: How Values Shape Human Progress.* New York: Basic Books, 2000.

Havel, V. *Disturbing the Peace: A Conversation With Karel Hvížďala.* Translated by Paul Wilson. New York: Vintage, [1986] 1990.

Hawken, P. *Regeneration: Ending the Climate Crisis in One Generation.* New York: Penguin, 2021.

Hayek, F.A. *The Road to Serfdom* (1944). Ed. Bruce Caldwell *Collected Works of F.A. Hayek*, vol. 2. Chicago: University of Chicago Press, 2007.

Hayek, F.A. *The Constitution of Liberty.* Chicago: University of Chicago Press, 1960.

Hayek, F.A. *Law, Legislation, Liberty.* Vol. 1, *Rules and Order.* London: Routledge, 1976.

Hayek, F.A. *Law, Legislation, Liberty.* Vol. 2, *The Mirage of Social Justice.* London: Routledge, 1976.

Hayek, F.A. *Law, Legislation, Liberty.* Vol. 3, *The Political Order of a Free People.* London: Routledge, 1976.

Healy, T. "The Measurement of Social Capital at International Level." OECD-paper, 2002. https://www.oecd.org/innovation/research/2380281.pdf (accessed February 18, 2022).

Heijne, S., and H. Noten. *Fantoomgroei: Waarom we steeds harder werken voor steeds minder.* (Phantom growth: why we have to work harder and harder while getting less and less). Amsterdam and Antwerp: Atlas Contact, 2020.

Helgeson, J. "American Labor and Working-Class History, 1900–1945." *Oxford Research Encyclopedia of American History.* Oxford: Oxford University Press, 2016. Online, https://doi.org/10.1093/acrefore/9780199329175.013.330

Henderson, R. *Reimagining Capitalism: How Business Can Save the World.* London: Penguin, 2020 (originally published as *Reimagining Capitalism in a World on Fire*).

Hendriks, M., M. Burger, A. Rijsenbilt, E. Pleeging, and H. Commandeur. "Virtuous Leadership: A Source of Employee Well-Being and Trust." *Management Research Review* 43, no. 8 (2020): 951–70.

Hengstmengel, J. *De homo economicus: een familiegeschiedenis* (Homo economicus: A family history). Amsterdam: Boom, 2020.

Hickel, J. *The Divide: A Brief Guide to Global Inequality and its Solutions.* London: Penguin Random House, 2017.

Hickel, J. *Less Is More: How Degrowth Will Save the World.* London: William Heinemann, 2020.

Hill, S. *Europe's Promise: Why the European Way Is the Best Hope in an Insecure Age.* Berkeley: University of California Press, 2010.

Hirschman, A.O. *Exit, Voice, and Loyalty: Responses to Decline in Firms, Organizations, and States.* Cambridge, MA: Harvard University Press, 1970.

Hirschman, A.O. "Rival Interpretations of Market Society: Civilizing, Destructive, or Feeble?" *Journal of Economic Literature* 20, no. 4 (December 1982): 1463–84.

Hodgson, G.M. *Conceptualizing Capitalism: Institutions, Evolution, Future*. Chicago: University of Chicago Press, 2015.

Hoekstra, R. *Replacing GDP by 2030: Towards a Common Language for the Well-Being and Sustainability Community*. Cambridge: Cambridge University Press, 2019.

Hofstede, G. *Culture's Consequences: Comparing Values, Behaviors, Institutions and Organizations Across Nations*. Beverly Hills: Sage, 2003.

Holslag, J. *De kracht van het paradijs: Hoe Europa kan overleven in de Aziatische eeuw*. (The power of paradise: How Europe will survive the Asian century). Antwerp: De Bezige Bij, 2014.

Holslag, J. *Van muur tot muur: De wereldpolitiek sinds 1989*. Amsterdam: De Bezige Bij, 2021 (originally published as *World Politics Since 1989*, Cambridge: Polity).

Hook, J. van. *Rebuilding Germany: The Creation of the Social Market Economy in Germany 1945–1957*. Cambridge: Cambridge University Press, 2004.

Horney, K. *The Neurotic Personality of Our Time*. London: Routledge, [1937] 1999.

Hummels, H., and E. Hilgers. *Anders groeien: Een medemenselijke aanpak van duurzaam en maatschappelijk ondernemen*. (Growing differently: A compassionate approach to sustainable and social entrepreneurship). Culemborg: Van Duuren Management, 2022.

Hummer, H. "Were the Lords Really All That Bad?" *Historical Methods* 43, no. 4 (2010): 165–70.

Hurst, A. *The Purpose Economy: How Your Desire for Impact, Personal Growth and Community is Changing the World*. Boise: Elevate, 2016.

Ifcher, J., and H. Zarghamee. "The Rapid Evolution of Homo Economicus: Brief Exposure to Neoclassical Assumptions Increases Self-Interested Behavior." *Journal of Behavioral and Experimental Economics* 75, issue C (2018): 55–65.

Institut Montaigne. *Responsible Capitalism: An Opportunity for Europe*. Paris, 2020.

International Federation of Red Cross and Red Crescent Societies (IFRC). *World Disasters Report 2020: Come Heat or High Water: Tackling the Humanitarian Impacts of the Climate Crisis Together*. 2020.

Jackson, T. *Prosperity without Growth: Foundations for the Economy of Tomorrow*. London: Routledge, 2009/2017.

Jackson, T. *Post Growth: Life after Capitalism*. Cambridge: Polity, 2021.

Jacobs, M., and M. Mazzucato, eds. *Rethinking Capitalism: Economics and Policy for Sustainable and Inclusive Growth*. Nashville: John Wiley & Sons, 2016.

Jaishankar, S. *The India Way: Strategies for an Uncertain World*. New Delhi: HarperCollins Publishers India, 2020.

Joas, H. *The Sacredness of the Person: A New Genealogy of Human Rights*. Washington, DC: Georgetown University Press, 2013.

Jong, E. de. *Culture and Economics: On Values, Economics and International Business*. London: Routledge, 2009.

Jong, E. de, ed. *Economic Ideas, Policy and National Culture*. London: Routledge, 2022.

Kahneman, D. *Thinking: Fast and Slow*. New York: Farrar, Straus and Giroux, 2011.

Kaiser, H.J. *In Ordinata Concordia. Het Subsidiariteitsbeginsel en de Geordende Eendracht in de Politieke Economie* (The principle of subsidiarity and ordered unity in political economy). Tilburg: Open Press Tilburg University, 2023.

Kal, V. *Alexander Doegin. Poetins filosoof* (Alexander Dugin: Putin's philosopher). Amsterdam: Prometheus, 2023.

Kallis, G., S. Paulson, G. D'Alisa, and F. Demaria. *The Case for Degrowth.* Cambridge: Polity, 2020.

Kakutani, M. *The Death of Truth: Notes on Falsehood in the Age of Trump.* New York: Tim Duggan Books, 2018.

Kant, I. "Idee zu einer allgemeinen Geschichte in weltbürgerlicher Absicht" (Idea for a Universal History with a Cosmopolitan Purpose). *Berlinische Monatsschrift* (November 1784): 385–411.

Kaptein, M. "The Moral Duty to Love One's Stakeholders." *Journal of Business Ethics* 180 (2022): 813–27.

Keane, J. *The Life and Death of Democracy.* London: Simon & Schuster, 2009.

Keefe, P.R. *Empire of Pain: The Secret History of the Sackler Dynasty.* New York: Anchor Books, 2022.

Kennedy, P. *The Rise and Fall of the Great Powers.* New York: Vintage Books, 1987.

Kets de Vries, M.F.R. *The Leader on the Couch: A Clinical Approach to Changing People and Organizations.* New York: John Wiley & Sons, 2006.

Kets de Vries, M.F.R. "Thought Leader Interview by Art Kleiner." *Strategy+Business* 59 (Summer 2010). https://www.strategy-business.com/article/10209.

Keynes, J.M. "Alfred Marshall, 1842–1924." *The Economic Journal* 34, no. 135 (1924): 311–72.

Keynes, J.M. *The General Theory of Employment, Interest and Money.* London: MacMillan, 1935.

Klamer, A. *Doing the Right Thing: A Value Based Economy.* London: Uniquity Press, 2016.

Klundert, T. van de. *Kapitalisme: Over de dominantie van kapitaal en de lange uitzondering.* (Capitalism: About the dominance of capital and the Long Exception). Utrecht: Eburon, 2019.

Koster, E. "Het Knowledge Filter: Leidt consensus tot betrouwbare kennis?" (The knowledge filter: Does consensus lead to reliable knowledge?) In E. Koster, ed., *Wat is wetenschap? Een filosofische inleiding voor levenswetenschappers en medici*, pp. 183–207. Amsterdam: VU University Press, 2019.

Kotilainen, K. *Perspectives on the Prosumer Role in the Sustainable Energy System.* PhD dissertation, Tampere University, 2020.

Kotkin, J. *The Coming of Neo-Feudalism: A Warning to the Global Middle Class.* New York: Encounter Books, 2020.

Kropotkin, P. *Mutual Aid: A Factor of Evolution.* London: Freedom Press, [1902] 2006.

Krugman, P. "How Did Economists Get It So Wrong?" *New York Times*, September 6, 2009.

Kuhn, T. *The Structure of Scientific Revolutions.* Chicago: University of Chicago Press, 1962.

Kupers, R. *A Climate Policy Revolution: What the Science of Complexity Reveals About Saving Our Planet.* Cambridge, MA: Harvard University Press, 2020.

Kuyper, A. "The Social Question and the Christian Religion" (1891). Republished in J.J. Ballor, M. Flikkema, and P. Heslam, eds., *On Business and Economics: Collected Works of Abraham Kuyper in Public Theology*, vol. 11, pp. 169–230. Bellingham: Lexham Press, 2021.

Landes, D.S. *Wealth and Poverty of Nations.* London: Little, Brown, 1998.

Latour, B. *Het Parlement der Dingen* (The parliament of things). Amsterdam: Boom, [1994] 2020. Translation of "Esquisse du Parlement des choses," originally published 1994, reissued in *Ecologie politique* 1, no. 56 (2018): 47–64.

Leyen, U. von der. "A Union that Strives for More: My Agenda for Europe," *Political Guidelines for the Next European Commission.* Brussels: European Parliament 2019. https://www.europarl.europa.eu/resources/library/media/20190716RES57231/20190716RES57231.pdf

Lipsky, M. *Street-Level Bureaucracy: Dilemmas of the Individual in Public Services.* New York: Russell Sage, 1980.

Luttwack, E.N. "From Geopolitics to Geo-Economics: Logic of Conflict, Grammar of Commerce." *The National Interest* 20 (Summer 1990): 17–23.

Machiavelli, N. *The Prince.* 1513/1532 (multiple editions, online and in print).

MacIntyre, A. *After Virtue: A Study in Moral Theory.* 3rd ed. Notre Dame: Notre Dame University Press, [1981] 2007.

Machlup, F. "Theories of the Firm: Marginalist, Behavioral, Managerial." *The American Economic Review* 57, no. 1 (1967): 1–33.

Mackey, J., and R. Sisodia. *Conscious Capitalism: Liberating the Heroic Spirit of Business.* Boston: Harvard Business Review Press, 2013.

Mahbubani, K. *Has the West Lost It? A Provocation.* London: Allen Lane, 2018.

Mahbubani, K. *Has China Won? The Chinese Challenge to American Primacy.* New York: Public Affairs, 2020.

Mandeville, B. *The Fable of the Bees.* 2 vols. Indianapolis: Liberty Fund, [1705/1714/1723] 1988.

Marx, K., and F. Engels. *Manifest der kommunistischen Partei* (The Communist Manifesto). London: Hirschfeld, 1848.

Marx, K. *Das Kapital: Kritik der politischen Ökonomie*, vol. 1. Berlin: Dietz Verlag, [1867] 1975.

Mauss, M. "Essai sur le don: Formes et raisons de l'échange dans les sociétés archaïques." *L'Année Sociologique* 1. Translated as *An Essay on the Gift: The Form and Reason of Exchange in Archaic Societies.* London: Routledge, [1923] 1950.

Mason, P. *PostCapitalism: A Guide to Our Future.* London: Allen Lane, 2015.

Max-Neef, M.A. *Human Scale Development: Conception, Application and Further Reflections.* New York: The Apex Press, 1991.

Mayer, C. *Prosperity: Better Business Makes the Greater Good.* Oxford: Oxford University Press, 2018.

Mazzucato, M. *The Entrepreneurial State: Debunking Public vs. Private Sector Myths.* New York: PublicAffairs, 2015.

Mazzucato, M. *The Value of Everything: Making and Taking in the Global Economy.* New Delhi: Allen Lane, 2018.

Mazzucato, M. *Mission-Oriented research and Innovation in the European Union.* Brussels: European Commission, 2018.

Mazzucato, M. *Mission Economy: A Moonshot Guide to Changing Capitalism.* New York: Allan Lane, 2021.

Mazzucato, M., and R. Collington. *The Big Con: How the Consultancy Industry Weakens our Businesses, Infantilizes our Governments, and Warps our Economies.* London: Allen Lane, 2023.

McCloskey, D.N. *The Bourgeois Virtues: Ethics for an Age of Commerce.* Chicago: University of Chicago Press, 2006.

McCloskey, D.N. *Bourgeois Dignity: Why Economics Can't Explain the Modern World.* Chicago: University of Chicago Press, 2010.

McCloskey, D.N. *Bourgeois Equality: How Ideas, Not Capital or Institutions Enriched the World.* Chicago: University of Chicago Press, 2016.

McCloskey, D.N. *Bettering Humanomics: A New, and Old, Approach to Economic Science.* Chicago: University of Chicago Press, 2021.

McGilchrist, I. *The Master and his Emissary: The Divided Brain and the Making of the Western World.* New Haven: Yale University Press, 2009 (expanded edition 2018).

McKillop D., D. French, B. Quinn, A.L. Sobeich, J.O.S. Wilson. "Cooperative Financial Institutions: A Review of the Literature." *International Review of Financial Analysis.* October 2020. doi: 10.1016/j.irfa.2020.101520

McLean, B. "Is Enron Overpriced?" *Fortune Magazine,* 143, no. 5 (2001), March 5.

Meier, U. "Der falsche und der richtige Name der Freiheit: Zur Neuinterpretation eines Grundwertes der Florentiner Stadtgesellschaft (13.-16. Jahrhundert)." In Klaus Schreiner/Ulrich Meier *Stadtregiment und Bürgerfreiheit.* Vol. 7, *Bürgertum,* pp. 37–83. Göttingen: Vandenhoeck & Ruprecht, 1994.

Milanovic, B. *Capitalism Alone: The Future of the System That Rules the World.* Cambridge, MA: Belknap/Harvard University Press, 2019.

Mill, J.S. "On the Definition of Political Economics; and on the Method of Investigation Proper to It" (1844). In *Essays on Some Unsettled Questions of Political Economy,* pp. 86–114. Kitchener: Batoche Books, 2000.

Mill, J.S. *On Liberty* (1859). In John Stuart Mill *Three Essays: On Liberty; Representative Government; The Subjection of Women.* Oxford: Oxford University Press, 1975 (multiple editions, online and in print).

Mills, P., and M. Schluter. *After Capitalism: Rethinking Economic Relationships.* Cambridge: Jubilee Centre, 2012.

Minow, M. *Between Vengeance and Forgiveness: Facing History After Genocide and Mass Violence.* Boston: Beacon Press, 1998.

Mishel, L. and J. Wolf, "DEO Compensation Has Grown 940% Since 1978," Research Paper *Economic Policy Institute* (2019), https://files.epi.org/pdf/171191.pdf

Moeller, B. "Piety in Germany around 1500." In S.E. Ozment, ed., *The Reformation in Medieval Perspective,* pp. 50–75. Chicago: Quadrangle Books, 1971.

Mokyr, J. *A Culture of Growth: The Origins of the Modern Economy.* Princeton: Princeton University Press, 2016.

Mollat, M. *The Poor in the Middle Ages: An Essay in Social History.* New Haven: Yale University Press, 1986 (originally published as *Les Pauvres au Moyen Age: Étude sociale,* 1978).

Moor. T. de. "The Silent Revolution: A New Perspective on the Emergence of Commons, Guilds, and Other Forms of Corporate Collective Action in Western Europe." *International Review of Social History* (2008): 179–212.

Moor, T. de. *Homo Cooperans.* Inaugural Lecture, Utrecht University. 2013. https://issuu.com/humanitiesuu/docs/gw_moor_tine_de_oratie_nl_definitie

Morseletto, P. "Restorative and Regenerative: Exploring the Concepts in the Circular Economy." *Journal of Industrial Ecology* (2020): 1–11.

Muijnck, S. de, and J. Tieleman. *Economy Studies: A Guide to Rethinking Economics Education.* Amsterdam: Amsterdam University Press, 2021.

Muijnck, S. de, E. Terragno Bogliaccini, and J.R. Surie. *Towards the Wellbeing Economy: Implications for Public, Environmental and Financial Policy.* Report, Future of Capitalism Project. Amsterdam: Vrije Universiteit; Utrecht: Our New Economy/Sustainable Finance Lab, 2021.

Naess, A. "The Shallow and the Deep, Long-Range Ecology Movement. A Summary." *Inquiry* 16, nos. 1–4 (1973): 95–100.

Nederlandsche Bank. "Trust in the Dutch Financial Sector Has Held Up during the COVID-19 Crisis." *Bulletins* May 3, 2021. Amsterdam: DNB.

Nedopil, C. "Countries of the Belt and Road Initiative," in *China Belt and Road Initiative (BRI). Investment Report 2022,* p. 25. Shanghai: Green Finance & Development Center, FISF Fudan University, 2022. https://greenfdc.org/wp-content/uploads/2023/02/Nedopil-2023_China-Belt-and-Road-Initiative-BRI-Investment-Report-2022.pdf

Nelson, R.R. "Intellectualizing about the Moon-Ghetto Metaphor: A Study of the Current Malaise of Rational Analysis of Social Problems." *Policy Sciences* 5 (1974): 375–414.

New Zealand Treasury/Te Tai Ohanga. *Te Tai Waiora. Wellbeing in Aotearoa New Zealand 2022.* https://www.treasury.govt.nz/sites/default/files/2022-11/te-tai-waiora-2022.pdf

Nicholls, A.J. *Freedom with Responsibility: The Social Market Economy in Germany 1918–1963.* Oxford: Clarendon Press, 1994.

Nisbet, R. *History of the Idea of Progress.* London: Routledge, 1994.

Noels, G. *Gigantisme: Van too big to fail naar trager, kleiner en menselijker.* Tielt: Lannoo, 2019.

Noels, G. *Capitalism XXL: Why the Global Economy Became Gigantic and How to Fix It.* New York: McGill-Queen's University Press, 2023 (translated and revised version of Noels, *Gigantisme*).

North, D., J.J. Wallis, and B.R. Weingast. *Violence and Social Orders: A Conceptual Framework for Interpreting Recorded Human History.* Cambridge: Cambridge University Press, 2009.

Nowak, M., and R. Hitfield. *Super Cooperators: Beyond the Survival of the Fittest.* New York: Free Press, 2012.

Nullens, P. *Hoop als kunst van verantwoord leiderschap* (Hope as the art of responsible leadership). Antwerp: Garant, 2021.

Nussbaum, M.C., and A. Sen. *The Quality of Life.* Oxford: Oxford University Press, 1993.

Oberhuber, S., and T. Rau. *Material Matters: Developing Business for a Circular Economy.* London: Routledge, 2022.

OECD. *Beyond Growth. Towards a New Economic Approach.* Paris: OECD, 2020.

Ogilvie, S. *The European Guilds: An Economic Analysis.* Princeton: Princeton University Press, 2019.

Olsthoorn, P. "Behalve gelijk hebben, ook gelijk krijgen." *Economisch Statistische Berichten (ESB).* 107/4816 (2022): 562–65. https://esb.nu/behalve-gelijk-hebben-ook-gelijk-krijgen/

O'Toole, J. *The Enlightened Capitalists: Cautionary Tales of Business Pioneers Who Tried to Do Well by Doing Good.* New York: Harper Business, 2019.

Ostrom, E.C.A. *Governing the Commons: The Evolution of Institutions for Collective Action.* Cambridge: Cambridge University Press, 1990.

Paape, L. *Maatschappelijke zorgplicht voor ondernemingen: Tien redenen waarom dat geen vraag zou moeten zijn.* (Due care for businesses: Ten reasons why this shouldn't be a question). Breukelen: Nyenrode Business University, 2022.

Pagel, M. *Wired for Culture: The Natural History of Human Cooperation.* London: Penguin, 2012.

Payne, K. *The Broken Ladder: How Inequality Affects the Way We Think, Live, and Die.* New York: Penguin, 2018.

Perkins, M.A. *Christendom and European Identity: The Legacy of a Grand Narrative Since 1789.* Berlin: De Gruyter, 2004.

Pettifor, A. *The Case for the Green New Deal.* London, England: Verso Books, 2019.

Philippon, T. *The Great Reversal: How America Gave Up on Free Markets.* Cambridge, MA: Belknap Press, 2019.

Phillipson, N. *Adam Smith. An Enlightened Life.* New Haven: Yale University Press, 2010.

Piketty, T. *Capital in the Twenty-First Century.* Cambridge, MA: Belknap/Harvard University Press, 2014.

Piketty, T. *Capital and Ideology.* Translated by Arthur Goldhammer. Cambridge, MA: Harvard University Press, 2020.

Pinker, S. *Enlightenment Now: The Case for Reason, Science, Humanism, and Progress.* New York: Penguin, 2018.

Plehwe, D., Q. Slobodian, and P. Mirowski, eds. *The Nine Lives of Neoliberalism.* London: Verso 2020.

Poel, I. van der. "The Relation Between Forward-Looking and Backward-Looking Responsibility." In N.A. Vincent, I. van der Poel and J. van den Hoven, eds., *Moral Responsibility: Beyond Free Will and Determinism,* pp. 37–52. Dordrecht: Springer, 2011.

Poel, I. van der, J.N. Fahlquist, N. Doorn, S. Zwart, L. Royakkers. "The Problem of Many Hands: Climate Change as an Example." *Science and Engineering Ethics* 18, no. 1 (2021): 49–67.

Polanyi, K. *The Great Transformation: The Political and Economic Origins of Our Time*. Boston: Beacon Press, [1944] 1957.

Polman, P., and A. Winston. *Net Positive: How Courageous Companies Thrive by Giving More Than They Take*. Boston: Harvard Business Review Press, 2021.

Pomeranz, K. *The Great Divergence: China, Europe, and the Making of the Modern World Economy*. Princeton: Princeton University Press, 2000.

Popper, K. *The Open Society and Its Enemies*. London: Routledge & Kegan Paul, 1945.

Pouw, N. *Wellbeing Economics: How and Why Economics Needs to Change*. Amsterdam: Amsterdam University Press, 2020.

Prak, M. *Citizens without Nations: Urban Citizenship in Europe and the World, c. 1000–1789*. Cambridge: Cambridge University Press, 2018.

Putnam, R.D. *Making Democracy Work: Civic Traditions in Modern Italy* Princeton: Princeton University Press, 1993.

Rajan, R., and L. Zingales. *Saving Capitalism from the Capitalists*. New York: Crown, 2003.

Rajan, R. *The Third Pillar: How Markets and the State Are Leaving Communities Behind*. London: William Collins, 2019.

Raworth, K. *Doughnut Economics: Seven Ways to Think Like a 21st-Century Economist*. London, England: Random House Business Books, 2017.

Reich, R. *Supercapitalism: The Battle for Democracy in an Age of Big Business*. London: Icon Books, 2007.

Reich, R. *Just Giving: Why Philanthropy is Failing Democracy and How It Can Do Better*. Princeton: Princeton University Press, 2018.

Rennert, K., et al. "Comprehensive Evidence Implies a Higher Social Cost of CO_2," *Nature* 610 (2022): 687–92.

Ricard, M. *Altruism: The Power of Compassion to Change Yourself and the World*. New York: Little, Brown, 2013.

Rifkin, J. *The European Dream: How Europe's Vision of the Future is Quietly Eclipsing the American Dream*. New York: Tarcher/Penguin, 2004.

Rifkin, J. *The Empathic Civilization: The Race to Global Consciousness in a World of Crisis*. Cambridge: Polity, 2009.

Rockström J. et al. "Planetary Boundaries: Exploring the Safe Operating Space for Humanity." *Ecology and Society* 14, no. 2 (2009): art. 32.

Rockström, J. and O. Gaffney. *Breaking Boundaries: The Science of Our Planet*. London: DK, 2021.

Roche, B., and J. Jakub. *Completing Capitalism: Heal Business to Heal the World*. San Francisco and Oakland: Berrett-Koehler, 2017.

Rodrik, D. *The Globalization Paradox: Democracy and the Future of the World Economy*, New York: W.W. Norton, 2011.

Rodrik, D. *Economics Rules: Why Economics Works, When it Fails, and How to Tell the Difference*. Oxford: Oxford University Press, 2015.

Röpke, W. *Civitas Humana: A Humane Order of Society.* London: William Hodge, 1948.

Röpke, W. *A Humane Economy: The Social Framework of the Free Market.* Chicago: Henry Regnery, 1960.

Rosanvallon, P. *The Demands of Liberty. Civil Society in France since the French Revolution.* Translated by Arthur Goldhammer. Cambridge, MA: Harvard University Press, 2007.

Rosling, H. *Factfulness: Ten Reasons We're Wrong about the World – and Why Things Are Better than You Think.* London: Sceptre, 2018.

Rostow, W.W. *The Stages of Economic Growth: A Non-Communist Manifesto.* Cambridge: Cambridge University Press, 1960.

Rotmans, J. and M. Verheijden. *Omarm de chaos* (Embrace chaos). Amsterdam: De Geus, 2021.

Sachs, J. *The End of Poverty: How We Can Make It Happen in Our Lifetime.* London: Penguin, 2005/2015.

Sacks, J. *The Home We Build Together: Recreating Society.* London: Continuum, 2007.

Sadin, E. *L'ère de l'individu tyran.* Paris: Grasset. 2020.

Sagan, C. *Pale Blue Dot: A Vision of the Human Future in Space.* New York: Random House, 1994.

Sandbu, M. *The Economics of Belonging: A Radical Plan to Win Back the Left Behind and Achieve Prosperity for All.* Princeton: Princeton University Press, 2020.

Sandel, M. *What Money Can't Buy: The Moral Limits of Markets.* New York: Farrar, Strauss and Giroux, 2012.

Sandel, M.J. *The Tyranny of Merit: What's Become of the Common Good?* London: Allen Lane, 2020.

Sanderson, H. *The Volt Rush: The Winners and Losers in the Race to Go Green.* London: One World Publications, 2022.

Satz, D. *Why Some Things Should Not Be For Sale: The Moral Limits of Markets.* Oxford: Oxford University Press, 2010.

Schenderling, P. *Er is leven na de groei: Hoe we onze toekomst realistisch veiligstellen* (There is life beyond growth: How we can secure our future in a realistic way). Voorschoten: Bot Uitgevers, 2022.

Schluter, M., and D. Lee. *The R-Factor.* London: Hodder & Stoughton, 1993.

Schomberg, R. van. "A Vision of Responsible Innovation." In R. Owen, M. Heintz, and J. Bessant, eds, *Responsible Innovation,* pp. 51–74. London: John Wiley, 2013.

Schön, D. *The Reflective Practitioner. How Professionals Think in Action.* London: Routledge, 1983.

Schulte Nordholt, H. *Is China nog te stoppen? Hoe een virus de wereldorde verandert* (Can China still be stopped? How a virus is changing the world order). Amsterdam: Querido, 2021.

Schmelzer, M., A. Vasintjan, and A. Vetter, eds. *The Future is Degrowth: A Guide to a World Beyond Capitalism.* London: Verso, 2020.

Schumacher, E.F. *Small is Beautiful. Economics as If People Mattered.* London: Blond & Briggs, 1973.

Sen, A. "Rational Fools: A Critique of the Behavioral Foundations of Economic Theory." *Philosophy & Public Affairs* 6, no. 4 (1977): 317–44.

Sen, A. "Adam Smith and the Contemporary World." *Erasmus Journal for Philosophy and Economics* 3, no. 1 (2010): 50–67.

Sennett, R. *The Culture of New Capitalism.* New Haven: Yale University Press, 2006.

Sennett, R. *Together: The Rituals, Pleasures and Politics of Cooperation.* New Haven: Yale University Press, 2012.

Sheikh, H. *Embedding Technopolis. Turning Modernity into a Home.* Amsterdam: Boom, 2017.

Sheikh, H. "Aanbevelingen voor een geo-economische wereld" (Recommendations for a geo-economic world). *Economisch-Statistische Berichten* 106, no. 4801 (2021): 407–9.

Siedentop, L. *Inventing the Individual: The Origins of Western Liberalism.* London: Allen Lane/Penguin Books, 2014.

Siame, M. "A Practical and Theoretical Approach to Social Venturing Entrepreneurship." In S.M. Brito, ed., *Entrepreneurship – Trends and Challenges*, pp. 83–104. Rijeka: InTech 2018. Open access: https://www.intechopen.com/chapters/58202. DOI: 10.5772/intechopen.72011

Simon, H.A. *Models of Man: Social and Rational.* New York: John Wiley, 1957.

Simons, L., and André Nijhof. *Changing the Game: Sustainable Market Transformation Strategies to Understand and Tackle the Big and Complex Sustainability Challenges of Our Generation.* London: Routledge, 2021.

Skidelsky R., and E. Skidelsky. *How Much Is Enough? Money and the Good Life.* London: Other Press, 2012.

Slobodian, Q. *Globalists: The End of Empire and the Birth of Neoliberalism.* Cambridge, MA: Harvard University Press, 2018.

Smith, A. *The Theory of Moral Sentiments.* Edited by D.D. Raphael and A.L Macfie. Indianapolis: Liberty Fund, 1759 (multiple editions, online and in print).

Smith, A. *An Inquiry Into the Nature and Causes of the Wealth of Nations.* Edited by Edwin Cannan. New York: The Modern Library, 1776 (multiple editions, online and in print).

Staveren, I. van, and P. Knorringa. "Unpacking Social Capital in Economic Development: How Social Relations Matter." Review of Social Economy 65, no. 1 (2007): 107–35.

Staveren, I. van. *Economics after the Crisis: An Introduction to Economics from a Pluralist and Global Perspective.* London: Routledge, 2014.

Steffen W. et al. "Planetary Boundaries: Guiding Human Development on a Changing Planet." *Science* 347, no. 6223 (2015). DOI:10.1126/science.1259855

Stigler, G.J., "The Theory of Economic Regulation," *Bell Journal of Economics and Management Science* 2 (1971): 3–21.

Stiglitz, J.E., A. Sen, and J.-P. Fitoussi. *Report by the Commission on the Measurement of Economic Performance and Social Progress.* 2009.

Stiglitz, J.E. *The Price of Inequality: How Today's Divided Society Endangers Our Future*. New York: W.W. Norton, 2013.

Stiglitz, J.E., J.-P. Fitoussi, and M. Durand. *Beyond GDP: Measuring What Counts for Economic and Social Performance*. Paris: OECD, 2018.

Stiglitz, J.E., J.-P. Fitoussi, and M. Durand. For Good Measure: Advancing Research on Well-being Metrics Beyond GDP. Paris: OECD, 2018.

Stiglitz, J.E. *People, Power, and Profits: Progressive Capitalism for an Age of Discontent*. London: Allen Lane, 2019.

Stiglitz, J.E., C. Dougherty and The Foundation for European Progressive Studies. *Rewriting the Rules of the European Economy: An Agenda for Growth and Shared Prosperity*. New York: W.W. Norton, 2020.

Stikker, M. *Het internet is stuk – Maar we kunnen het repareren* (The internet is broken – but we can fix it). Amsterdam: De Geus, 2019.

Stoelinga, F. *India: Land van de toekomst* (India: Country of the future). Amsterdam: De Kring, 2019.

Storper, M. "Community and Economics." In A. Amin and J. Roberts, eds., *Community, Economic Creativity, and Organization*, pp. 37–68. Oxford: Oxford University Press, 2008.

Streeck, W. *How Will Capitalism End?* London: Verso, 2016.

Sustainable Finance Lab. *De Purpose van Nederlandse Financiële Instellingen*. Position Paper. Utrecht: SFL, 2020.

Sverdrup, H., and K.V. Ragnarsdottir. "Natural Resources in a Planetary Perspective." *Geochemical Perspectives* 3, no. 2 (2014): 129–341.

Sztompka, P. *Trust: A Sociological Theory*. Cambridge: Cambridge University Press, 1999.

Sztompka, P. "Moral Capital: An Important Prerequisite for Social Change and Successful Modernization." *China Academic Journal Electronic Publishing House*. 2016 (access terminated from outside of China per March 2023).

Taplin, J. *Move Fast and Break Things: How Facebook, Google, and Amazon Cornered Culture and Undermined Democracy*. New York: Little, Brown, 2017.

Taylor, C. *Sources of the Self: The Making of the Modern Identity*. Cambridge, MA: Harvard University Press, 1989.

Taylor, C. *A Secular Age*. Cambridge, MA: Belknap/Harvard University Press, 2007.

Thatcher, M. "No Such Thing as Society". Interview by Douglas Keay for *Woman's Own*. 23 September 1987. Available at Margaret Thatcher Foundation, https://www.margaretthatcher.org/document/106689.

Think Tank of Young Economists of the Future of Capitalism Consultation (S. de Muijnck, E. T. Bogliaccini, and J.R. Surie). *Towards the Wellbeing Economy: Implications for Public, Environmental and Financial Policy*. Amsterdam: Vrije Universiteit, 2021. https://www.moralmarkets.org/wp-content/uploads/2021.04.10_Towards-the-Wellbeing-Economy.pdf

Think Tank of Young Economists participating in the Future Market Consultation. *Renewing the Welfare State: The Right Mix of Ensuring Jobs, Income and Services*. Amsterdam: Vrije Universiteit, 2021. https://www.moralmarkets.org/

wp-content/uploads/Renewing-the-welfare-state-the-right-mix-of-ensuring-jobs-income-and-services.pdf

Thunberg, G. *The Climate Book*. London: Allan Lane/Penguin, 2022.

Tieleman, J. et al., *Thinking Like an Economist? A Quantitative Analysis of Economics Bachelor Curricula in the Netherlands*. Rethinking Economics NL (2018); https://www.rethinkingeconomics.nl/

Tierney, B. "Religion and Rights: A Medieval Perspective." *Journal of Law and Religion* 5, no. 1 (1987): 163–75.

Tilburg, R. van, et al. "Financiële beleidsinterventies voor een circulaire economie" (Financial policy interventions for a circular economy). In *Sustainable Finance and Government Policy*, pp. 27–70. Topics in Corporate Finance Series 27. Amsterdam: Amsterdam Center for Corporate Finance, 2019.

Tirole, J. *Economics for the Common Good*. Translated by S. Rendall. Princeton: Princeton University Press, 2017.

Tocqueville, A. de. *De la démocratie en Amérique*. 1830–1835. English translation: *Democracy in America* (multiple editions, online and in print).

Trebeck, K., and J. Williams. *The Economics of Arrival: Ideas for a Grown-Up Economy*. Bristol: Policy, 2019.

Trompenaars, F., and C. Hampden-Turner. *Riding the Waves of Culture: Understanding Cultural Diversity in Business*. London: Nicholas Brealey, 1997.

Tulder, R. van, and E. van Mill. *Principles of Sustainable Business: Frameworks for Corporate Action on the SDGs*. London: Routledge, 2023.

Tyler, T.R. *Why People Cooperate*. Princeton: Princeton University Press 2011.

Ullmann, W. *Medieval Political Thought*. London: Penguin, 1975.

Verbrugge, A. *De gezagscrisis. Filosofisch essay over een wankele orde* (The crisis of authority: A philosophical essay about a vulnerable order). Amsterdam: Boom, 2023.

Verburg, R. *Greed, Self-Interest and the Shaping of Economics*. London: Routledge, 2018.

Verburg, R. *The Mission of Economists*. Forthcoming.

Volberda, H.W., J. Jansen, M. Tempelaar, and K. Heij. "Monitoren van sociale innovatie: Slimmer werken, dynamisch managen en flexibel organiseren" (Monitoring social innovation: Working smart, manage dynamically, organizing flexibly). *Tijdschrift voor HRM* 1 (2011): 85–110.

Volberda, H.W., J. Sidhu, P. Vishwanathan, and K. Heij. *De winst van Purpose: Hoe ondernemingen het verschil kunnen maken* (The profit of purpose: How companies can make the difference). Amsterdam: Mediawerf, 2022.

Vries, B. de. *Ontspoord kapitalisme: Hoe het kapitalisme ontspoorde en na de coronacrisis kan worden hervormd* (Derailed capitalism: How capitalism derailed and can be reformed after the corona crisis). Amsterdam: Prometheus, 2020.

Vries, P.H.H. "Are Coal and Colonies Really Crucial? Kenneth Pomeranz and the Great Divergence." *Journal of World History* 12, no. 2 (Fall 2001): 407–46.

Vuyk, K. *Oude en nieuwe ongelijkheid: Over het failliet van het verheffingsideaal* (Old and new inequality: About the breakdown of 'leveling up'). Utrecht: Uitgeverij Klement, 2017.

Waal, F. de. *The Age of Empathy: Nature's Lessons for a Kinder Society.* London: Souvenir Press, 2010.

Weber, M. *The Protestant Ethic and the Spirit of Capitalism.* New York: Charles Scribner's Sons, 1958 (originally published as *Die protestantische Ethik und der Geist des Kapitalismus,* 1905).

Weber, M. *Wirtschaft und Gesellschaft.* Tübingen: J.C.B. Mohr, [1920] 1972.

Weisbrod, B.A. *The Voluntary Nonprofit Sector: An Economic Analysis.* Lexington: Lexington Books, 1977.

Wieland, J. *Relational Economics: A Political Economy.* Cham: Springer, 2020.

Wijk, R. de. *De slag om Europa: Hoe China en Rusland ons continent uit elkaar spelen* (The battle for Europe: How China and Russia are dividing our continent). Amsterdam: Balans, 2021.

Wilkinson, R. and K. Picket. *The Spirit Level: Why Equality is Better For Everyone.* London: Penguin Books, 2010.

Wilkinson, R. and K. Picket. *The Inner Level: How More Equal Societies Reduce Stress, Restore Sanity and Improve Everyone's Well-being.* London: Allen Lane, 2018.

Witte, J. *The Reformation of Rights: Law, Religion, and Human Rights in Early Modern Calvinism.* Cambridge: Cambridge University Press, 2007.

Wolf, M. *The Crisis of Democratic Capitalism.* New York: Penguin, 2023.

Wood, D. *Medieval Economic Thought.* Cambridge: Cambridge University Press, 2002.

WRR (Wetenschappelijke Raad voor het Regeringsbeleid/ Netherlands Scientific Council for Government Policy), *Samenleving en financiële sector in evenwicht* (Finance and Society: Restoring the Balance). The Hague: WRR, 2016.

Wu, T. *The Master Switch. The Rise and Fall of Information Empires.* London: Atlantic Books, 2012.

Wu, T. *The Attention Merchants: The Epic Scramble to Get Inside Our Heads.* New York: Knopf, 2016.

Xi Jinping, *The Governance of China* (3 vols). Beijing: Foreign Language Press, 2014-2021.

Young, S.B., *Moral Capitalism: Reconciling Private Interest with the Public Good.* San Francisco: Berrett-Koehler Publishers, 2003.

Young, S.B. *The Road to Moral Capitalism.* Minneapolis: Waterside Press Publisher, 2014.

Yunus, M. *A World of Three Zeros. The New Economics of Zero Poverty, Zero Unemployment, and Zero Net Carbon Emissions.* New York: PublicAffairs, 2018.

Zak, P.J. *Moral Markets: The Critical Role of Values in the Economy.* Princeton: Princeton University Press, 2008.

Zingales, L. *A Capitalism for the People: Recapturing the Lost Genius of American Prosperity.* New York: Basic Books, 2012.

Zuboff, S. *The Age of Surveillance Capitalism: The Fight for the Human Future at the New Frontier Of Power.* Manchester: ProFile, 2019.

Index of Names

Index of Subjects

About the authors

Jan Peter Balkenende is Minister of State and was from 2002 to 2010 Prime Minister of the Kingdom of the Netherlands. He is now External Senior Advisor to EY and involved in Corporate Responsibility, Chair of the Dutch Sustainable Growth Coalition, and of the Noaber Foundation, Associate Partner at Hague Corporate Affairs, Member of the Club de Madrid, and Professor Emeritus at Erasmus University Rotterdam.

Govert Buijs is a political philosopher and currently holds the Goldschmeding research chair 'Societal and Economic Renewal' at the Faculty of Humanities of the Vrije Universiteit Amsterdam. He recently supervised an interdisciplinary Templeton Research project on Markets and Morality, a collaboration between the universities of Amsterdam-VU, Rotterdam, Nijmegen, and Tilburg.

Printed and bound by CPI Group (UK) Ltd, Croydon, CR0 4YY

16/04/2025

14658433-0001